W9-DAE-318

DATE DUE

The Awakening Twenties

GORHAM MUNSON

The
Awakening
Twenties

A MEMOIR-HISTORY
OF A LITERARY PERIOD

1935 1985

LOUISIANA STATE UNIVERSITY PRESS
BATON ROUGE AND LONDON

Designer: Joanna Hill
Typeface: Cloister
Composition: Moran Colorgraphic

Library of Congress Cataloging in Publication Data

Munson, Gorham Bert, 1896–1969.
    The Awakening Twenties.

    Bibliography: p.
    Includes index.
    1. American literature—20th century—History and
criticism. 2. United States—Intellectual life—20th
century. 3. United States—History—1919–1933.
I. Title.
PS223.M8   1985   810'.9'0052   84-14316
ISBN 0-8071-1201-1

Several chapters herein appeared earlier, often in revised versions and sometimes under differing titles, in the following journals: "Alfred Stieglitz and '291'—A Creative Source of the Twenties," *Forum*, Fall and Winter, 1960; "Greenwich Village That Was," *Literary Review*, Spring, 1960; "Herald of the Twenties: A Tribute to Waldo Frank," *Forum*, 1961; "Magazine Rack at the Washington Square Book Shop," *Studies in the Twentieth Century*, Fall, 1969; "A Comedy of Exiles," *Literary Review*, Autumn, 1968; "Chaplinesque," *Forum*, 1967; "The Classicism of Robert Frost," *Modern Age*, Volume 8, Number 3, 1964; "A Weekend at the Chateau du Prieure" (part of "Orage in America"), *Southern Review*, Volume 6, Number 2, n.s., 1970; "Woodstock, 1924," published in *Hartford Studies in Literature*, Volume 1, No. 3, 1969.

To Melville Cane

I have declared my belief in the imminence of an American Risorgimento. I have no desire to flatter the country by pretending that we are at present enduring anything except the Dark Ages.

A Risorgimento means an intellectual awakening. This will have its effect not only in the arts, but in life, in politics, and in economics. If I seem to lay undue stress upon the status of the arts, it is only because the arts respond to an intellectual movement more swiftly and more apparently than do institutions, and not because there is any better reason for discussing the first.

Ezra Pound, Patria Mia, 1913

Contents

Contents

PART THREE   *The Writers*

Illustrations

Illustrations

Publisher's Note

When Gorham Munson died suddenly in August of 1969, he had completed a draft of *The Awakening Twenties*. It was no rough draft. The manuscript was close to perfection, because its author was a perfectionist. No rewriting was needed for stylistic polishing. The manuscript offered a near-flawless study of a fascinating period in literary history, written from the unique perspective of a participant-observer whose craft, indeed whose very life, was language, the written word.

To copyedit the prose of such a skilled craftsman would have been intimidating under the best of circumstances, when the author himself could have reviewed any small suggestions for change. But to edit the work of a stylist like Gorham Munson, without the reassurance of having him check and respond to one's recommendations, is awesome. And to realize a substantial reduction in the length of the original text—a change that comments more on present economic times than on the book itself—again, without the comfort of the author's concurrence in words, phrases, or paragraphs selected for deletion, was unusually difficult.

It would have been impossible, but for the author's widow. Elizabeth Delza Munson enabled us to shorten the book without sacrificing its heart or losing the powerful presence of its author. How she accomplished this merits some brief comment here.

Elizabeth Delza stands just five feet high—and that when she breathes deeply and holds herself upright, which she does with grace and charm. A professional dancer in her youth, she still teaches dance. And she conveys a dynamic sense of *joie de vivre*, appearing far too young and active to have been Gorham Munson's wife when he and the others in this book were coming of age in the 1920s. She is clearly a woman who has lived, and continues to live, her own life of creativity and artistry.

But she is also a remarkable partner to the deceased author of this book. Elizabeth Munson is exceedingly knowledgeable of the book's subject matter, because she lived and studied and worked throughout the Twenties within the literary-artistic circle about which Munson has written. She is intimately in touch with who and what her husband and his peers were.

Serving as proxy for the author, Elizabeth Munson carefully reviewed every page of the manuscript as it was readied for publication. She knew why each word mattered, and she knew which words mattered more than others. In responding to editorial questions and suggestions, she consistently spoke with the voice her husband would have used. When deletions from the original manuscript had to be made and transitional sentences had to be created, those changes reflected as profoundly as was possible, given the circumstances, the original work.

Because of Elizabeth Munson's thoughtfully energetic cooperation in the editorial process, this is Gorham Munson's book. It is written in his voice, with his spirit.

Preface

This is a book of related essays on subjects that were formative of the literary period known as the Twenties in America. Part of the relationship among the essays is made by fibers of memoir, which are, of course, personal and subjective. I have intended these filaments of memoir to serve as connective tissue, but the memoir element nevertheless affects the selection of material for evaluation and even determines emphasis on a few occasions. There is, too, a historical relationship that holds the essays together. But the book is not a comprehensive history, nor does it have a steady and balanced view of the historical Twenties. In short, the essays are only freely related to each other.

Yet *The Awakening Twenties* does, I think, give a sufficiently coherent account of the creative sources of the decade in that brief preceding period I have called the American resurgence (or America's coming-of-age, if you wish). And the evaluative essays on figures and events of the early Twenties—again, I think—cohere strongly enough to convey the mood of awakening that was more characteristic of the time than the moods vulgarly known as "flaming youth" or "lost generation."

In my account, the Twenties began with an enormous release from the tension of war on November 7, 1918; the new period turned round in the pivotal year of 1920 when America cast off the Genteel Tradition and embraced the New Realism. In an unspecific way, the book ends with the remarkably pregnant situation of 1924, a historical moment unusually rich in possibilities of renascent achievement.

The reader will observe that the treatment of some of the principals in the 1924 situation includes their works and activities for a number of years after that date. These figures—notably Hart Crane, Charles Chaplin, Robert Frost, and A. R. Orage—were all potent in 1924, but it would have been unnatural to have cut off consideration of their work at precisely that date. I have therefore continued their stories into the Thirties and beyond.

This book has been several years in the writing, being combined as it was for four years with full-time teaching and part-time editorial duties. It has been completed under ideal conditions for research and writing at the University of California, Davis, and at the Center for Advanced Studies, Wesleyan University. My warm thanks to Gerry Baker, of the Department of English, University of California, Davis, for her efficient helpfulness in preparing the final version of chapters 1 through 10, and to Joan Farrell and Barbara Satton, of the Center for Advanced Studies, for their technical preparation of the second half of a long typescript.

G.M.

The Awakening Twenties

The Birthday of the Twenties

The literary phase of the period called the Twenties began in a reprieve to the younger generation that came on November 7, 1918. This false report of an armistice was nevertheless a true carrier of the reprieve, and the delirious joy it set off turned into hope confirmed.

On that day I was a resident master at the Riverdale Country School which was situated a half mile beyond the Van Cortlandt Park terminus of the subway line running to Times Square and the theater district of New York. The few boarding pupils and I had rooms on the top floor of a large wooden building a few steps away from the new, one-story brick building in which classes were held and meals were taken.

I remember nothing of that day except two hours in the afternoon, which I shall presently recall. I must have glanced at a morning newspaper—the New York *Times* probably—and learned from its headline that "GERMANS SEEK-ING TRUCE REACH ALLIED LINES." Because everybody knew that the end of the war was near, the United Press announcement made shortly after noon of November 7 that an armistice had been signed was instantly believed.

At 1 P.M. a lone whistle blew high above Manhattan, then another, and another, and soon there was a tremendous chorus of whistles above the streets and on the waterways around the island. Newsboys, shouting "the war is ovah," hit the streets with "Extras." Out at Riverdale we heard the whistles faintly, and all afternoon there came to us a low roar from the great city to our south.

Riverdale Country School did not, however, break out in celebration. The schedule of afternoon activities and evening study period went calmly on. It was my turn to stay on the grounds, to supervise afternoon play, and to preside over study hall. I did not repine at being assigned to the school grounds, for I did not know until the next day what I was missing: not just a big celebration but the very greatest celebration in New York's history.

It was a halcyon day—calm, an intense blue sky, temperature in the mid-fifties. I led my charges down the hill into Van Cortlandt Park and set them to playing soccer. Over on the northern side of the playing field I sat down, and there something took me by surprise. The state of joy that came over me was like no psychological state I had felt before and like none I have felt since. For an hour or more I sat on a clump of grass, letting my charges play by themselves, while suffusion after suffusion of peace filled me. That hour or two of what I have since called the enjoyment of a halcyon state of mind is all that I can remember of the day when the end of World War I was prematurely reported.

The next morning I read about what had happened below the Harlem River while I sat blissfully on a tussock in Van Cortlandt Park. I read how Fifth Avenue was closed to traffic as crowds surged up the roadway from curb to curb and how there was singing and cheering and much bussing by women of the men in uniform. Businesses closed, school children were sent home, impromptu parades started all over Manhattan. From the tall buildings a storm of ticker tape, confetti, streamers of paper towels, scraps of paper fluttered down; there was a record paperfall, 155 tons of paper, to be swept up the next day. The State Department issued denials of the United Press cable but the crowds, refusing to comprehend, went on celebrating. The lights went up on Broadway that evening, liquor was illegally served to men in uniform, and New Yorkers drank copiously to the end of the war and the piping times of peace.

The extraordinary thing about this greatest of all New York celebrations except the celebration of the true armistice four days later was the absence of ugliness. "There ran an unwonted spirit of delicacy and tenderness," I read in the New York *Tribune* on November 8. "There was none of the rowdiness associated with election and New Year's jubilations. No one was handled roughly." The *Tribune* reporter saw many eyes glistening with tears that afternoon, and a steady stream of thankful persons left the noise of Fifth Avenue to pray in St. Patrick's. On the East Side people called out "Shalom! Shalom!"

Shortly before all the whistles and sirens of ships and factories let out their high roar, the liberal journalist Harold Stearns had joined his publisher Horace Liveright for lunch. The roar broke out while they were on the street, and they saw Enrico Caruso come out on a small balcony at the Knickerbocker Hotel where he lived and throw roses down on the crowd. "As I myself remember it," Stearns wrote seventeen years later, "the expressions of even the dullest and most sordid people's faces really changed; countenances lighted up with new hope, new assurance. There was a new look in everybody's eyes. It was the dawn of a new world—and everybody knew it, whether they were articulate or reticent."

On that day the makers and expressers of the most characteristic moods of the literature of the coming decade were all surely exalted by the premature announcement of an armistice. Even T. S. Eliot in London must have felt that war's end was very near, although his duties at Lloyd's Bank, Ltd., were not remitted because no false report of a cease-fire was spread in England. Only four years after this halcyon afternoon the young man on the tussock in Van Cortlandt Park would be reading Eliot's precipitation of a postwar mood of disillusion that would be named "the waste land mood."

In Greenwich Village a young woman from Maine had recently published a quatrain—"The First Fig"—that would become the most-quoted quatrain of the 1920s: "My candle burns at both ends." Edna St. Vincent Millay would be the symbol of the "flaming youth mood."

Even more representative of the oncoming young generation of writers and readers was Second Lieutenant F. Scott Fitzgerald who was now relieved of the prospect of overseas service (which he craved). His infantry unit had been brought up from the South to Camp Mills on Long Island, and had actually been marched onto a transport and then marched off. He had already begun writing about parties in the "jazz age mood."

In Italy a young midwesterner, briefly apprenticed to newspaper work, was convalescing from wounds suffered while serving in the Italian infantry. A few years later Gertrude Stein was to say to him, "You are all a lost generation," and in a novel Ernest Hemingway would precipitate the "lost generation mood."

On this November seventh the happiest man in Baltimore—certainly the most relieved—may have been the thirty-eight-year-old bachelor and editor of the *Smart Set*, Henry Louis Mencken, who had registered for the draft two months earlier and was glumly awaiting his call to fight in a war about which he was skeptical and antipathetic. The nearness of conscription had for once shaken the mood of the diverted spectator, the mood of hearty entertainment, which Mencken would make popular in the Twenties.

Mencken's friend, Theodore Dreiser, was lumbering about Greenwich Village in these days. He did not know that his conflicts with Comstockery were over, and the mood of naturalism—agnostic, deterministic, scientific—in which he brooded over his novels was on its way to dominating the work of many American writers.

Sinclair Lewis was thirty-three on this birthday of a new period; married, the father of a boy, he was a free-lance writer who had not yet expressed the critical mood that would make him internationally famous—the mood of satire, the mood of "debunking," to use that crude word coined in the Twenties.

Last of the great expressers of the moods of the Twenties was Eugene O'Neill who on this joyous day seems to have been living soberly in New Jersey, having earlier visited Greenwich Village to attend rehearsals of his one-act play, *Where the Cross Is Made*. Exempt from military service because of his tubercular history, O'Neill held violent antiwar sentiments. More than any other mood, he had been expressing the mood of bohemia—before his second marriage he had lived in a little room above a saloon in Greenwich Village—but after he became a Broadway dramatist, his general mood might be characterized as psychoanalytic. It was not necessary to have a profound understanding of psychoanalysis—and O'Neill never acquired such understanding—to express the general air, the circumambient mood, of the new schools of the "unconscious" that O'Neill expressed. He disseminated the mood of psychoanalysis while insisting that he had read comparatively little of Freud, Jung, and Adler.

Of these eight voices of the Twenties' moods, the young man of twenty-two whom we left on the sideline of the boys' soccer game had read only three. He avidly read Mencken each month in the *Smart Set*; he had a slight acquaintance with Eliot from the *Little Review*; and he had read an O'Neill short story and had seen *Where the Cross Is Made* at the Provincetown Playhouse. He had heard of Dreiser and of Edna St. Vincent Millay, but he had not yet read their work. Of Sinclair Lewis, although Lewis had written popular novels, he had never heard; his eye had simply not noted the advertisements. Nor had he heard of Scott Fitzgerald or Ernest Hemingway, for they had not yet made their debuts before the general reading public.

4

Four days later came the true armistice. Mark Sullivan, a writer of contemporary history, caught the impressions of Kenneth Mayo, an American officer at the front. The Germans, Mayo said, made a demonstration, but in the American sector where he was, "when the noise of battle ceased there was a restful peace that passeth man's understanding or his ability to describe: there was no hilarity or jubilation."

What was this restful peace that passed this young officer's ability to describe? I believe that it was what I too, a civilian with weak eyes, felt that afternoon in Van Cortlandt Park—the feeling of youth restored, of rich possibilities regained. Consider what had been the black state of the young generation, the generation that was to set the tone of the Twenties. This generation had been coming of age with an exciting sense of potentiality. English thought and letters just before 1914 had been atingle with expectancy of a new age. Despite the war in Europe, America seemed to be a seedbed for a national revival in the arts. America's entrance into the war was a sudden constriction of potentiality. Early in 1918 Scott Fitzgerald had written from training camp to his cousin: "It looks as if the youth of me and my generation ends sometime during the present year, rather summarily—If we ever get back, and I don't particularly care, we'll be rather aged—in the worst way. . . . Every man I've met who's been to war, that is this war, seems to have lost youth and faith in men."

But now on November 7, 1918, came the promise, to be confirmed four days later, of a quick release from the awful threat to the possibilities of youth. The restrictions of war would soon be lifted, and the shadow of mass death would disappear. Vocations would open up, and the rotogravure sections of the Sunday newspapers would stop their "Died on the Field of Honor" gallery of photographs of the youthful casualties.

The wonderful times of peace were at hand, and the young generation in America looked to the future with a confidence that would be impossible to the generations that followed; the young generation that entered the depressed thirties, and the young generation that entered the armed forces in the early forties would not know this confidence.

There was hilarity, there was jubilation on the birthday of the Twenties, but beneath the celebration, flooding the beings of many young men and young women was the sudden feeling that the opportunity to rebel and to fulfill themselves had indeed come. Youth was being given back to us. So it seemed on

5

that afternoon of November 7, 1918, when the feeling of being at war was succeeded by the feeling of being at peace.

But a full understanding of what this birthday of the Twenties, this rebirth of youth, meant to its writers requires some retrospective on the artistic-literary-political community that was beginning to flourish in America before the war began. Comprehending the power of this new peace requires a look backward—to the halcyon days of American resurgence.

PART ONE

The American Resurgence
1912 – 1919

CHAPTER I

Reveille in the Arts

"America will never be the same again." So opined the New York *Globe* after the official opening of the 1913 Armory Show. This became the central assertion in the legend that kept green the memory of the show for fifty years and more. The legend said that American art had been provincial before 1913. Then modernism—postimpressionism, Fauvism, cubism—had made a sensational descent upon New York. Thereafter American art entered into a period of renascence and achieved international recognition.

The International Exhibition of Modern Art, which opened on February 17, 1913, at the Armory of the Sixty-ninth Regiment on East Twenty-sixth Street in New York, was an undertaking of the Association of American Painters and Sculptors (AAPS), a group of twenty-five founded in January of 1912. Three men performed most of the work in organizing the large exhibition—about thirteen hundred works—which opened a year later. They were the president of the AAPS, Arthur B. Davies; the secretary of the AAPS, Walt Kuhn; and the Paris representative, Walter Pach. Each was gifted for his special role in the great enterprise.

Arthur B. Davies (1862–1928) at fifty-one had unquestioned standing as one of America's leading painters. He had a good knowledge of art, a broad and refined taste that transcended his own style of "poetic" painting (nymphs in frieze-like compositions), and useful connections with wealthy patrons. He was adventurous and courageous. When he saw the catalog of the Sonderbund Show held in Cologne in the summer of 1912, he sent it to Walt Kuhn with a note: "I wish we could have a show like this."

Walt Kuhn (1880–1949) was the very man for the mission to Europe to secure paintings and sculpture like those shown at Cologne. "Go ahead, you can do it" were Davies' parting words as Kuhn sailed. When Kuhn reached Paris he called on another member of the AAPS, sculptor Jo Davidson. "Walt was dynamic and tireless," Davidson remembered in his autobiography. "He loved a show. He had been in circuses and had organized them. He was the main spirit of the Kit-Cat Club, and he went at the job of organizing the Armory Show with the same enthusiasm as he did for the Kit-Cat Ball. He was a born showman." Thirty-three-year-old Kuhn had a marked talent for publicity, and for painting circus clowns, as the world found out when the Armory Show opened in February of 1913.

Walter Pach (1883–1958), a thirty-year-old painter and art writer in Paris, helped Kuhn and Davies to round up the most daring examples of contemporary French art. He took them to see the avant-garde collection of the Steins, Gertrude, Leo, Michael, and Sarah; Leo lent a Matisse and two Picassos, Michael and Sarah two Matisses. Pach would later explain the cubist movement to the public aroused by the Armory Show. "The Cubists," he explained, "are the men who propose to bring the graphic arts to the level which the race long ago attained in music most of all, and in architecture." Music had developed from a rudimentary stage of imitation (primitive sounds) to the complex structures of sonatas and symphonies. In painting, however, in the nineteenth century it was evident that the very perfection to which realism in painting had attained revealed the futility of realism alone. Pach declared that "the men in search of the great essentials should demand anew an art which should be not an imitation, but what it has eternally been—expression." The core of his explanation was that "the pictures and sculptures in our Exhibition show that, in a short period of time, the men badly named 'Cubists,' have followed an exactly similar direction to that which was found in the art of music, and, as in the latter art, the possibilities of expression were infinitely increased with the change from the representation of the actual to the use of the abstract. I think that the men conferring a similar increase in freedom in the graphic arts, would be entitled to our profoundest gratitude."

Young Walter Pach here struck the vein that was to be enlarged in his critical writing in the Twenties. "He was at home in all epochs and schools from the high days of Egypt, the Chinese, the Greeks, the Aztecs and the Mayans," said Van Wyck Brooks, Pach's companion on many walks and gallery tours;

"and he saw no dichotomy between the work of any of them and that of the sculptors and painters he had encountered in Paris. . . . His deep sense of tradition involved an unwavering faith that his 'masters of modern art' continued it."

Others who lent a hand to Kuhn and Davies in Paris were Alfred Maurer, then forty-four years old, and Jo Davidson, who was about to turn thirty. It should be noted that the Armory Show was the undertaking of young artists, people in their thirties and early forties, with Arthur B. Davies the senior member of the organizing team.

Frederick James Gregg, a newspaperman, was engaged to promote the show. He secured the prestigious financial aid of the salon mistress, Mabel Dodge, who was made an honorary vice president of the Association of American Painters and Sculptors. Other honorary vice presidents were Alfred Stieglitz and Joel Elias Spingarn. Gregg himself was made an honorary member of the AAPS, as was John Quinn.

John Quinn, lawyer, battler against censorship, patron of writers, art collector, addressed the crowd on opening night. The International Exhibition of Modern Art, he boasted, "is the most complete art exhibition that has been held in the world during the last quarter century." It was a reasonable boast.

When I saw the recreated Armory Show, at its fiftieth anniversary exhibition in 1963, there was not, of course, the same shock of recognition or thrill of novelty that some open-minded viewers had felt on the opening night of 1913. Many of the paintings and sculptures in 1963 were familiar from display in the Metropolitan Museum, the Museum of Modern Art, and other great galleries. But how fresh, how vital, how revolutionary still was the general impression produced in 1963. The art that had grown stale with time was not there. The works chosen for the fiftieth anniversary were undiminished in vitality, were still spectacularly alive on the burlap-covered walls.

Here were the works of the greatest of the Fauve painters: Matisse's *Red Studio* and *Goldfish and Sculpture*, which had often been displayed at the Museum of Modern Art. Picasso's *La Femme au Pot de Moutarde* was as striking as the day it left the painter's studio for the dealer. Cézanne's solidity of form had the impact that was described by Leo Stein, Willard Huntington Wright, and other advanced critics at the very time of the original Armory Show. One lingered before *Portrait of Madame Cézanne* and *La Colline des Pauvres* even though one had studied them several times. *La Colline des Pauvres* had been the first

11

Cézanne to be purchased by the Metropolitan Museum—for $6,700 at the Armory Show. Kandinsky was represented in the reconstructed show by *Improvisation No. 27*, Gauguin by *Words of the Devil*, Van Gogh by *In the Woods*. And one soon came on Brancusi's pure forms in the sculpture *The Kiss*.

But had a certain picture been omitted from the 1963 exhibition, that show could not have been called a reconstructed Armory Show. That one picture, the most controversial one in 1913, was inescapably there in the path of the perambulating spectator; and it was still as exciting as it had been annoying to the old guard academician Kenyon Cox who wrote that "the things [his eyes saw] are quite indescribable and unbelievable." The old guard called Marcel Duchamp's *Nude Descending a Staircase* "an explosion in a shingle factory," meaning to libel it. But today we find this description more perceptive than libelous since, as John Canaday has pointed out, "we can say, in art lingo, that the composition of *Nude Descending a Staircase* is based on the idea of breaking natural forms into a series of kinetic planes." Today we enjoy the prankishness of Duchamp. He titled his clever pastiche of cubism, futurism, and predadaism *Nude Descending a Staircase*, and thereby sent the conventional art lover on a wild goose search through the nonrepresentative forms to find suggestions of representation. Theodore Roosevelt, turning art critic in the *Outlook*, called the title "a rather cheap straining after effect" and declared that the Navajo rug in his bathroom was infinitely ahead of the Duchamp composition from the standpoint of artistic merit.

The French painters, the future Ecole de Paris, won most of the attention and most of the glory, but there were a few American painters who were distinctively avant-garde in their exhibited works—notably Marsden Hartley represented by two still lifes in the 1963 show and John Marin whose water colors of the Woolworth Building have survived the Armory Show in their pristine originality. Charles Sheeler and Joseph Stella and Stuart Davis can still be praised for their early work. The committee selecting American works for 1913 unaccountably passed over Winslow Homer and Thomas Eakins, but redeemed themselves in picking five works by Albert P. Ryder who became the American "discovery" of the International Exhibition of Modern Art. From contemporary accounts we learn that the screens of Robert W. Chanler made a hit with reviewers and public, probably because he appeared modern without being extreme and thus suited the middle-of-the-road taste of many visitors to the Armory of the Sixty-ninth Regiment.

12

The original Armory Show closed with a snake dance led by the regimental fife-and-drum corps. The popping of champagne corks followed and there was an impromptu dance, the artists whirling the women attendants around the great hall. Well might they celebrate, for the Armory Show had been successful in all respects. It was probably the most jubilant occasion in American art history.

In point of attendance, the doors had to be closed for two hours during the last afternoon, because the Armory was filled; and it was estimated that from ten to twelve thousand crowded in on the final day. Total attendance from February 17 to March 15 was placed at about 85,000. (The show, cut to 634 works, went on to Chicago for three and a half weeks and attracted, with the aid of some free admission days, nearly 189,000 visitors. In Boston the show was reduced to about 300 works of foreign origin, and the attendance dropped below 13,000.)

In point of sales, the Armory Show was also acclaimed a success. Sales in New York, Chicago, and Boston totalled $44,148 divided into sales of foreign works ($30,491) and sales of American works ($13,657). All in all, 174 works of art were sold; 123 were by foreign artists, 51 by American. The best-selling painter was Redon (13 paintings and pastels, 20 prints). After Redon, the three Duchamp-Villon brothers were the most successful in sales (Raymond Duchamp-Villon, three sculptures; Marcel Duchamp, four paintings; Jacques Villon, nine paintings).

In point of publicity, the Armory Show got all the breaks. Was it derided in the press? The butt of cartoonists? Denounced as "immoral" and "degenerate"? It was indeed, and every knock became a publicity boost. The more the show was ridiculed and denounced, the more the public wanted to see it. Jerome Myers described the peak attendance on the last day as "the wildest, maddest, most intensely excited crowd that ever broke decorum in any scene I have witnessed."

Even the arguments among the critics drew crowds. Kenyon Cox was extreme in declaring that "this thing is not amusing; it is heartrending and sickening"; Frank Jewett Mather, whose criticism was more reasoned and restrained, nevertheless asserted that cubism was either "a clever hoax or a negligible pedantry." The defense of the new was carried on by Alfred Stieglitz, Hutchins Hapgood, and Joel Elias Spingarn—among others.

In manifesto-style, Stieglitz wrote in the New York *Times* that "the dry bones of a dead art are rattling as they never rattled before. The hopeful birth of a new art that is intensely alive is doing it. A score or more of painters and sculptors who decline to go on doing merely what the camera does better, have united in a demonstration of independence—an exhibition of what they see and dare express in their own way—that will wring shrieks of indignation from every ordained copyist of 'old masters' on two continents and their adjacent islands." Thus did Stieglitz greet "the anti-photographic," the complement to photography.

The vigorous open-minded columnist of the New York *Globe*, Hutchins Hapgood, saluted in the Armory Show a remarkable manifestation of life force—the life force of art. Joel Elias Spingarn, the American champion of Benedetto Croce and his philosophy of expression, said extravagantly in the New York *Evening Post*:

> The opening night of the International Exhibition seemed to me one of the most exciting adventures I have experienced, and this sense of excitement was shared by almost everyone who was present. It was not merely the stimulus of color, or the riot of sensuous appeal, or the elation that is born of a successful venture or the feeling that one has shared, however humbly, in an historical occasion. For my own part, and I can only speak for myself, what moved me so strongly was this: I felt for the first time that art was recapturing its own essential madness at last, that the modern painter and sculptor had won for himself a title of courage that was lacking in all the other fields of art.

There is no doubt that the Armory Show dealt the mortal stroke to the National Academy of Design. Although a few of them belonged to the National Academy, the members of the American Association of Painters and Sculptors were almost unanimous in their revolt against the academy, which gave honors to painters like Cecilia Beaux, Edward Redfield, and John W. Alexander. The National Academy, whose plan to erect a building in Central Park had been defeated, had become unpopular with the press; it was ready for the *coup de grâce* of the Armory Show.

However, the realists (the Ashcan School) were an unanticipated casualty of the explosion at Lexington Avenue and East Twenty-sixth. Robert Henri and his associates—John Sloan, George Bellows, George Luks, and Jerome Myers—lost status. After the Armory Show they were no longer in the vanguard of American art. Of Henri, Milton W. Brown said: "The former standard bearer of progressive art was in eclipse and his troops were irretrievably scattered."

While the representative painters of the realist school were thus slipping in status, the nonrepresentative or distortionist artists around Alfred Stieglitz—Marsden Hartley, John Marin, Abraham Walkowitz, and others—rose in status in the decade following the Armory Show. The show had been an introduction to modern art (a revelation, in truth) for a whole generation of artists, and the younger artists were breaking with the past and experimenting in the new directions. For the American painters who would dominate the Twenties, the Armory Show was reveille for the "New Spirit" symbolized by the pine tree on the catalog.

Two other important effects were on the galleries and on collectors. Nine months after the Armory Show an ex-bartender, Charles Daniel, assisted by an occasional poet, Alanson Hartpence, opened the Daniel Gallery, which became famous during the Twenties for its hospitality to the American avant-garde. Macbeth had shown the Eight (realists) before the show and continued to show the new art after it, as did Stieglitz's more radical gallery, "291." Macbeth and "291" were presently joined by N. E. Montross, Folsom Galleries, and a new gallery, the Bourgeois Gallery, in giving exhibitions of modern art. In March, 1914, the Carroll Gallery, backed by that angel of modern artists, John Quinn, joined the group of galleries promoting the new, and in October of the next year the Modern Gallery opened with an exhibition of Braque, Picabia, and Picasso. Walter Conrad Arensberg, poet and patron of modern art, was the backer of the Modern Gallery. Its manager was Marius de Zayas, caricaturist and critic, erstwhile of the Stieglitz circle.

As for the effect on collectors, the Armory Show incited a number to buy the new art. Foremost was Miss Lillie P. Bliss, a friend of Arthur B. Davies, whose collection eventually became the nucleus of the Museum of Modern Art. Others were John Quinn, who acted as lawyer for the AAPS; Arthur Jerome Eddy of Chicago; Arensberg, whose collection became the Louise and Walter Arensberg Collection of the Philadelphia Museum of Art; Katherine S. Dreier, whose Société Anonyme gallery in the early Twenties was a haven for the new artists; and the young collectors—Albert E. Gallatin, Dr. Albert C. Barnes, Stephen C. Clark, Edward W. Root, and Hamilton Easter Field—who made modest beginnings at the Show.

The Armory Show was a reveille for American writers, too. For the first time in American literary history there was cross-fertilization between the art world and the literary world. Writers were friends and companions-in-arms with painters, as Van Wyck Brooks was with John Sloan and Walter Pach. Gertrude Stein was writing a kind of literary cubism and composed portraits of Matisse and Picasso that Stieglitz published in *Camera Work*. Her portrait of Mabel Dodge was already notorious, and Mabel Dodge wrote an appreciation of Gertrude Stein that was timed for the arrival of the Armory Show. In the public mind Gertrude Stein and the Armory Show were associated tendencies. Writers and painters mixed at the headquarters of Alfred Stieglitz. Waldo Frank, Paul Rosenfeld, Alfred Kreymborg, and William Carlos Williams learned about Cézanne and Marin, Matisse and Weber, Picasso and Maurer at "291." As a critic, Willard Huntington Wright spanned the fields of painting and belles-lettres, while Marsden Hartley often indited poems or essays on art. The *Little Review* office (the apartment of the editors) was another meeting place for avant-garde painters and writers, with Joseph Stella a favorite visitor. In Paris Ernest Hemingway learned secrets of descriptive writing from hard study of Cézanne canvases. And certainly one should speak of the painter-poet E. E. Cummings, who was a fine example of modern painting and modern letters.

The *Seven Arts* magazine in 1916, the *Dial* in 1920—were they not beneficiaries of the shock and stimulation that the Armory Show dealt creative endeavor in many related fields? Joel Elias Spingarn, who had been thrilled at the Armory Show, contributed rousing words on freedom to the *Seven Arts*, and in the *Dial* Henry McBride reported sympathetically each month on the forces set in motion by the Armory Show.

But was not the last word on the Armory Show uttered by Alfred Stieglitz a fortnight before the show opened? Referring to the painters and sculptors who had united in a demonstration of independence, Stieglitz said the last word for then and for a half-century later: "If a name is necessary in writing about these live ones, call them 'Revitalizers.' That's what they are, the whole bunch." The Armory Show began the revitalization of the arts in America that was to make the Twenties a second "Golden Day" in the enhancement of our national culture.

CHAPTER 2

The New Freedom and
the New Nationalism

Political turmoil in 1912 signified a political awakening in the Republic. The Republican party split—the conservative faction staying with William Howard Taft for president, the progressive faction bolting to nominate Theodore Roosevelt. The Democratic party nominated the governor of New Jersey, Woodrow Wilson, to run for president in this three-cornered race.

Wilson was a most interesting candidate in that he was an intellectual running for the highest office in the land. He feared that he lacked Roosevelt's appeal to the public imagination. Deprecating himself, he said that in the public imagination he must be "a vague, conjectural personality, more made up of opinions and academic prepossessions than of human traits and red corpuscles." But his campaign speeches, published under the title of *The New Freedom* (Englewood Cliffs, New Jersey, 1961), fired the hopes and enthusiasm of enough voters to elect him, even though the combined vote for Taft and Roosevelt exceeded Wilson's.

Undeniably an intellectual, and not at all a vague, conjectural one, Wilson was an educator who made a national reputation as president of Princeton. A productive scholar throughout his academic career, Wilson attempted to lead, as August Heckscher phrased it, "through the power of style and more particularly through style in oratory." From his senior year at Princeton, Wilson had worked for excellence in the arts of persuasion,* but it was an intellectual

---

* His style remained too formal to reach the effectiveness of the informal styles of Franklin Roosevelt and John Kennedy. He didn't achieve the clarity and warmth of "fireside oratory."

excellence more than an emotional one. Throughout his political life, he was devoted to the ideal of acting on principle.

But Wilson, who distrusted intellectuals in government, did not form a "brain trust" to advise him on policy. The exception to this distrust—a great exception—was Boston attorney Louis D. Brandeis whom Wilson appointed to the United States Supreme Court in 1916. Brandeis, an enemy of industrial and financial monopoly, persuaded Wilson to base his 1912 campaign on the trust question and formulated the economic doctrine of Wilson's New Freedom speeches.

The New Freedom was defined in Wilson's flowery language as "a Liberty widened and deepened to match the broadened life of man in modern America, restoring to him in very truth the control of his government, throwing wide all gates of lawful enterprise, unfettering his energies, and warming the generous impulses of his heart,—a process of release, emancipation, and inspiration, full of a breath of life as sweet and wholesome as the airs that filled the sails of the caravels of Columbus and gave the promise and boast of magnificent Opportunity in which America *dare not fail*."

Wilson's New Freedom speeches were keyed to the rousing theme of "the old order changeth." He thrilled his listeners by saying that "we are in the presence of a new organization of society." He asserted that "a new social age, a new era of human relationships, a new stage-setting for the drama of life" are at hand. In truth, "we are upon the eve of a great reconstruction."

The great change was greater than Wilson and those who responded enthusiastically to his speeches could have imagined in 1912. American society was well on the way from an agrarian to an urban society, and American industry was accelerating for the leap from the machine age to the power age that would take place during World War I. Even though Wilson's program did not measure up to these stupendous changes, it was still on a great enough scale to enlist a mighty effort from the electorate.

Wilson declared war on the "special interests" that controlled the federal government. He proposed an end to the state of affairs in which the United States government was a mere foster child of special interests. Candid debate should be encouraged. "What we need is a universal revival of common counsel." In fact, utter publicity was needed.

Wilson denounced the protective tariff and aimed his biggest guns of oratory at the giant trusts. His remedy? Not the regulation of the big trusts that

Roosevelt was calling for, but the restoration and regulation of competition. And, of course, Wilson was an unremitting foe of the bosses, something he proved by deed in disowning New Jersey boss Jim Smith, as well as by defiant words.

He carefully disclaimed making charges of a bankers' conspiracy to control the economy and politics of the nation. But his finest moments of oratory were spent on hints of a monopoly of credit. "Some of the biggest men in the United States, in the field of commerce and manufacture, are afraid of somebody, are afraid of something. They know that there is a power somewhere so organized, so subtle, so watchful, so interlocked, so complete, so pervasive, that they had better not speak above their breath when they speak in condemnation of it." More precisely, he declared that "the great monopoly in this country is the monopoly of big credits," and in this he anticipated the analysis of the New Economics* of the 1930s.

> A great industrial nation is controlled by its system of credit. Our system of credit is privately concentrated. The growth of the nation, therefore, and all our activities are in the hands of a few men who, even if their action be honest and intended for the public interest, are necessarily concentrated upon the great undertakings in which their own money is involved and who necessarily, by reason of their own limitations, chill and check and destroy genuine economic freedom. This is the greatest question of all, and to this statesmen must address themselves with an earnest determination to serve the long future and the true liberties of men.

How often were these words quoted in the course of the Great Depression by the followers of C. H. Douglas and Frederick Soddy who claimed that the Federal Reserve Act of 1913 had not, definitely had not, settled "the greatest question of all."

"Emancipate business," Wilson cried as he campaigned in 1912. "Liberate the vital energies of the American people" was another potent rallying-call. Historians today may calmly say that the general theme of the New Freedom was the restoration of a type of economic individualism and political democracy that was believed to have existed earlier in America and to have been destroyed

---

* The New Economics of financial heretics, not Keynesian economics which was not then called the New Economics.

by the great corporations and corrupt political machines; but the New Freedom in its time was headier stuff than that. It preached the adventure of change. Our life has broken away from the past, Wilson repeated again and again, and "we are just upon the threshold of a time when the systematic life of this country will be sustained, or at least supplemented, at every point by governmental activity."

Wilson spoke truly in his first inaugural address when he said to the nation: "We have been refreshed by a new insight into our life." Reviving the custom, abandoned since 1801, of addressing Congress in person, he told that body, "Only new principles of action will save us from a final hard crystallization of monopoly." In a couple of years he signed into law a considerable number of bills designed to make effective the New Freedom program.

In 1909 a seminal work in political science was published that marked the appearance of "the first important political philosopher ... in America in the Twentieth Century." This tribute to Herbert Croly (1869–1930) came from Walter Lippmann, who augmented it by declaring that Croly's "*The Promise of American Life* was the political classic which announced the end of the Age of Innocence with its romantic faith in American destiny and inaugurated the process of self-examination."

At various times between 1886 and 1899 Hebert Croly studied at Harvard, chiefly philosophy, in the classrooms of George Herbert Palmer, Josiah Royce, George Santayana, and William James; and it was William James who gave him a philosophy—pragmatism—for facing a changing America. From 1900 to 1906 Croly was editor of the *Architectural Record*; his architectural taste was shown in the beautiful old Chelsea house in New York in which the *New Republic* was installed. He was not quite forty when he produced his seminal book, *The Promise of American Life*, which Theodore Roosevelt called "the most powerful and illuminating study of our national conditions which has appeared for many years."

Croly was, in fact, the philosopher of the New Nationalism which Roosevelt as leader of the Progressive party was pitting against Wilson's New Freedom in the 1912 campaign. There was popular understanding of this philosophic role, as was shown in the *American Magazine* which published a full-page photograph of Croly with the caption: "The man from whom Colonel Roosevelt got his 'New Nationalism.'" The caption exaggerated Croly's influence. Croly was a philosopher, Roosevelt was a politician; and the two complemented each other on ideas they held in common and had perhaps reached independently. Charles Forcey even believes that "Croly's book merely clarified and strengthened ideas that had long been part of Roosevelt's thought. And Roosevelt's own performance as President had been a major source of Croly's ideas." Croly had only in passing called his philosophy the "New Nationalism." Roosevelt took up the phrase in the 1912 campaign and injected it into the mainstream of American politics.

What was the New Nationalism? As defined by Croly, "the higher American patriotism . . . combines loyalty to historical tradition and precedent with the imaginative projection of an ideal national Promise." American life "is committed to the realization of the democratic ideal; and if its Promise is to be fulfilled, it must be prepared to follow whithersoever that ideal may lead." Croly argued for "the transformation of the old sense of a glorious national destiny into a sense of a serious national purpose which will inevitably tend to make the popular realization of the Promise of American life both more explicit and more serious."

In Croly's eyes, the man of the future would be a "disinterested and competent individual . . . formed for constructive leadership." "For better or worse," Croly wrote on the last page of *The Promise of American Life*, "democracy cannot be disentangled from an aspiration toward human perfectibility, and hence from the adoption of measures looking in the direction of realizing such an aspiration."

And so Herbert Croly stood with Theodore Roosevelt at Armageddon when the New Nationalism fell before the New Freedom. But Wilson's administration was progressive, and Croly became a Wilsonian liberal who supported Wilson's war policy in 1917.

I have called *The Promise of American Life* a seminal work because, although its sale was small, only 7,500 copies, it impregnated an unusual number of very good minds with its "extremely clear and interesting presentation of a central theme, the necessary association of the American national idea with American democracy" (Robert Morss Lovett). Among the minds thus impregnated were those of Dorothy and Willard Straight, who were impelled by the force and weight of Croly's political philosophy to establish the *New Republic* as a weekly journal for the expression of that philosophy. Organizing the journal gave Croly

21

an opportunity to try to reform and awaken American intellectual life which he had depicted as being "just about as vigorous and independent as that of the domestic animals." "American intelligence," he had insisted, "has still to issue its Declaration of Independence." Now Dorothy and Willard Straight were placing in Croly's eager hands the resources needed to organize a declaration of intellectual independence. American intelligence, Croly had said, "had still to proclaim that in a democratic system, the intelligence has a discipline, an interest, and a will of its own, and that this special discipline and interest call for a new conception both of individual and of national development. For the time being the freedom which Americans need is the freedom of thought. The energy they need is the energy of thought. The moral unity they need cannot be obtained without intensity and integrity of thought."

Thus Croly prescribed for America an intelligentsia which in Russia had meant a class of well-educated, articulate persons who constituted a self-conscious social enclave within a nation and sought to assume the guiding role of an intellectual, social, or political vanguard. But the word *intelligentsia* had no currency in America until the final year of World War I. *Intellectuals*, meaning persons devoted to matters of the mind and especially to the arts and letters, came first; *Intellectuals* (upper case) had entered journalistic writing about 1914 when the *New Republic* was founded and obtained a vogue for a while when used in an elite sense. Herbert Croly may be called the first Intellectual—self-conscious and elitist—in American history. (He was not, of course, the first intellectual, lower case.) And he gathered around him in the pages of the *New Republic* kindred Intellectuals such as Learned Hand, Walter E. Weyl, Felix Frankfurter, Harold J. Laski, Walter Lippmann, John Dewey, Morris R. Cohen, and, most self-conscious of all, the junior staff member Randolph Bourne.

The appearance of the Intellectuals in the wake of the New Freedom–New Nationalism debate was one of the certain signs of the imminence of an American risorgimento which Ezra Pound predicted was coming. "The thesis I defend is: that America has a chance for Renaissance," said Pound in 1913. The prophet, however, missed the significance of the appearance of the Intellectuals. In fact, he never made friendly reference to them in the Twenties, and certainly was unfriendly in later decades. But, pace Pound, the Intellectuals did much to foster the literary revival of the Awakening Twenties.

CHAPTER 3

Randolph Bourne— Hero of the Young Intellectuals

Randolph Bourne was youth's partisan in the generational conflict that culminated in disillusionment at America's rejection of the League of Nations. Since 1920, there has not been the full-scale confrontation of generations that marked the period of American resurgence and ended in the triumph of young America. In this fathers-and-sons confrontation Bourne was spokesman for the young generation.

How well I remember the courage roused in me when I read Bourne's first book, those essays of 1911 to 1913 which he had written at Columbia, published in the *Atlantic Monthly*, and then collected in *Youth and Life*. I had just moved into Greenwich Village with only a small bank balance and a substitute teacher's job to support my budding literary career, and I urgently needed spiritual support. This I received from "Youth," the first essay in *Youth and Life*; and I am certain that a number of my coevals were similarly emboldened for "the adventure of life" that Bourne described in another essay. "To face the perils and hazards fearlessly, and absorb the satisfactions joyfully, to be curious and brave and eager,—is to know the adventure of life"; this had an Emersonian ring that cheered us new candidates for American scholar.

My copy of *Youth and Life* was borrowed, so instead of underscoring the sentences that electrified me, I copied them into a notebook.

> One thing, at least, it [youth] clearly is: a great, rich rush and flood of energy. . . . At twenty-five I find myself full of the wildest radicalisms, and look with dismay at my childhood friends who are already settled down. . . . Youth's thirst

for experience is simply that it wants to be everything, do everything and have everything that is presented to its imagination. . . . Prudence is really a hateful thing in youth. A prudent youth is prematurely old. It is infinitely better, I repeat, for a boy to start ahead in life in a spirit of moral adventure, trusting for sustenance to what he may find by the wayside. . . . Youth, therefore, has no right to be humble. The ideals it forms will be the highest it will ever have, the insight the clearest, the ideas the most stimulating. . . . Youth puts the remorseless questions to everything that is old and established,—Why? What is this thing good for? . . . Youth's attitude is really the scientific attitude. . . . The whole philosophy of youth is summed up in the word, Dare! Take chances and you will attain! . . . It is the glory of the present age that in it one can be young. Our times give no check to the radical tendencies of Youth. On the contrary, they give the directest stimulation. A muddle of a world and a wide outlook combine to inspire us to the bravest of radicalisms.

Some of my elders by five years had thrilled to *Youth and Life* when it had come out in 1913. To Carl Zigrosser who had roomed with Bourne at Columbia, it seemed that here was "a man of 'virtu,' a universal man who did many things well and easily—writing, music, conversation."

Among Bourne's earliest friends was Alyse Gregory who was then studying singing and was later to be managing editor of the *Dial*. Alyse Gregory was attracted by the essay on "The Excitement of Friendship" and wrote Bourne about her disagreement on two minor points. When she met Bourne, she discovered him to be a hunchback, but her first impression was quickly minimized. "He had," she tells us in her memoirs, "a fine intellectual forehead, blue eyes of extraordinary intelligence, ironical and childlike, and long, slender, nervous hands in which one could almost feel the pulse beating. I had been so delighted by his exciting mind that I felt, after leaving him, as if my life had taken a new turn."

Later Bourne took Miss Gregory to the rooms of his friend, Paul Rosenfeld, for dinner and high talk. "Human intercourse," Miss Gregory notes, "is rarely regarded as an art. Paul Rosenfeld was one who treated it as such." And so did Randolph Bourne in the evenings when his friends—Van Wyck Brooks and Agnes de Lima were soon among them—dropped by his Greenwich Village flat. That league of youth that Van Wyck Brooks says was the desire of Randolph Bourne was started by the first enthusiastic readers of *Youth and Life* who were impelled to seek out the author.

And what was Bourne's criticism of the older generation? He said that the social agitation and religious heresy of the men and women between twenty and thirty were making their parents and uncles and aunts uncomfortable.* The foundation of the older generation's religion, Bourne granted, might be religious, but the superstructure was almost entirely ethical. "Most sermons today are little more than pious exhortations to good conduct." As for the moral ideals of sacrifice and service, extolled by his elders, Bourne argued that these ideals were intensely selfish. He attacked sharply the "canalized emotions" of the ideal of duty. "Social service" was an insidious compromise. Moreover, "the entire Christian scheme is a clever but unsuccessful attempt to cure the evils of inequality by transposing the values."

Warming to his indictment, Bourne said: "I deliberately accuse the older generation of conceiving and greatly strengthening these ideals [duty, sacrifice, service] as a defensive measure. Morals are always the product of a situation; they reflect a certain organization of human relations which some class or group wishes to preserve." In short, Bourne objected to the ethical philosophy of the older generation as too individualistic and too egoistic.

On the other hand, Bourne faulted the general intellectuality of the older generation for not being individual enough. "Intellectually the older generation seems to me to lead far too vegetative a life." It never speaks of death, it shies away from sex issues, it is incurious about the motives and emotions of people. Quite flatly, he charged, "The older generation has grown weary of thinking." In short, "The older generation still uses the old ideas for the new problems."

Bourne's early essays in the *Atlantic Monthly* were what the editor of that magazine today would call "think-pieces"—that is, essays of opinion, not researched and documented articles on the radical wing of the young generation. Yet we young radicals saw truth in his sketches of our conforming and conventional elders and of our own nonconformist and unconventional personalities that found a haven in Greenwich Village where Bourne might be seen walk-

---

* What follows is a condensation of "This Older Generation," an essay later than *Youth and Life* but in harmony with the brief descriptions of the older generation scattered throughout that volume.

ing on Charles Street in a black student's cape brought back from his wanderyear in Europe.

The birth injury that disfigured the left side of his face was a strong determining factor in the life of Randolph Silliman Bourne, born at Bloomfield, New Jersey, in 1886. Even more of a determinant was the childhood illness that retarded his growth and left him a hunchback. In what may be the best of his essays, for it survives the topical interest of his war essays—I mean, of course, "A Philosophy of Handicap," which should be in the anthologies of great essays—Bourne shows with warm objectivity how these determinants drove him inward to cultivate his intellect and his literary and musical talents and also drove him outward to cultivate friendship and social sympathy. His grotesque appearance, which so often gave a fatal first impression, forced him to meet life as a challenge. He refused to settle for making the best of a bad bargain but sought out satisfactions in art and friendship and the struggle for a better social order that he could look on, not as compensations, but as positive goods. As Louis Untermeyer testified after meeting Bourne in the days of the *Seven Arts*, "You forgot the misshapen dwarf with the long wooden face, the mangled ear and the torn mouth, as the fine eyes flashed and the small hands punctuated some particularly devastating criticism. There was not only a noble fire in what Bourne said, there was an exquisite courtesy in his manner."

Bourne got very little stimulation from a classical education. Almost from the first moment of his intellectual awakening, he was a modern. It was William James who introduced him to a critical testing of ideas, and it was William Lyon Phelps who introduced him to the "modern novel" of Hardy, Meredith, Tolstoy, and Turgenev. Soon he was interested in the progressive educational ideas of John Dewey, and he ultimately wrote two books about educational experiments. He was impressed by Charles A. Beard, then a Columbia professor, and author in 1913 of *An Economic Interpretation of the Constitution of the United States*. Bourne became an undoctrinaire socialist or, perhaps more accurately, a literary radical, as he called himself, who often detected class-interest and class-bias in the books he reviewed. In 1914 he became a junior member of the *New Republic* staff, and he wrote some three hundred pieces for it before resigning because of the journal's stand on American entrance into the war.

In a long essay on Newman, Bourne defined himself as an intellectual. "We are passing out of the faith era, and belief, as an intellectual attitude, has almost

26

ceased to play an active part in our life." Bourne's paternal grandfather had been a Congregationalist minister; Randolph had been brought up in the Presbyterian church; he had slipped over to the Unitarians; but by maturity he had shed all these influences and become completely secular.

> In the scientific attitude there is no place whatever for belief. We have no right to "believe" anything unless it has been experimentally proved. But if it has been proved, then we do not say we "believe" it, because this would imply that an alternative was possible. All we do is to register our common assent to the new truth's incontrovertibility. Nor has belief any place in the loose, indecisive issues of ordinary living. We have to act constantly on insufficient evidence, on the best "opinion" we can get. But opinion is not belief, and we are lost if we treat it so. Belief is dogmatic, but opinion has value only when it is tentative, questioning. The fact is that in modern thinking the attitude of belief has given place to what may be called the higher plausibility.

Insofar as Bourne had any religion at all, it was the religion (I would say, pseudoreligion) of humanitarianism. He dedicated himself to social salvation, not personal salvation; nor was he ever Thoreauvian in his attitude toward himself. "This, then, is the goal of my religion,—the bringing of fuller, richer life to more people on this earth."

As a humanitarian and a modern, Bourne counterattacked when the Platonist Paul Elmer More and his follower, Stuart P. Sherman, attacked Bourne's rising generation. "The world has grown too wide and too adventurous for Mr. More's tight little categories." And Stuart P. Sherman "would do even less adequately. His fine sympathies were as much out of the current as was the specious classicism of Professor Shorey."

But Bourne distinguished something new, something American and praiseworthy in the books of Theodore Dreiser. Bourne sought to subdue puritanism as a ruling force in American culture, and Dreiser had become the *bête noir* of the degenerate puritans who backed the Society for the Suppression of Vice. Bourne also sought to diminish the colonial nature of American culture; he opposed chiefly the colonialism of what he called "the ruling class of Anglo-Saxon descendants in these American States." Bourne welcomed Dreiser because "his emphases are those of a new America which is latently expressive and which must develop its art before we shall really become articulate. For Dreiser is a true hyphenate, a product of that conglomerate Americanism that springs from

27

other roots than the English tradition. . . . There stirs in Dreiser's books a new American quality. It is not at all German. It is an authentic attempt to make something artistic out of the chaotic materials that lie around us in American life."

Antipuritan though he was, Bourne deplored H. L. Mencken's obsession with puritanism as a literary force. Casting himself as Miro, the literary radical, he saw "Mr. Mencken and Mr. Dreiser and their friends, going heavily forth to battle with the Philistines, glorying in pachydermous vulgarisms that hurt the polite and cultivated young men of the old school." And he saw these violent critics, in their rage against puritanism, becoming themselves moralists, "with the same bigotry and tastelessness as their enemies."

Bourne had analyzed the "puritan's will to power" and concluded that "the puritan is a case of arrested development." Though puritans remain a danger and a threat, let us not, Bourne pleaded, become obsessed with them, for "when are we going to get anything critically curative done for our generation, if our critical rebels are to spend their lives cutting off hydra-heads of American stodginess?" The question was addressed to Mencken.

It was critically curative, Bourne urged, to perform surgery on the colonial attitudes of America. But this was not to be done by advocates of the melting pot theory of American society. The melting pot had simply not melted the diverse nationalistic and colonial feelings of Germans, Scandinavians, Bohemians, Poles, and other elements of America's great alien population. In fact, the nationalistic feelings of the hyphenated Americans in World War I showed that the melting pot had never existed.

Bourne challenged Woodrow Wilson's contention that "the great melting-pot of America, the place where we are all made Americans of, is the public school, where men of every race and of every origin and of every station in life send their children, or ought to send their children, and where, being mixed together, the youngsters are all infused with the American spirit and developed into American men and women." On the contrary, Bourne told his contemporaries, "we have all unawares been building up the first international nation."

In his own generation, Bourne claimed that colonialism had "grown into cosmopolitanism," and the motherland was no one nation but "all who have anything life-enhancing to offer to the spirit." He strove to make his concept of transnational America clear but only made it picturesque. "America is coming to be not a nationality but a transnationality, a weaving back and forth, with the other lands, of many threads of all sizes and colors." A cooperation of cultures—that would be the goal; and "in the current Jewish ideal of Zionism," Bourne added, "we shall find . . . the purest pattern and the most inspiring conceptions of trans-nationalism."

In April of 1917 Woodrow Wilson, who had been reelected because he had kept America out of war, led America into war with the Central Powers. The liberals of the *New Republic* followed Wilson, and Randolph Bourne resigned and proceeded to write for the *Seven Arts*, the *Masses*, and the fortnightly *Dial*. To the *Seven Arts* he contributed those brilliant, forceful essays on intellectuals and the war—notably "The Collapse of American Strategy" and "Twilight of Idols" — that gave him heroic reputation among the intellectuals after the war. To Bourne the issue for intellectuals was: "The war—or American promise: one must choose. One cannot be interested in both. For the effect of the war will be to impoverish American promise." In the end he found the instrumental philosophy of Dewey criminally inadequate for meeting the inexorability of war. "We are in the war because an American government practised a philosophy of adjustment, and an instrumentalism for minor ends, instead of creating new values and setting at once a large standard to which the nations might repair."

At the time Bourne's war essays appeared, they had little effect, as he himself recognized. Walter Lippmann took leave from the *New Republic* to become an assistant to Secretary of War Newton D. Baker. John Dewey wrote apologies for the course of the American government. Colonel E. M. House acted as liaison between the White House and the *New Republic*; and the *New Republic* gained the undeserved reputation of being an unofficial voice of the Wilson administration. Bourne lost his engagement with the intellectuals.

Nevertheless, a few months after the Armistice Randolph Bourne was acclaimed the hero of the intellectuals—a posthumous elevation, for Bourne died, aged only thirty-two, in the terrible influenza epidemic of the closing months of 1918. He left a long unfinished essay on "The State." With impassioned logic, he declared, "War is the health of the State," a key sentence that has been quoted so often that one is surprised not to find it in Bartlett.

Bourne bequeathed a renaissance role to postwar intellectuals. They were exhorted to be value-creators, who should follow "the allure of fresh and true ideas, of free speculation, of artistic vigor, of cultural styles, of intelligence suffused by feeling, and feeling given fibre and outline by intelligence." Scofield Thayer, a wealthy young intellectual, had been very sympathetic to Bourne's

29

war essays in the *Seven Arts*, and backed Bourne for a place on the fortnightly *Dial*. More or less consciously, Thayer aspired to carry out the bequest of Bourne. He planned to make a monthly out of the fortnightly *Dial* and to present in it "the allure of fresh and true ideas . . . of artistic vigor . . . of intelligence suffused by feeling"; within a year of Bourne's death Thayer was assembling his first monthly number, the lead-off feature of which was "An Autobiographic Chapter" by Randolph Bourne. For several years thereafter, the *Dial* could be regarded as the continuator of Bourne's heroic endeavor to rally a new fellowship in the younger generation—the generation of Lewis Mumford and John Dos Passos and Paul Rosenfeld—that would pledge itself to the purpose of creating, in the words of Bourne's colleague Van Wyck Brooks, "a fine, free, articulate cultural order."

Bourne's writings on World War I and the intellectuals had been timely and strictly applicable to a precisely defined situation. But situation and time had changed. He never expressed the philosophy of pacifism; he was never a pacifist absolutist. Nor was he an isolationist, forerunner of the America First persuasion. Admitting that he had an irreconcilable animus against war, he stood for American neutrality *and* the positive use of the neutrality to bring about a negotiated peace in Europe. Thus he was not a pure noninterventionist. He supported Wilson's "peace without victory" speech and even had good words for "armed neutrality," but the American declaration of war he regarded as the collapse of American strategy. He bitterly lamented that America as a belligerent power could no longer use her great neutral power to bring the warring nations to a negotiated peace that would really be a peace without victory. He was friendly and hopeful toward the Kerensky government, but it is likely that he would have turned against the Bolshevik tyranny, not at once but probably about the time that Bertrand Russell and Emma Goldman were reporting their disillusionment.

The League of American Writers, a notoriously pro-Russian organization, unscrupulously violated the memory of Bourne by using him as a stage property in the first years of World War II. Propagandizing for pacifism and nonintervention on the part of the USA, the league sought American heroes to lend patriotic prestige to their cause; they thought of Randolph Bourne. Had he not been pacifist and noninterventionist in World War I? The league established the Randolph Bourne Memorial Award to honor those who were guided by the Hitler-Stalin pact in their attitude toward the Allies; and in 1941 the award was given to Theodore Dreiser, who was virulently anti-British and rabidly pro-Russian. Then Hitler attacked Russia. Overnight the members of the league called for intervention and soon they were agitating for a "second front" to divert the fury of Hitler's attack from Russia. No more was heard of the Randolph Bourne Memorial Award. And indeed Bourne was not usable by any group in the situation that preceded America's entrance into World War II. He had ceased to be a contemporary.

Whereas Bourne was once ahead of the times, the times caught up and went ahead of him in the third and fourth decades of the century. He played a big role in the brief American resurgence, but died too soon to leave work that would perpetuate his value to the whole period between the two world wars. The very words that had an idealistic tinge in his short career—words like *intelligentsia, intellectuals, radicals*—fell into disuse; by the time of the League of American Writers, they had been replaced by words like *liberals, communists, fellow-travellers, anticommunists, lefts,* and *avant-garde*. The radicals had become heterogeneous, and that fine word no longer seemed to fit all the warring factions of the left, to say nothing of an intellectual right. Thus, when we call Bourne a literary radical, as he called himself, or an undoctrinaire socialist, it makes him sound dated; and he was dated in the sense that his contribution to American life was quickly consumed and passed into the cultural stream of the Twenties.

But if we cannot go back to Bourne for renewal in approaching the crises of the present, as we can go back in certain respects to a figure like Thoreau, we can still feel grateful to Bourne for being the keenest spirit of what has been facetiously called the "Apostolic Student Movement" of the resurgent decade. Brooks, Waldo Frank, James Oppenheim, and Paul Rosenfeld were part of this group which opposed the values of a business civilization dominated by gigantic corporations. These men and others like Scofield Thayer and Lewis Mumford were a prophetic minority in their generation which could fitly be called the American Promise generation. It was a generation working in the little theater movement, in the new magazines, in the realistic novels, and the free verse of the period that was bent on the realization of the promise of American life.

Bourne is still treasured in the hearts of those who once belonged to the young generation that he led forth to battle their elders who were upholding the standard of the genteel tradition. He taught us how to dodge the social and family pressures that made for a narrow life. He led the way for us—*his* generation—in the adventure of life. Alive with curiosity, ardent in pursuit of modern ideas, in love with the future, Bourne was indeed the hero of *Our America*, the pathbreaking book Waldo Frank was to write soon after Bourne's death, a book about the revised traditions and new literature and fresh social thought that Bourne cherished as the promise of America.

CHAPTER 4

Alfred Kreymborg and Others

After the first issue of *Others* in July, 1915, the thirty-one-year-old editor Alfred Kreymborg received a letter, postmarked London, from Ezra Pound. The expatriate, alertly scanning new books and magazines coming from his native land for signs of the risorgimento he had predicted, wrote of the first issue of *Others*: "While I concede this to be the liveliest sheet that has ever come out of the states, quite a few exhibits are frankly impossible." He offered a group of his own poems and begged the editor to accept "the strange poem inclosed"— "Portrait of a Lady" by T. S. Eliot.

A few months earlier Pound had written to Harriet Monroe: "*My gawdd!* *This* IS *a* ROTTEN *number of Poetry.*" Founded in 1912, *Poetry* had failed to spearhead the "new poetry movement" that people had begun to talk about. What was needed in America, Walter Conrad Arensberg confided to Kreymborg one day in 1914, was a poetry magazine that would dedicate its energies to experiment throughout. That was the day *Others* was conceived; it was born in the following summer. Harriet Monroe came to consider *Others* a radical offspring of *Poetry*, "the more so," Kreymborg noted, "as a number of her contributors appeared in the newer periodical—with poems, on more than one occasion, she had rejected and regretted rejecting."

Others, in fact, became a focal center of the American resurgence. It was at the center of the free verse explosion of the decade, but it may be added that all the lines of the poetic revival passed through it. Its motto was: "The old expressions are with us And there are always Others." *Others* had a place for the traditional and space for attempts to satisfy the craving for novelty. It recognized the validity and permanence of traditional forms of expression, but its *raison d'être* was experimental writing. It promoted efforts to invent new forms and extend the resources of poetic language.

Alfred Kreymborg was the chief promoter of the excitement of the "new poetry." Ezra Pound would later refer to Kreymborg as an example of "anemia of education." Although not too severely handicapped for an interesting career in poetry and playwrighting, Kreymborg was a dropout after only two years of high school. His father was a German-born "segar-packer," and his mother's parents had come from Germany. The father was Roman Catholic, the mother Lutheran; their son Alfred escaped church attendance almost entirely and became a gentle pagan.

Nevertheless, Alfred managed to get a fair self-education. In music, which he loved, he learned to play the mandolute. In literature—except for Walt Whitman whom he uncritically worshiped—he preferred minor writers to major ones. In art—he was a frequenter of "291" and present at the big Alfred Stieglitz luncheon tables at the Prince George and Holland House. And in writing—he even subsidized his forgotten first book, a collection of paragraphs on life and love, published by Grafton Press, which also published Gertrude Stein's *Three Lives*, an author-financed book that would become famous. He never acquired any skill in literary criticism; in fact, throughout his career he eschewed criticism, being more promoter than editor in the various publishing ventures he planned and sometimes executed. He explained his refusal of critical office by saying that he had "a preference for inconclusive conclusions to human problems" and that he found "more meat in suspended opinions than . . . in finalities."

Chess was his major intellectual interest, and he was formidable at the chessboard. He once tied Capablanca in a tournament of the New York State Chess Association, losing in the play-off by the slightest of slips in the end-game. He even earned a sort of livelihood by prowess in chess. But as a composer of free verse, he was consistently rejected and yet persistent for years in submitting poems to unreceptive editors.

Alfred Kreymborg was wistful and lonely, seemingly unwanted in the literary world. He sought out the company of other undiscovered artists and writers: Marsden Hartley, "the long lean eagle from the hills of Maine," he called him; Alanson Hartpence who was to become the assistant of the avant-garde Daniel

Gallery in the Twenties; Man Ray who quite soon revealed an intriguing originality.

Poet and art collector Walter Arensberg offered to underwrite the printing bills of *Others* for one year. The printer, an energetic anarchist in the Bronx who called himself Mr. Liberty, promised to print five hundred copies of each issue at cost, which he estimated at $23 per issue. He explained that he refused to extract any profit from a job for "redicals."

The first number, sixteen pages with a goldenrod cover, presented poems by Wallace Stevens, Mary Carolyn Davies, Mina Loy, Orrick Johns, Horace Holley, Ezra Pound, William Carlos Williams, and Alfred Kreymborg. It set off a surprising fuss in the newspapers. Mina Loy, who had lived in Paris and Florence and known Guillaume Apollinaire and F. T. Marinetti, attracted most attention, chiefly derisive, and Alfred Kreymborg's poems called "mushrooms" were irresistible to parodists.

In the second number appeared Stevens' "Peter Quince at the Clavier" and several poems by William Carlos Williams, who would play a vigorous role in future issues. The third number introduced T. S. Eliot, John Gould Fletcher, Maxwell Bodenheim, and Walter Arensberg. The fourth was devoted to the Choric School, whose attempt to associate dancing with poetry was explained in a foreword by Ezra Pound.

With the backing of Mr. Liberty's successor, John Marshall, a bookshop partner, *Others* appeared with an unusual regularity for a "little magazine." The subscription list grew to 250, and the print order at times reached 1,000 copies. Jeers and applause greeted the young poets each time an issue appeared.

Pound was, of course, right in saying that "quite a few exhibits are frankly impossible." Part of the file of *Others* is indeed a burial ground for what Max Eastman stigmatized as "lazy verse." Some of the poems expired even as they saw the light of day. But the publication of William Carlos Williams' "Tract" more than atoned for the impossible exhibits.

The dominant tone of *Others* was a mixture of playfulness, good workmanship, and exciting discovery. The venture came at the time of the *vers libre* explosion, for which Pound had propagandized as he fostered the school of imagism. Amy Lowell, on her return to America, shouted masterfully for free verse, making more stir than Pound. Since what she wrote seemed easy and was easy, the cult of *vers libre* was as catching as was Spanish influenza in the last year of the resurgence. Finally, T. S. Eliot was obliged sternly to remark that no *vers is libre* to the man who does an honest job.

In short, there was a small wave of popular enthusiasm for free verse. Upon the crest of this wave *Others* had been rushed forward to the shores of light. Its thirty issues contain most of the good free verse of the time, and, all allowances made, surprisingly little of the great quantity of bad free verse that was poured out in those adventurous days.

In the spring of 1916 the editorial staff expanded to include William Carlos Williams, Helen Hoyt, Maxwell Bodenheim, and Alanson Hartpence as associate editors, and the new contributors included Amy Lowell, Carl Sandburg, Conrad Aiken, Marianne Moore, Edgar Lee Masters, Padraic Colum, Witter Bynner, Benjamin De Casseres, Kenneth Burke, and even the pseudonymous poets Emanuel Morgan and Elijah Hay of Spectra hoax fame. A Spanish-American number was brought out and then America entered the war. *Others* suspended publication until December, 1918.

From that date until it died of loss of spirit in July, 1919, it was managed by Kreymborg and three associate editors: Lola Ridge, William Saphier, and Dorothy Kreymborg—to whom were soon added Orrick Johns and, as art editor, William Zorach. Among the discoveries in this final period were Evelyn Scott, Marsden Hartley, Wallace Gould, Yvor Winters, and Emanuel Carnevali.

It will be seen that in a broad manner the poets in *Others* were united, but the principle of their coming together was too broad to justify critics labeling them a group or a school. In one of the later issues of *Others* the editors objected to this labeling tendency. "It has been said in many places that the contributors to *Others* (magazine or anthologies) are members of a group, a school. This is not true. Collectively or separately, they eschew everything which approximates ismism. Any one is free to come in or stay out of the magazine, subject of course to the none-too-infallible judgment of the editors."

This chronicle of the history of *Others* should include mention of certain undertakings that sprang from the magazine. There were three *Others Anthologies*, 1916, 1917, 1919, which preserved in more permanent form the best poems printed in the magazine. There was the Others Theatre, in which the Millay sisters, Edna and Norma, acted, and Rihani (Kathleen Cannell) danced, with music by Julian Freedman and sets by William Zorach. It had a brief successful run at the Provincetown Playhouse and a brief disastrous run at the Bramhall Playhouse. And there was the Others Lecture Bureau, under whose auspices

Lola Ridge, Conrad Aiken, Alfred Kreymborg, and William Carlos Williams toured the Middle West.

Paradoxically, the death of *Others* was its most vital act. "*Others* has come to an end," wrote William Carlos Williams, who compiled and edited the final number in 1919. "I object to bringing out another issue after this one. *Others* is not enough. It has grown inevitably to be a lie, like everything else that has been a truth at one time. I object to its puling 4 × 6 dimension.* I object to its yellow cover, its stale legend. Everything we have ever done or can do under these conditions is being done now by any number of other MAGAZINES OF POETRY! *Others* has been blasted out of existence. We must have a new conception from the bottom up or I will not touch it."

At the back of that issue was a fiercely uttered supplement entitled "Belly Music," also by Williams. He complained harshly of the deficiencies in the poetry magazines of the day. "How is one to go about getting something done in this welter? In the first place—although it was not true five years ago—all the 'good stuff' there is to print does somehow get upon the page in some crazy fashion today." He attacked the vogue of the "lovely" and demanded more awareness.

> Poets have written of the big leaves and the little leaves, leaves that are red, green, yellow and the one thing they have never seen about a leaf is that it is a little engine. It is one of the things that make a plant GO. . . . He [the poet] writes in order to escape the mechanical perfection of sheer existence. He writes to assert himself above every machine and every mechanical conception that seeks to bind him. He writes to free himself, to annihilate every machine, every science, to escape defiant through consciousness and accuracy of emotional expression. . . . The mark of a great poet is the extent to which he is aware of his time and NOT, unless I be a fool, the weight of loveliness in his meters. . . . To think means to stop singing only when you deny the power of release in thought.

Williams damned the critics as sophomoric and nonsensical. He said of himself that he was "one who slips back at last with savage resentment—like a beast with a bone in his throat," and his last growl in *Others* granted that "with the help of a real critic the work that even a small group, such an inadequate

* Actually *Others* had a 7 × 10 format.

group as the OTHERS could swing would have at least the beginnings of that splendor which—would be so out of place in America, like J. P. Morgan's watch chain! There is not a whisper of protest. There are only salaried employees of GREAT magazines who try to get radical stuff into their masters' periodicals when they are able to or the budget allows."

In fact, Williams was already on fire to start a new magazine, though it would be a year before he and Robert McAlmon would get out *Contact*. Kreymborg was now ready to conclude that *Others* had had its day and must stop. But a magazine which had presented at the moment it did the work of T. S. Eliot, Marianne Moore, Ezra Pound, Wallace Stevens, and William Carlos Williams—first rank all by the time the decade of the Fifties had come—had won a secure and honorable place in the literary history of the first quarter of the twentieth century. Kreymborg rightly believed that "a definite milestone had been laid" and that the contributors to *Others* could now "express themselves independently of one another."

CHAPTER 5

Robert J. Coady, Soil
and the Skyscraper Primitives

When *Soil: A Magazine of Art* suspended publication in July, 1917, probably very few thought that its force would persist for another decade. Painters had been interested in the reproductions *Soil* showed: Cézanne, Van Gogh, Picasso, Henri Rousseau, Poussin, Seurat, African sculpture, and other works generally ignored by the official art world of America. And painters had been startled by photographs of locomotives, cranes, and steam hammers appearing in an art magazine. Perhaps there *was* something for the esthetic eye in the forms of machinery. Although *Soil* published Wallace Stevens, Maxwell Bodenheim, and Gertrude Stein, this magazine meant less to the writers of its brief day. Either the writers missed it altogether or they saw it as merely another expression of the ferment of the times. It attained a circulation of five thousand copies, vanished, and for several years was seemingly forgotten.

But in 1922 *Soil* rose from the limbo of little magazines. References to partial phases of its program began to appear in *Broom*, come to America from its European residence. To *Broom* Robert Alden Sanborn contributed an article on the founder of *Soil*, Robert J. Coady, after which Coady became almost but not altogether legendary. Sanborn, who had been a principal contributor to *Soil*, declared that "*The Soil* was Coady."

Exactly who was Robert J. Coady? He founded an independent art gallery on Washington Square which became a haunt of Alfred Kreymborg. "The pugnacious, red-headed Irishman," Kreymborg wrote in *Troubadour*, "not only had incisive ideas about modern art, but a year or two later, founded an aggressive magazine called *The Soil*, which ran through five brilliant numbers and more or less prophesied the advent of several subsequent publications."* At one point Coady had invited Kreymborg to become literary editor of *Soil*, combining it with *Others*. Kreymborg, supported by William Carlos Williams, gratefully declined the alliance. Coady's temperament was belligerent. He has been described by an art critic who knew him as a man whose brow suggested intelligence while his mouth suggested a racetrack tout. And Coady was indeed immersed in certain expressions of American life that some might have called more congenial to touts.

Coady had an appetite for city life where that life was naive, forceful, broad, and sportive. As Robert Alden Sanborn tells us:

> Bob Coady knew intimately the amusement side of his New York. He read the cartoons and sporting pages of the yellow sheets; he prowled about lower Third Avenue, preferring the serials and slapstick comedies of the smelly little East Side movie theatres to the pretentious musical and feature programs of the amusement places of Broadway; he was a devotee of the old Chinese theatre on Doyer Street, and spoke with bitter regret of its passing; he delighted in the live Seurats and Lautrecs which he found in the smoky galleries of the burlesque houses on 14th Street; he rediscovered the *Comédie Humaine* amongst the employees and patrons of McCann's restaurant on Myrtle Avenue, Brooklyn; he sought the glory that was Greece on the Polo Grounds, and in Madison Square on fight nights; and in the playful colorings of Negro children he found the crude beginnings of a more representative art than was ever hung in the National Academy.

Coady's gaze at American life was intelligent. He looked for an indigenous life, for an indigenous art, for the possibilities of an indigenous art. He realized that the America of the early twentieth century yearned toward the big city, toward New York. Although some Americans lived from generation to generation in rural regions, there seemed to be no deep attachment to the soil. There was no really deep settling down, no enmeshing of birthplaces in the various expressions of agrarian culture. The American farmer was no longer making legends or folk songs, if he ever had; and he was not creating architecture that was solid and harmonious with his land. Nor did he arrange and manage

---

* Kreymborg may have had in mind an art magazine called *The Blind Man*, *Broom*, and *The Seven Lively Arts* by Gilbert Seldes.

his farm with the beautiful economy of the French peasant. His wife was equally uncreative in cookery, dress, or lace-work. His speech was generally more corrupt than racy.

Increasingly, isolation from the metropolis was disappearing. Railroads, automobiles, newspapers, the radio, manufactured goods flooded the countryside with metropolitan aspirations, standards, and culture. Materials were lavish, but culture did not seem to arise from the sprawling diffuseness.

New York was different. Here the American reached the apex. Because there was no other place to go, he settled. New York was confined. The city had volcanic energy but it was confined by conditions: the desire to take root, and the short supply of materials. Thanks to a stricture in land, New York gave birth to the skyscraper. Coady chose New York as his cultural base.

At the time of Coady's magazine, Van Wyck Brooks was saying that highbrow and lowbrow divided American life between them, and left no common middle ground of usable experience. Coady did not accept that thesis. The central rhythm in American life was coming from business and industry. It was a rhythm that affected everybody; everybody had to make some kind of adjustment to it, had to incorporate it in his experience. The excessive pounding of this rhythm could be said to be America's peculiarity among the nations.

The goal of the rhythm was not a creative or experiential one. It was naked acquisition. But the acquisitive motive does not function in purity. Other imperious desires crowd in and strike off at tangents. The acquisitive drive is leavened by humor; it demands entertaining or violent relief; it affords room for the esthetic sense to express courage or aspiration or strength; it taxes invention and energy; it enforces economy and coordination. The business-industrial rhythm may deprive people of normal physical exercise, but it provides sport as a balance. There are fruitful accidents. Coady was alert in perceiving the creative byproducts of an essentially acquisitive drive; and he saw that the kind of vitality, the qualities of life, that energized these byproducts constituted usable experience common to all Americans.

"There is an American Art," he asserted. "Young, robust, energetic, naive, immature, daring and big spirited. Active in every conceivable field." As examples, he named many things beyond the pale of academic art: the skyscraper, colonial architecture, the steel plants, the bridges, Indian beadwork, sculpture, decorations, music and dances, Bert Williams, Ragtime, the Buck and Wing and the Clog, syncopation and the cakewalk, football, Coney Island, the *Police*

41

Gazette, the sporting pages, Krazy Kat, Nick Carter, Walt Whitman, Poe, William Dean Howells, Artemus Ward, Gertrude Stein, Pennsylvania Station, railroad signals, boxers, dialects, and slang. It is true he also named cigar store Indians, Prospect Park, and the zoo. His appetite was ravenous. "This is American Art. . . . It has grown out of the soil and through the race and will continue to grow. It will grow and mature and add a new unit to art. . . . Our art is, as yet, outside of our art world. It's in the spirit of the Panama Canal. It's in the East River and the Battery. It's in Pittsburgh and Duluth. It's coming from the ball field, the stadium and the ring. Already we've made our beginnings, scattered here and there, but beginnings with enormous possibilities. Where they will lead, who knows? To-day is the day of moving pictures, it is also the day of moving sculpture." (Alexander Calder's mobiles swung gently in the not distant future.)

Coady used words loosely, but one has no difficulty grasping his vigorous intent. One can also feel his reservations. Coady knew that he was often acclaiming potentials rather than achievements. But "the point about *The Soil,*" wrote its literary editor, Enrique Cross, in rebuke to *Broom,* "was, as its name implied, that it must shoot its seed, not at the honest skulls of the public ubiquitously, though that was good, but at the nurseries where public skulls gather— this for terrain in lieu of circulation."

Coady had critical insight, an awareness of the inherent properties of the various media he and his contributors discussed. Thus Coady denied that the motion picture was properly either photography or drama. "A motion picture is a medium of visual motion." Some years later Slater Brown of *Broom* refined Coady's statement by arguing that the inherent and special trait of the movies is the deformation of motion. With this lead in, Brown commented on the art of Charlie Chaplin. Chaplin, notable in his shuffle, deformed natural motion and showed his intuitive sense of the nature of the medium.

The content of Chaplin's pictures was accounted for by a paper Chaplin himself wrote for the first number of *Soil.* Chaplin pointed out that the successful comedian must be a psychologist first of all. He must know how to make the Chinese and the Brazilian and the Armenian laugh at the same thing; he must learn the secret of universal laughter. Chaplin explained that he sought to give spontaneous and vital release to the suppressed rebelliousness in every breast. He found that by upsetting symbols of authority such as policemen or by pulling the whiskers of pompous capitalists, he succeeded everywhere in making people laugh. *Soil* never gave a complete solution to the problems it raised; but almost always, as in the instance of Chaplin's article, it starts us on the right track.

The dime novel was seriously discussed. A feature serial of *Soil* was *The Pursuit of the Lucky Clew* by the author of *Nicholas Carter*. *Soil* proclaimed that the dime novel was a genuine "American reflect, chaste as Sunday School, good where it was naif and better always than the Winston Churchills," referring to popular American novelists like the author of *The Inside of the Cup*. Mr. Rothstein of Street and Smith was quoted: "They [dime novels] are typically American. The characters grow out of our local environment, the actions result from local laws, ordinances and customs. The situations could not happen anywhere else. The plots are no better or worse than the so-called serious stories, they have less technic and more life. The characters are set in motion from the start and they tell the story by their actions. The result is that the reader is in direct contact with them and not held away by 'clever composition.'" The Editor's Note repeated that "they draw sustenance wholly from this soil, hence their influence is formative." But the dime novel was not praised in *Soil* at the expense of serious literature. It was admitted that at times the dime novel strained our credulity, that it revealed a half-demoded, half-puritanic piety toward women, and that its impersonal, direct, swift style overindulged in short, choppy sentences.

Another instance of the feel for inherent properties was given in an article on the Woolworth Building. George Simpson said: "I like to see a building that shows its construction. There are some steel-constructed buildings that look like wall-constructed and often they are but it is stupid to make them so, because they are neither one thing nor the other. . . . The skyscraper is positively an outgrowth of American conditions. . . . (It abolishes the Gothic arch). . . . Windows were a boon, ornamentally, and could be used to secure lightness, airiness of aspect as at least one step toward the characterization of a new style. . . . The Woolworth Tower looms up, at right angles to antiquity." That is what one could read about skyscrapers in *Soil* in 1917.

Robert J. Coady lived in a skyscraper wilderness, and he accepted that wilderness as an environment for culture to master. He groped about it to familiarize himself with its exuberant fauna and wild flora. He took hold avidly of this particular and that. He did not construct a system. He was a "skyscraper primitive."

Soil was Robert J. Coady; and Coady was vigorous, independent, open to new materials and new forms, intensely nationalistic. His reservations and insights were not subtle, but sufficient to save him from the grosser errors that apostles of the new sometimes commit. He never declared that the past was a bucket of ashes. He was not profound or comprehensive, though very inclusive within the range of his enthusiasms. After his death, he remained as an inciter to new cultural actions that Americans must undertake.

To fully comprehend the American resurgence one might search out a file of *Soil*, December, 1916–July, 1917. It was an amazing magazine. *Soil* was more aggressively American than its nationalistic contemporary, *Seven Arts*. It roared New York; it roared America. And it was a source, not for a literary school that might be called the skyscraper primitives and that tried to get born when Malcolm Cowley and Matthew Josephson turned *Broom* into an American Dada magazine, but it was a source—or perhaps better a forerunner—of the "lively arts" critics of the early 1920s.

Soil suspended publication a few months before *Seven Arts* stopped. Enrique Cross went to Mexico, Robert Alden Sanborn continued writing, and Robert J. Coady enlarged his "constructive program for the development of a real American tradition."

Shortly before Coady's death at the unripe age of thirty-nine, a large dinner was given to honor him. For this occasion Coady printed a thirty-two-page pamphlet which was a call to form the American Tradition League and to publish a monthly magazine devoted to the development of American culture. The call was addressed to actors, amusement experts, architects, cartoonists, composers, critics, dancers, dieticians, directors, doctors, editors, hygienists, illustrators, musicians, painters, philosophers, photographers, physical culturists, poets, scientists, sculptors, writers and laymen.

The members of the American Tradition League were to support fifteen general propositions.

> That the world is not ugly.
> That life is a great privilege.
> That man has developed through instinct and intelligence into various degrees of culture.
> That culture is the quality of human happiness.
> That human happiness is that state of being in which man's faculties find their fullest expression.

That culture should dictate all political and economic activities and establish health, wealth and beauty of the world.

That the United States favored by Providence with a vast geographical field for unity, freedom and expansion, a geological abundance, a climate of widest variety, a sociology and physiology of unlimited combinations and a psychology as broad as humanity, has the foundation for a great and distinct race and a culture of enormous possibilities.

That the world is today in need of our culture.

That the European tragedy has practically made us the pivot of human progress.

That our responsibilities are tremendous.

That we are undergoing the acid test.

That our immediate actions will declare us a great nation or a great abortion.

That our case is imperative.

That all our ills are due to the lack of sufficient culture and the preponderance of racial, group, class and individual greed.

Coady's manifesto was extremely unsophisticated. "It is time the reign of greed should end," but "neither the Democratic nor the Republican party will end the reign of greed." At the same time one could not put trust in radical politicians, because "the policies of our radicals, treating symptoms instead of causes, will not accomplish even their limited aims." Certainly Coady did not feel that Soviet Russia had solved the problem of good legislation. Paraphrasing Thomas Jefferson, he declared that "the best legislation is least legislation."

Coady was at one with H. L. Mencken in his hostility to puritanism. "The Puritan interpretation of democracy is utilitarian and material, and has interfered with the development of our culture," whereas "tolerance is the basis of democracy." Coady saw our national purpose not as an Anglo-Saxon "gentility" but as "a new and distinct race and a new and distinct culture, made up of, and produced by one hundred per cent of Americans." At the heart of the manifesto was Coady's proud faith in America. "We are an immigrant nation" and "immigration is necessary to our maturity and to our present existence."

Coady passed from his Whitman-like faith in America to a remedial program for the league that was somewhat less grand than his credo. There were the usual planks of progressivism that called for the repeal of the espionage laws, amnesty for political prisoners, election of judges, the dissemination of sex hygiene, and the modification of prohibition. Then came planks that bore the stamp of Coady's flamboyant personality—among them the suggestion that "our national anthem be changed from 'The Star Spangled Banner' to 'Dixie'" and the proposal that one million dollars be the limit of individual ownership.

But for all the cultural flag-waving, the American Tradition League never got off the paper it was written on. According to Kreymborg, Coady was planning to start a four-page daily newspaper reporting on the arts, popular and fine, when death came. For a few years a few people remembered Coady's vivid personality, and it seemed that he might become a legend. But he didn't make it. His views lost their novelty and many won acceptance. By the end of the Twenties, the skyscraper was accepted as an architectural masterwork, and Coady was forgotten.

He had not been an American Apollinaire, for he was not a poet and propagandist of the modern movement—only a propagandist. Nor was he comparable to Alfred Stieglitz, artist in a new medium and propagandist; again Coady was only a propagandist. His propaganda for "skyscraper primitivism" was successful, but certainly not because of his efforts alone. "Skyscraper primitivism," though not under that name, was absorbed into the mainstream of American criticism. Coady was forgotten, but his part in the awakening years of American resurgence is worth remembering.

CHAPTER 6

Alfred Stieglitz and "291"—A Creative Source of the Twenties

On that False Armistice Day when the Twenties began, a posthumously famous art gallery at 291 Fifth Avenue had been closed for eighteen months. Little has been said to explain why Alfred Stieglitz abandoned in spring, 1917, the two gray rooms he rented on the top floor at 291 Fifth.

Paul Rosenfeld, a devout member of the Stieglitz circle, declared that "291" had accomplished its pioneer work by 1917. It had only attracted a few permanent members from the public. "It was," he wrote rather awkwardly, "because of the smallness of the artists that it had to be destroyed. They were closing the door on freedom. The pictorial photographers were betraying the machine; photography the living issue was non-existent. And the colorists were playing against the spirit of art." Moreover, Rosenfeld asserted, French painters had been incapable of understanding "291"; they regarded it as a salesroom. And the American artists were knifing each other and looking on Stieglitz as a source of cash. Even Cézanne, who had had a sensational early showing at "291," had by 1917 become the new academy.

Closed the doors of "291" were when the Twenties dawned. But impulses from "291" were powerfully alive and forward-thrusting as the new decade unfolded. In heralding the advent of the Twenties, Waldo Frank in *Our America* (p. 183) said of the younger generation of artists: "The present brilliant generation is unthinkable without this home ["291"] and this man, Stieglitz." And "291" was indeed a creative source of the Twenties; creative vitality stemmed from it throughout the period.

America in the second decade of the twentieth century was, to a new generation of workers in the arts, a "Sahara of the Beaux Arts," to borrow Mencken's description of the South; and in this cultural desert "291" was an oasis. So it seemed to the memoirist Mabel Dodge Luhan when she returned to New York in 1912 from the brilliant life, with Gertrude Stein as star guest, that went on at her villa in Florence. She was hating New York for its noise, its business, and its rawness, when the nonconformist journalist Hutchins Hapgood took her to "291." Luhan later wrote of "291":

> It was one of the few places where I went. It was always stimulating to go and listen to him [Stieglitz] analyzing life and pictures and people—telling of his strange experiences, greatly magnifying them with the strong lenses of his mental vision. . . . He was always struck by the Wonder of Things, and after a visit to him, one's faith in the Splendid Plan was revived. I owe him an enormous debt I can never repay. . . . At "291" I met people who became the friends of a lifetime. There we gathered over and over again, drawn and held together by the apparent purity of Stieglitz's intention. He was afraid of nothing, and always trusted his eyes and his heart. . . . There were always attractive people at Stieglitz's place. . . . What a dauntless spirit he had!

Many attempts to define "291" have been made. Just as Robert J. Coady was said to have been *The Soil*, so Belle Greene and others declared that Stieglitz was "291." Who then was Stieglitz? It would be hard to improve on his own succinct description of himself: "I was born in Hoboken. I am an American. Photography is my passion. The search for Truth my obsession."

Born on New Year's Day, 1864, at Hoboken, New Jersey, Alfred Stieglitz was the son of a well-to-do German Jewish immigrant who took a lively interest in the arts and in sports, especially in horse racing. The Stieglitz family had a summer place at Lake George, the site of many of Stieglitz's famous "cloud pictures" in the Twenties.

From age seventeen to age twenty-six Stieglitz lived in Europe, chiefly Germany. There he received the best technical education of the times. He learned about optical science and the chemistry of photographic processes, as well as the techniques of picture-taking and print-making. He was also immersed in music and art and books. But he did not go the expatriate way of Henry James and James McNeill Whistler. He came back to the United States in 1890 with a good European education fused with his native upbringing. For five years he was in the photoengraving business. He left that in despair over the decaying spirit of good craftsmanship.

His real career in the 1890s was in photography. He won medal after medal in the international camera shows, and by 1900 he was recognized as a young master in a medium for which the status of an art was being claimed. The old controversy—photography: is it an art? — expired sometime in the Twenties. The controversy was impossible to continue in the face of *Spring Showers, Horsecar Terminal, The Steerage, Ferryboat, The Two Towers,* and other Stieglitz photographs that were indubitably works of art. Of course, it was not Stieglitz's photographs alone that settled the issue. There were others—Julia Margaret Cameron, Edward Steichen, Paul Strand. At the beginning of photography there had been that remarkable master David Octavius Hill. Because of Stieglitz's great achievement in photography, though, Waldo Frank wrote in 1919, "He is perhaps to-day the one major American in art."

What marked Stieglitz off from other photographers was his finding in photography a way of life. He found in it not less than a philosophy of living. For him photography was a dedication to truth and art. "Every photograph," he declared, "was really nothing more than an experiment in life—and in technical work."

In 1903 Stieglitz began to edit and publish a quarterly magazine, *Camera Work,* and with that venture, followed by the opening in 1905 of the Photo-Secession Gallery at 291 Fifth Avenue, the impact of Stieglitz began to be felt in literary circles as well as in photographic and art circles. Or rather Stieglitz began to attract writers to the pages of *Camera Work* and the exhibitions at 291, and then they experienced the impact of the man.

In design, paper, and printing *Camera Work* was a beautiful magazine. It was specially packed and sent by registered mail to the small list of subscribers. Naturally, with such pains, it cost more to fill a subscription than the annual price of eight dollars. "Each copy of *Camera Work* was mailed in perfect condition," Alfred Stieglitz told me some years after the quarterly's demise, "but I have always regretted that I could not have been present to check on the condition when the subscriber unpacked his copy." The number of readers considerably exceeded the subscribers, for copies were passed around, treasured for years, and then shown to the generation too young to have personally known "291."

On an August afternoon in 1920, when I was the only visitor at the Woodstock Art Gallery in the Catskills, the director, William Murrell Fisher (who had contributed a poem and a note to *Camera Work*) brought forth a special number published in 1912 and enthusiastically suggested that I read aloud then and there the portraits of Picasso and Matisse by Gertrude Stein which were, according to Stieglitz, the *raison d'être* of the special number. I did not know as I read aloud to Fisher the strangely insistent writing that these "continuous statements" on Picasso and Matisse were the first publication of Gertrude Stein's work.*

In January, 1915, Stieglitz brought out a special number of *Camera Work*, dated July, 1914. Punctuality was not a virtue of this publication. This number, carrying no pictures, was composed entirely of answers to the question of what "291" was. "Art gallery" was not inclusive enough, not dynamic enough, for what went on at 291 Fifth Avenue. "I could do my work just as well tending bar as running an art gallery," Stieglitz remarked to me on the second occasion I met him in 1923, and he handed me the "What is '291' " number. I studied the issue to find out what had already inspired the legend of "291," a legend so potent to a young writer like myself that I had painted 291 on the steamer trunk I took to Europe in 1921. I put the numerals on for easy recognition of my trunk at French and Italian railway stations, but they were more magical than utilitarian to me.

The anarchist poet and sculptor Adolf Wolff, writing from prison, had said: "Next to my own little studio '291' is for me the freest and purest breathing place for what is commonly called the soul." Djuna Barnes conveyed excitement: "291 is the Attic near the Roof. It is nearer the roof than any other attic in the world. There insomnia is not a malady—it is an ideal."

Hutchins Hapgood gave a good description when he said, " '291' to me is a 'Salon,' a laboratory, and a refuge—a place where people may exchange ideas and feelings, where artists can present and try out their experiments and where those who are tired of what is called 'practical life' may find a change of spiritual atmosphere. . . . I go there to see Alfred Stieglitz, to live for an hour in his spirit, to realize his pure courage and to feel his genuine attempt to get at what is called the truth, which is something that may be felt but never defined." Man Ray's statement in that special number was even better.

For a year, from March, 1915, to February, 1916, Stieglitz fathered a second magazine out of "291." This publication, measuring about twenty inches by twelve, numbering four to eight pages, was published monthly and sold for ten cents a copy, one dollar by the year. It would not have been a Stieglitz enterprise had it not offered a second edition, printed on special paper, which sold

* Not counting *Three Lives*, which was an author-financed book.

for one dollar a copy, five dollars by the year. The name of this magazine was *291*, and when I first saw it—Stieglitz gave me the September-October, 1915, number which contained his photograph *The Steerage*—I called it a pre-Dada review. I was fresh then from the manifestations of Dada in Europe, and the typographical audacities of *291* seemed to have anticipated Tristan Tzara and his outlaws. And indeed Stieglitz had anticipated Dada in presenting an "ideo-gramme" by Apollinaire, a "caligramme" by J. B. Kerfoot, several drawings by Picabia, a typographical spree in French by Marius De Zayas, a poem in French by Ribemont-Dessaignes, and "La Vie Artistique" in two installments by Max Jacob. French representation was very strong in *291*, and the spirit of Dada was already stirring in its forerunners like Picabia and Jacob. But the American half of *291* was "constructive" and dead serious. Agnes Ernest Meyer argued that scientific criticism of art had become possible. Katharine N. Rhoades wrote about the ecstatic moment in listening to music. Marin did a blue, white, and black cover that had no flippancy such as Picabia was delighting in. De Zayas wrote on Negro art. And there was the great affirmation, the Whitman-like promise, of *The Steerage* photograph. *291* was more a post-Armory Show mag-azine than a pre-Dada review.

Camera Work and *291* were not the core of the phenomenon called "291." At the core was *Stieglitz talking*. When you met Stieglitz you met a monologist, and much has been written about his incessant talk, which interfered with the visitor's contemplation of the art on the walls of his gallery. It was as if the pictures were only bait to lure people within the range of Stieglitz's voice. There were some—probably many, and I among them—who could not listen indef-initely to Stieglitz's monologues. That required a passivity, a discipleship. Her-bert J. Seligmann, who seemed to have that capacity, was often there when I called on Stieglitz. He would sit for hours without saying a word, silently ab-sorbing like blotting paper all that Stieglitz said. I used to think that he wrote down Stieglitz's "conversation" after every exposure to it. Perhaps he did* but I also used to ask what there was to recall and write down? Stieglitz said little that was rememberable. Mostly it was a flow of unmemorable talk under pres-sure: it was the pressure of the man behind the talk that made it effective—if it was effective.

In *America and Alfred Stieglitz: A Collective Portrait* (1934), Dorothy Norman

---

* *Alfred Stieglitz Talking: Notes on Some of His Conversations* by Herbert J. Seligmann was published in 1966.

records three statements by Stieglitz that fashion a key to the understanding of why he talked *at* people so much and with so little of the give-and-take conversation. These are those key statements:

> I am the moment. I am the moment with all of me and anyone is free to be the moment with me. I want nothing from anyone. . . .
>
> When I am no longer thinking but merely am, then I may be said to be truly living; to be truly affirming life. Not to know, but to let exist what is, that alone, perhaps, is truly to know. . . .
>
> You will find as you go through life that if you ask what a thing means, a picture, or music, or whatever, you may learn something about the people you ask, but as for learning *about* the thing you seek to *know*, you will have to sense it in the end through your own experience, so that you had better save your energy and not go through the world asking what cannot be communicated in words. If the artist could describe in words what he does, then he would never have created it.

Place these thoughts of Stieglitz in the strong light cast by Nietzsche's great essay *The Birth of Tragedy*—which Stieglitz quite possibly read—and one gets a revelation of the man. Stieglitz was the anti-Socratic man. Socrates' form was the dialogue; the result he aimed at was knowledge. Stieglitz, it seemed to his listeners, talked almost incessantly. His form was the monologue; the result he aimed at was a quickening of being. Himself on the side of Dionysus, and I think we may even call him a true Dionysian, Stieglitz was anti-Socratic in the form, method, and purpose of his talk.

Stieglitz was more advanced in being than in knowledge; that is, he was more like a saint of art than a sage of art. It seems highly significant that Stieglitz said, "I refuse to identify seeing with *knowing*. Seeing signifies awareness resulting from inner experience."

This much can certainly be said about Stieglitz's talk: it was challenging; it labored against self-deception; it put pressure on the listener to seek and clarify experience. Stieglitz was not a prophet, though it is very tempting to dramatize him as the prophet of the Twenties. When he talked to people, or rather at people, he did not ask questions, he did not use the Socratic dialectic, he did not hold dialogues. Stieglitz wanted people to experience, not to formulate, and the purpose of his monopolizing talk was to awaken his listener and to impel him to experience.

Stieglitz resembled a teacher but actually he wasn't. The closest I can come to characterizing the unique role he played is to call him a peculiar sort of guru *manqué*. Several have called him a prophet, but what he lacked was precisely a revelation. But a guru *manqué*, an unorthodox religious teacher lacking the gift, yes.

What made Stieglitz so extraordinary a person? Why did a poet like my friend Hart Crane return from his visits to Stieglitz and write him: "You don't know how much I think about my essay and your work. . . . *I am your brother always.*" What impelled Paul Rosenfeld to write "Alfred Stieglitz is of the company of the great affirmers of life"? It was because he was a source-person, because he formed around himself a creative source of the Twenties, the phenomenon known as "291."

It is both easy and hard to show this source-influence of Stieglitz. It is perhaps an overstatement to say that in retrospect one sees written across the decade's achievements the strong handwriting of Alfred Stieglitz, that masculine, black calligraphy with the heavy down-strokes, "as if drawn with a burnt match," as Melville Cane once remarked to me. His is certainly one of the signatures of the makers of the Twenties, but still he is only one of the major influences, and it is very hard to say how widely his light was refracted through those in his immediate circle.

The visual arts owed most to him. In 1925 he opened a new small gallery, the Intimate Gallery, which continued until 1929, the year in which the Twenties began to die, though the curtain did not go down until 1931. In the decade Stieglitz concentrated on only seven artists—John Marin, Marsden Hartley, Georgia O'Keeffe, Arthur G. Dove, Charles Demuth, Paul Strand, and himself. And these were the most vital of the period; Marin, Hartley, and Dove are today acclaimed as the best painters of the time. Stieglitz gave or found financial support for them; gave them exhibitions; shared with them his spirit of search, his exacting standards, his passion for truth. Drop the Stieglitz group from the Twenties and you make a great vacancy in the twentieth-century history of American art. Even better as a final word on Stieglitz's art is the statement of Ananda K. Coomaraswamy: "His photographs are 'absolute' art, in the same sense that Bach's music is 'absolute' music."

CHAPTER 7

Waldo Frank—Herald of the Twenties

They had a strong sense of the part they were destined to play, that generation of writers who were in their early thirties when the 1920s dawned and who celebrated their seventy-fifth birthdays in the 1960s, sometimes with extensive public honor. They were conscious of themselves as a generation in revolt against the Genteel Tradition of American letters. They saw themselves as the young generation, *les jeunes*, the moulders of the future. They were aware that a new period was starting with them, and very soon they voiced this awareness. Just as there was a young France, a young Ireland, a young Spain, so there was a young America emerging from the bankruptcy of man's political hopes at Versailles and launching a revival in literature and the arts.

The arrival of the young generation was signaled by the appearance in November, 1919, of a remarkable manifesto: *Our America* by Waldo Frank. In this book Waldo Frank played herald of the Twenties, as the reviewers acknowledged at the time—and as the retrospective writers forgot thirty years later in the twenty-fifth anniversary number of the *Saturday Review of Literature*. Yet at the onset of the Twenties, Frank probably did more than any other writer of the avant-garde to reveal the opportunity for a new turning of our culture. His resume of the American past and his prospectus for a new America were heady draughts indeed for young America; a second printing of *Our America* was called for before 1919 ended, and a third printing was ordered a few months later.

Waldo Frank had been well educated for his role as announcer of a new literary period. In *Our America* he spoke of the leaven of European thought and culture at work in New York City. "New York," he said, "lies between invading Europe and America. A frontier city. And a self-conscious one." Frank grew up in a New York family in which German and French were spoken. Between high school and college he spent a year at a Swiss school. At Yale he wrote a book on the spirit of modern French letters that Yale University Press was willing to publish after revision, though the young author never completed the revision. After college Frank lived for a while in France and met some of the young French writers. By the time he alighted in Greenwich Village in 1913 Frank was a Europeanized American who had rejected the expatriate's way and who was acting on a program to put his roots deeper in America.

Frank's preparation for a career in the arts was not exceptional in his generation. More than any generation since the Twenties, his coevals were at least bilingual; they studied in Europe, knew European literature and the life in the capitals of Europe. Van Wyck Brooks, for instance, had spent a year of his boyhood in Germany, France, and England. After college he had practiced as a journalist in England for a year and a half, and he had had his first book published there. In 1913 he had returned to England and had written *America's Coming of Age* before the war forced his passage back to New York. Even the most native of our poets, Robert Frost, went abroad; he lived in England for nearly three years, and it was there his first book was published and the first "shock of recognition" of his poetry happened. And the leaven of Europe could be seen at work in the *Seven Arts* magazine, of which Waldo Frank was associate editor while Robert Frost served on the advisory board, as did Van Wyck Brooks for several months.

The *Seven Arts*! There it lay on the reading table of the college library on a November afternoon in 1916, unannounced, never before heard of—its simple, tasteful cover by Rollo Peters quietly displaying the title of a salutatory essay, "America and the Arts," by Romain Rolland. To how many young men and women, I wonder, did the first sight of this magazine give the thrill of discovery, the thrill of knowing at once that here was a new vein of gold of the spirit, a lode for the pioneers of a new age to search? I have experienced the emotion of discovery a number of times in a life of intellectual and artistic adventure, but never more keenly, more expansively, than when I first turned the pages of Volume I, Number I, of *Seven Arts*, subtitled *An Expression of Artists for the Community*.

Some were prepared for the appearance of the new magazine. A letter from the editor had been mailed in the summer of 1916 to prospective contributors, informing them that "it is our faith and the faith of many, that we are living in the first days of a renascent period, a time which means for America the coming of that national self-consciousness which is the beginning of greatness. In all such epochs the arts cease to be private matters; they become not only the expression of the national life but a means to its enhancement. Our arts show signs of this change. It is the aim of the *Seven Arts* to become a channel for the flow of these new tendencies: an expression of our American arts which shall be fundamentally an expression of our American life."

How good *Seven Arts* was is easily shown. Long after its demise, when the interim judgment of time has been made, one may look through the file of the magazine's single year of publication and select the contents for a *Seven Arts Reader* that would interest the contemporary reader because of artistic merit or historical value or biographical worth. Two pieces alone would make the *Seven Arts Reader* a success: a one-act play, "A Way Out," by Robert Frost, and a short story, "Tomorrow," by Eugene G. O'Neill.* The Frost play is his only known excursion into the theater, although around 1927 he was still entertaining the idea of writing plays. The O'Neill story is laid at a dive near South Street, Tommie the Priest's, and is a preliminary sketch of the characters at Jimmie the Priest's, the milieu of *The Iceman Cometh*.

In the verse section of the *Seven Arts Reader* one would put "The Bonfire" by Robert Frost; "Grass" by Carl Sandburg; "The Broncho That Would Not Be Broken of Dancing" by Vachel Lindsay; "Guns As Keys: And the Great Gate Swings" by Amy Lowell; "The Headland" by Arthur Davison Ficke; verse by Louis Untermeyer, Jean Starr Untermeyer, Alfred Kreymborg, and by three undergraduate poets—Stephen Vincent Benét, Babette Deutsch, and Robert Silliman Hillyer.

In the story section the most interesting American selections—the magazine published fiction by the English writers D. H. Lawrence and J. D. Beresford—would be "Queer," "Mother," and other stories by Sherwood Anderson that subsequently appeared in *Winesburg, Ohio*; and several stories by Waldo Frank, such as "Rudd," which later appeared in *City Block*, and "Bread-Crumbs," which was dropped from the *City Block* cycle. To these would certainly be added "The Song of Ariel" by a then very young writer, S. N. Behrman.

(But at least half the fiction published in *Seven Arts* and most of the one-act plays would not make the grade of our *Reader*. An exception would be a one-

* Although O'Neill would never allow a reprinting of his story, the Frost play was published by Harbor Press in 1929.

act play, "The Dream," by Theodore Dreiser, because the massiveness of Dreiser's achievement lends interest even to his minor efforts.)

The strongest section of the *Reader* would be the essays. This would include "Life, Art and America" by Theodore Dreiser; "The Dreiser Bugaboo" by H. L. Mencken; "Twilight of the Acrobat" and "Albert P. Ryder" by Marsden Hartley; "Aesthetic Form" and "Turgenev" by Willard Huntington Wright; "Meanings" and "American Optimism" by Leo Stein; and "In a Time of National Hesitation" and "H. G. Wells, Theological Assembler" by John Dewey. These all have durable interest, and to them might be added a rather "dated" article on "Young Spain," because its author, John R. Dos Passos, is not "dated." There remain three groups of essays that would confer distinction upon the *Seven Arts Reader.*

One group, along with "This Unpopular War" by John Reed, was responsible for the alienation of the subsidizer of *Seven Arts*. It consists of the antiwar essays of Randolph Bourne: "The War and the Intellectuals," "A War Diary," "Below the Battle," "The Collapse of American Strategy," "The Twilight of Idols," and other stinging, impassioned attacks on the pragmatic justifications of American entrance into World War I.

A second group was by Waldo Frank. "Emerging Greatness" announced the significance of Sherwood Anderson; "Concerning a Little Theatre" was an attack on the Washington Square Players; "Vicarious Fiction" exposed the shallowness of the British novel in the hands of Bennett and Wells; "A Prophet in France" was about Jules Romains. But all these essays were filled with the "faith . . . that we are living in the first days of a renascent period."

Finally, there were the essays of Van Wyck Brooks: "Enterprise," "The Splinter of Ice," "Young America," "Our Awakeners," "Our Critics," and "The Culture of Industrialism." If the new generation was entering upon its tasks with a heightened consciousness of the American past and an intensified awareness of goals, it was in considerable part due to these essays, and to Brooks's book that had preceded them: *America's Coming of Age* (1915).

Of course, the *Seven Arts Reader* should have an introduction to tell the inside story of this short-lived but remarkably influential magazine, but that introduction should not be James Oppenheim's "The Story of the *Seven Arts*" (*American Mercury*, June, 1930). "Looking back on it," Oppenheim wrote, "I believe I wasn't 'culturally' there with my colleagues." The writer of our hypothetical introduction should be Waldo Frank, for as Van Wyck Brooks has

said, Frank "was the real creator of *The Seven Arts*." Everything I have heard
about the conduct of that publication bears out Brooks's assertion, although
Oppenheim says that Frank was called an editorial tyrant in the second six
months of the magazine's existence.

Oppenheim was generally content with writing editorials, and *Seven Arts*'s
associate editor Waldo Frank was free to mould the magazine into what he
thought it ought to be. There is no doubt that he dreamed that *Seven Arts* could
and would do in America what the *Nouvelle Revue Française*, founded in 1909,
had succeeded in doing in France. Frank had a personal acquaintance with the
publishing house and theater affiliated with the *Nouvelle Revue Française* and felt
that they expressed a group that had *organically* (his emphasis) come into being.
He noted that the contributors to the *Nouvelle Revue Française* were the new
generation in French letters. And he hoped that something like this could happen in America.

Van Wyck Brooks has told us of Frank's aspiration for the *Seven Arts*. "Now,
on our new magazine," he says in *Days of the Phoenix*, "Waldo 'yearned to join
the ranks of an army' that, as he said, was 'not yet in existence'; and he was
looking for a criticism that would draw the battleline and release the young 'into
the joy of consecrated war.' . . . and Waldo regretted that we had no 'groups'
such as he had known in France, in the circle of the Vieux Colombier theatre,
for example."

Frank came very near to realizing his aspiration. A glance back at the contributors to our phantom *Seven Arts Reader*, with the addition of such other *Seven
Arts* writers as Carl Van Vechten, Kenneth Macgowan, Hendrik Van Loon,
Witter Bynner, and Lee Simonson, will reveal that many of the new generation
of American letters had found a common front—with certain conspicuous ex-
ceptions (Willa Cather, T. S. Eliot, Ezra Pound, Marianne Moore, for instance). The advisory board was filled out with Edna Kenton, David Mannes,
and Robert Edmond Jones. After a few months Van Wyck Brooks was moved
up from the advisory board to the working editorial staff, becoming an associate editor but not sharing in the managerial function Frank continued to exercise.

"Whitman, who made one feel at home in every corner of the United States,
was the tutelary genius of the paper," Van Wyck Brooks has remembered, and
the magazine had besides an inspiring genius in Alfred Stieglitz. To the first
number Peter Minuit (Paul Rosenfeld) contributed an informal piece about "291

Fifth Avenue" in which he observed that "the painting and the sculpture and the photography shown there are but the means. For in the heart of Alfred Stieglitz is the desire to procure America what she most needs—self-consciousness."

Suppose that *Seven Arts* had flourished and survived until the end of the Twenties. Suppose, that is, that *Seven Arts* had succeeded in taking a position in America for fifteen years analogous to that actually taken by the *Nouvelle Revue Française* in France. Suppose that *Seven Arts*, with its national aspiration and emphasis, had not been replaced by the *Dial*, with its cosmopolitan spirit and international gallery of contributors, but had continued to be the leading review of the new generation—would, then, the literary history of the Twenties have been different? Undoubtedly the Whitman-Stieglitz tendency would have been strengthened; Waldo Frank, the chief critical voice of that tendency, would have consolidated the leadership he temporarily won with *Our America*; there would have been a difference, of course. But only, it seems to me, of reputations, not of production of works of literature. The stream would have been much the same, but critical esteem for some of the components would have been modified upward or downward. But this is the idlest of idle speculations, introduced only to refresh our perspective on *Seven Arts*.

The inescapable truth is that the magazine could not possibly have survived after its first year. Six months after the magazine's birth, America entered World War I; and the editors and leading contributors could not evade speaking their minds about the crisis of their generation and their nation. They could not and they would not be silent on the war. Their utterances were critical, pacifistic, antiwar—but never unpatriotic. No issue of *Seven Arts* was censored or barred from the mails. No indictment for conspiracy to obstruct enlistment or for sedition was ever brought, though at least two contributors, Randolph Bourne and Hendrik Van Loon, were shadowed by the police.

The vulnerability of *Seven Arts* lay in the donor, Mrs. A. K. Rankine, whose relatives owned a big food industry. She is said to have regarded the editorial position of her magazine as "pro-German" and to have been offended by the burning antiwar essays of Randolph Bourne, and especially offended by John Reed's "This Unpopular War." "It was [Bourne's] writing largely," says Van Wyck Brooks in *Days of the Phoenix*, "that killed *The Seven Arts*, for the donor could not accept this anti-war position, nor," adds Brooks, "could I, for it seemed to me to oppose the war was scarcely less futile than opposing an earthquake.

Besides, was not Pan-Germanism a terrible menace?" Mrs. Rankine, who was an admirer of the war president, Woodrow Wilson, was unwilling to continue her subsidy unless the editors relinquished some of their freedom. Van Wyck Brooks has confessed that "I could not see why a magazine that served the arts should throw away its life for any such reason [antiwar propaganda]." But Frank, who had registered for the draft as a conscientious objector, and Oppenheim felt strongly about editorial freedom and would accept no curtailment.

Thus, to the offices of *Seven Arts* in the fine town house on the southwest corner of Madison Avenue and 31st Street came anxiety and the gloom of war and the threat of suspension; under that strain came dissension among the editors as efforts were made to raise capital. An appeal went to Amy Lowell who said she would help support the magazine if the editors would pledge themselves to abandon criticism of the Wilson administration and to forego discussion of the war. This was, of course, unacceptable to Oppenheim and Frank; Brooks retired to his office and shut the door while the argument was waged.* Other possible backers—Scofield Thayer has been mentioned among them— stipulated an editorial reorganization in which the titular head, Oppenheim, should take a place of equality with the other editors. This Oppenheim would not consent to. In fact, as he remembered it, "Frank actually offered to make me his assistant editor!" According to Frank, Oppenheim had the legal power to kill the magazine, and he killed it; and this pre-Twenties attempt to promote "the idea of a literary community," in Brooks's phrase, came to an end with the twelfth issue. It had achieved a circulation of five thousand, very good for the time, and larger, it should be noted, than our literary quarterly reviews achieve today. It found the audience that would grow and support the younger publishing houses of the Twenties—firms like Boni and Liveright and Alfred A. Knopf and B. W. Huebsch, which were already in existence when *Seven Arts* was started and which would in the Twenties publish best-selling works by Dreiser and Sherwood Anderson and Van Vechten.

In another respect Waldo Frank was an *avant-courier* of the Twenties. His early fiction struck a new note. In 1915 the *Smart Set*, edited by Mencken and George

---

* Brooks's second wife, Gladys, observed that Van Wyck did not pick up the gauge of battle when she introduced Allen Tate to him. "It was as though Van Wyck chose to retreat until the danger of altercation had passed."

Jean Nathan who were then the pacesetters in discovering new talent in fiction, published two novelettes by Frank. But it was not until 1917, while *Seven Arts* was in full course, that Frank's novel, *The Unwelcome Man*, came out. This novel had been written in 1914 and 1915, but fourteen publishers had rejected it. By the time the fifteenth brought it forth, the author had grown remarkably beyond the immaturity of his novel. Although *The Unwelcome Man* is a pretty poor novel, it was nevertheless a harbinger of the 1920s and as such should be briefly examined.

"It's one of the forerunners of a new style, a new note, in fiction," was the prompt report of Clarence Day, Jr. Day called it "a history of Quincy Burt's Unconsciousness and of how it directs him," and psychoanalysis was indeed one of the components of the new note. True, Frank did not make much use of psychoanalysis, yet it was evident that the novelist had read Freud and Jung and that his view of his characters had been affected by their teachings. Possibly *The Unwelcome Man* could be described as the first psychoanalytic novel in our literature.

More justly, though, it could be called one of the earliest American novels of social criticism, for its criticism of the American small town, of New York, of college and business life, and even of the American landscape was more prominent than the attack on the psychology of the family. As a critic of Main Street, Frank was three years ahead of Sinclair Lewis.

There was a serious quality about *The Unwelcome Man* that seemed new, a quality that Van Wyck Brooks felt was Russian. The book made him think of Ivan Aleksandrovich Goncharov's *Oblomov*: "Mr. Frank's Quincy Burt is a sort of American Oblomov, a character which is quite as typical in his own time and place, but of which all the terms are seen, as it were, in reverse. For America is simply Russia turned inside out." Brooks went on to observe that "Russia, without her novelists, might have become conscious of the vacuity of her life; but it was the novelists nevertheless that made her actively conscious of it, conscious enough to seek values and create them. *The Unwelcome Man* belongs to the small group of American novels that promise to play the same part in our life."

How hungry we were then for fiction that would portray, reveal, and criticize American life! So starved were we that we could dismiss the tedious faults of *The Unwelcome Man*. "His book isn't faultless," Day remarked, and Brooks summed it up as being "rather an extremely interesting than a successful work of art." And we could generally declare with Brooks that "the vitality of Mr. Frank's conception is shown by the fact that it provides a concrete touchstone for most of the problems of our contemporary civilization." But to reread *The Unwelcome Man* after satiety from several decades of social criticism is to be overcome by those tedious faults we so generously dismissed in 1917.

Frank may have been striking a new note in his content, but in form and style his novel was Victorian. Using the limited omniscient point of view, Frank indulged in the Victorian privilege of walking on stage to comment on action, characters, and theme. The great technical advance of the contemporary novel has been the achievement of spontaneity, whereby the author writes himself out of the story and his novel seems self-propelled. But Frank repeatedly relaxes the tension between subject and form by editorializing, moralizing, and, above all, wiseacring.

Even worse than the wiseacring interruptions was the author's often-expressed pity for his chief character, Quincy Burt. Frank has told us what he intended Quincy Burt to be: a common child, an everyman, a seed that rots in the ground. Brooks, as we have seen, thought that Frank had created an American Oblomov, a symbol of the ineffectual side of the American character. In *The Novels of Waldo Frank*, William Bittner says that Frank is obviously the chief character of *The Unwelcome Man*, but quickly adds that the story of Quincy Burt is not the author's, not a symbolic American's, not an American everyman's; Quincy is not any of these because Quincy Burt is not a created character. He is a totally uninteresting character, without the spark of fictive life, without an appearance of actuality.

Quincy, to be blunt about it, is what blunt people call a "little tin Jesus." His chief feature demands recognition and welcome as an exceptional human being—"the messiah complex"—but he is uninteresting because he does not grow; his essence does not develop.

Clearly *The Unwelcome Man*, harbinger though it was of the fiction of the Twenties, was nevertheless a transitional novel. Its theme of failure—the seed that rotted in the sour soil of industrial America—was to be succeeded even before the Twenties began by the theme of escape and search—of the man who one day walks out of his office in disgust and takes to the open road to find himself. Not Frank but Sherwood Anderson would be the first to compose fiction on a characteristic Twenties theme.

In style, too, *The Unwelcome Man* was less realistic than the major style of the Twenties. What was to come was a sense-based style marvelously conforming to the physical world that gave a powerful illusion of actuality. Frank's style tended to be metaphorical, emotional, turgid. Although he wrote within the realistic convention, his style never *firmly* touched the physical world.

The Unwelcome Man, written, be it again noted, in 1914 and 1915, was the last work of Frank's apprenticeship to letters. Thereafter he matured with great rapidity and intensity. But Frank thought *The Unwelcome Man* better than prentice work, for he permitted its reissuance in 1923. He said then that "it is the expression of the years in which it was conceived and written," which is why the date of its composition has been stressed. "The author," Frank went on, "has long since been absorbed in a widening organism. Absorption, in one form or another, is the true term for death. The author of this novel is therefore dead." The novel, too, was dead in the estimation of the public, for extremely few copies of the new edition were demanded.

The story of how Waldo Frank came to write *Our America* is an interesting illustration of the valuable offshoot that may come out of wartime cultural exchanges between allies. The French High Commission recalled actors from the front and sent the Theatre du Vieux Colombier to New York as a cultural means of strengthening American love for France. The Nouvelle Revue Française publishing house then commissioned Frank to write a long essay, "The Art of the Vieux Colombier," which it published in New York late in 1918. This was followed by an overture to Frank from Gaston Gallimard, of *Nouvelle Revue Française*, and Jacques Copeau, of the Vieux Colombier, to write a book about young America for the French public. Frank said that he would write it *for* his country and *to* his country, and the French publishing firm readily agreed. He thereupon wrote the book at top speed in the early months of 1919, revised it in April and May, and aroused the enthusiasm of his adventurous New York publisher, Horace Liveright, who speeded up production and released the book in November, about nine months after Frank had penned the first words.

The book dazzled my immediate generation. We were then two or three years out of college and more recently out of military service. We had taken no course in American literature; only courses in English literature were given by departments of English which were generally colonial in spirit. We felt obstructed by puritanism in expression of our vision and interpretation of life. Puritanism in the guise of Comstockery was a rampant force and had suppressed Dreiser's *The "Genius"* on incredible Nice-Nellyish grounds. Prohibition, which was overt, crusading puritanism, loomed before us. We were "sort of socialistic"; we had read *New Worlds for Old* and I suppose that many of us could be described as H. G. Wellsian Socialists, which meant that we weren't serious students of Marx. We had read Freud's *Interpretation of Dreams* and were very hopeful for the advance of psychology.

We were distinctly young hopefuls, and estheticism and the precious had some appeal. We had started to read Oscar Wilde in college, and we read book after book by James Huneker, introducing us to the musicians, painters, writers, and philosophers of contemporary Europe. Favorite books were Romain Rolland's *Jean Christophe*, Samuel Butler's *Way of All Flesh*, and George Moore's *Confessions of a Young Man*.

We had no grasp of our national letters. Mark Twain? We thought of him as a buffoon who amused our parents against whom we were rebelling. Melville was in limbo. We had begun to read Whitman, and we went to the one-act plays the Provincetown Players staged. Some of us had come across Randolph Bourne's *Youth and Life* with its incitement to radical life. We were readers of the *Little Review*, the fortnightly *Dial* lately come to New York from Chicago, the *Nation*, and the *New Republic*. We were reading the *Liberator*, a replacement for that war casualty, the *Masses*, and we were buying *Pearson's* every month to read Frank Harris.

We were the newcomers to Greenwich Village; we played small roles in fly-by-night little theaters like Duncan Macdougall's Barn Theatre. We wrote short stories, precious "prose poems," and *vers libre* in the little magazines; we contributed brief reviews to the *Dial* and *New Republic*, and began to think about the novels and plays we would write.

In short, we were a very plastic generation. We were ready for eloquence on the promise and the dream of America. Waldo Frank came swiftly to proclaim that promise and dream; his was the voice that spoke thrillingly of a conception of America to be created by the young writers and artists.

He discovered for us that "the soul of Mark Twain was great." He made us resolve then and there to read *Huckleberry Finn* when he said that this book is "the voice of American chaos, the voice of a precultural epoch. . . . Huckleberry Finn is the American epic hero. . . . One rises from the book, lost in the beat of a great rhythmic flow: the unceasing elemental march of a vast life, cutting a continent, feeding its soil." Nor were we downcast by the harsh judgment of the American soul that followed. "And upon the heaving surface of this Flood, a human child: ignorant, joyous and courageous. The American soul like a midge upon the tide of a world." We would make use of this masterpiece in the conception of America to be created, for which *Our America* was the manifesto.

Our wealth in Lincoln was revealed in a new light. His transfiguration, Frank told us, was a miracle. "Abraham Lincoln prophesies the break from the materialistic culture of pioneer America: personifies the emergence from it of a poetic and religious experience based on the reality of American life—and in terms so simple that they have become the experience of all. This is our true wealth in Lincoln. . . . What lives in Lincoln is the miracle of his achievement of spiritual values from the crude life about him."

Another "hidden treasure" was Thoreau, "the great *ingénu* of our land . . . like cold, clear water against our fever." *Walden*, Frank declared, was "America's first great prose" and "the first conscious 'Yea' of the Puritan world." Whitman, of course, was the great cache of treasure. "For the song of Whitman's vision was the orchestra of life." *Democratic Vistas* was our greatest book of social criticism, just as clearly as *Leaves of Grass* was our greatest poem. Finally, among the hidden treasure was a great American painter, Albert P. Ryder, who had died as recently as 1917. All these gave us an inspiring past, and moreover, a usable past which Van Wyck Brooks had been desiderating for the new American literature.

Our America had a powerful negative argument about our culture, and the young people who read the work applauded it. "Cultural America in 1900," the argument began, "was an untracked wilderness but dimly blazed by the heroic ax of Whitman." America, Frank told us and later told the French when *Notre Amérique* appeared and the English when Hugh Walpole introduced the English edition, is the land of the pioneer. The pioneer, he pointed out, had "had to abhor Wholes, in order to be equal to the infinite detail of his existence. . . . Experience was the foe of the Pioneer." And so a utilitarian conviction fastened on religion and on the universities. Our native philosophy was pragmatism; "it emerged from its panoply of liberal phrase as a mere extension of the old pioneering mood. . . . The legs of the pioneer had simply become the brains of the philosopher." American optimism was a heritage from the pioneer: "The pioneer must hope. Else, how can he press on?"

Dovetailed with this analysis of the pioneer was an analysis of the puritan. Bourne and others had written of the puritan's will to power. As Frank put it,

> The Puritan had begun by desiring power in England. This desire had turned him deviously into austere ways. He had soon learned the sweets of austerity. Now he became aware of the power over himself, over others, over physical conditions which the austere life brought with it. A virgin and hostile continent demanded whatever energy he could bring to bear upon it. A frugal, self-denying life released that energy far better than could another. . . . Pioneer and Puritan met on a basis of psychological and temperamental unity. They merged and became one. The Puritan's nature fitted him superbly to be a pioneer. The pioneer existence made permanent the Puritan's nature.

Under Frank's hands the pioneer-puritan thesis became comprehensive. He devoted a whole chapter to the Jew in America, in which he maintained that "the Jew simply was caught up in the continental rhythm. He became a pioneer: in many ways . . . he was a Puritan already." The Society for Ethical Culture he stigmatized as a poor substitute for the synagogue; it offered "a completely commercialized religion."

Then there were the "buried cultures" Frank wrote of. "The Indian is dying and is doomed." In the Southwest "the Mexican is already lost in the spell of the tin-can and the lithograph." Indeed, the old puritanism had itself become a buried culture, and the Reverend Billy Sunday was its strident voice. In a climactic statement, Frank declared that "American Industrialism is the new Puritanism, the true Puritanism of our day."

The denunciation of America continued. "Chicago is the dream of the industrial god. Chaos incarnate. . . . New England is a tragedy of ambition." The denunciation grew shrill, but we early readers were too sympathetic to object to the tone. "America is the extraverted land. New York its climax. Here the outside world has taken to itself a soul—a towering, childish soul: and the millions of human sources are sucked void."

America's big-circulation magazine? "A mere decked-out carrier for advertisers." American universities? "Incubators of reaction." The Broadway

66

theater? Terrible. American politics? "Bryan was a voice without a mind. Speaking in 1896, as if Karl Marx had never lived."

One hears the socialist accent in an occasional sentence in *Our America*, and in fact the book was written from a consciously held socialist point of view. Frank, it is true, never speaks of a Their America—the America of the Founding Fathers, the pioneers, the puritans, the industrialists. But a Their America is implied throughout as a contrast to Our America, the America of cultural radicals and social radicals, "the men who listen to Stieglitz, and have not quite joined him in their mind with the example of Bill Haywood" and "the readers of socialistic pamphlets [who] have not heard of '291.' " For Frank, Charles A. Beard's *An Economic Interpretation of the Constitution of the United States* had discredited the Founding Fathers. They belonged to Their America, whereas Our America began with Thoreau, Lincoln, and Whitman. Their America was enveloped in "the whole set of myths required by a democracy in which five per cent of the people owned sixty-five per cent of the world they lived in."

How innocent was this socialist point of view! But its innocence was not to become apparent until twelve years later, at the very end of the Twenties. Frank was too near to World War I to see that the Western world had passed in that crisis from the machine age to the power age. The great shift of the work load from the backs of men to the backs of machines had taken place at an accelerated tempo, and labor had assumed more and more a catalytic role in production. A tremendous leap in productive capacity had occurred. In England a few advanced economists were to see as early as 1920 that the power age had been born and were to lay the foundations of the new economics. But Frank— and nothing more could have been expected—was innocent of perception and knowledge of all this; he wrote his book with unshaken confidence in the old economics, socialist division. Maldistribution was the curse, and "fair" distribution would be the blessing. Frank's mind was dominated by the concepts of the age of scarcity and was unforeseeing of the age of plenty producible by the new technology.

But if Frank was innocent in his economic views in 1919, his readers were equally so and equally ignorant of "the flaw in the price system" discovery of the new economics leaders in Great Britain. We cheered Frank when he implied that ownership of capital was synonymous with control of capital. We didn't know then that the assumption that ownership means control is the pathetic

Marxist fallacy in a financial-credit society, and we were to be fearfully slow to learn this. Frank himself was to continue mired in Marx to the day of his death.

What moved us, the young generation of the Twenties, far more than the negative argument of *Our America* was the portrayal Frank made of the generation just preceding us, a generation that had rejected the old gods but not found new ones. This was a generation in the transition of revolt, and Frank wrote brilliantly about its leading figures: Edgar Lee Masters, whose *Spoon River Anthology* had been a sensation in 1915; Theodore Dreiser, author by then of five novels, *Sister Carrie, Jennie Gerhardt, The Financier, The Titan,* and *The "Genius"* and Henry Adams, whose *The Education of Henry Adams* had been privately printed in 1907 and posthumously published in 1918.

Masters, born in 1868, and Dreiser, born in 1871, Frank regarded as a pair of brothers. His immediate judgment of Masters needs no revision today. "The whole burden of Masters' song," Frank said, referring to *Spoon River Anthology,* "is of the burial of love and life beneath the crass deposits of the American world." Frank saw that "the *Anthology* is not great poetry" and this was not contradictory of the claim of Masters' early champion, John Cowper Powys, who had hailed Masters as "a poet of enduring depth and originality." True, said Frank, *Spoon River Anthology* has no wings and is eyeless, "but it is a great book, precisely because it is so noble an expression of the winglessness and eyelessness of him who wrote it: and of the generation whose voice he is."

Frank's description of the ponderous, brooding Dreiser as he lumbered onto the literary scene has never been bettered. "Perhaps the most majestic monument of this transition by which America needed to journey upward into birth is in the novels of Theodore Dreiser." Frank perceived that "the stuff of Dreiser's novels corresponds with amazing clearness to the stuff of our American life. It is unlit and undifferentiated." Nevertheless, his novels had form. "His books have the crude form of massiveness. . . . His books move. But they move like herds . . . they have the rhythm of inchoate, undifferentiated life." Dreiser and Masters were brothers, for Frank, in that they "mark the transition of revolt. They have denied the old gods. But we shall not be free of the old, till we have found the new."

Frank heralded the men who had found new gods to serve, the men who represented the promise of America, the men who were expressing the dream of young America. One of these thus heralded, Randolph Bourne—"the chief humanist of our wistful generation," Frank called him—was already untimely dead at the age of thirty-two, but posthumous collections of his writings continued the steeling influence he had exerted on the temper of the new generation. Two others, fiction writer Frederick Booth and pianist/composer Leo Ornstein, had dropped out. Also James Oppenheim, whom Frank called "the laureate of our immediate, distraught world," would die as the "exhorter" rather than the poet.

But what a group of revivers of the national spirit Frank had named: Van Wyck Brooks, Alfred Stieglitz, Carl Sandburg, Sherwood Anderson, Paul Rosenfeld, Amy Lowell.

It was, of course, not a literary group in the French sense. Its members were separated by geography. It might have become an organic group such as Frank dreamed of if the members had all lived in a single literary capital, for these six and Frank and Bourne shared a common aspiration for cultural revival in America.

Too individualistic for any group were Robert Frost and H. L. Mencken. Frank saw that Sandburg and Anderson were "more conscious prophets," but "Frost is the more perfect artist." Mencken he described as "a sort of capering Saint George come to slay the Puritan dragon." Others in the advancing company of the men of the decade whom Frank hailed were the causerie writer Philip Littell, the reviewers Francis Hackett and Clarence Day, Jr., and the scene designer Robert Edmond Jones. Lastly, Frank heralded Charlie Chaplin as "our most significant and most authentic dramatic figure. . . . Chaplin is our sweetest playboy, our classic clown, sprite of our buried loves." Was this the first praise of Chaplin to come from an intellectual? I suppose not, but it was the first this once-young reader of *Our America* had encountered.

It seemed to me then that this inspiring book bore out the motto from Walt Whitman that preceded its text: "I say that the real and permanent grandeur of These States must be their Religion." And I marked in the margin for its profundity the dictum that "the one true test of values in the world is the hierarchy of Consciousness." That gave the work a deep critical foundation and saved it from being a rapidly written piece of journalism to acquaint the foreigner with new currents in American life. The last paragraph of the work was an eloquent summons to the fulfillment of Our America: "We must begin to generate within ourselves the energy which is love of life. For that energy, to whatever form the mind consign it, is religious. Its act is creation. And in a dying world, creation is revolution." Fit words for prologue to the pivotal year of 1920!

CHAPTER 8

Greenwich Village That Was— Seedbed of the Twenties

The fiftieth anniversary of the Armory Show in 1963 had recaptured the spirit of vitality that this original exhibition of modern art had offered in 1913. Still fresh, still revolutionary in fact, was the general impression of the art works shown. But fifty years took a heavier toll on Greenwich Village. That haven of the young artists and intellectuals of the first two decades of this century had become almost unrecognizable by the 1960s—if not much earlier.

In the classes that were graduated just before America entered World War I, literary undergraduates heard rumors of Bohemia in New York and yearned to go there. I remember how, on my first stroll through the Washington Square area, the place seemed to speak liberty and love and art. In college I had come upon the poetry of William Vaughn Moody who had once lived on Waverly Place, and I had shouted assent—as if I really knew life—to his lines, "Save sacred love and sacred art, / Nothing is good for long." When I returned to the Wesleyan campus, I wrote up this visit to Bohemia, and the piece, "Lunch at Polly's," came out in the college literary monthly in the fall of 1917, after I had been graduated.

I had found Polly's—the formal name was the Greenwich Village Inn—on West 4th Street and had been charmed by the summer custom of outdoor service in the backyard. Seated at a plain deal table, I had enjoyed a Spanish omelet. An awning overhead protected the guests from the dripping wash strung above the yard. I had seen the waiter Mike chase a cat from a table top, and I had seen Polly Holliday minding the cash register at the door. In my account I described her as a "large-featured girl, with a pasty complexion." Agnes

Boulton's memory is more flattering: "Polly Holliday dominated the scene," Boulton wrote in recalling her life with Eugene O'Neill, "tall, dark-eyed, and calm . . . she gave her place the air of a club."

Edmund Wilson, out of Princeton in the class of 1916, must have been living on West 8th Street at this time. He was visited in February of 1917 by F. Scott Fitzgerald of the Princeton class of 1917. Fitzgerald immediately liked the Village; it was, he thought, a man's world "released . . . from all undergraduate taboos." After his discharge early in 1919 from military service, Fitzgerald, like many an artist and writer of his generation, wished to live in the Village. He proposed to John Peale Bishop (Princeton, 1916) that they set up an apartment there. "Will you honestly take a garret (it may be a basement but garret sounds better) with me somewhere near Washington Square?" Bishop had replied. Fitzgerald never did become a Villager, but he was typical of his generation in wanting to be one. By the end of January, 1919, Edna St. Vincent Millay (Vassar, 1917) had reached the Village and was writing letters from 139 Waverly Place. Soon she would be the poet of the Village in *A Few Figs from Thistles*. In "Macdougal Street" she gave a physical impression:

> The fruit-carts and clam-carts were ribald as a fair,
> (Pink nets and wet shells trodden under heel).

Mabel Dodge, with her second husband, the architect Edwin Dodge, had returned late in 1912 to America from her villa in Florence. Already a practiced salon mistress, she took the second floor of the General Daniel Sickels house at 23 Fifth Avenue. The old Civil War general—he had lost a leg at Gettysburg—was then ninety-two and kept himself in a temper by reading newspapers all day long on the ground floor. Soon, with the aid of friends Carl Van Vechten, Hutchins Hapgood, and Lincoln Steffens, Mabel Dodge filled her white drawing room—brilliant white woodwork, heavy white wallpaper, white bearskin rug, white porcelain Venetian chandelier for candles, white marble mantlepiece, white linen drapes—with the brightest and blithest spirits of the "New Freedom" period of Woodrow Wilson.

The salon has not been an American institution. There have been few in our history, and only two in my lifetime—Mabel Dodge's during the first Woodrow Wilson term and Muriel Draper's in the Twenties and early Thirties. But of these the greatest exception to our lack of salon life was Mabel Dodge's. In a chapter of his diverting novel, *Peter Whiffle*, Carl Van Vechten describes an

evening at Edith Dale's (Mabel Dodge's), and it transmits to us the stimulation, the cross-fertilization of ideas, the ardor for social change, the conversational excitement, the bohemian manners that the Mabel Dodge evenings as-
suredly had. With the people attracted to 23 Fifth Avenue it could not have
been otherwise. To be met there were: Walter Lippmann, already brilliantly
launched on political writing; Jo Davidson "with his jovial black beard, Bacchus
or satyr in evening clothes," as Van Vechten described him in *Peter Whiffle*;
John Reed, with whom Mabel Dodge was to sail away to Europe, Edwin Dodge
having left in the early days of the salon; Robert Edmond Jones, the new scene
designer; Marsden Hartley, whose paintings hung on the walls of the drawing
room; shy Edwin Arlington Robinson and shy Ridgeley Torrence, poets; Max
Eastman, poet and radical, and Ida Rauh, his wife; Andrew Dasburg, painter
who went to the Southwest in the mid-Twenties; Charles Demuth, another rising painter; Frank Harris who introduced himself, "I am Frank Harris, the son
of man!—and the son of God"; Dr. A. A. Brill, pioneer disciple and translator
of Sigmund Freud; Neith Boyce, Edna Kenton, Helen Westley, Henrietta
Rodman, Margaret Sanger; Emma Goldman and Alexander Berkman, anarchist leaders; Big Bill Haywood, IWW leader; Harry Kemp, bohemian poet, and
Hippolyte Havel, bohemian anarchist. "Hippolyte, sweet, blinking amblyoptic
Hippolyte, his hair as snarly as Medusa's," in Van Vechten's description. It
was Hippolyte Havel—the model for the cursing anarchist Hugo Kalmar in
O'Neill's play *The Iceman Cometh*—who defined Greenwich Village as a state
of mind, and that state of mind came into being in the years 1913 and 1914 at
Mabel Dodge's salon.

And the mistress of these gatherings? "Edith [Mabel]," says Van Vechten
in *Peter Whiffle*, "was the focus of the group, grasping this faint idea or that
frail theory, tossing it back a complete or wrecked formula, or she sat quietly
with her hands folded, like a Madonna who had lived long enough to learn to
listen. Sometimes she was not even at home, for the drawing-room was generally occupied from ten in the morning until midnight. Sometimes—very often, indeed—she left her guests without a sign and went to bed. Sometimes—
and this happened still oftener—, she remained in the room without being
present."

It would seem that Mabel Dodge (after 1923 Mabel Dodge Luhan) had the
ideal personality for a salon mistress and was ideally circumstanced, being
wealthy, for the role. Hers was a catalytic personality; she induced activity around

her. Things began to happen, and sometimes they were big things like the Madison Square Garden pageant for the Paterson strikers, which she and John Reed organized.

In *I Thought of Daisy*, that finest of novels about Greenwich Village, Edmund Wilson was surely thinking of Steffens and Reed and Eastman and the others who came to 23 Fifth Avenue when he had his narrator ruminate on the early Village: "There they had come, those heroes of my youth, the artists and the prophets of the Village, from the American factories and farms, from the farthest towns and prairies—there they had found it possible to leave behind them the constraints and self-consciousness of their homes, the shame of not making money—there they had lived with their own imaginations and followed their own thought."

Of what was the early Greenwich Village clearly the source? Most clearly, I suppose, of a new movement in the American theater, for out of the Village came the Washington Square Players, the most successful little theater of the second decade of the century. And from the Washington Square Players came the Theatre Guild in 1920. Equally germinative was the Provincetown Playhouse and its great gift to the American theater, Eugene O'Neill, whose *Beyond the Horizon* opened on Broadway in 1920.

Less clearly, the early Village had an effect on book publishing. One of the important new firms, one that was to introduce new methods and many of the major authors of the Twenties, was Boni and Liveright. Albert and Charles Boni had been publishing downtown in the Village as early as 1913 when they issued Alfred Kreymborg's magazine, the *Glebe*.* Although the Bonis did not stay long with Horace Liveright, the stamp of Greenwich Village on the list remained after their withdrawal to set up the firm of A. and C. Boni which was located in the Village of the Twenties.

But the largest role played by Greenwich Village was the spearheading of the revolution in manners and morals which all agree took place in the Twenties. Although, of course, not the only and perhaps not the greatest provocator, the feminist movement was one of the most potent forces preparing for the revolt of the young generation in the Twenties; the bachelor girls and their male

---

* In which Ezra Pound's first Imagist anthology was published and which later became *Others*.

sympathizers had invaded and captured the Village as early as the Mabel Dodge *soirées*. The prototype of the Greenwich Village woman was a New York schoolteacher, Henrietta Rodman, who advocated women's suffrage (a goal attained in 1920), female dress reform, birth control, free love, the right of workers to strike, and, for a time, nudism. Floyd Dell gave a quick sketch of Henrietta Rodman, under the name of Egeria, in *Love in Greenwich Village*: "Egeria had the rare gift of being able to start things. Some people, it is true, said that what she inevitably started was trouble; but that was scarcely just to her. . . . [She was] a *Candide* in petticoats and sandals, she did always manage to involve herself in complicated difficulties; but she faced those difficulties serenely, and fought her way out of them—into some new thorn-patch. . . . She invented Greenwich Village—the Greenwich Village whose gay laughter was heard around the world. It wasn't at all what she had meant it to be—for she was a very serious young woman, and it was incurably frivolous. But still—she did it!"

The bachelor girl wore batiks and sandals; she bobbed her hair and smoked cigarettes when few women smoked; she earned her livelihood, and at Bertolotti's on West 3rd street she stood at the bar with the men. She read Ellen Key and Freud; she made speeches at the Liberal Club and got herself arrested for birth control propaganda; she acted in little theaters and painted cubistic pictures and wrote *vers libre*. She was a good companion to the young men who were crowding into the Village. They were young men in revolt against the small-town culture of America (*Main Street* was only five or six years away), and they were eager to do battle against the prevailing puritanism of American life. The short-haired girls and the long-haired men were caricatured—Irvin Cobb and Samuel Merwin and even Sinclair Lewis in *Hobohemia* were to libel them for bourgeois guffaws—but they were to prevail. The trails they blazed, the oncoming young generation in the Twenties was to follow.

Much of the trail-blazing was performed in the Village magazines. This was especially true of the *Masses* which in 1912 moved from a lower Manhattan office to 91 Greenwich Avenue and came under the chief editorship of Max Eastman. In his autobiography, *From Another World*, Louis Untermeyer, who was associated with the *Masses* from the early editorship of Piet Vlag to the second conspiracy trial in 1918, makes the strange assertion that "the *Masses* had its habitat in the Village, but it was not a part of it." This is a curious statement about a publication that included on its editorial staff such conspicuous Villagers as John Reed, Mary Heaton Vorse, Robert Carlton Brown, John Sloan, Stuart Davis, and Floyd Dell, the managing editor, not to mention Eastman himself. Indeed, on the masthead of the *Masses* was flaunted a manifesto of the uncommercial, antibourgeois, self-expressive spirit of Bohemia. "This magazine," it proclaimed, "is owned and published cooperatively by its editors. It has no dividends to pay; nobody is trying to make money out of it. A revolutionary and not a reform magazine—a magazine with a sense of humor and no respect for the respectable. Frank, arrogant, impertinent, searching for the true causes. A magazine directed against rigidity and dogma wherever it is found; printing whatever is too naked or true for a money-making press; a magazine whose final policy is to do as it pleases and conciliate nobody—not even its readers."

But there was another magazine that also had the Village for its habitat and was as much *of* it as the *Masses*. This magazine has never received its due from the chroniclers of little-magazine history. The *Pagan* called itself "A Magazine for Eudaemonists" (adherents of the Aristotelian conception of happiness) and carried the motto: "Hang your lantern in yon nook, / Drink and laugh at priest and shah," which sounds more hedonistic than eudaemonistic. It was founded in May, 1916, by Joseph Kling who supported it and himself in a mysterious manner (some said he was a schoolteacher). He began with a circulation of five hundred, claimed that he had two thousand at the end of the first year, and somehow kept the magazine alive until 1922. In 1919 Kling opened a bookstore at 23 West 8th Street in conjunction with his magazine, and it was in this combined office and shop that I first met Hart Crane.

There was in those years a neighborhood magazine called the *Greenwich Village Quill*, and in it appeared verse by Bobby Edwards that twitted the editor of the *Pagan* and proprietor of the Pagan Book Shop. The verses give us the flavor of the Village of 1919.

> Oh, pagan, Pan-like Joe
> How sylvan-like you go
> And manufacture woe
> When ladies say you no:
> Oh, pagan thing
> Oh, singing Kling
> 'Tis Spring!

Oh, Pagan publisher
Whom poet-maids prefer
Into your little shop
May many ladies stop.

Although Hart Crane soon outgrew the *Pagan* (he was to include no poem from it in *White Buildings*), Kling continued to be the target for young writers, and he was surprisingly receptive to new talent. Among the many contributors of prose and poetry to the *Pagan* were such writers as Paul Eldridge, DuBose Hayward, Mary Carolyn Davies, Malcolm Cowley, Edward J. O'Brien, Gustav Davidson, James Rorty, Mortimer J. Adler, Herbert S. Gorman, Louis Zukofsky, Joseph Moncure March, and Joseph Wood Krutch. Whatever adjective might be applied to the youthful work of these and other writers whom Kling published, "fetid" is the most inappropriate and "promising" would be the most likely.

For many of the *Pagan*'s writers, the magazine was a training-school, a novitiate of sorts. For Hart Crane it was a literary high school. Kling gave Crane what he most needed at the age of seventeen: the encouragement of publication. But he could not give him guidance. Kling was himself insensitive to the new writers in the *Little Review*—Joyce, Pound, Eliot, Wyndham Lewis, William Carlos Williams, William Butler Yeats—who were to be so stimulating to Crane. Kling's taste had been formed earlier, and whatever policy the *Pagan* had was only Kling's personal taste, which liked the Russian realists of 1900, the Yiddish humorists of the Café Royal, and the Continental and English aesthetes of the Yellow Book period. Nor could Crane and the rest of us learn anything from Kling's own literary technique, which was simple, impressionistic, staccato. As a rule, editorials were as absent from the *Pagan* as was the copyright notice. But occasionally Kling exploded with short expostulations against war, against censorship, and against religion. He wasn't much of an editor, and yet the welcome Joseph Kling extended to the new generation that was to give the Twenties so much of its tone and aura should not be undervalued.

At 23 West 8th Street, the Pagan Book Shop had started with a small stock of new and secondhand books. A few steps to the west had been a rival bookseller Kling hated; he was Samuel Roth, fresh from Columbia and later, notorious for the piracy of *Ulysses* and for his troubles with the government over the publishing of allegedly obscene books. A few steps to the east was the

Washington Square Book Shop. Nearby was the Strunsky cafeteria, Three Steps Down, where the *Pagan* editor would go for a hurried lunch.

Kling would open his shop in midmorning and pounce on his mail. Unlike most editors, he read manuscripts at once, sitting at his battered desk or standing beside it. It was a performance I can see and hear now, for Kling would read aloud passages he liked and would punctuate his editorial consideration with audible comments, gruntings, and chuckles.

He was then in his early thirties, a short, thickish man, with black hair and a harsh voice. There was a pronounced bulge at the corner of his right eye, and one shoulder rose higher than the other, so that he had a distorted look. He liked to wear a green eyeshade and to strip off his coat. In vest and shirtsleeves, then, standing and reading quickly one manuscript after another, he would make up his mind instanter about each of them. When a manuscript particularly struck his fancy, he would chortle and exclaim to his audience: "Goddammit, boy, that's got gissum!"

Inelegant, but it did express the warmth with which the old Villagers greeted the oncoming writers of the Twenties. The Village prepared the way and in 1920 the popular audience was to join in the welcome.

When did the Village die? For Greenwich Village in its role of Latin Quarter *is* dead beyond a peradventure, succeeded by a quarter that is solidly bourgeois with its high-rent apartment buildings and disagreeably commercial with its tourist attractions. But the death of the Latin Quarter Village did not occur as early as some have dated it. Already in the Twenties there were those who said the "real" Village was dead. In *Love in Greenwich Village*, Floyd Dell gave 1924 as the date for the passing of the Village. This was to mistake his retirement to Croton-on-Hudson for the fall of the Village. Despite the defection of Dell and some other first-generation Villagers, the Village flourished and persisted throughout the Twenties and did not start to die until the Great Depression. The pre-Twenties quarter about which Dell wrote so sentimentally was in fact the seedbed of the Village of the Twenties that Edmund Wilson was to depict so realistically in *I Thought of Daisy*.

One block of the Washington Square quarter that was very much alive in the Twenties still stirs up powerful memories of the old Bohemia for me. That block is West 13th Street, from Sixth to Seventh Avenue; and in the Twenties it was Montparnassian. Still standing fifty years later, near the Sixth Avenue corner, is the brick house in which the eccentric John Brooks Wheelwright had his silly row with the landlord. And just a few doors west is the beautiful old brick house in which B. W. Huebsch published, from 1920 to 1924, the great weekly, the *Freeman*. A little farther along were the offices of Roger Baldwin and the American Civil Liberties Union, which had been organized in World War I.

Then came a speakeasy favored by the literati of the Twenties, Mario's— still there in the sixties, legitimized after 1933. I was introduced to Mario's by Lincoln MacVeagh, head of the Dial Press at 152 West 13th. Over a bottle of prohibition "red ink" he told me his recollections of Robert Frost for the biography I was writing. Then came the building of the progressive school, the City and Country School; and last, near the Seventh Avenue corner, was the building housing the *Dial* magazine, with the Dial Press in the basement. There then, on this block, were the magazines the young writers of America aspired to write for, the school to which the Village intellectuals sent their children, the speakeasy patronized by gourmets like Ford Madox Hueffer (not yet Ford), and the homes of editors and poets. It was representative of the flourishing Village of the Twenties.

But the very heart of Bohemia is gone. That wonderful French hotel—not Americanized French, but real French—the Hotel Brevoort, headquarters for the state of mind called Bohemia, is no longer standing. That was where a farewell dinner for Emma Goldman and Alexander Berkman had been held in 1919. And the Walt Whitman Society met there each year to celebrate the anniversary of his birth. Another absent landmark is the Lafayette Hotel on University Place. The game room of this French hotel was more popular than the Brevoort, because more affordable to us.

A walk around the Square today, though, would be crushing to one's sentiment for the past, for Washington Square has become what the opponents of the expansion of New York University warned it would become—the campus of NYU. On East Waverly Place, which runs out of the Square, one always cast a glance at Number 29, home of Frank Harris. Now there is no Number 29; in its stead stands a great pile of bricks called One University Place.

The old south side of the Square, except for the Judson buildings, is completely gone. Gone is Number 61, Madam Branchard's where Frank Norris and Theodore Dreiser had lived. Gone is Bruno's Garret at Number 58, and Number 46 where Bobby Edwards had his studio. Neither has Macdougal Street survived. That row of old houses on the west side—the Liberal Club, the Dutch Oven restaurant, the converted stable in which Pegasus was hitched that became famous as the Provincetown Playhouse, producer of Eugene O'Neill's early plays—all are gone.

The portents of doom that Floyd Dell saw even as the Twenties dawned were waxing all during the Twenties. As Dell noted: "Seventh Avenue was being extended southward, the new subway was being laid; in a little while the magic isolation of the Village would be ended." And so it was by 1920. Greenwich Village, Dell declared, "was to become a side-show for tourists, a peep-show for vulgarians, a commercial exhibit of tawdry Bohemiansim"; and he cited the rash of "atmospheric" restaurants, the exploitation of the Village balls at Webster Hall, and the counterfeit Villagers like Tiny Tim, the "psychic candy" hawker. But this process of commercializing Bohemia went on more slowly than Dell anticipated and was not completed until World War II. Inexorable, though, was the change from a low-rent community to a high-rent one that was fatal to the spirit of impecunious Bohemia. "The beautiful crumbling houses of great rooms and high ceilings and deep-embrasured windows would be ruthlessly torn down to make room for modern apartment buildings; the place would become like all the rest of New York City—its gay, proud life would be extinguished."

Dell has sung of this change in "The Ballad of Christopher Street."

"Is it still there, I wonder, down in Christopher Street,
That little rickety house of ours where life was young and sweet?"
No, my dear, they've torn it down, a year and a day ago;
There's nothing there but an empty lot where the purple burdocks grow.

That would be about 1919, and then sometime in the early Twenties began a building boom.

Builders will come, with riveters, and rivet loud till noon,
And call it a day, and go away, leaving against the sky
A great brand-new apartment-building fourteen storeys high.
And women with dogs, and men with cars, will quarrel and sleep and eat,
After the fashion of their kind, at Eleven Christopher Street.
For the days that we knew are dead, my dear, and never in all time's turning
Shall there burn in the hearts of Christopher Street the fires that we felt burning
When in that little house of ours life still stayed young and sweet. . . .

The Village of the Twenties, which grew from the prewar Village, exists no more.

Randolph Bourne. Line drawing by Arthur G. Dove, from the Death Mask by James Earle Fraser. Reproduced from Paul Rosenfeld's *Port of New York*, Harcourt Brace.

Alfred Stieglitz. Photograph by Paul Strand. Reproduced from Paul Rosenfeld's *Port of New York*, Harcourt Brace.

Georgia O'Keeffe. Photograph by Alfred Stieglitz. Reproduced from Paul Rosenfeld's *Port of New York*, Harcourt Brace.

John Marin. Photograph by Alfred Stieglitz. Reproduced from Paul Rosenfeld's *Port of New York*, Harcourt Brace.

Jean Toomer. Courtesy Special Collections, Fisk University Library.

Marsden Hartley. Photograph by Alfred Stieglitz. Reproduced from Paul Rosenfeld's *Port of New York*, Harcourt Brace.

Gaston Lachaise. Reproduced from *The Sculpture of Gaston Lachaise*. Courtesy Eakins Press, Publishers, New York, and the Lachaise Foundation.

Man Ray in 1920. Reproduced from Man Ray's *Self-Portrait*, Little Brown and Co.

Waldo Frank. Photograph by Alfred Stieglitz. Reproduced from Gorham Munson's *Waldo Frank*, Boni & Liveright.

PART TWO

The Pivotal Year, 1920

CHAPTER 9

Magazine Rack of the
Washington Square Book Shop

In 1920 the Washington Square Book Shop was already living on its original reputation as a launching-pad for flights into the theater, little magazines, and book publishing. On Macdougal Street it had been a center for creative enterprise. But after its removal to West 8th Street, just off Fifth Avenue, it was less of a club and more of a business; its old role of seedbed was resumed uptown by the Sunwise Turn Book Shop.

Even so, the Washington Square Book Shop, presided over by Egmont Arens and Josephine Bell, was during the Twenties the Greenwich Villagers' favorite shop for browsing and even for purchasing books when the price could be afforded. A number of us impecunious young writers were regular patrons of its magazine stand. Magazines priced at fifteen cents to thirty-five cents we could afford, and many an exciting quarter hour was spent looking over the new issues displayed on the rack just inside the shop's entrance.

It was a very selective rack. One could not find the big-circulation magazines like *American Magazine* and *Saturday Evening Post*. In Middletown, U.S.A.,* one out of five families received the *American*; one out of six received the *Saturday Evening Post*. But not many in Middletown ever saw the magazines on display at the Washington Square Book Shop. About fifteen copies of the *New Republic* went each week to Middletown, a city of 35,000; about three copies of the monthly *Dial* supplied Middletown's demand. Most of the fifteen or so magazines carried by the Washington Square had no circulation whatever in Middletown.

* Muncie, Indiana

In what a high-pitched anticipatory mood we ducked into this book shop once or twice a week to see what was new on its magazine rack. Here were the publications of the new movements in American art and thought and literature. Here were the reviews that were stimulating the young. Here were the magazines we wanted to write for—were, in fact, already writing for one or two. Even before the issue containing a book review we had contributed could reach us by mail, it would be on sale in the Washington Square Book Shop rack; and when that happened, the excitement of our visit was doubled.

New Republic

In January of 1920 the weekly magazine I watched for most eagerly was the *New Republic*. I was then reviewing books for it, and there was each week a chance that a short review of mine would be printed. That was the case when I turned the pages of the January 7, 1920, issue and found in the back pages my unfavorable notice of a novel by Alexander Black.

On the front cover of the *New Republic*'s first issue of the new decade, in large type, was a sort of keynote-editorial:

1920

In Europe the greatest famine of modern times, in Asia disturbances from the Urals to the Sea, on the southern border the beginnings of a desperate adventure, the world over schism and distrust, at Washington a deadlock of office holders, no single measure of reconstruction achieved, a Presidential year. It will not be an easy year. It will not be a possible year if thought is suppressed and terrorized, if the censors, the propagandists and bigots have their way. 1920 will leave the world better than it found it only if free men insist upon their freedom.

And the masthead:

Editors

Herbert Croly

Francis Hackett

Alvin Johnson

Charles Merz

Walter Lippmann

Philip Littell

The editors were listed as equals but it was known then, as it had been known at the founding of the journal in 1914, that first among equals was Herbert

Croly. He wrote the leading editorial each week, formulated policy, and guarded integrity. In 1919 he had made a courageous decision, full of risk. The circulation of the *New Republic*, under 1,000 when it started, had risen to 43,000 by 1919. It had been thought to be—but wasn't quite—the unofficial voice of the Wilson administration. But Croly denounced the Treaty of Versailles and repudiated the League of Nations, and precipitously in 1920 the circulation dropped 40 percent from its peak. Now in the first month of the year the *New Republic* ran chapters from John Maynard Keynes's new book, *The Economic Consequence of the Peace*; and the editorial, "Europe on the Rack," in the January 21 issue was clearly inspired by Keynes's book. It would be many years before the *New Republic* would climb back to a circulation above 40,000.

Too much has been said against Croly's "heavy" and "abstract" style. Formal and abstract it was, but it was not labored, even though laboriously composed. It was effective, and on at least one occasion (*New Republic*, February 8, 1920), it achieved anthology rank of a permanent kind. Croly wrote a tribute to Abraham Lincoln after seeing John Drinkwater's legendary drama. Could any editor of that day have bettered Croly's words on Lincoln as the embodiment of the spiritual promise of democracy?

> Hence it is that Lincoln is at once the most individual and the most universal of statesmen. In externals he fairly reeks of Middle-western life during the pioneer period. No man could reflect more vividly the manners and the habits of his day and generation. He is inconceivable in any other surroundings. But with all his essentially and intensely Middle-western aspect, he achieved for himself a personality which speaks to human beings irrespective of time and country. Already he is being more carefully studied and more discriminately appreciated in England than in America, and the interest of Englishmen is prophetic of that of other peoples. Wherever throughout the world Democrats look for a hero or a seer whose life and sayings embody the spiritual promise of a democracy, they will turn to Lincoln.

The promise of American life, the spiritual promise of democracy—this was the object of Croly's study throughout his life, and this was the theme that gave the *New Republic* motive power and cohesion during the decade and a half of its greatness. That first issue of the *New Republic*, dated "Saturday 7th November 1914," advertised on its cover in large display type: "A Journal of Opinion which Seeks to Meet the Challenge of a New Time." Croly was forty-five then. One of his editors, brilliant Walter Lippmann, was only twenty-five; but he had already founded his reputation for political insight with *A Preface to Politics* (1913). In his senior year at Harvard, Lippmann had been an assistant to George Santayana; after graduation he worked for a while as a special investigator for Lincoln Steffens on *Everybody's Magazine*. He had become a Socialist and in 1912 went to Schenectady, New York, to serve as private secretary to George R. Lunn, the Socialist mayor. From 1914 to 1920 he contributed greatly to the *New Republic's* meeting "the Challenge of a New Time"; and it was even rumored that he had drafted Wilson's Fourteen Points (not true, though he may have helped in the drafting). Now, in 1920, Lippmann sized up for *New Republic* readers the various presidential candidates. I do not know whether it was he or Croly who wrote the *New Republic's* endorsement of Herbert Hoover as presidential timber (eight years too soon for history), but he went along with this early forwarding of Hoover's name.

The *New Republic* editor who most interested this prentice reviewer in 1920 was Francis Hackett. An Irish immigrant at eighteen, he had made a bright name for himself in Chicago; he made journalistic history in his editorship of the weekly book section of the Chicago *Evening Post*. Croly invited Hackett to join the *New Republic* for its first number. And this act conspicuously showed Croly's sagacity in selecting editorial associates, for Hackett proceeded to make the literary part of the new journal as fresh and powerful and exciting as Lippmann made the political part. Hackett's lead reviews were, I thought then, the most brilliant that were coming out in America; and they have stood the rigorous test of time as few reviews to meet a weekly deadline ever do. I reread them forty-five years later, and they were as fresh and final as they had seemed in 1920, these reviews of Dreiser, Sinclair Lewis, Floyd Dell, and other writers of the revival.

Take this judgment, for example, of Dreiser in a review of *Hey-Rub-a-Dub-Dub* (May 26, 1920). It needs no correction in the perspective of time:

> He drives along like a springless truck, sparing neither himself nor his passenger. And yet, heavy and turgid and monotonous and sensuously obtuse as he seems to be, he makes his discussion interesting. . . . His sincerity is the salt of his nature. It makes even of his manner a sort of virtue. . . . The truth seems to be that Theodore Dreiser's mind is formless, chaotic, bewildered. . . . In short, our leading novelist is intellectually in serious confusion, and needs a deeper philosophy than—hey rub-a-dub-dub.

The other editors on Croly's brilliant team were Charles Merz, who became editor of the New York *Times* in 1923, Philip Littell, who wrote urbane causeries; and Alvin Johnson, who had been active in founding the New School for Social Research in 1919. Johnson, who specialized in fiscal and trade problems and was ultraorthodox in his economics (he had many reservations about John Maynard Keynes), regarded himself as a Midwestern liberal in a camp of Eastern liberals; he came more and more into conflict with Croly over the future course of the New School for Social Research and finally resigned from the *New Republic* in 1923. But in 1920 he was reviewing to Wells's dissatisfaction the best-selling *Outline of World History* and stirring readers to think hard on the postwar economic situation of the "Punic Peace," as he called it before Keynes called it the "Carthaginian Peace."

New Republic continued on its high level of editorial statesmanship throughout the 1920s. Croly died in 1930, and after that the inspiration of "the promise of American life" weakened; his statesmanship was followed by merely political editing.

Nation

Stacked in rivalry beside the current *New Republic* would be the current *Nation* on the rack of the Washington Square Book Shop. The *Nation*, we understood, was a revived weekly, but to us it seemed a new journal of opinion. Founded in 1865, it had been, we were told, a great weekly under the editorship of E. L. Godkin. Had not Henry and William James, and Henry James, Sr., and Lowell, Longfellow, and Whittier, and Thomas Wentworth Higginson and Charles W. Eliot reviewed for it? Latterly it had declined in circulation and influence. For a few years it had been edited by Paul Elmer More, a dodo if you took the word of Mencken and Brooks.

But in 1918 it had been taken over by Oswald Garrison Villard and dedicated anew to liberalism. This, in our estimation, made it a new magazine, for it had now gained a new and much larger public, having risen within eighteen months from a circulation of a few thousand to a printing of 53,000.

In its first issue of 1920, the masthead of the *Nation* had listed Villard as editor, Henry Raymond Mussey as managing editor, and William MacDonald, Arthur Warner, Freda Kirchwey, and Mabel H. B. Mussey as associate editors. But we noticed changes all that year. In March, the Musseys resigned. Earlier

Carl Van Doren had been listed as literary editor. In April, Arthur Gleason became an associate editor. In May, Lewis S. Gannett became an associate editor, and Ernest H. Gruening replaced Mussey as managing editor. In August, Ludwig Lewisohn, who was the journal's dramatic critic, became an associate editor.

Thus it was in 1920 that the "Van Doren dynasty" began. Carl was away from his *Nation* office a good deal and deputized his younger brother Mark to perform the literary editor's duties. Carl's wife Irita also had a staff connection at the *Nation* that grew into the literary editorship when Carl went to the *Century* in 1922. She was herself succeeded by Mark Van Doren in 1924. Dorothy Van Doren, Mark's wife, in due course joined the *Nation* staff. The dynasty spread during the Twenties; Carl was one of the founders of the book club, the Literary Guild, and Irita joined *Books*, the literary review the New York *Herald Tribune* set up for Stuart P. Sherman in 1924.

"It was an exciting office in which to work," Lewis S. Gannett has remembered. "I doubt that there was ever another such journalistic heaven as was *The Nation* in the early post-war years. I came back from France . . . with one ambition in all the world: to land a job on Villard's *Nation*. I knew what I wanted, and was blissful when I got it: half-time at first, and small pay."

Of the regular contributors in that election year of 1920 when the *Nation* declared that the voters faced "a choice between Debs and dubs," I remember best Henry G. Alsberg, who wrote letters from Russia; he was to head the Federal Writers Project of the New Deal years and to initiate the great series of *American Guides*.

A circulation-building feature was the documentary International Relations section. "We were the first to print," Lewis Gannett boasted, "the new Russian constitution, the anti-imperialistic treaties, new land laws in the border republics, as well as to expose secret treaties pre- and post-war, suppressed reports of pogroms in Poland, and documents on skulduggery in five continents."

Readers who preferred the *Nation* to the *New Republic* argued its superiority from the training of Oswald Garrison Villard in newspaper writing. Villard, they said, had a fine news sense and a flair for finding able newspapermen to write for him. And indeed Villard himself criticized Croly for lack of newspaper experience. In the *Dictionary of American Biography*, Villard wrote that "as a journalist [Croly] suffered from a lack of newspaper experience. . . . His freedom from financial exigencies made him less concerned with timeliness and journalistic enterprise."

I was among those who found the *New Republic* more nourishing than the *Nation*. This was precisely because Croly was the philosopher of liberalism, whereas Villard was the journalist of liberalism. Villard, a grandson of William Lloyd Garrison and the author of a biography of John Brown, was truly in the abolitionist tradition of journalism and pamphleteering. He had reforming and crusading zeal. He espoused causes but had no great overmastering cause. Croly had the great cause of fulfilling the promise of American life, and this was a more thrilling summons to the young generation than the exposé articles of the *Nation*.

Freeman

Under date of March 17, 1920, the first issue of a new weekly appeared on the rack of the Washington Square Book Shop. It had an English-looking format and was called the *Freeman*. A scholarly book publisher has claimed that is was "America's most stimulating venture in periodical literature," and its editor has claimed that "it was quite generally acknowledged to be the best paper published in our language," the *New Age* of London, I should remark, being past its prime when the *Freeman* rose to preeminence. Neither the publisher, B. W. Huebsch, nor the editor, Albert Jay Nock, could be called impartial—but what they said was true.

As I glanced at the double-columned front page of the review I had plucked from the rack, I was smitten by the first paragraph of "Current Comment," which was the first department of the *Freeman*. I was then drifting from literary socialism to philosophic anarchism, and this paragraph—later revealed to be Albert Jay Nock's—led me to drop anchor in anarchism; thereafter I abstained on principle from voting until the fourth time that Franklin Roosevelt ran for the presidency. Because it struck perfectly the keynote of the new venture, I reproduce the paragraph that had this crystallizing effect on me.

> So far the utterances of Presidential aspirants are not worth serious attention. Everyone knows, of course, that the primary object of the major parties is this year the same as it has been for over forty years, namely, to prevent a real issue being brought before the people; and they will certainly succeed unless labour [*Freeman* affected British spelling], the agrarians, and other disaffected special interests unite to force upon the country a simple statement of fundamental eco-

nomic fact—as simple and fundamental, for example, as the tentative programme offered them by the Committee of Forty-Eight. It does not seem probable, however, that anything like this will take place. Between the two major parties, as again everyone knows, there is not a pin to choose in respect of principle. Their working policies, motives, intentions, and ideals are identical. The only real difference between them is that one is in and wants to stay in, while the other is out and wants to get in. This precisely, and none other, is the situation that confronts the electorate. It is not new; it has confronted them, as we have said, for more than forty years.

I accepted at once the political cynicism without identifying the "statement of fundamental fact" as Henry George's theory. It was enough for me that the *Freeman* was friendly toward revolutionary labor and the new Russian experiment and was opposed to repression in all of its chief forms.

In its third issue the *Freeman* said forthrightly: "*The Freeman* is not a liberal paper; it has no lot or part with liberalism"—and this set the hook in my allegiance. "The *Freeman* is a radical paper," the unsigned editorial (later ascribed to Nock) continued; "its place is in the virgin field, or better, the long-neglected and fallow field, of American radicalism; its special constituency, if it ever has any, will be what it can find in that field."

The editorial went on to describe the fundamental differences between liberalism and radicalism. Whereas for the liberal, the state was essentially social and capable of change effected by political means, the radical adjudged the state "fundamentally anti-social and is all for improving it off the face of the earth, not by blowing up office-holders, as Mr. Palmer [A. Mitchell] appears to suppose, but by the historical process of strengthening, consolidating and enlightening economic organization."

This editorial clearly marked off the *Freeman* from the reformist *Nation* and the politics-centered *New Republic*. In economics, "the practical difference between the radical and the liberal is quite as spacious. The liberal appears to recognize but two factors in the production of wealth, namely, labour and capital; and he occupies himself incessantly with all kinds of devices to adjust relations between them. The radical recognizes a third factor, namely, natural resources, and is absolutely convinced that as long as monopoly-interest in natural resources continues to exist, no adjustment of the relations between labour and capital can possibly be made."

94

Whence arose this new star in the small constellation of periodicals of the left? All we young writers knew at the time was that the paper was heavily supported by meat-packing money in Chicago, "hog-butcher of the world." Its editors, Francis Neilson and Albert Jay Nock, were scarcely known. Nock was extremely averse to publicity, and it was not until 1946 that an account of the founding of the *Freeman* became public. By then two of the three principals in publishing the paper were dead. The third, Francis Neilson, in telling the *Freeman* story, pressed incredible accusations against the deceased second principal, Albert Jay Nock—which makes it desirable to relate in some detail the facts about the founding and first year of the *Freeman*.

The *Freeman*'s angel was Helen Swift Neilson. Born the daughter of Gustavus Franklin Swift, meat-packing king, she had grown up in the business society of Chicago and had married Edward Morris of Morris and Co., another large meat-packing firm. Edward Morris died in 1913, and in 1917 his very wealthy widow married a recently divorced Englishman, Francis Neilson. It was, said Neilson in his memoirs, "a wedding without the usual courtship and without the pledge of lovers." Noting that no congratulations were received from the relatives or friends of Helen Swift, Neilson said that Helen's twenty-four-year-old son had said to him, "You can never be a father to me."

Helen Swift Neilson had a slight, delicate literary gift. A graduate of Wellesley, a student of Browning in Jenkin Lloyd Jones's class, she liked to go "woodsing" on her country estate; and she wrote nature sketches that appeared in the *Freeman* after its second year. She wrote three books: *Where Green Lanes End*; *Zack Jones, Fisherman-Philosopher*; and *My Father and My Mother* (privately printed). She was an undemonstrative woman, Francis Neilson observed, and "had a masculine mind." She was interested in psychoanalysis and in her husband's political and economic ideas. She was not, however, a patron of the type of Willard and Dorothy Straight, the angels of the *New Republic* who were devoted to the policy and ideas of that paper. Helen Swift Neilson was devoted to her husband.

Francis Neilson was a pacifist who distrusted the modern state and advocated the single tax. How much of an antistatist and Georgist his wife was of her own conviction is unclear, but there is no doubt that Helen Swift Neilson wanted to provide a paper for her husband to spread abroad *his* views.

Francis Neilson (born Francis Butters, son of a waiter) had been born in Birkenhead, across the Mersey estuary from Liverpool, and had been brought up by grandparents in Shropshire. He had come to the United States at eighteen and worked as a day laborer and clerk. Then he found jobs on the stage as a "super" and wrote articles on the theater. Later he studied with Dion Boucicault, joined the company of William Gillette, and became a protégé of Anton Seidl, the Wagnerian conductor. In 1897 Neilson returned to England with Gillette in *Secret Service* and was commissioned to be Charles Frohman's representative in London. For four seasons he was manager of the Royal Opera in Covent Garden.

In 1904 Neilson quit the opera for the hustings and managed liberal campaigns for Parliament until 1910 when he himself ran for Parliament in Cheshire and was elected. He remained in the House of Commons until 1915. Because he opposed British participation in World War I, he resigned from politics and returned to America.

His book *How Diplomats Make War* was published in New York in 1915, with an introduction by Albert Jay Nock. But because the book was unsigned—it was credited to "A British Statesman"—the name of Francis Neilson gained no *réclame*. Nor did Neilson make a literary reputation in America with *A Strong Man's House* and other novels and plays he wrote. He contributed a number of editorials and several "Miscellany" causeries to the early numbers of the *Freeman*, but these too were anonymous and did nothing to enlarge his slight reputation.

The sum of the knowledge we of the younger generation had of Albert Jay Nock was that he had been an associate editor of the *Nation* for a short time. A few of our elders remembered that Nock had been a staff writer for the *American Magazine* during its hard-hitting muckraking years, but even they did not know that he had been an Episcopalian minister for a decade or so. Did we hear the intriguing rumor that Nock had once been a semiprofessional baseball player or was that a later addition to the legend, for legendary Nock became during the *Freeman* years.

When the war broke out, he had been sent to Europe by Secretary of State Bryan. Nock made a mystery of his mission—as he made a mystery of many things in his life—but he saw Robert Dell in France and Ramsay MacDonald in England and finally came to Liverpool to call on the dissident Member of Parliament, Francis Neilson. Brand Whitlock provided the note of introduction. Nock brought away the manuscript of *How Diplomats Make War*, which he soon placed with B. W. Huebsch. In a powerful introduction Nock indicated the officeholders of the warring governments and declared that it was time Americans knew something about the men behind the talk of war aims. Soon Neilson arrived with his family in America and went about lecturing on the war. Neilson and his first wife were divorced in 1917; shortly afterwards Helen Swift Morris and Neilson were married.

Nock visited the Neilsons several times and had conversations with Mrs. Neilson about the future of her husband. Nock is alleged to have planted the idea that the *Nation* might be bought, whereupon Villard came to Chicago to see the Neilsons. According to Neilson's reminiscences in 1946, it was arranged that Nock should join the staff of the *Nation* and Mrs. Neilson should be responsible for his salary. This arrangement was discontinued after a while, and Nock in the autumn of 1919 visited the Neilson farm in Wisconsin for new discussions with Mrs. Neilson. "I little dreamed it was to be a momentous visit," wrote Neilson. After a week, Mrs. Neilson said to him at dinner, "We have a great surprise for you. We're going to start a paper of our own."

Neilson's thoughts, published after both Mrs. Neilson and Nock were dead, were aggrieved. "When Nock put that idea [of purchase] into Helen's head about *The Nation*, he was certainly looking to the future. I would not do him an injustice, but it must be understood that he was in touch with a very rich woman and a man who, he thought, would enable him to obtain a position which he undoubtedly believed he was capable of filling. It seems to me now that the place I held at the time was absurd, for it was not until after *The Freeman* had been issued for two years that I learned from my wife the inwardness of the story." Neilson then proceeded to make preposterous charges of sciolism, plagiarism, indolence, ignorance of foreign languages, faulty memory, and even mental illness (attributed to the male climacteric). "Poor Frank!" wrote Brand Whitlock to a friend. "He was so much nicer before he got rich"—comment sufficient on Neilson's jealous attack on Nock.

The matter for reflection in this belated disclosure is that the *Freeman* had from the outset a seed of antipathy between Neilson and Nock that would thwart the paper's longevity. Mrs. Neilson was backing a husband, not a policy and idea. The husband, unaccustomed to riches, was suspicious of his colleague's designs. And Nock had to steer the ship through annual deficits of $80,000 and a circulation that was elite but too small, only 7,000. The disunity of the editors was so well concealed that it was a surprise and a shock to the *Freeman's* readers when the paper suspended publication on its fourth anniversary. But we

97

can now see that it was doomed from the start, for it was only a question of time before the jealous husband would advise his wife "to bring the paper's course to a speedy end."

We who aspired to write for the *Freeman* knew somehow that it was Nock's paper. Neilson never seemed to be in the office, and in fact he was traveling abroad much of the time. It was Nock who engaged the staff. It was Nock who set the Jeffersonian tone of the paper. He himself wrote hundreds of pieces, employing the strengths of a mind fortified with the ideas of Herbert Spencer, Matthew Arnold, Franz Oppenheimer, and Henry George and warmed by the democratic faith of Jefferson. Nock often called himself an anarchist but defined the word in his own way. With him, it was "the State, our enemy," but in reply to a newspaper he said: "Government will continue on this earth. As if any person in his right mind ever doubted it!"

A test of Nock's courage came six months after the *Freeman* started. The Red Scare was virulent, and Attorney-General A. Mitchell Palmer was hunting witches on a scale greater than Joseph McCarthy's efforts thirty years later. On September 16, 1920, there was a shattering explosion directly across from J. P. Morgan and Co., at 23 Wall Street. A bony horse pulling a red wagon stopped at noon in front of the United States Assay Office in which was stored nearly one billion dollars in gold. The driver jumped from the wagon and disappeared into lunchtime crowds. Seconds later, there was a blinding blue-white flash and a roar like a big German shell. When the yellow sulphurous smoke cleared away, there were thirty-three dead and three hundred injured.

Hysteria followed. Reds and anarchists were furiously blamed, and vengeance on radicals was sought. Almost alone, the *Freeman* rejected terrorist suppositions and advanced alternative conjectures. It took great courage to dissent from Red-baiting at this moment, for mobs were impatient during the Palmer era. But on October 27, the *Freeman* observed that "To the relief of many, and the possible disappointment of a few, this famous expert [Dr. Walter Scheele, an eminent authority on explosives] is convinced after 'a careful analysis of all the fragments of metal found at the scene of the explosion' that the catastrophe could not have been caused by a terrorist organization." The *Freeman* had kept cool. Nothing more was heard of the Wall Street explosion that was at first vehemently blamed on the Reds.

In Volume I, Number 1, the *Freeman* named only Francis Neilson and Albert Jay Nock as editors. But Nock engaged a strong staff and in six weeks the

Freeman ran up their names on the masthead as associate editors: Van Wyck Brooks, Walter G. Fuller, Clara La Follette, Geroid Robinson. Sometime later Walter G. Fuller, an Englishman and husband of Crystal Eastman, was listed as managing editor. But a year later all outward signs of rank disappeared; the masthead simply listed the six names in alphabetical order as editors.

"It was Nock's wish that *The Freeman* should be an Abbey of Theleme," Van Wyck Brooks has written, "and his motive for us all [editors] was 'Do what you like,' for he hoped to realize the old humanists' dream of a human association existing in a state of absolute freedom. . . . For two years, in the last page of the paper, I spoke up for socialism with never a word from Nock that this doctrine was abhorrent to the species of anarchist that he was himself."

Brooks was the greatest asset the *Freeman* had, for with many writers and readers, he counted more weightily in their esteem for the paper than did the little-known Nock. Brooks was then at the height of his "letters and leadership" period. Decidedly a programmatic critic, he sought to foster a national culture of self-fulfillment that should be implemented, as Frederick W. Dupee has pointed out, in terms of an *organized intelligentsia.*

An example of the effectiveness of Brooks's programmatic criticism was his elevation of the discussion of expatriation which enlivened the *Freeman* in the last five months of 1920. The discussion was opened by Harold Stearns in a vulgarly provocative article, "What Can a Young Man Do?" (*Freeman*, August 4, 1920). Our irreconcilable young men are going to Europe, he declared, because rebellious youth is not wanted in the United States. Stearns inveighed against the dismal towns and rural horror of America—how obsolete is this standard complaint of the early Twenties—and saw in the Eighteenth Amendment a dire symbol. Youth has no chance to change this environment. "If his interest is in literature, he must either become popular or starve; if in art, he must choose between flattering the vanity of silly rich people or enduring the lowest common denominator of Broadway or the movies or put all his energies into the struggle to make a bare living."

Brooks quickly lifted the discussion from this level and enlarged it. Readers had written in, predictably saying: "Make your struggle for freedom where you stand" and "why run to Europe when there is so much to be done in this country." The editors had replied that the readers' contention, as against Mr. Stearns, had slight value; and the stage was set for an unsigned editorial, "Go Abroad, Carissimo!" which must certainly have been written by Brooks. The editorial took its text from Ibsen who had written to Bjornson: "Go abroad, carissimo! Both because distance gives a wider range of vision, and because much more value is set upon the man who is out of sight." This, the editorial said, is the plainest common sense. In America expatriation has been a breach of the tribal law, but now let writers set their minds at rest. "We live in a new epoch; the time has come to perceive that through the self-fulfillment of its constituent individuals alone a nation can become great."

The editorial insisted that the essential matter is that "the choice spirit should, by whatever means, attain his fullest development. . . . Everything else, even, or rather especially, from the point of view of patriotism, is of secondary importance. For the more we develop the more we become ourselves, and the more we become of our race." Ibsen had lived in exile for twenty-seven years, but Norway paid him a pension. "A poet," Ibsen said, "belongs by nature to the race of the longsighted. Never have I seen home, and the living life of home so distinctly, so circumstantially, and so closely as from a distance and in absence." Therefore the *Freeman* said: "Let them [emigrés], by whatever means they can, escape from the living death of the village crank, the weary journalist, the benighted provincial wit, knowing that self-fulfillment is the quintessence of patriotism. Where one lives and under what conditions is, in a word, solely a question of experience." The artist must follow his instinct, as Goethe did in going to Italy and Delacroix to Morocco, whereas Thoreau's "over-determination kept him the provincial that he was." Robert Frost and Hamlin Garland had reversed the "go west" trend. "For without experience of a life wider, richer, more enlightened than that of his environment, how can the young provincial growing up in the tideless, dolorous midlands of America, discover himself or his vocation, or the glory of any vocation?" Life in Europe, the *Freeman* concluded, contains more of the universal than life in America. "As they [writers] find themselves, America will find itself in them."

Correspondents continued to send unsympathetic letters about Stearns's account "of the difficulties besetting the spirit which finds itself alien to our civilization," and the *Freeman* made a further effort to sweeten the topic in an Arnoldian sense. In an editorial, "Culture and Freedom" (September 8, 1920), the writer, who seems to have been Brooks with a Nock accent, affirmed that creative spirits had no duty to remain in America. "A good case could be made out for the thesis that the interests of general culture are better served intensively, by strengthening the centres of culture than by scattering one's energies about its hinterland."

100

With charm and clarity Brooks contributed his views each week in "A Reviewer's Notebook." His recurrent themes were the historical defeats of the American writer and the need to create "a usable past," the prophecy of Whitman and the role of leadership an intelligentsia should assume. It soom became noticeable in the *Freeman* that Brooks was the head of a new school of critics; the chief members, Newton Arvin and Lewis Mumford, often sounded a Brooksian note in the middle articles of the journal.

Dial

In 1919 the *Dial* was a fortnightly edited by Robert Morss Lovett. Clarence Britten was the editor who made the assignments, a brisk, bright man whose untimely death was a distinct loss to liberal journalism. There were rumors that summer of impending changes at the *Dial*, and by December an announcement told of a change so great that the *Dial* would virtually be a new magazine when next it appeared on the rack of the Washington Square Book Shop.

In the 1950s E. E. Cummings noted this transformation, or rather metamorphosis. "Through Harvard I met Scofield Thayer; and at Harvard, Sibley Watson—two men who subsequently transformed a do-gooding periodical called The Dial into a first rate magazine of the fine arts; and together fought the eternal battle of selfhood against mobism; the immortal battle of beauty against ugliness." It was unfair to call the old *Dial*, founded at Chicago in 1880 by Francis F. Browne and moved to New York in 1918 by his successor, Martyn Johnson, "a do-gooding periodical." The old *Dial* correctly called itself a fortnightly journal of "Criticism and Discussion of Literature and the Arts." Its editors in 1918 were not professional "do-gooders," but were of the new breed of intellectuals—Clarence Britten, George Donlin, Harold Stearns, and Scofield Thayer; and a supplementary group—John Dewey, Thorstein Veblen, and Helen Marot. But Cummings' comment stirs memory of the ubiquity of Harvard men in the American resurgence, as the years from 1912 to 1918— from the founding of *Poetry* in Chicago to the moving of the *Dial* from Chicago to New York—have been named by Richard Chase.

Walter Lippmann on the *New Republic* and John Reed on the *Masses* had come from Harvard at about the same time; Van Wyck Brooks on the *Seven Arts* had preceded them by a year or so. T. S. Eliot had been graduated from

Harvard in 1909 and had emigrated to England. Harold Stearns had grubbed his way through Harvard a few years after Eliot and had been taken on the *Dial* by Martyn Johnson. If a Harvard graduate, fresh from courses by Santayana and Babbitt, Briggs and Copland, had real talent and wanted to enter on a literary career, he found Harvard friends and connections already established in strategic editorial positions and sometimes received help from them, but only if deserving, in getting their careers launched. So it was with Scofield Thayer of the class of 1913.

Born in 1888, Thayer was the only son of a man who had made a fortune in textiles at Worcester, Massachusetts. He had received an excellent education—at Milton Academy where T. S. Eliot was a sixth-former when he entered, in Europe where he was accompanied by a tutor, at Harvard where he was an editor of the *Harvard Monthly* and from which he was graduated *cum laude* in 1913, and finally at Magdalen College, Oxford, for study in the classics and philosophy. The war disrupted his postgraduate studies, and he returned to the United States and began his career as patron of artists and writers. He sent money to James Joyce in Zurich when Joyce was in dire need of a thousand dollars. In the winter of 1917/18 he bought stock in the *Dial* and lent money, intended as a gift, to it. Fortunately for the welfare of the arts in America, Thayer was exempted from military service and left free to develop his interest in the *Dial*.

When I first heard of Scofield Thayer, he was living at one of the choicest places in the Village—on the top floor of the Benedick (now occupied by New York University) on the east side of Washington Square. It was said that his bookshelves were stacked with first editions and rare books and his walls decorated with Aubrey Beardsley drawings. A fine view of the whole of Washington Square, then still Henry Jamesian in character, could be had from a high, narrow windowseat.

My impression of Scofield Thayer on the one occasion I met him—at tea in John Cowper Powys' rooms—was that of a literary dandy. He dressed with studied taste. This impression of dandyism one also receives from the Adolph Dehn caricature of Thayer in dressing-gown, quill pen in hand, which was reproduced in the *Dial* for June, 1926, and captioned "Le Byron de nos jours." And the E. E. Cummings caricature, *S. T. at the Dial*, reproduced in Nicolas Joost's *Scofield Thayer and the Dial* (1964)—suggests a Parisian dandy of the brothers Goncourt time.

Thayer was "slender of build, swift of movement, always strikingly pale," noted Alyse Gregory in her reminiscences of the American resurgence and the early *Dial* years. He had "coal-black hair, black eyes veiled and flashing, and lips that curved like those of Lord Byron." Alyse Gregory said that he seemed to many "the embodiment of the aesthete with over-refined tastes and sensibilities" but this she felt was far from the case. "He was ice on the surface and molten lava underneath," she declared, and added that "his mind was inflammable and satirical, and it was at the same time sober and sad." This is helpful in dispelling any notion that Thayer was a butterfly but gives no clue to the mental disaster that was to overwhelm him in the later Twenties.

It will be recalled that Scofield Thayer was an admirer of Randolph Bourne, the emergent leader of the young intellectuals. Thayer bought stock in the *Dial* mainly because Bourne was an unofficial contributing editor. Both men believed that the young intelligentsia was crucial to the perpetuation of ideals through art and literature. Both were convinced that "the world will never understand our spirit except in terms of art. When shall we learn that 'culture,' like the kingdom of heaven, lies within us, in the heart of our national soul?" Thus was Thayer guided toward that serious aesthetic role, with its touchstone of intensity, which he was to act superbly as editor of the new *Dial*, from 1920 to 1925.

Thayer associated with himself on the old *Dial* another wealthy young man from Harvard—James Sibley Watson, Jr., of Rochester, New York. Watson came on as president of the Dial Publishing Company. Thayer was secretary-treasurer. When the final agreement was made on November 15, 1919, for the two Harvard aesthetes to take control of the *Dial*, Watson retained the title of president and Thayer took the title of editor. But President Watson, who was taking a degree in medicine (radiology) at New York University, was a very important editorial associate as well. He was, in fact, more avant-garde in taste than Thayer.

The magazine Thayer and Watson acquired late in 1919 was a fortnightly with a circulation of about ten thousand. They changed it into a monthly magazine of the arts, international in scope and aesthetic in outlook, that was to affect us like an entirely new publication when the January, 1920, number appeared on the rack of the Washington Square Book Shop. It had a new format, designed by Bruce Rogers; and it was new in impact. There had never been anything like it in the history of American magazines. The impact of this January, 1920, number was chiefly made by the opening contributions: a Gaston

Lachaise frontispiece, "An Autobiographic Chapter" by Randolph Bourne, and seven poems and four line drawings by the Harvard poet and artist E. E. Cummings.

In an unfinished novel, Bourne had written about a six-year-old boy named Gilbert, essentially himself, and had depicted the child's expanding life and his going to school. Any unpublished fragment by Bourne was eagerly read in 1920, but the most exciting writer in this first number was E. E. Cummings. The typography of his poems was revolutionary but, as we soon perceived, not arbitrary. His lyricism had a freshness that we tried to describe by saying that it was of the time of Queen Elizabeth. "O Distinct / Lady of my unkempt adoration"—this gave the thrilling note of the new lyrist.

To the next number of the *Dial* Cummings contributed an essay on the sculpture of Gaston Lachaise that reinforced the impact of the frontispiece of the January number. Lachaise, Cummings said, is "inherently naif, fearlessly intelligent, utterly sincere." Casting aside moderation, he praised him for what he called the negating of OF with IS. Accompanying this essay were drawings by Lachaise and two photographs of his sculpture. One reader of the *Dial* who was powerfully affected by the work of Lachaise was Hart Crane who later became a worshipful friend of Gaston and Madame Lachaise.

With this second number Gilbert Seldes was appointed an associate editor (later changed to managing editor). Another Harvard man, Seldes was to add brilliance to the *Dial* in its Theatre Chronicle and its book review section, and to participate in its editorial attitudes and practice.

The *Dial* was an education in the arts for an advanced public that had been forming during the resurgence and emerged after the war. The *Dial*'s circulation at the end of the first year of Thayer's editorship numbered about six thousand. By the end of 1922 it had reached nearly fourteen thousand. It was an expensive undertaking for Thayer and Watson. The deficit at the end of the first year was about $100,000.

But the greatest service of the *Dial* to American culture was its impact upon American writers. It conducted to them new impulses of modern arts and letters that instigated their own creative efforts. What made the *Dial* thrilling was its discovery of the best new writers coming out of undergraduate literary magazines like the *Harvard Monthly* and the short-lived *Sansculotte* at Ohio State University where Ludwig Lewisohn taught; out of the American Ambulance Service in France and Italy; and out of postwar Greenwich Village.

The great discovery of the *Dial*, next to Cummings, was Kenneth Burke, whose short story "Mrs. Maecenas" came out in March. "Mrs. Maecenas" told of the hunt for a genius in the student body carried on by a college president's widow and how she placed her hopes on seventeen-year-old Siegfried and urged him on to "experience," and in the end reacted in distaste to the pimples on his adolescent chin. It was an elaborate and artificial tale with fine conversational gambits and clever quotations from Siegfried's writings. Its ivory tower ambience enchanted two young writers, Hart Crane and me, who were cover-to-cover readers of the *Dial*—notes on contributors, briefer mentions, advertisements and all—who compared notes with each other after every issue of the *Dial* for several years. We forthwith decided to wager on the rise of Kenneth Burke to literary leadership in our generation, "this youngest generation" as it was soon to be dubbed.

In April, Kenneth Burke reviewed the autobiographical fiction of John Cournos and exclaimed: "Heaven alone knows what is to become of the novel"—a cry that was to be repeated and amplified with the publication of *Ulysses*. In July, Burke had another story, an artificial, very literary thing called "The Soul of Kajn Tafha," which did not in the least shake the Crane-Munson estimate of Burke's promise, even though it had a kind of artificiality Burke would soon outgrow.

Crane and I also noted the reviews of Malcolm Cowley in February and April, but they had little impact on us. Cowley's effect on "this youngest generation" was to come two years later. Impact, however, was definitely what Cummings' review of *Poems* by T. S. Eliot had in the June number. Cummings called the slim volume "an accurate and uncorpulent collection of instupidities" and spoke in a phrase I long remembered of "the positive and deep beauty of his skilful and immediate violins." Cummings declared, "Before an Eliot we become alive or intense as we become intense or alive before a Cézanne or a Lachaise," and he summed up the volume as "an extraordinarily tight orchestration of the shapes of sound."

In that same June number there was an essay that intoxicated Crane and excited me, and had a lasting effect on both of us. This was "Some Remarks on Rimbaud as Magician" by W. C. Blum (Sibley Watson). There have been many essays and translations of Rimbaud since Dr. Watson's—translations by W. C. Blum of *A Season in Hell* and *Illuminations* followed in the July and August numbers—but Watson's pioneer efforts to introduce Rimbaud to American writers and readers have not been superseded as were Pound's notes in the *Little Review*. Rimbaud, Blum (Watson) stated, wished to be "a true wizard of dreams consciously working changes in his receptive apparatus, trying to regain and perfect that omnipotence of thought which Freud attributes to the savages." This staggered Crane's imagination, and he became completely intoxicated when Blum quoted Rimbaud's famous declaration: "I say it is necessary to be a *seer*, to make oneself a SEER! The poet makes himself a *seer* by a long, immense, and reasoned *derangement of all the senses*. . . . For he reaches the *unknown!*"

W. C. Blum followed up his introduction of Rimbaud with a review of P. D. Ouspensky's *Tertium Organum* (September, 1920), which also made a powerful impression on Crane and me, though neither of us went to Ouspensky's pages at once. "What [Ouspensky] has accomplished," said Blum, "is an artistic synthesis of certain liberating implications of the new mathematics with the very old affirmations of the mystics." Blum summed up *Tertium Organum* as "a rather strong statement in favour of freedom."

The *Dial* set a high standard in book reviewing and didn't miss noticing any important book either. An interesting example of its alertness was its review (October, 1920) of a new revolutionary economic text. Both the *New Republic* and the *Nation* had overlooked it, and the *Freeman* had merely listed it as a book received. But the *Dial* described this new analysis of financial economics—*Economic Democracy* by C. H. Douglas—and promptly assigned it to an important reviewer. Ordway Tead noted that a new outlook on the confusing problem of finance and credit was required. Although he failed to grasp the constructive part of Douglas' book, he did imply that *Economic Democracy* should be required reading for open-minded students of postwar economic problems.

I have been noting the formative impact the *Dial* had on two of its young readers, one of whom was a poet of genius. But both of us were representative of the oncoming "men of the Twenties." Now I should stress the truly catholic education the *Dial* gave to public taste.

What rich fare the *Dial* spread before its enthusiastic readers all during 1920. Provocative of future controversy were two chapters from Brooks's *The Ordeal of Mark Twain*, a pioneering literary application of psychoanalysis that *then* seemed brilliant. Memorable too was Sherwood Anderson's short story "The Triumph of the Egg," perhaps his best. Ezra Pound was represented by "Fourth Canto" and "Hugh Selwyn Mauberly"; Marianne Moore by two poems. And then there was a series of notebook jottings, "Dust for Sparrows" by Rémy de Gourmont, an idol of Kenneth Burke and other youthful aesthetes. In the October number appeared "The Approach to M. Marcel Proust" by Richard Aldington and "Saint-Loup: A Portrait" by Marcel Proust; and in November, T. S. Eliot offered "The Possibility of a Poetic Drama." That number also carried ten poems by William Butler Yeats. And there was a charming serial of literary reminiscences by Ford Madox Hueffer.

It should be possible to understand now why it is said that the *Dial* provided a higher education in the arts and letters of the twentieth century. But often, I must repeat, it was education with impact, as was true of the serial publication of "Belphegor: An Essay on the Aesthetic of Contemporary French Society" by Julien Benda. This essay was a forerunner of the attacks on romanticism that would be unloosed at the end of the Twenties by the New Humanists. Benda declared in italics that *"modern French society requires of art that they make it experience emotions and sensations and no longer expects to realize from works of art any kind of intellectual pleasure."* He vigorously attacked Bergson and "the purely emotional conception of art." His was a salutary influence on some of us young romantics who would later become more classical in taste.

We, the younger writers, knew the *Dial* was a great magazine while it was happening. We concurred at once with the judgment of the English editor A. R. Orage, which the *Dial* quoted in its house advertising: "Perhaps the most fully realized of all the promising literary magazines now current in the world. It is in all probability considerably in advance of the American reading public for whom it is intended, but it is all the better on that account. Culture is always being called upon to sacrifice popularity, and, usually, even its existence, in the interests of civilization."

Malcolm Cowley recalled that "for the young American writer, it was marvellous to have a magazine that would publish his best work, and pay him for it." But the last word on the *Dial* was spoken by one who helped it to achieve the editorial brilliance of its five years under the active editorship of Scofield Thayer. *"The Dial* made a noise in the world," wrote Gilbert Seldes. "It directly affected the artistic life of a generation, and indirectly the life of our whole time."

Little Review

Of the little magazines displayed on the rack of the Washington Square Book Shop in this pivotal year of 1920, the most famous and the best was *Little Review*. Ranged beside it were *Pagan, Quill, Plowshare, Modern School, S4N,* and

Contact; but *Little Review* was easily the front runner of these small, unsubsidized, uncommercial, avant-garde publications. It had, in fact, gained a big head start in its Chicago period, 1914–1917.

The founder had been Margaret Anderson, a young woman of beauty and vivacity who had rebelled against family life in Columbus, Indiana, and escaped to Chicago. At Columbus, Margaret Anderson, just out of Western College for Women, though not a graduate, wrote: "I had a green room overlooking lilac bushes, yellow roses and oak trees. Every day I shut myself in, planning how to escape mediocrity (not the lilacs and roses but the vapidities that went on in their hearing)." And escape she did—to Chicago.

In Chicago, Margaret Anderson did miscellaneous book reviewing for a religious weekly and for Francis Hackett on the Chicago *Evening Post*. Then she got a very minor editorial job on the old *Dial* and also did some clerking in Browne's Book Store, which Frank Lloyd Wright had designed. On the *Dial* she was "initiated into the secrets of the printing room—composition (monotype and linotype), proofreading, make-up. This practical knowledge was indispensable when I began the *Little Review*." Floyd Dell succeeded Francis Hackett at the Chicago *Evening Post*. Margaret Anderson reviewed books for Dell and went to a sort of salon his first wife, Margery Currey, created.

These soirées at the Dells were golden in Harry Hansen's memory when he wrote his sketches of Chicago literary life in *Mid-West Portraits* (1923). He recalls the talkers—Sherwood Anderson with his drawl; Theodore Dreiser, always folding and unfolding a handkerchief; John Cowper Powys, rhapsodic on great writers; Arthur Davison Ficke from Dell's home city of Davenport, Iowa; Maxwell Bodenheim with his snarl; Edgar Lee Masters who looked like Thackeray; Carl Sandburg, newspaperman and poet, and many many others. Of this circle Margaret Anderson has written: "Floyd Dell and I talked of Pater and of living like the hard gem-like flame. . . . I liked Sherwood—because he, too, was a talker of a highly special type. . . . Sherwood and Floyd would talk to chairs if they had no other audience. . . . But Dreiser had no more wit than a cow."

The Dell circle was Margaret Anderson's preparation for founding a little magazine in 1914. As she tells it in *My Thirty Years' War*: "If I had a magazine I could spend my time filling it up with the best conversation the world has to offer." That was Margaret Anderson's editorial platform and policy, her editorial standard and goal. She aspired to be the mistress of a salon-in-print, and it was a man from the Dell salon—a certain Dewitt whom she called "Dick"—who gave her part of his salary each payday to start her magazine-salon.

Members of the Dell circle were often represented in the early numbers of the *Little Review*. Sherwood Anderson wrote about "The New Note"; Vachel Lindsay contributed a poem, "How a Little Girl Danced," inspired by Lucy Bates; George Burman Foster wrote a series of articles on Nietzsche; Arthur Davison Ficke contributed poems on Japanese prints; Margery Currey reviewed Ellen Key; Llewellyn Jones wrote on Bergson; notes on John Cowper Powys' lectures appeared. It all had the flavor of a soirée at the Dells. Of herself at this time, Margaret Anderson recalled that she "spoke only in gasps, gaps and gestures," and her editorials were like that—excited and breathless.

Then Emma Goldman came to Chicago. Margaret Anderson heard her lecture and had just time to turn anarchist before the third number of the *Little Review* closed. This conversation cost "Dick's" support but Eunice Tietjens gave a diamond ring, Frank Lloyd Wright gave a hundred dollars, others chipped in, and the *Little Review* precariously continued. "I became increasingly anarchistic," Margaret Anderson has told us. "Anarchism was the ideal expression for my ideas of freedom and justice. . . . I decided that I would make my life a crusade against inhumanity." But in a year or so her highly personal enthusiasm for Emma Goldman cooled and a new stimulus, a Chicago art student out of the Midwest, walked into the *Little Review* salon-in-print—Jane Heap.

"There is no one in the modern world whose conversation I haven't sampled, I believe, except Picasso's," said Margaret Anderson. "So I can't say it isn't better than Jane Heap's. But I doubt it in spite of his reputation. I felt in 1916 and feel today that Jane Heap is the world's best talker."

Jane Heap (who signed her editorials "jh") became an associate editor under the singular title of "Advisory Board" (singular because there were no others on the board), and from then on: "Jane and I began talking. We talked for days, months, years. . . . We formed a consolidation that was to make us much loved and even more loathed."

In 1917 the *Little Review* salon moved from Chicago to New York, and there Margaret Anderson "found the same difference between the quality of talk in Chicago and New York (in Chicago's favor) that I found later between that of New York and Paris (in New York's favor)." A snobbish "motto" appeared on the front cover—Making No Compromise with the Public Taste—which flaunted the feeling of superiority and exclusiveness of the salon-between-covers. But with the appointment of Ezra Pound to the post of foreign editor, the *Little Review* began to lose some of the random improvisation that a salon mistress encourages and to achieve more coherence as a magazine. Margaret Anderson had corresponded with Pound who was an exile in London, and "when he wrote suggesting that *The Little Review* employ his talents as foreign editor we hailed the occasion."

When we recall the major writers Pound brought into the *Little Review*, we see that Margaret Anderson and Jane Heap could hardly fail to make history in "little magazine" publishing. First, there was T. S. Eliot represented by a cerebral fiction, "Eeldrop and Appleplex." Pound himself was a regular contributor: "A Study in French Poets," "The Chinese Written Character" (mostly by Fenollosa), "De Gourmont: A Distinction," and other critical forays. Pound also sent over frequent contributions by Wyndham Lewis, poems by William Butler Yeats, prose by Ford Madox Hueffer. He edited a whole number devoted to Henry James. But the greatest catch he made for the *Little Review*, the leviathan of letters he hooked, was James Joyce. Serial publication of *Ulysses* started in 1918 and in the pivotal year of 1920 came the famous Gerty McDowell episode, after which Margaret Anderson and Jane Heap were haled into court.

But by January, 1920, when the younger patrons of the Washington Square Book Shop searched the magazine rack with the keenest expectancy for the new issue of the *Little Review*, Pound's name had gone from the masthead. The January, 1920, issue carried an un-Poundian debate over the "Art of Madness" between Evelyn Scott and jh. As a mad personality, the Baroness Else von Freytag-Loringhoven had captivated Margaret Anderson and Jane Heap. But the young poet Hart Crane who lived in the same building above the *Little Review* hid in a doorway when he saw the baroness coming down the street, preceded by three dogs, her arms clanking with cheap bracelets, two tea-balls bouncing on her bosom, and long-handled spoons affixed to her black velvet tam-o'-shanter.

The baroness was, in fact, regarded even by sympathetic subscribers as a *Little Review* aberration, a "crush" of its editors, and their rave notes on her art fell on deaf minds. It had been very different when Margaret Anderson and jh had raved about Mary Garden. Carl Van Vechten had bought one hundred copies of the *Little Review* to distribute the "rave" to friends. But this infatuation with the baroness' poems was adjudged by us otherwise devoted readers to be an extremely silly sentimentality.

The *Little Review* in 1920 carried only two or three pages of advertising in an issue, but a full-page advertisement of Crane's Mary Garden Chocolates excites interest long after this candy has disappeared into oblivion. This advertisement was secured by Hart Crane from his father, a prosperous candy manufacturer in Cleveland. The layout consisted simply of a picture of the opera singer and a box of candy and an endorsement—"Your chocolates are the finest I have ever tasted anywhere in the World"—over Mary Garden's signature. One may suspect that Hart Crane had something to do with the naming of the chocolates and the endorsement, as well as with the placement of the advertisement in a medium that gave a print order of only four thousand copies.

But it was Joyce's *Ulysses* that issue after issue made the *Little Review* preeminent in the avant-garde arena. A naturalistic short story writer named Israel Solon often spoke out in the *Little Review* salon in a department reserved for "the reader-critic," and Solon spoke for most of the writers who followed the *Little Review* when he declared (January, 1920) that "James Joyce is beyond doubt the most sensitive stylist writing in English. There is enough skill and matter in a single episode of *Ulysses* to equip a regiment of novelists. . . . He gives me more than I can ever carry away." Such was the effect of Joyce on those who were serious about experimental writing, and one ventures to say that they all read the *Little Review*.

The magazine, however, had other readers who were disgusted by experimental virtuosity. Wrote one of them to Margaret Anderson after reading Leopold Bloom's musings about Gerty McDowell: "I think this is the most damnable slush and filth that ever polluted paper in print." Margaret Anderson sat up all night to answer this letter—"such was my hurt for Joyce, my own hurt." She said that she regarded Joyce's *Ulysses* as "the high water-mark of the literature of today" and fired back: "He is not writing for you. He is writing for himself and for the people who care to find out how life has offended and hurt him." For once Margaret Anderson's repartee was weak, and it was to be weak again when she commented explosively on her approaching day in court by publishing *Ulysses*.

More than once the Post Office had confiscated copies of the *Little Review* containing installments of *Ulysses*. A new attack came in the fall of 1920 when

John S. Sumner, secretary of the Society for the Suppression of Vice, moved against the editor for publishing the Gerty McDowell episode. He served papers on the Washington Square Book Shop for selling the offending number, and Miss Anderson and Miss Heap sought the help of John Quinn, art patron and militant lawyer, to defend the case. Quinn appears to have considered it a lost cause from the start, but he was a friend of Joyce and Pound and a financial backer of the *Little Review* (to the extent of $1,600), and he armed himself to fight the dragon of Comstockery. Powerful Anthony Comstock had died in 1915 and his successor, Sumner, was not as fanatical; but the dragon was still formidable and usually victorious over artists. The artists, as a matter of fact, did not know how to combat the dragon.

You have no sense, Quinn told the editors of the *Little Review*, and exacted a pledge that they would not open their mouths when they came before the three judges. This was wise, for Margaret Anderson was bursting with a "defense" that was nothing but a defiance of the sort that many Americans were then showing against Prohibition. "I am not in the defy business but in the law business," Quinn reminded her.

Margaret Anderson's defense was a haughty attack upon the stupid law and the stupid public. It brought out all her snobbery. The artist was superior to the public and had no responsibility to the public. Her attack was all founded on the fancied superiority of one psychological type over other types and on ignorance of inspired common sense applied to the question of censorship. But we were all unsophisticated in those days on a question that had been argued by Plato and Hobbes, Milton and Mill; and the defiant emotionalism of the *Little Review* constituted our stand, too, against Comstockery.

At the trial Quinn put on three witnesses—John Cowper Powys, who denied that *Ulysses* was capable of corrupting the minds of young girls; Philip Moeller, who offered a psychoanalytical apologia for *Ulysses*; and Scofield Thayer, who admitted under examination that he would have taken legal advice before publishing *Ulysses* and then wouldn't have published. Quinn got his three clients off with the minimum fine of one hundred dollars.

It was reserved for Judge John M. Woolsey in 1933 to rise to the historic occasion and hand down a classic decision on the charge of pornography brought against Joyce. In 1920 Margaret Anderson simply could not rise to the occasion. It was perhaps enough that she had recognized the genius of Joyce; she should not have been expected to found a criticism of Joyce as well. She set out to fill her magazine with "the best conversation in the world," and she succeeded by inviting the very best into her magazine-salon. She shall be known to the literary historian as an editor of genius when it came to picking the best writers of her time.

Vanity Fair

It is amusing to recall that *Vanity Fair* was a sister of the *New Republic*—the chic fashionable sister of the young serious intellectual. In his first editorial (March, 1914), Frank Crowninshield wrote, "*Vanity Fair* has but two major articles in its editorial creed: first, to believe in the progress and promise of American life and, second, to chronicle that progress cheerfully, truthfully, and entertainingly." The two magazines came on the scene of the American resurgence in the same year. One was political and progressive, the other social and tolerant; but both were expressive of the Twenties when that period dawned in 1918.

Crowninshield, who had been publisher of the *Bookman*, editor of the *Metropolitan*, editor of *Munsey's*, and art editor of the *Century*, had formulated the kind of magazine he wanted. "There is no magazine," he said, "which covers the things people talk about at parties—the arts, sports, humor, and so forth." He proceeded to edit a magazine that "will print humor, it will look at the stage, at the arts, at the world of letters, at sport, and at the highly vitalized, electric, and diversified life of our day from the frankly cheerful angle of the optimist, or, which is much the same thing, from the mock-cheerful angle of the satirist." Such was the announced intention in 1914, and by 1920 when young writers stopped at the Washington Square Book Shop to look over the magazine rack, *Vanity Fair* had sparklingly carried out this intention.

In January, 1920, the humor was provided by Stephen Leacock and G. K. Chesterton. Chesterton was starting a series of twelve essays with "The Soul of Skylarking," subtitled "Thoughts on the New Renascence and the Structure of the Future." Dorothy Parker looked at the stage, Pitts Sanborn wrote about music, George W. Sutton, Jr., reviewed "Some of the High Spots of a Year of Motor Boating," and there were six pages of "Smart New Motor Cars You Will See at the Automobile Show." There were features by Thomas Burke, Giovanni Papini, A. A. Milne, and John Jay Chapman. In the department "For the Well Dressed Man," it was noted that in 1919 there had been a reaction against stiff collars and the soft collar had come in—to stay, as it proved.

"A true vintage of the Twenties," said Elizabeth Janeway, long afterwards when she reviewed the history of this sparkling, winning publication. And she remarked that *Vanity Fair* bore the stamp of one man's mind, Frank Crowninshield's. Quite true, if we include his ability to pick editors who were imbued with the new spirit of the decade. The masthead of the January, 1920, number listed Robert C. Benchley as managing editor. On the staff were Dorothy Parker and Robert E. Sherwood. They would leave soon, and their places would be taken by John Peale Bishop and Edmund Wilson, Jr. Much credit should go to these young editors, especially to Bishop and Wilson, for making *Vanity Fair* "a true vintage of the Twenties."

Bishop contributed verse and essays and reviews. "The Golden Age of the Dandy" might well be called the ideal *Vanity Fair* essay for its lightly carried historical learning, its subject matter, its suave, entertaining style. In this essay Bishop was as civilized as Aldous Huxley, another *Vanity Fair* contributor, and not unworthy of Max Beerbohm, nominated for the Hall of Fame in *Vanity Fair* for May, 1920. Bishop was prompt in his favorable review of O'Neill's *Beyond the Horizon*.

Wilson contributed more often than his associate Bishop. To the March, 1920, number he contributed "The Inevitable Literary Biography"; in August he wrote on "The Progress of Psychoanalysis"; in September he concerned himself with Henry James in "The Gulf in American Literature"; "Things I Consider Overrated" was his October contribution; "The Anarchists of Taste" (mostly about Carl Sandburg) followed in November.

Other *Vanity Fair* contributors in that year were F. Scott Fitzgerald, who had been at Princeton with Bishop and Wilson, and Edna St. Vincent Millay, with whom both young editors fell in love and to whom one proposed. Arthur Symons' essay on Edgar Saltus revived interest in an out-of-print author and stimulated a hunt in secondhand bookstores for *Mr. Incoul's Misadventure* and *The Imperial Purple*.

A taste-forming feature of *Vanity Fair* was the Hall of Fame nominations, which proposed in 1920 William Butler Yeats, Max Beerbohm, George Ade, Harriet Monroe, Walter Lippmann, Henri Matisse, Isadora Duncan, and James Gibbons Huneker among others. Yeats's poems had been appearing in the *Little Review* and the *Dial*. *Vanity Fair*'s nomination read: "W. B. Yeats—Because he has been a force in the Irish renaissance; because, unlike many poets, he has kept on experimenting and has achieved in his latest book, *The Wild Swans at Coole*, a Dantesque beauty quite different from his early iridescence; because he is the greatest poet writing English today." By such striking encomia *Vanity Fair* was a principal taste-maker of the Twenties. Harriet Moore rated kudos for founding *Poetry* in Chicago in 1912 and publishing Yeats and other rising poets. Walter Lippmann began writing articles for *Vanity Fair* after being nominated for the Hall of Fame. Isadora Duncan and James Gibbons Huneker had been, like Crowninshield himself, forerunners of the Twenties.

There was, in fact, a good deal of cross-fertilization in the leading magazines of the revival of the Twenties. Soon after the *Dial* had praised the sculpture of Gaston Lachaise, *Vanity Fair* was introducing it to its larger audience. Marsden Hartley, contributor to the *Seven Arts* and the *Dial*, wrote on Vaudeville in *Vanity Fair*. Other figures whose reputations would be writ large in the Twenties were Willa Cather, Louis Untermeyer, and Robert Edmond Jones; they were all in *Vanity Fair* in 1920. So was Hugh Walpole, who led off the year with "William Somerset Maugham: A Pen Portrait by a Friendly Hand." Ten years later appeared Maugham's novel *Cakes and Ale* which was alleged to contain a pen portrait of Hugh Walpole by an *unfriendly* hand.

And for those young writers in the Village who bought magazines at the Washington Square Book Shop, *Vanity Fair* was the top market for their wares. They thought they had no password to enter the *Saturday Evening Post*, citadel of the Philistines; nor could they breach the *Atlantic Monthly*, bastion of the genteel tradition. But *Vanity Fair* was sympathetic, and they aimed to join its cheerful company. In the next two years *Vanity Fair* welcomed to its pages Heywood Broun, Floyd Dell, Sherwood Anderson, Paul Rosenfeld, Donald Ogden Stewart, Stephen Vincent Benét, John R. Dos Passos, Djuna Barnes, Gilbert Seldes, and Kenneth Burke. And so in 1924, when it came to naming "the five readable magazines in the United States," the *Dial*, counting itself among the five, named *Vanity Fair* to the select group—the others being the *Nation*, the *New Republic*, and (unexpectedly) the *Yale Review*. Had the *Dial* made its list a few months earlier, it would have named the *Freeman* in place of the *Yale Review*, and there were certainly strong affinities between *Vanity Fair* and the avant-garde quarter of the *Dial, Freeman, Nation,* and *New Republic*. A regular writer in one was likely to appear in any of the others in the course of the decade.

Modern School

Diagonally across the street from the Washington Square Book Shop stood the old Hotel Gonfarone on the corner of Macdougal and 8th Streets. I remember the tail end of a dinner there on a Friday evening in February, 1920. The dinner had been organized "principally to discuss the present status of *The Modern School* magazine, and to collect funds for its maintenance." Being insolvent, I had stayed outside until the appeals for money were over; then I slipped into the group as they began to break up. Under a pseudonym, I had submitted "The Document of a Disillusioned Schoolmaster" to the *Modern School,* and I wanted to meet the editor, Carl Zigrosser, who had for several years made this publication a little magazine of real distinction. Among the departing diners were such luminaries of the anarchist movement as Hippolyte Havel and Hutchins Hapgood. They had heard Lola Ridge read her revolutionary poems and listened to speeches by Harry Kelly, leader of the Stelton, New Jersey, anarchist colony; Harry Weinberger, aggressive attorney for anarchists; and Anna Strunsky Walling and Dr. Cecile Greil.* I sought out Zigrosser and complimented him on his tribute to Randolph Bourne that had appeared in the *Modern School* the month before my document about teaching in boarding schools. Zigrosser told me of having roomed with Bourne at Columbia. In the *Modern School* tribute, he had written:

> What memories, too, of musical evenings. Wagner, Schumann, Debussy, occasional tastes of the Russians Moussorgsky, Scriabine, the noble violin sonata of César Frank, the three of Brahms, Bach suites and Swedish folksongs! It was

---

* Some years later Dr. Greil was to be my personal physician. She had been Dreiser's, she told me, and had started Dreiser on his handkerchief accordion-making routine when he was breaking himself of the smoking habit. But Dreiser's biographers do not substantiate her claim. Anyway Dreiser was a nonsmoker.

his [Bourne's] good fortune, in music as in writing and talking, to perform easily and without effort. He was an extraordinarily quick reader of music, and his execution was in no sense amateurish. A thorough study of the piano in his youth and the year he spent making music-rolls before he came to college, laid the foundation of a technic that never deserted him. He never practiced, yet he was always in good form. His playing was always correct and musicianly in spirit, and although he never rose to superb emotional heights, his interpretation never fell below a uniformly high standard. ... His rendition of the MacDowell or Brahms sonatas or the Schumann Etudes Symphoniques left little to be desired.

The subtitle of the *Modern School* was "A Monthly Magazine Devoted to Libertarian Ideas in Education," but Zigrosser had broadened it into an avant-garde magazine with emphasis on progressive education. He had a cover—a spreading tree with two innocent deer beneath its branches—designed by Rockwell Kent, who also designed a set of initial letters to adorn the contents. Zigrosser, who subsequently became a print authority, had a good eye for new poets; he had published poems by Wallace Stevens, Hart Crane, Padraic Pearse, Lola Ridge, and Alfred Kreymborg, as well as fables by Padraic Colum. There had been articles by Hiram K. Motherwell, Evans Clark, Margaret Naumburg, Leonard D. Abbott, Jacques Copeau, Albert Gleizes and Ananda K. Coomaraswamy. New ideas had been welcomed in reviews of guild socialism and the "conscious control of the individual" system of F. Matthias Alexander (which Bourne, Dewey, Waldo Frank, and other avant-garde thinkers were heralding).

Modern School was a good magazine—adventurous, vital, imbued with resurgent spirit, a libertarian monthly that lasted ten years (1912–1922). When Frank V. Anderson succeeded Zigrosser in the editor's chair in 1920, the *Modern School* was converted into a sort of house organ for the Ferrer Modern School at Stelton, New Jersey. The Modern School Association of North America, located in the anarchist colony at Stelton, had been the publisher of the *Modern School* from the first number, but the editorial policy had transcended the tiny educational experiment at the Ferrer School. In 1920 there were signs that the journal would narrow its policy somewhat, but we haunters of the Washington Square Book Shop still watched eagerly for its appearance and found its January-March issue full of light and fire. The light came from Coomaraswamy's article on "Guild Education in India"; the fire came from articles by Everett Dean Martin, Algernon Lee, and others attacking the notorious Lusk educational bills at Albany and from intensely anarchistic poems by Lola Ridge. "How It Feels to Teach at Stelton" by Spencer Trask was, however, a harbinger of what the magazine would be like in its final year of publication.

Plowshare

Born in 1912 as the *Wild Hawk*, christened *Plowshare* in 1916, this little magazine was an art colony magazine. It was published at Woodstock, New York, on the fringe of the Catskill mountains, and it was sponsored by a group of Woodstock writers and artists. The chief editor was Hervey White, founder of the Maverick colony on the outskirts of the village. Most of *Plowshare*'s contributors were Woodstock residents, year-round or summer. In those years Woodstock ranked with Provincetown as a colony of painters (William McFee, Andrew Dasburg, Eugene Speicher, Henry McFee, Ernest Fiene) and writers (Walter Weyl, Edwin Bjorkman, Allan Updegraff, playwright Lawrence Langner, Richard LeGallienne), and it was possible to assemble an interesting "periodical of beauty and freedom" as the *Wild Hawk* styled itself, from this community.

Hervey White, editor-in-chief, was also the printer of *Plowshare*. He had acquired a small press of the kind that ocean liners used to print menus and bought enough fonts to print a 32-page (as I remember) magazine. In his Maverick cabin he set the magazine by hand, bound it, and mailed it to a small list of subscribers and to a few bookstores like the Washington Square Book Shop or Laukhuff's in Cleveland where Hart Crane pounced on little magazines.

To some extent White was living on a reputation of having preceded Dreiser as a naturalist. He had written an early novel, *Quicksand*, in the 1890s, but had soon abandoned naturalism. Repentant, he turned to the composition of lighter, more romantic novels which he printed, one a year, on his little press during the long, shut-in Woodstock winters. In due course White detested Waldo Frank's *Our America*, which praised Dreiser and other naturalists. And I argued with him through the mails about what seemed to be an antisemitic attitude.

On the basis of having spent a few days in Woodstock in 1919, I submitted short stories and essays to White. Hart Crane wrote me about these as they appeared, but he never mentioned an essay by William Murrell in the January, 1920, *Plowshare* that Crane's biographers have wished that he had, for it lies at the base of a perplexing mystery. Rack my memory as I will, I cannot recall anything that would serve as proof that Crane read this essay in the early part of 1920. The essay was an appreciation of a young East Side poet who had died of tuberculosis and poverty, and it was illustrated by unpublished poems of the poor young man. The writer, William Murrell (full name: William Murrell Fisher), had befriended the stricken poet and had inherited his sheaf of poems in manuscript. The poet's name was Samuel Greenberg. Some years later Crane was to write me: "This poet, Greenberg, whom Fisher nursed until he died of consumption at a Jewish hospital in NY, was a Rimbaud in embryo." And later Crane was to assimilate phrases, metaphors, and lines from Greenberg's manuscripts into the "Voyages" poems and "Emblems of Conduct," causing some to cry "plagiarism"—a foolish charge refuted by Brom Weber.

One thing is certain: I did not exchange views with Crane about the William Murrell essay in the January, 1920, number of *Plowshare*, because I did not take it seriously. I thought that Fisher was making an imaginary portrait and had composed the wild verses himself. Fisher was an art critic who had written for *Seven Arts* under the name of William Murrell and had retired to Woodstock in 1917/1918. Occasionally he contributed to *Plowshare* imaginary or half-imaginary portraits of artistic personalities, so there was excuse for my surmise that Samuel Greenberg was invented. I thought the verse "terrible" and exhibited by Murrell only for a satirical purpose. As Crane described the verse in 1923: "No grammar, nor spelling, and scarcely any form"; but I did not see the "quality that is unspeakably eerie and the most convincing gusto" that Crane detected. I was sure that William Murrell was hoaxing us.

Plowshare was suspended in December, 1920. Revived in 1934, it was soon suspended a second time and received burial in a one-hundred-word notice in *The Little Magazine*. Altogether inadequate for the only magazine that published the poetry of poor Samuel Greenberg, "the hobbling yet really gorgeous attempts," in Crane's words, that were to have an effect on Crane himself when he met William Murrell Fisher at Woodstock in 1923.

Smart Set

I cannot remember if the *Smart Set: A Magazine of Cleverness* was stacked in the rack at the Washington Square Book Shop alongside *Vanity Fair* and *Dial*. It appealed strongly to the shop's patrons, but I believe we had to buy it on news company stands. One spotted its masked devil cover on the subway stands, and there paid thirty-five cents—as aristocratic a price as *Vanity Fair*'s—for entree to the best literary vaudeville of the decade. We have had nothing like it since Mencken and Nathan sold the magazine to Hearst in 1923.

By 1920 I was an addicted reader of *Smart Set* but it eludes me how I found it the first time. It looked like the other pulp magazines, the "louse" maga-zines* such as *Snappy Stories*, which I scorned, and indeed it had started out in 1900 as a magazine for the literary efforts of society women, its founder being Colonel William D'Alton Mann, publisher of the scandalmongering *Town Topics*. Colonel Mann didn't make a go of *Smart Set*, and John Adams Thayer, publisher of *Everybody's*, had then tried to make something of it. Thayer had given a book review department to a lively young Baltimore newspaperman named Henry Louis Mencken and the drama department to a cosmopolitan young graduate of Cornell named George Jean Nathan. Later he tried out a young editor from the West Coast named Willard Huntington Wright with damaging results in loss of readers and loss of advertisers. Thayer had there-upon unloaded *Smart Set* on his principal creditor, the head of a paper company, and the creditor appointed Eltinge F. Warner, already the publisher of *Field and Stream*, to be publisher of the property so hastily dropped on him. Warner promoted Mencken and Nathan—this was in the year World War I broke out—to coeditors, and *Smart Set* proceeded gaily to assault the Genteel Tra-dition.

Most of this background was unknown to the young writers of 1917 and 1918 who became aware of *Smart Set* for the first time and began to fire manu-scripts at it. To us *Smart Set* had sprung full-grown from the iconoclastic forehead of "Our America." We passed the word around that here was a mag-azine that welcomed new writers. We noted that it published James Joyce, D. H. Lawrence, Lord Dunsany, Waldo Frank, Ben Hecht, Louis Untermeyer, and James Branch Cabell. Its rates of payment were low, but decisions were wonderfully prompt. One submitted little fables, epigrams, plays, short stories, and *within four days* one received payment for an acceptance or the returned

---

* Mencken and Nathan cynically set up two of these "louse" magazines (the adjective is theirs), *Parisienne* and *Saucy Stories*, and the profits paid off *Smart Set*'s deficits.

manuscript. For young writers living hand to mouth, this promptness was an overwhelming inducement to submit to *Smart Set* first.

A return to the January, 1920, issue of *Smart Set* will show that here free men were "insisting upon their freedom"—as *New Republic* had advised—under the leadership of that vigorous disturber of the bourgeois peace, H. L. Mencken. In that issue of *Smart Set* there was a clever, frivolous one-act play, "Porcelain and Pink," by F. Scott Fitzgerald, who would four months later become a celebrity. There was a short story, "The Perfume Counter," by Thyra Samter Winslow, and an essay by Carl Van Vechten on "Variations on a Theme by Havelock Ellis," about how badly musicians write and how well painters write. A department of wit and cynical wisdom, "Répétition Générale," was dashed off by Mencken and Nathan. A theater department, captioned "The Coming of the Censor," was Nathan's responsibility, and a book department, captioned "The Flood of Fiction," Mencken handled.

Said Mencken in his corner of this issue: "Bierce is dead, and in America, at least, the post is vacant. I have a fancy that James Branch Cabell will enter into enjoyment of its prerogatives and usufructs. . . . If he ever had a chance for popularity, his new book, *Jurgen* has ruined it. *Jurgen*, estimated by current American standards, whether of the boobery or of super-boobery, is everything that is abhorrent. . . . *Jurgen* is the modern man in reaction against a skepticism that explains everything away and yet leaves everything inexplicable. He is the modern man in doubt of all things, including especially his own doubts."

This was the tone that justified Gerald W. Johnson's characterization of Mencken as "the kettle-drummer of the revolt of the twenties." In that tone, Mencken attacked Paul Elmer More in "The Diary of a Reviewer," in the February, 1920, issue. "More's book [*With the Wits*], in general, is dull stuff—correct and virtuous, but deadly dull. . . . [More] is a perfect specimen of the civilized Puritan—pulled in one direction by the lascivious lures of the bozart, and in the other direction by his inherited fears of beauty." This was devastating criticism to us who had not read More and were now determined not to. How were we to know that is was unfair?

It is easy to convince a later generation of the merits of *Smart Set* in 1920 by merely listing some of the writers who appeared in it, but we must remember that these writers were unknown then in comparison with their reputations only a few years later. In fact, *Smart Set* was instrumental in making their reputations. F. Scott Fitzgerald was all over the file that year, once with two stories in one issue. One of his best stories, "May Day," appeared in the summer. Other fiction was contributed by Lawrence Vail (known to the Provincetown Playhouse audience as an occasional actor), Winthrop Parkhurst, Solita Solano (later a member of the *Little Review* coterie), Lilith Benda, Elizabeth Sanxay Holding, and Stephen Vincent Benét. In August, 1920, there was a novelette, "Coming, Eden Bower!" by Willa Sibert Cather. There were one-act plays from F. Scott Fitzgerald, S. N. Behrman, and Aldous Huxley ("Among the Nightingales"). As for verse, there were lyrics from Sara Teasdale, Babette Deutsch, Louis Untermeyer, and Harry Kemp—but no *vers libre*. *Smart Set* looked like a high-priced shoddy pulp magazine; but once opened, the pulp paper gave off freshness and vitality and youth and sophistication.

And always, at the back, were the taste-forming departments of Nathan and Mencken. Nathan was the first powerful champion of Eugene O'Neill. In the July, 1920, issue, after O'Neill had given *Beyond the Horizon* to Broadway, Nathan wrote: "Eugene O'Neill: the one writer for the native stage who gives promise of achieving a sound position for himself. And by sound position I mean a position, if not with the first dramatists of present-day Europe, at least with the very best of the European second raters. . . . He has a sense of world theme, a sense of character, and he knows how to write. . . . He sees life too often as drama. The great dramatist is the dramatist who sees drama as life."

At about the same time Mencken in his monthly book department was reviewing *This Side of Paradise*. "The best American novel that I have seen is also the product of a neophyte, to wit, F. Scott Fitzgerald. . . . In *This Side of Paradise* he offers a truly amazing first novel—original in structure, extremely sophisticated in manner and adorned with a brilliancy that is as rare in American writing as honesty is in American statecraft. . . . Fitzgerald is a highly civilized and rather waggish fellow. Not since Frank Norris has there been a more adept slapping in of preliminaries." Overpraise, but it expresses the high spirits of the generation that was coming into power in literary America.

Ezra Pound, Mencken told *Smart Set* readers, "is perhaps the most extraordinary man that American literature has seen in our time, and, characteristically enough, he keeps as far away from America as possible." Mencken himself has written a just account of the *Smart Set*, 1914–1922. We find it in "A Personal Word," a 16-page promotional booklet once widely distributed but now so scarce that it is locked away in the Rare Book Room of the New York Public Library. It was never intended, Mencken explained, to make a popular magazine of *Smart*

Set. Nathan and he "always sought to print, not the most popular stuff we could find, but the best stuff." Because they could not compete with the more popular magazines in bidding for manuscripts, it was the endeavor of Mencken and Nathan "to maintain a hospitable welcome for the talented newcomer—to give him his first chance in good company, and to pay him." And it was true, as Mencken claimed, that they had "brought out . . . more novices of first-rate ability than any other American magazine."

In a succinct statement of editorial policy Mencken wrote, "Both of us are against the sentimental, the obvious, the trite, the maudlin. Both of us are opposed to all such ideas as come from the mob, and are polluted by its stupidity: Puritanism, Prohibition, Comstockery, evangelical Christianity, tin-pot patriotism, the whole sham of democracy. Both of us, though against socialism and in favor of capitalism, believe that capitalism in the United States is ignorant, disreputable and degraded, and that its heroes are bounders. Both of us believe in the dignity of the fine arts, and regard Beethoven and Brahms as far greater men than Wilson and Harding. Both of us stand aloof from the childish nationalism that now affects the world, and regard all of its chief spokesmen, in all countries, as scoundrels."

The name of the magazine, Mencken confessed, had been a handicap in gaining serious attention to its offerings. People thought it was an all-fiction magazine of smart society, and it was mostly sold to newsstand buyers. As a matter of fact, half of each issue was nonfiction, and the publisher wished to convert a substantial part of the newsstand circulation to subscriptions; that, said Mencken, "would lead us into easier waters, and enable us to improve the magazine." And indeed, if *Smart Set* had been called *Blue Review*—a name Willard Huntington Wright, Mencken, and Nathan had picked for a literary magazine they dreamed of founding—it would surely have made an even greater impact upon American taste and the encouragement of native belles lettres.

In 1920 H. L. Mencken reached the crest of a wave of personal influence that had been rolling since the Armistice of 1918 released him from muzzling his bellicose pro-Germanism. He had been awaiting a draft summons to fight on the side he didn't believe in—and then the Twenties had been born and he was free to galvanize the postwar spirit of revolt. The voltage of that spirit had been raised by Mencken's remarkable essay on "Puritanism as a Literary Force," and in *Our America* (1919) Waldo Frank predicted that Mencken was "a sort of capering St. George come to slay the Puritan Dragon." The slaying of the

Comstock dragon was his mission, and he accomplished it with gusto and humor. More than that, he galvanized the whole revolt of the young against the Genteel Tradition in life and letters.

In a few years Walter Lippmann was to write that Mencken was "the most powerful personal influence on this whole generation of educated people." In 1920 he was on his way to that position. He was on the move from the role of literary critic, which was salutary, to the role of political and social sage, which was to prove too big for his capability. He was not a Voltaire, but as a stimulator of vital literature in 1920 he could not be beat.

But it was the many little magazines and reviews we found in the Washington Square Book Shop that seemed so very special to us in that pivotal year. The book shop remained a fountainhead throughout the Twenties; but in the first year of the decade, it was so much a part of our own beginnings as writers that its value can hardly be overstated. Whether we looked for and found ourselves or our compatriots in the pages of those first little magazines, the experience was uniquely invigorating. These were the magazines of the young intelligentsia; these were *our* magazines. And this was our magazine rack in our book shop.

CHAPTER 10

New Publishers

"The crying need in the book-trade," said the editorial in *Publishers' Weekly* of January 3, 1920, "is better and more complete distribution, not merely more sales but more markets." This was the persistent theme of *Publishers' Weekly* throughout the Twenties. At the end of the decade, defeat was acknowledged. The celebrated Cheney Report, titled *Economic Survey of the Book Industry, 1930–1931,* found that "no entirely new distribution system is at present possible, but the existing machinery, under present conditions, is incapable of handling a reasonable volume profitably."

All the same, publishers were ever hopeful. Year after year they expressed the sentiment of that 1920 editorial. "Book publishers enter the new year with both confidence and apprehension—confidence that it will be a notable year, apprehension lest they prove unable to take full advantage of the hopeful conditions." But *Publishers' Weekly* saw that "until the impulse to buy a book and the chance to buy it are brought close together, book publishing will always be unsatisfactory." The editorial concluded that "1920 is bound to be a notable year for books and reading; let us hope, too, that it will be notable for progress in the scope and efficiency of book selling machinery."

Statistics, however, do not show 1920 as a notable year for books and reading. There was only a modest increase over the figures for 1919 when new books and new editions had totaled 5,741 titles. A total of 6,187 new books and new editions appeared in 1920—about half the number published in the postwar years of the late Forties and about one-quarter of the number published in the mid-Sixties. We must remember that per capita consumption of new books was distressingly low in 1920.

Best-seller lists were also distressing to those who hoped for a quickening and uplifting of American taste. In fiction the best-selling authors in order of sales magnitude were Zane Grey, Peter B. Kyne, Harold Bell Wright, James Oliver Curwood, Irving Bachellor, Eleanor H. Porter, Joseph C. Lincoln, E. Phillips Oppenheim, Ethel M. Dell, and Kathleen Norris. No sign here of a literary revival. Adventure stories in the great open spaces, preachy novels, sentimental romances—that was what the big public seemed to want—not realism. The nonfiction best-seller list represented the new times better. It was led by Philip Gibbs's *Now It Can Be Told*, followed by John Maynard Keynes's *The Economic Consequences of the Peace*, two books about Theodore Roosevelt who had died the year before, and a travel book, *White Shadows in the Southern Seas*, by Frederick O'Brien.

There was more excitement in a "Noteworthy Fiction of 1920" list of thirty-six novels drawn up by *Publishers' Weekly*. Some of the noteworthy titles that can be recalled with interest half a century later are: *September* by Frank Swinnerton, *The Dark Mother* by Waldo Frank, *Treacherous Ground* by Johan Bojer, *This Side of Paradise* by F. Scott Fitzgerald, *Interim* by Dorothy Richardson, *Mitch Miller* by Edgar Lee Masters, *The Rescue* by Joseph Conrad, *Miss Lulu Bett* by Zona Gale, *Potterism* by Rose Macaulay, *Poor Relations* by Compton Mackenzie, *The Young Physician* by Francis Brett Young, *Hunger* by Knut Hamsun, and *Night and Day* by Virginia Woolf. Other authors on this "Noteworthy Fiction" list were St. John Ervine, Vincente Blasco Ibañez, Catherine Carswell, Elizabeth Sanxay Holding, and Anne Douglas Sedgwick.

Scanning *Publishers' Weekly* for that pivotal year, one finds at intervals a bugle-cry announcement of the new spirit in American and British letters. In January there was Charles Fort's *Book of the Damned*, introduced by Theodore Dreiser. In February the publisher advertised that it was "receiving over 3,000 a week of this book [*Economic Consequences of the Peace*], but shall be continually behind in our orders for a fortnight." Also in that month were advertisements of *Beyond the Horizon* by Eugene O'Neill and *Instigations* by Ezra Pound. In March there was bugling for *This Side of Paradise*, *Miss Lulu Bett*, and *The American Credo* by H. L. Mencken and George Jean Nathan. In June Carl Sandburg's *Smoke and Steel* was advertised. In July there was a full page announcement of *Main Street* by Sinclair Lewis.

126

In September one publisher announced a second book within the year by Fitzgerald, *Flappers and Philosophers*, reporting happily that *This Side of Paradise* had reached its eighth printing. Toward the end of September another publisher announced the forthcoming publication of *Moon Calf* by Floyd Dell and *Youth and the Bright Medusa* by Willa Cather.

Thus, despite the small growth shown by trade statistics and the inferior literary quality of the best-seller list, publishers were right that 1920 was "bound to be a notable year for books and reading"—although the notability would not come from the old-line established houses.

In fact, most American publishers were not responding to the changing times. They were unadventurous and provincial in their response to American literature; some were stodgy. Their trade organization, the American Publishers Association, had disintegrated after losing a costly battle with R. H. Macy & Company over price maintenance; they regrouped cautiously in 1920 as the National Association of Book Publishers. The new association was afraid of antitrust legislation and ruled out any involvement in retail price maintenance. In fact, the association did little more than expend $50,000 a year for institutional advertising and general book trade promotion. But it justified its existence in 1931 when it engaged an outside specialist to make a detailed analysis of the economics of book publishing (the aforementioned Cheney Report).

And yet the publishing situation in 1920 was highly favorable to the new literary movement. Some five or six young publishers, who would ultimately rejuvenate the whole industry, welcomed the new realists, the new critical voices, the new poets—and thereby became partners in the creation of a period. It takes three parties to make a period—authors, publishers, and readers. Authors were emerging from the American resurgence and were being joined by the youngest generation of writers demobilized from World War I; readers in growing numbers were ready for them; and a handful of publishers linked the new authors to the new reading public. Not enough honor has been given by literary historians to Scribner's, Alfred A. Knopf, Boni & Liveright, B. W. Huebsch, and Harcourt, Brace & Howe, for their part in the creation of the Twenties. In 1920 Scribner's brought out 201 new titles,* Knopf brought out 82 titles, Boni & Liveright 45, Huebsch 40, and Harcourt, Brace 83. These houses published Fitzgerald, Mencken, Dreiser, O'Neill, Sherwood Anderson,

---

* Figure supplied to Elizabeth Munson by Charles Scribner, Jr.

Sinclair Lewis, T. S. Eliot—representative writers who set the literary tone of the Twenties. These few publishers themselves set the tone of publishing in the new decade. They raised standards of book manufacturing; they insisted on more attractive jackets; they pursued more persuasive advertising; and they stepped up publicity for their authors and titles. Paced by them, American publishing became progressive and enterprising. By the end of the Twenties it no longer held back from literary rebellion.

Scribner's

F. Scott Fitzgerald, thinking of his publisher, Charles Scribner's Sons, wrote that he had enjoyed "the curious advantage to a rather radical writer in being published by . . . an ultra-conservative house." But Scribner's, though it was a conservative house, was never ultra-conservative; it had in fact manifested a liberal strain in part of its list. Founded in 1846, it was nearly seventy-five years old when this minor liberal strain suddenly became pronounced and, a few years later, dominant. A thirty-six-year-old editor, Maxwell Evarts Perkins, was the transforming influence. He was the editor who discerned the promise of Fitzgerald and proceeded to pick such representative Twenties authors as Ernest Hemingway, Ring Lardner, "S. S. Van Dine," and Thomas Wolfe, the last arrival of the Twenties.

Perkins' predecessor was a distinguished literary adviser, William C. Brownell, who had brought much distinction to Scribner's list. During his forty years Scribner's published Robert Louis Stevenson and Henry James, George Meredith and James M. Barrie, H. G. Wells and John Galsworthy, Theodore Roosevelt and Max Eastman, Edith Wharton and James G. Huneker—names that brightened the respectable reputation that such authors as Henry van Dyke, John Fox, Jr., Thomas Nelson Page, and F. Hopkinson Smith had given the house of Scribner. Brownell was a fine critic, author of *French Traits*, *Victorian Prose Masters*, and *American Prose Masters*; he was associated with the New Humanists, but he was never inflexible. Even Mencken had to concede that he was a "worthy if somewhat gummy man," and Huneker warmly admired him as an important critic of literature and the fine arts. Brownell's *Standards* appeared in 1917, *The Genius of Style* in 1924, both sustaining the judgment of Stuart P. Sherman that Brownell was "the critical representative of our literary aristocracy." Thus, Scribner's could never have been justly called ultra-conservative as many of the older American publishers were in 1920. It is known that some of Scribner's older salesmen and office staff were shocked by Fitzgerald's being on the list, but the firm's head, Charles Scribner, Sr. ("C. S.") was not a hidebound president.

"C. S. had, like all good publishers," observed Edward L. Burlingame, "an intuition about public demand. He knew the seasons of its ripeness . . . he realized the public trend after the first World War and published the books of Scott Fitzgerald, Hemingway and others against all the discreet tradition of the firm."

The rising man at Scribner's as the Twenties opened was Maxwell Evarts Perkins, grandson of William Maxwell Evarts, the lawyer who defended President Andrew Johnson at the impeachment proceedings, served as secretary of state under Rutherford B. Hayes, and was elected United States senator from New York in 1885. Max Perkins—he was never called Maxwell in publishing circles—was usually thought of as a New Englander. He did live in Connecticut; but he was born in New York City and grew up in Plainfield, New Jersey, where he knew a boy named Van Wyck Brooks. Perkins went on to St. Paul's in New Hampshire and entered Harvard in the class of 1907. Brooks, by now Perkins' best friend, was in the class of 1908 but completed his degree requirements in three years and was graduated in 1907. For a time Perkins was a reporter for the New York *Times* and won attention with a thrilling story about a ride with auto racer George Robertson, the Vanderbilt Cup winner in 1908.

Then one day, armed with a letter from Professor Barrett Wendell of Harvard, Max Perkins called at Scribner's. He was hired as advertising manager at the age of twenty-six—the year was 1910—and at Scribner's he stayed until his death thirty-seven years later. "Oh, I've always been at Scribners," he used to say to authors who asked when he had started there. In 1914 he had become editor under William C. Brownell. He continued to rise during the Twenties, becoming a director and secretary, and finally a vice-president after the Twenties closed. But let us fix our attention on Max Perkins at one moment on September 16, 1919, when he was composing a special delivery letter to a young author in St. Paul, Minnesota.

This moment was the climax of a story of hopeful literary endeavor that went back two years to Princeton. Here an undergraduate who was repeating his junior year had shown the manuscript of a novel to Dean Christian Gauss with the request that the dean submit it to his publisher, Charles Scribner's Sons. But Gauss had felt that the novel was not ready for submission. The undergraduate had then been commissioned second lieutenant in the regular army and left Princeton for officers' training at Fort Leavenworth.

There, in three months, he wrote the first draft of *The Romantic Egotist*, a novel bearing some undefined relation to the one Dean Gauss had seen. This draft was sent to an Irish author, Shane Leslie, who was teaching at the Newman School near Hackensack, New Jersey. Leslie, who was published by Scribner's, sent *The Romantic Egotist* to his own publisher. It was returned to the author with a long letter of encouragement and suggestions for revision. Perkins, it seemed, liked the manuscript and suggested transposing it to the third person. The young officer tried to meet the suggestions and returned the manuscript to Scribner's for a verdict. At the end of October, 1918, it was finally rejected. Only Perkins favored it, Brownell couldn't stomach it, and Edward L. Burlingame described it as "hard sledding."

A few days later came the celebrations of the false and the true Armistice and the birth of the Twenties during the revels. The following February the young officer-author was demobilized—the second officer in his regiment to be let go, being "unusually disposable," according to a more skillful comrade-in-arms. He proceeded for some months to rewrite, alter, and add to *The Romantic Egotist*. And on September 3 Fitzgerald sent the manuscript, now entitled *This Side of Paradise*, to Scribner's. Thirteen days later Max Perkins, having, with the aid of Charles Scribner, Jr., won out against the older editors, was able to write F. Scott Fitzgerald, "I am very glad, personally to be able to write you that we are all for publishing your book, 'This Side of Paradise.' The book is so different that it is hard to prophesy how it will sell, but we are all for taking a chance and supporting it with vigor." This was a decisive moment in three careers—in the career of an author, in the career of an editor, and in the career of a publisher.

But suppose that at this observed moment on September 16, 1919, Perkins had written to decline *This Side of Paradise*. It is not at all certain that another publisher would have accepted it. The conservative houses—the great majority—would have disliked the book's rebelliousness, and the few progressive houses might well have objected to its glaring faults of style and construction. Brownell of Scribner's was right in his poor opinion of the book's artistic pretensions. Editors might well have been unanimous in judging this first novel a failure, though some of them would have hoped to see the second novel.

Max Perkins saw the faults of Fitzgerald and his immaturity as clearly as anyone did, but he also saw the splendid promise of the man and thereby began to show the editorial genius that made him the outstanding editor of the Twenties. By the end of his career Perkins was known as the book editor who had guided the greatest number of young talents to ripeness in the American literary revival. He had started with Fitzgerald; he was concluding with Marcia Davenport.

Not only must a great editor have an intuition of the development of an author; he must also have an intuition of the rising generation that will possibly set the tone of the coming decade. Somehow Perkins knew that the Genteel Tradition was fading and that the red banners of Youth would soon be streaming from Provincetown and Greenwich Village to Carmel and Hollywood. *This Side of Paradise*, Mark Sullivan noted, "had the distinction, if not of creating a generation, certainly of calling the world's attention to a generation." Perkins, who had been at Harvard in 1907, was a little older than this generation whose writers came out of Princeton, Harvard, and Yale in the classes of 1916, 1917, 1918. But he was keenly responsive to the poetry of campus life they evoked, and he had a kindred understanding of their liberal American dream. He felt the imminence of the Jazz Age, as Fitzgerald was to name it.

He could not tell how large a public was ready for *This Side of Paradise*, but he had a hunch that it was there and that a resolute promotion of the book would pay. It did. *This Side of Paradise* sold nearly 33,000 copies in the first seven months and better than 50,000 in its first three years. Perkins' gamble on Fitzgerald was therefore decisive in his editorial career. It ensured authority and power for him in the conduct of Scribner's publishing through the Twenties and afterwards.

With the successful launching of Fitzgerald, Scribner's changed. Fitzgerald recruited authors for the house and Perkins signed them to contracts. Thomas Boyd, author of the war novel *Through the Wheat*, was first. Then came Ring Lardner with *How To Write Short Stories*, Fitzgerald again being the recommender. Next, eagerly recommended by Fitzgerald, was Ernest Hemingway; he brought *The Torrents of Spring*, which ridiculed Sherwood Anderson and was therefore unacceptable to Anderson's publisher; Perkins caught Hemingway on the rebound from Boni & Liveright. In 1926 Scribner's began publishing the detective fiction of S. S. Van Dine (Willard Huntington Wright), and again Perkins' sales sense was vindicated; whereas detective novels usually sold only a few thousand, the first three S. S. Van Dine novels hit over 60,000 each. Finally, in 1929 Perkins accepted the much-rejected novel of Thomas Wolfe, *Look Homeward, Angel,* and consolidated forever the reputation of Scribner's as one of the progressive publishers of the Twenties. The seed from which this reputation grew was that letter Perkins wrote to Fitzgerald on September 16, 1919.

Knopf

In the early spring of 1919 I made a desultory search for a job. Among other applications I applied to the young publishing firm of Alfred A. Knopf at its small office in the Candler Building, 220 West 42nd Street. I was poorly prepared to interview the publisher who was already rejuvenating the industry. After I got into his office, I had no idea how to present my application to Mr. Knopf. He treated me with courtesy, but it did not take him long to decline my proffered services. Nevertheless I was stimulated and filled with hope for the new literary life in America even if Mr. Knopf had dismissed me so quickly. I declared to myself as I left that the 27-year-old Knopf was, in the collegiate phrase of the day, "a prince of a fellow." I did not know then that one of Knopf's authors, Carl Van Vechten, had phrased his first impression in a more fitting manner: Knopf, he said, "resembled a prince from a Persian miniature."

I had met a tall, romantically handsome young man wearing a pink shirt (in an office!) and a black tie that matched his jet black mustache and black hair. His elegantly tailored suit was by Wetzel, no doubt. The princely impression was to persist through the years of Knopf's distinguished publishing career. "We call him Belshazzar," an editor remarked to me at an American Booksellers Association luncheon in the early 1940s when the colorfully dressed Knopf passed by our table. And in the jacket painting of Volume I of the privately printed *Portrait of a Publisher,* a Typophiles production in 1965, Warren Chappell has depicted Alfred Knopf as a richly dressed Sultan.

Knopf had been well prepared for the role he was playing in 1919 when literary young men wanted to hitch their wagons to this bright rising star of publishing. A New Yorker, he had attended Columbia College in the class of 1912 and had had his mind turned toward publishing by Joel Elias Spingarn. The influence was indirect. Spingarn's course was comparative literature, and Knopf's publishing was to be characterized by his broad interest in many literatures— French, German, Scandinavian, Polish, Spanish, Latin American, Japanese, and several others. Spingarn offered a personal prize for an essay on a contemporary writer by a student in his course, and young Alfred Knopf competed, choosing John Galsworthy for his subject. From this choice "way [led] on to way" until Knopf landed in publishing and not in the law, as he had first intended. Knopf wrote to Galsworthy for biographical information. By sending Galsworthy a copy of his essay, he won his friendship, though Randolph Bourne won the Spingarn prize. Galsworthy invited his young admirer to his cottage in Devonshire when he came to England in the summer of 1912; there Galsworthy pressed on him the writings of Joseph Conrad and W. H. Hudson. And in London, hanging around Dan Rider's book shop that was frequented by writers, Knopf began to be attracted toward the career of publisher.

Back in New York, the young Knopf secured employment in the accounting department of Doubleday, Page & Company, then opening their Garden City, Long Island plant. His wages were only eight dollars a week—raised to twelve after a year—but the opportunity for a basic course in publishing procedures was unusual and excellent. "I went through the place like a shot," Knopf has said. "From accounting to manufacturing, then to advertising, and then to sales, where I was allowed to tangle a little with the editorial department." He has recalled that "Doubleday, Page & Company was an exciting place for a youngster just out of college. I was allowed to sit in on the weekly editorial meetings . . . and I was allowed to take the manuscript of [Conrad's] *Chance* home and to be the first to read it." He was then given a chance to show what talent for book promotion he might have. He was permitted to send advance copies of *Chance* and to solicit tributes to Conrad from leading American writers—Basil King, Rex Beach, Louis Joseph Vance, Winston Churchill (the novelist), Robert W. Service, George Barr McCutcheon, Jack London, Meredith Nicholson, Mary Austin; but three turned him down: Theodore Dreiser, William Dean Howells, Harold Bell Wright. Then Knopf was allowed to write and sign a booklet on Conrad which was distributed widely by Doubleday, Page. The result was a coup of promotion that earned applause from publisher George H. Doran, who declared that "to Knopf more than to any one other person, Conrad owes his fame and popularity and the reading public a debt of gratitude."

After this coup Knopf went to work for Mitchell Kennerley as general assistant at twenty-five dollars a week and stayed with him for fourteen months. All this while he saved money toward a business venture of his own. With the added income of an allowance from his father, Knopf amassed two thousand dollars. His father added three thousand to those savings, and Knopf was then ready to break with Kennerley and set out under his own imprint. Even allowing for the very great differences in purchasing power, wage-and-price levels, and the like between May, 1915, when Alfred Knopf founded his own company and October, 1965, when that company celebrated its fiftieth anniversary, the success Knopf realized with an initial capital of only five thousand dollars is still a marvel.

Almost from the outset Knopf had an assistant, a young woman of remarkable talent for the business, who became Mrs. Blanche Knopf in the second year and virtually a partner in the developing enterprise.

Knopf struck at once the cosmopolitan note for which his house became famous. Of the eleven books published in the first year, ten were translations. In course of time he was the publisher of no fewer than six Nobel Prize winners. Cosmopolitanism was to be as great a trait of the Twenties as was the interest of that period in a revival of national literature. The cosmopolitan James Gibbons Huneker would be just as much of a forerunner as would the midwesterner Theodore Dreiser who was founding by example a school of American naturalism. In a general way, the period threw off its English colonialism and turned to Europe for sustenance in its coming-to-independence. Malcolm Cowley has rightly suggested that "Knopf was trying to create a public for Continental authors partly because of a notion that it would also be a public for American authors with Continental standards of taste, candor, and invention. Such a public, free from provincialism, would help to carry American writing into the mainstream of world literature." The one book on Knopf's first list that was not a translation was the most successful. That was a reissue of W. H. Hudson's *Green Mansions* which Galsworthy had recommended. "*Green Mansions* was the book that put us in business, but not in a very flush kind of way," Knopf told a *New Yorker* writer.

Knopf books are called Borzoi Books after the Russian wolfhound trademark he adopted for his firm; and Borzoi Books mean handsome, well-made books. "I love books physically," Knopf confessed in an early catalog, "and I want to make them beautifully. I do no one a serious injustice when I say that American books are *not* beautiful." He proceeded to improve vastly both taste and style in American bookmaking. "I have found the prevalent idea that a good-looking book must necessarily cost too much to manufacture wholly fallacious. Good-looking books do cost—the publisher's time and thought. And so I have experimented with boards printed up in brightly colored Continental designs, with Italian hand-made papers, with French papers, with a Russian artist's idea for a binding."

In his second year of publishing Knopf engaged the architect and artist Claude Bragdon to advise him on bindings, end papers, jackets, and design. Authors appreciated the pains Knopf took to make their books handsome. Book buyers were appreciative too. It was publisher George H. Doran in *The Chronicles of Barrabas* who justly appraised Knopf's service to the industry. "In mechanical artistry of production Knopf set a new standard of excellence."

In his third year Knopf clearly showed that his cosmopolitan tastes would not overshadow his interest in new American writers. In 1916 he published a little book, *Art Versus Journalism*, by Max Eastman; and two years later he published Eastman's volume of verse, *Colors of Life*. In 1917 he "magnetized" Joseph Hergesheimer away from Kennerley, as it has been expressed, and published his novels henceforward, beginning with *The Three Black Pennys* which sold quite well. *Gold and Iron* came in 1918, and in 1919 there were three Hergesheimer titles: *Java Head, The Happy End*, and *Linda Condon*. Ezra Pound was also a notable pick-up in 1917. That year appeared *Lustra of Ezra Pound, with Earlier Poems* and *"Noh" or Accomplishment: A Study of the Classical Stage of Japan* by Pound and Fenollosa. Pound's *Pavannes and Divisions* was on the 1918 Knopf list. *Others, An Anthology of the New Verse*, edited by Alfred Kreymborg, was another sign of Knopf's interest in 1917 in new American poets. Conrad Aiken made the list in 1919 with *Scepticisms: Notes on American Poetry*.

The phenomenal best-selling author Knopf acquired in those early years began as a very poor-selling author. Witter Bynner had taken Knopf to lunch in 1916 to meet a Syrian-American mystic who lived in Greenwich Village. Kahlil Gibran had published parables in *The Seven Arts* magazine and already had a small following among the intelligentsia. It was so small that only a few hundred copies were sold of *The Madman*, which Knopf published in 1918. The following year Knopf brought out *Twenty Drawings* by Gibran at five dollars a copy but it sold even less than *The Madman*. Nor did *The Forerunner* in 1920 do any better. One wonders why Knopf stayed with an author whose first three books sold so poorly, but he seems to have had a personal fondness for Gibran—despite a certain reserve toward his philosophy. He had no hunch about popularity for Gibran when he published *The Prophet* in 1923; nor did the first year's sale of this famous book—1,159 copies—indicate that it would not also fall into the remainder market. The miracle of word-of-mouth recommendation, which no publisher can work, began spontaneously to manifest itself in 1924 when sales of *The Prophet* unexpectedly doubled and then doubled again in 1925. The steadily increasing sale of *The Prophet*—in 1965 the sale passed the 2-million mark—naturally revived the unprofitable Gibran titles of 1918 and 1920.

More to Knopf's personal taste than the watery, pseudo-mysticism of Gibran were the books of Carl Van Vechten. *Music and Bad Manners* appeared in 1916 and *Interpreters and Interpretations* in 1917. There were two in 1918: *The Merry-Go-Round* and *The Music of Spain*. Knopf appears to have relied on Van Vechten's judgment about manuscripts, for in the Twenties he published a large number of authors recommended by the music critic: Langston Hughes, James Weldon Johnson, Rudolph Fisher, Miguel Covarrubias, Wallace Stevens, Neith Boyce, Isa Glenn, M. P. Shiel, Chester Himes, H. B. Fuller, and Arthur Machen.

By 1920 H. L. Mencken was firmly a Knopf author. As Mencken recalls it, "It must have been in 1913 or thereabout that I first met [Knopf]—a very tall, very slim young fellow, but lately out of college, with a faint and somewhat puzzling air of the exotic about him." Knopf had come to talk about the promotion of Conrad at Doubleday, Page, but he gave Mencken the impression that he was too idealistic to succeed in publishing. It has been said that Mencken was still skeptical of "Noff," as he called him, when Knopf started his own firm. Not until 1917 did he come aboard the Knopf enterprise, "taking a modest room on D deck," metaphorically speaking. His first publication with Knopf was *A Book of Prefaces*, which contained a long essay on Conrad. In the same year Knopf put out a lively pamphlet, *Pistols for Two* by Owen Hatteras, a pseudonym for H. L. Mencken and George Jean Nathan. *Pistols for Two* profiled the two editors of *The Smart Set*.

Relations were a little strained in 1918 but in 1919 Mencken came back wholeheartedly and was given better accommodations than a room on D deck. (Eventually he was to occupy one of the best suites.) There are many who believe that Mencken will be valued most and longest for his philological works. In 1919 Knopf presented the first of these, *The American Language*; and it made an immediate impression of value and usefulness on even the authoritative academic philologists. "A book to be taken seriously," said Brander Matthews. "Well planned, well proportioned, well documented, and well written." Twenty-five years later critical opinion would hold that *The American Language* had become a landmark in a new era of American linguistic studies. For good measure of Mencken, Knopf also published *Prejudices: First Series* in 1919.

Thus in five years Alfred A. Knopf, starting with no American authors and only small capital, had risen to the highest prestige with the generation of American authors coming to power in the Twenties. He had maintained his leadership in the publication of foreign books—his big foreign novel in 1920 was Knut Hamsun's *Hunger*—but he was also ahead of the older firms in attracting upcoming American novelists, poets, and essayists. Consider the strength of his 1920 list: Joseph Hergesheimer, *San Cristobal de la Habana*; Clarence Day, Jr., *This Simian World*; T. S. Eliot, *Poems*; Willa Cather, *Youth and the Bright Medusa*; Carl Van Vechten, *Interpreters, In the Garret, The Tiger in the House*; H. L. Mencken and George Jean Nathan, *Heliogabulus, The American Credo*; and H. L. Mencken, *Prejudices: Second Series*.

In 1940, after twenty-three years of association with Knopf, Mencken paid warm tribute. "He is, by my standards, the perfect publisher," Mencken concluded. A number of other authors who had assisted in setting the tone of the Twenties were in agreement with the "Sage of Baltimore."

Boni & Liveright

Horace B. Liveright was as much a representative man of the Twenties as Scott Fitzgerald. As a publisher, he was no less in tune with the Zeitgeist than were Scott Fitzgerald, Edna St. Vincent Millay, and John Barrymore. One of his authors, Waldo Frank, writing in the *New Yorker* under the pseudonym of Search-Light, declared that "no record of [the Twenties] can be complete, that fails to reckon with HBL . . . erratic, tangential, generous, inspired . . . this trader in letters, this gambler in aesthetics, this marketer of poets, this poet of marketers."

Liveright came to publishing out of Philadelphia in the first place, then out of paper manufacturing, and finally out of Greenwich Village. He had gambled on Wall Street; he had sought patents for paper novelties; he had met in Greenwich Village the patent lawyer and theater enthusiast Lawrence Langner and the book shop enterpriser Albert Boni. Greenwich Village was then one of the incubators of American culture, of the American soul—such was Waldo Frank's claim when profiling Horace Liveright for the *New Yorker*.

Albert Boni had a dream of reprinting *modern* books cheaply. It was to be a sort of "Everyman's Library" for the modern, with his interest in contemporary literature and the literature of the preceding century. And it would feature revolutionary and iconoclastic writers who were not yet acceptable to the slow-moving Everyman's Library. Boni first discussed this idea with Alfred Wallerstein and then infected Horace Liveright with enthusiasm.

Lawrence Langner recalls in his memoir, *The Magic Curtain*:

> Albert Boni with whom I had shared the Washington Square Book Shop, called at my office and asked my advice as to whether he should go into partnership with Horace Liveright in the book publishing business. "I strongly advise you against it, Albert," I said. "Horace is a wonderful promoter and will bring a great deal of enthusiasm to the firm, but you will need a partner who can work fifteen hours a day, if necessary, reading manuscripts and making editorial decisions." A few days later Horace came to see me and asked my advice as to whether he should enter into a partnership in the publishing business with Albert Boni. "I strongly advise you against it, Horace," I said. "Albert is a wonderful promoter and will bring a great deal of enthusiasm to the firm, but you will need a partner who can work fifteen hours a day, if necessary, reading manuscripts and making editorial decisions." They immediately formed the firm of Boni & Liveright and remained together as partners for barely six months, after which they quarreled violently.

In 1917, Alfred Wallerstein bowed out, and Albert Boni and Horace Liveright put in $6,250 each to start the new firm. They launched the Modern Library—reprints of such authors as Samuel Butler, Bernard Shaw, Friedrich Nietzsche, Fyodor Dostoyevsky, Ivan Turgenev, Oscar Wilde, George Moore, and Max Beerbohm, put forth in smelly, oily, limp leatherette bindings at the low price of sixty cents a volume. The Modern Library was a boon to the young people who would soon give a tone of youthful sophistication to the decade of the Twenties. In time it became one of the great achievements of American publishing.

At the end of its first year Boni & Liveright had a net profit of $10,000, remarkable for a firm with no back list. Thomas Seltzer, an uncle of Albert

Boni, joined the firm early but, as noted by Langner, dissension broke out after the first six months and continued for two years. Finally a coin was tossed to determine who would buy out whom. Boni won the toss to buy out Liveright and Seltzer but was nevertheless obliged to relinquish his claim and sell to Liveright. Horace Liveright was permitted to keep the joint imprint but agreed to surrender it if and when Albert Boni returned to publishing.* A former editor of *The Century*, T. R. Smith, became Liveright's chief editor.

By 1920 Boni & Liveright had been heard as a clarion in the publishing world. To the book trade the firm represented the new ferment and the new figures in American letters. In its fourth year, Liveright brought out the respectable number of 45 titles, leading off with a book he was reluctant to publish, Charles Fort's *The Book of the Damned*. Theodore Dreiser, Liveright's "big author" and one of the most difficult authors in the history of publisher-author relations, insisted that Liveright publish Fort if he was to continue publishing Dreiser's books. Although *The Book of the Damned* sold quite modestly, Fort's attack on scientific orthodoxy was sensational and his books were revived in 1941 in an omnibus volume that went through six printings. Dreiser's own entry on Liveright's 1920 list was *Hey Rub-A-Dub-Dub*, a crudely philosophical work that received bad reviews and sold slowly, passing the 3,100 mark by the end of the decade. Dreiser would become a very substantial literary property but that was a few years off and his relations with Liveright were to culminate in a great outburst of suspicion and anger during negotiations for sale of the motion picture rights to *An American Tragedy*. Another author whose books would sell in high figures but would start slowly with Liveright was Eugene O'Neill whose first Broadway play, *Beyond the Horizon*, published in February of 1920, bore the Liveright device of a cowled monk seated at a writing table. "I have often wondered," said Louis Kronenberger who worked there for a while, "who thought up this most misleading of office symbols, for never in publishing, and seldom anywhere else, has there been an atmosphere so unmonastic, so unstudious, so unsolitary as at Liveright's." In that same February, Liveright published Ezra Pound's *Instigations*; and toward the end of the year, he published T. S. Eliot's *The Sacred Wood*.

A Boni & Liveright failure was Waldo Frank's novel *The Dark Mother*,

---

* When A. & C. Boni, Inc., was formed in 1923, Liveright was asked to relinquish the joint imprint. He refused, but some years later he dropped "Boni" and became Horace Liveright, Inc.

launched in August and expected to score in the wake of *Our America*. But *The Dark Mother* received a damaging review in the influential *Dial* by Frank's colleague of *The Seven Arts*, Paul Rosenfeld, and sold fewer than 1,250 copies during the whole decade of the Twenties. The critic found Frank deficient in character-creation. Frank's novels, Rosenfeld alleged, were fantasies written with an air of detachment to justify the author's own sense of painful election. My own critical study of Waldo Frank, published by Boni & Liveright in 1923, challenged Rosenfeld's criticism of *The Dark Mother*. I called the novel "an exciting failure," though I later came to question what I had thought was exciting about its sluggish narrative flow, its uninteresting characters, its pre-Jamesian method of telling, and its strained style.

Horace Liveright was already a good showman in 1920. He had an effective style in advertising. Heavy black borders and very bold type made his advertisements stand out. And the informal copy, written in a kind of inter-office-memo style, gave him a dashing individual character. In those days his offices were in the Tilden Building, 105 West 40th Street. In 1923 he moved to a brownstone house at 61 West 48th Street where it has been said that "Boni & Liveright was an actual *part* of the speakeasy world." Not only were there six speakeasies to one publishing house on the block, but they were virtually all B & L branch offices.

The most popular branch office was a speakeasy almost next door as one walked toward Sixth Avenue. It was here that I met several of the B & L staff who would establish their own firms upon "graduation" from 61 West 48th. After Liveright had published my first book, the monograph on Waldo Frank, Julian Messner and Donald Friede took kind notice of the fledgling author whose sale was microscopic. I did not meet Richard Simon and Bennett Cerf, who were supposed to sell the little "turkey" I had written. Manuel Komroff, Liveright's production manager, I did meet when my book was being manufactured; but I missed Edward Weeks, Lillian Hellman, and Beatrice Kaufman who were helping to make the name of Liveright noted for audacity in sales methods and editorial enterprise.

Publishers of that day were wary of the censor. But not Liveright. Although John Sumner and the Society for the Suppression of Vice were still powerful, Liveright jauntily bucked their power in 1919 with Hutchins Hapgood's *The Story of a Lover* and successfully fought off the Clean Books Bill that came up for passage in the New York State Legislature in 1923.

It is a pity that Liveright's attempt to write his autobiography failed to produce a publishable book. It is a further pity that the biography of Liveright projected by Manuel Komroff in the 1940s was never carried through for lack of encouragement. Legends about the unconventional office on West 48th Street, the drinking and the parties that went on in it, are largely true. But the legends tend to distract attention from the great service to American letters that Liveright performed in his encouragement of the literary revival of the Twenties.

B. W. Huebsch, Inc.

On August 1, 1925, the publishing firm of B. W. Huebsch, Inc., lost its identity, merging with the newly formed Viking Press. At the time of the merger B. W. Huebsch, Inc., had published nearly five hundred titles during twenty or more active years. The exact date of its start is not easy to fix, for this firm was originally a printing business that printed diaries and yearbooks before moving very gradually into the publishing of a list of books.

B. W. Huebsch was certainly one of the makers of the favorable climate, the favorable milieu, for American literature in the Twenties. Born in New York City, the son of a rabbi who had come to the United States from Germany, Ben Huebsch somehow acquired a very good education without going to college. In his youth he was apprenticed to a lithographer and studied art at Cooper Union. He also studied the violin under the well-known conductor Sam Franko, and turned this part of his education to account when he wrote, for a time after 1900, a music criticism for the New York *Sun*. He became a truly cultivated gentleman and contributed gracefully pointed notes on culture to *The Freeman*, of which he was also the publisher.

Ben Huebsch was influenced in the direction of a publishing career by a remarkable uncle, Samuel Huebsch, who had emigrated from Hungary to the United States. Samuel Huebsch has been described as a philosopher, linguist, and printer; and it was he who directed Ben Huebsch toward printing and then publishing. Ben began work in his brother's printing shop, and in 1900 he and his brother Daniel printed and *distributed* a previously rejected manuscript, *The New Humanism*, by Edward Howard Griggs. Thereafter publishing was in the blood of Ben Huebsch; by 1907 he was set up as a publisher with a small clerical staff in offices at the corner of Nassau and Spruce streets. The previous year he had published Gelette Burgess' delightful and devastating foray against "chestnuts," as rubberstamp expressions were then called. Burgess, by the way, invented the term *blurb*, which entered the language at large and stuck tenaciously in the vocabulary of the publishing world. Burgess defined a blurb as "self-praise; to make a noise like a publisher," but he did not have his own publisher in mind, for B. W. Huebsch was a modest blurbist. His emblem was a seven-branched candlestick, designed by Charles B. Falls, with the subscription "This Mark on Good Books"; his dust-jackets were sedate, a plain cream color; his advertising was modest and in quiet good taste. He was always inclined to let a good book speak for itself.

Early in his publishing life Huebsch took a special interest in the education of booksellers. He organized a bookselling course in New York and was one of the founders of the National Association of Book Publishers in 1920. In politics as in publishing he was a liberal. In 1916 he had sailed to Europe on the Henry Ford Peace Ship. Shortly afterwards he was one of the founders of the American Civil Liberties Union.

Huebsch was the publisher of Maxim Gorky, Herman Sudermann, Gerhardt Hauptmann, August Strindberg, Jules Romains, and Mikhael Artzibashef. Other Europeans he published were Ellen Key, Henri Bergson, and Georges Sorel. In the Twenties Huebsch was famous for having published James Joyce and D. H. Lawrence before the decade began. As early as 1916 he was publishing Joyce, bringing out in the same year both *Dubliners* and *A Portrait of the Artist as a Young Man*. *Chamber Music* and *Exiles* followed in 1918. D. H. Lawrence shared 1916 with James Joyce. Huebsch published four Lawrence titles, including *The Rainbow*, in that one year.

New American writers fared well with Huebsch, too. He published George Jean Nathan's first book of which he was sole author, *Another Book on the Theatre*, in 1915. And he fostered the emergent forces in American literature by the publication in 1915 of Van Wyck Brooks's formative work, *America's Coming-of-Age*. Brooks was again on his list in 1918, with his equally formative book, *Letters and Leadership*. As far back as 1910, Huebsch had published James Oppenheim (*Wild Oats*) and Horace Traubel (*Optimos*). He had picked up books by Willard Huntington Wright (*Misinforming a Nation*, 1917), Francis Hackett (*Ireland*, 1918), and Thorstein Veblen (*The Higher Learning in America*, 1918). But Huebsch made his stongest bid for fame as a discoverer of new American authors in 1919 when he published Sherwood Anderson's *Winesburg, Ohio*. Not

The Pivotal Year, 1920

only did Huebsch accept that much-rejected manuscript, he also hit upon a fine title for it. *Winesburg, Ohio* was the first of Anderson's books to produce "the shock of recognition."

The younger generation of American writers came to look upon Huebsch as one of *their* publishers. "When I get *The Bridge* done, or something of equal length," Hart Crane said, "I think it will be time to try Liveright or Huebsch or Knopf for a collected publication." And again Crane wrote that Huebsch "certainly is the most cultured publisher here. I am thinking of submitting my book to him when it is ready."

In 1919 Huebsch had moved his offices to 32 West 58th Street, in what *Publisher's Weekly* called "the Mitchell Kennerley Building." The following year he took the fine old building on West 13th Street which housed *The Freeman* as well as his book firm. "It was Huebsch who assured *The Freeman* a place in the front lines when he wrote to Van Wyck Brooks, then living in California, to ask him to join the magazine as literary editor"; so we read in *A History of the Freeman* by Susan J. Turner.

In the pivotal year of 1920 B. W. Huebsch had a larger list than usual—forty titles. He rarely published more than twenty-five in a year, but in 1920 he was moving with the expanding times as were Liveright and Knopf. His number one book was *Poor White* by Sherwood Anderson. The new D. H. Lawrence book was *New Poems*. Another important book was Randolph Bourne's *The History of a Literary Radical*. Bourne, whose *Untimely Papers* Huebsch had published in 1919, was the right kind of author for the kind of selective publishing Huebsch was attempting. Other good titles on his 1920 list were a translation from the Russian of Alexander Blok's poem *The Twelve* and Gorky's *Reminiscences of Tolstoy*. A bitter attack on Woodrow Wilson, *The Story of a Style* by William Bayard Hale, expressed the postwar attitude of liberals toward the president they charged had led them into war after promising to keep them out.

When B. W. Huebsch died in 1964 at the age of 88, G. Thomas Tanselle recalled that he had provided "one of the great examples of the personal, one-man publishing firms." Obituary writers noted Huebsch having once said that he'd "rather publish good books than do anything else." In 1936 he had said: "I cannot think of publishing merely as a means of earning a living." A publisher must "choose from amongst the works offered for publication by creative minds." Huebsch had published only works that had appealed personally to him, which is probably something few commercial publishers of his time could say.

As the American Twenties flowered spendidly, B. W. Huebsch, publisher of Brooks, Bourne, and Anderson, could well feel that he had been one of those who prepared the soil and nurtured the growing forces that would make the period distinctive. But he was too modest to make creative claims for his role. He liked to let his authors' books speak for themselves. His publishing record speaks for itself too and quietly proclaims him a creative force in the making of the Twenties.

Harcourt, Brace & Howe

Columbia University was the nest from which the publishing firm of Harcourt, Brace & Howe came. Alfred Harcourt and Donald C. Brace, from upstate New York villages, were friends in the class of 1904; both made the staff of the campus newspaper, the *Columbia Spectator*. One of their inspiring professors was the controversial Joel Elias Spingarn who was to declaim manifestos on the "new criticism" and who would be their adviser when they launched their own publishing company. Alfred Harcourt's roommate at Columbia was John Fisher who married Dorothy Canfield, a best-selling novelist on an early Harcourt, Brace & Howe list. Another Columbia friend was Melville Cane of the class of 1900. Cane, a light versifier in college, had entered the law, and it was he who drew up incorporation papers for Harcourt and Brace in 1919. Cane matured into the writing of serious poetry, which was published by his Columbia friends from 1926 on. As corporate director, Cane served the firm for many years, even after it became Harcourt, Brace, Jovanavich.

Donald Brace, born into the printing business, went to the publishing house of Henry Holt & Co. soon after his graduation from Columbia and in due course became assistant treasurer and head of the production department. Alfred Harcourt followed Brace to Henry Holt, as a salesman for the trade book department. He was permitted to make scouting trips to England to acquire British titles, work that benefited him greatly in establishing contacts for his own publishing venture a few years later. He too rose at Holt, becoming secretary and a director in his last years there.

Alfred Harcourt has been given credit for the discovery of Robert Frost at Holt. The story has often been told of how Mrs. Henry Holt sent a copy of the English edition of *North of Boston* to Harcourt, recommending publication, and how Harcourt sent the book to Dorothy Canfield Fisher for a report and at once ordered a small edition from England when that Vermont woman urged publication. When Harcourt left Holt to publish for himself, Frost was tempted to go with him, but could never quite make up his mind to leave Holt.

Carl Sandburg had no such reluctance. Harcourt had liked *Chicago Poems* so much that he resorted to a trick to get the book accepted at Holt. There were perhaps six poems in the manuscript that might have antagonized Holt's poetry reader, W. P. Trent of Columbia. Harcourt removed these poems before sending the collection to Trent, then replaced them after Trent had voted for Sandburg. Trent apparently never reread the book after publication. In time Sandburg became one of the "big authors" at Harcourt, Brace & Howe.

"Mr. Holt was nearly seventy when I went to him [1904]," Alfred Harcourt said in his privately printed reminiscences; "and his highly creative period was past, but the fearlessness was still there, the highest business principles, and an uncompromising loyalty to quality. Like all of us at seventy, this one-time 'radical' was beginning to disapprove of some of the new ideas." Harcourt was the conduit into the old firm of the new ideas that were making some men—socialists and anarchists—dream of a new age, and he brought Bertrand Russell's *Proposed Roads to Freedom* into the house. Luckily for him the Russell exposition of guild socialism and other roads to freedom sold forty thousand copies. But despite this sale, old Henry Holt was unhappy. "I saw," Harcourt wrote, "I was not going to be able to publish books dealing with the new ideas with which the world was seething, and that Henry Holt would never feel safe with me again. . . . On May 8, 1919 I resigned. I think he was somewhat shaken but we parted friends."

Harcourt was acting on the principle that "neither do men put new wine into old bottles," a principle that was guiding the new publishers: B. W. Huebsch, Alfred A. Knopf, and Boni & Liveright. However, Maxwell Perkins at Scribner's was showing that a new-old publishing house was possible, even if Henry Holt couldn't take an infusion of youth. Harcourt was thirty-eight when he left Holt on May 8, 1919, and began to think about setting up a new company. The average age of the new publishers, counting Maxwell Perkins among them, was about thirty-four. That was the age of Harcourt's friend Sinclair Lewis, who had spent several years in publishing at Frederick A. Stokes and George H.

Doran. Lewis came east and told Harcourt: "Start your own business. I'm going to write important books. You can publish these. I've got a little money saved up and you can have some of that. Now let's start making plans."

Things moved fast. Within two months Harcourt had signed contracts for thirteen books. Frederic Melcher, editor of *Publisher's Weekly*, recommended Will Howe of the University of Indiana to head the textbook division, and on July 29, 1919, the firm of Harcourt, Brace & Howe was incorporated. The three took offices in an old Georgian house set well back from the street— No. 1 West 47th Street.

Old hands at publishing urged them to establish bank credit relations. "But Don [Brace] and I thought differently," Alfred Harcourt has written; "we were country boys. We believed that when we used bank credit, we went into debt, and a fear of debt was part of our whole makeup. I knew that bank loans would worry me so much that they might vitiate my publishing judgment." (Being in debt to the banks might well have made Harcourt hesitate to publish one of his first-year titles, C. H. Douglas' *Economic Democracy*, a revolutionary work that aroused much covert opposition in British banking circles.) "All the money I had," Harcourt continued, "was in Henry Holt and Company stock which I had bought several years before. . . . I sold the Henry Holt stock back to them and put the proceeds into my own business. It was a small list of people who originally invested in Harcourt, Brace, and there were changes almost immediately. The largest amount of paid-in capital we ever had was $123,500 and from the first we discounted our bills."

The first book under the Harcourt, Brace & Howe imprint was *Organizing for Work* by the pioneer industrial engineer H. L. Gantt, who was formulating the new science of industrial management. The first best-seller the new firm published (in January, 1920) was John Maynard Keynes's *The Economic Consequences of the Peace*. Felix Frankfurter had tipped Walter Lippmann off on the importance of the Keynes arraignment of the Versailles treaty; and Lippmann, who was an adviser to Harcourt, Brace, recommended Keynes's book to Alfred Harcourt. Negotiations were complicated, but in the end Keynes was so thoroughly satisfied by Harcourt's treatment that he advertised the fairness of his publisher to his friends in the Bloomsbury group, and several—Lytton Strachey, Virginia Woolf, E. M. Forster, Clive Bell, *et al.*—became Harcourt, Brace authors.

In 1920 the Harcourt, Brace list attained the sizable number of eighty-three titles, one more than Knopf and over twice the number of Huebsch titles. Among the Harcourt, Brace offerings was Carl Sandburg's *Smoke and Steel* which was published in June of that year. Sales volume jumped from $19,372 for the last five months of 1919 to $261,681 in 1920. The following year the jump was phenomenal—up to $720,262. The biggest factor in this enormous sales expansion was the publication on October 23, 1920, of Sinclair Lewis' *Main Street*.

The legend that Sinclair Lewis, after writing six novels intended as popular, turned his back on commercial success and wrote out of anger a novel that he thought wouldn't sell but would be truthful and an artistic success—that legend is only half true. He had played with the idea of *Main Street* intermittently for several years. Then in 1919 he buckled down to the job and wrote 100,000 words. He finished the first draft of over 200,000 words by the first of March, 1920. But he kept up his popular-commercial writing during this time, publishing *Free Air* as a *Saturday Evening Post* serial and as a Harcourt, Brace novel in 1919. When he delivered on July 17, 1920, the revised manuscript of *Main Street*, he hoped it would sell 10,000 copies. (*Free Air* had sold just over 8,000.) Alfred Harcourt thought it would sell as many as 20,000 copies. At one point something was said about the sale of *Main Street* equaling the 40,000-copy sale of Arnold Bennett's *Old Wives' Tale*, and Lewis was excited. Certainly he had always hoped to sell better than his early novels had.

The book trade ordered cautiously, guided by Lewis' previous sales, and unwilling to believe that a novel attacking the American small town could be a runaway best seller. But Heywood Broun, the New York *Tribune* book reviewer, broke the publication release date by three days with a burst of applause for the truthfulness of the new novel. And then the miracle happened. There was an immediate run on the bookstores. Booksellers thought the demand would drop in a short time, but it kept up in the East and then spread to the West. In 1921 *Main Street* took and held, month after month, first place on the best-seller lists. Sales in that one year reached 295,000 copies.

What had happened? Certainly something more than a shift in the taste of the novel-reading public. America had been turning as on a pivot from an agrarian society to an industrial society. In 1920 what was called "the revolt of the village" came to a head, and it was Sinclair Lewis who struck the final blow against the ruling tradition of the sweet, wholesome American village, the tradition of "Friendship Village."

There had been books before that had attempted to destroy the myth—

E. W. Howe's *Story of a Country Town*, touted by Mencken, Hamlin Garland's *Main Travelled Roads*, Harold Frederic's *The Damnation of Theron Ware*, Edgar Lee Masters' *Spoon River Anthology*, and Sherwood Anderson's *Winesburg, Ohio*. But *Main Street* was the culmination of the attack on middle-class complacency in the country towns. And it swept the nation—the clearest possible proof that America was pivoting into a new period of letters and morals.

Main Street was the first best seller of the Twenties. Mencken read the book "with great joy" and pronounced it "the best thing of the sort that has been done so far." Scott Fitzgerald wrote to Lewis: "I want to tell you that *Main Street* has displaced [*The Damnation of*] *Theron Ware* in my favor as the best American novel. The amount of sheer data in it is amazing! As a writer and a Minnesotan let me swell the chorus—after a third reading. With the utmost admiration."

With *Main Street* Sinclair Lewis assumed the leadership of the new movement in American literature, and H. L. Mencken was his philosopher. As Mencken had belonged to Knopf, so Sinclair Lewis was the proud possession of Harcourt, Brace & Howe. And *Main Street* was the success that established this new publishing firm's role in the decade.

Hart Crane. Photograph by
Walker Evans, ca. 1930. Repro-
duced from John Unterecker's
Voyager: The Life of Hart Crane.
Courtesy Farrar, Straus &
Giroux.

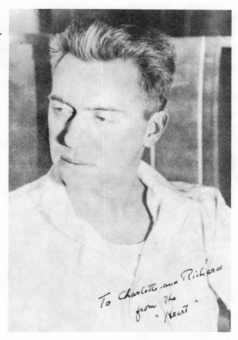

Hart Crane. Drawing by Willy
Lescaze.

Charlie Chaplin, 1925. Photograph by Edward Steichen. Reprinted with the permission of Joanna T. Steichen.

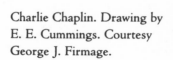

Charlie Chaplin. Drawing by E. E. Cummings. Courtesy George J. Firmage.

Robert Frost. Photograph by
Doris Ulman. Reproduced from
Gorham Munson's *Robert Frost*,
courtesy George Doran & Co.

Kenneth Burke, in the Twenties.
Courtesy Elspeth Burke Hart.

Kenneth Burke, with his first wife, Lily Mary Batterham, and his two daughters, left to right, Eleanor Dava and Jeanne Elspeth. Courtesy Elspeth Burke Hart.

Wallace Stevens, circa 1916. Courtesy Holly Stevens and the General Research Division, The New York Public Library, Astor, Lenox and Tilden Foundations.

William Carlos Williams, self-portrait. From book jacket for William Carlos Williams' *A Recognizable Image*. Courtesy New Directions, New York.

Drawing of A. R. Orage by F. E. Jackson. Reproduced from *A. R. Orage: A Memoir* by Phillip Mairet. Courtesy University Books, New Hyde Park, New York.

A. R. Orage, 1928. Photograph
by Ansel Adams. Reproduced
from *A. R. Orage: A Memoir* by
Phillip Mairet. Courtesy University Books, New Hyde Park,
New York.

G. I. Gurdjieff. Photograph from
Thomas de Hartmann's *Our Life
with Gurdjieff*, Cooper Square,
Publisher, Inc., New York.

PART THREE

The Writers

CHAPTER 11

A Comedy of Exiles

The "lost generation" of expatriates permanent and pro tem has been preserved for posterity in Hemingway's first and best novel, *The Sun Also Rises*. In it one encounters the emotional casualties of World War I, the playboys and young writers of the postwar period, the dabblers in the arts and the cafe sots that infested the Left Bank. The mood of the novel: "One generation passeth away, and another generation cometh, and the earth abideth forever. . . . The sun also ariseth, and the sun goeth down."

One of the first characters we meet in *The Sun Also Rises* is Harvey Stone who was derived from Harold Stearns, self-appointed recruiter for the exodus of writers from the United States in 1920/21. Harvey Stone is a café sot, who is always "borrowing" money and piling up saucers at the café. He goes out to the horse races. That is what the original of Harvey Stone did: in course of a few years of exiledom, Harold Stearns, who had left the states after editing a big symposium, *Civilization in the United States*, became Peter Pickem, an accredited Paris racing editor.

This was a sordid descent for a man who had tried, after Bourne's death, to be the spokesman for the young intellectuals of America. In *America and the Young Intellectual* (1921) Stearns had declared that the postwar generation "*does* dislike, almost to the point of hatred and certainly to the point of contempt, the type of people who dominate in our present civilization." In 1921 he had organized and edited the "first of the symposiums": among the thirty or so contributors to *Civilization in the United States* were H. L. Mencken, Van Wyck Brooks, Lewis Mumford, Robert Morss Lovett, John Macy, Ernest Boyd and

J. E. Spingarn; they gave America a good roasting. Stearns was proud of this book, which was published in 1922 after he had escaped to Europe; but some reviewers yawned at its continuous expression of dissatisfaction with American life. Albert Jay Nock, for one. "Its plan," Nock wrote in the *Freeman*, "makes for sterility. It takes a cross-section of American life in general, poses it starkly, and makes a report upon it; and hence inevitably it adduces little that is not already quite well known, it gives voice only to dissatisfactions already quite articulate, and suggests little that is not already obvious."

Clearly the editing of *Civilization in the United States* emptied Stearns of plans for symposia and writing. With a flourish of rejection, he sailed for England on July 4, 1921, but he was already bankrupt in ideas when the *Berengaria* dropped her pilot, and he had no projects in mind to accomplish when he reached London. From there he crossed to France and sank into Bohemia, sending over a little correspondence to American papers, going broke, landing a job on the Paris *Herald*, dallying through several affairs with women, throwing up his Paris *Herald* work because he was bored, and finally becoming Harvey Stone in chapter six of *The Sun Also Rises*. Harvey had a pile of saucers in front of him, and he needed a shave. It would seem as if Stone-Stearns needed the irritating environment of the states to make him produce his polemical articles and his programmatic books. Removed from the irritations, he fell into lassitude.

One cannot say much for the literary projects of the expatriate writers in the quarter of *The Sun Also Rises*, aside from Gertrude Stein, Ezra Pound, and the Britisher Ford Madox Ford. Most of the American expatriates were minor writers—very minor—and they were not in Hemingway's *roman à clef*. But they could have been perfectly cast in the book as supernumeraries. Robert MacAlmon, Lawrence Vail, Allan Ross MacDougall, Harry Crosby—they were the life that Hemingway imitated.

There were also the expatriates pro tem who have written books about their Paris years—Malcolm Cowley, Matthew Josephson, and one of these two-to-five-year exiles, Harold Loeb, who was the original of a major character, Robert Cohn, in *The Sun Also Rises*. Robert Cohn backed a review of the arts. "The review commenced publication in Carmel, California, and finished in Provincetown, Massachusetts. By that time Cohn, who had been regarded purely as an angel, and whose name had appeared on the editorial page merely as a member of the advisory board, had become the sole editor. It was his money and he discovered he liked the authority of editing." Harold Loeb, like Cohn, backed a review of the arts. He had nine thousand dollars from the sale of his interest in the Sunwise Turn Book Shop, and he started *Broom: An International Magazine of the Arts* in Rome. It later moved to Berlin and finished in New York. In his book *The Way It Was*, Loeb relates the history of *Broom* from Kreymborg to Josephson, and in so doing writes unflatteringly about Gorham Munson, expatriate pro tem and founder in Vienna of an avant-garde review, *Secession*.

Avant-Garde Review of the Twenties

It is now very difficult to feel oneself back in 1921. One way of recovering the past is to think of two or three authors whose reputations have suffered drastic deflation, but who were flying high that year. Amy Lowell and Carl Sandburg will do but a better example might be Sherwood Anderson. He was to receive the first Dial Award at the end of 1921; lengthy essays were written about his "art"; he was prominent in the new surge forward. In fact, he was ripe to be spoiled by overpraise, ready to fall from simplicity into simplism, about to lose his artlessness for a silly, affected word-naiveté. In what state was our literary criticism, our reading taste, that a writer like Anderson could be so overrated? Our critics, I felt in 1921, were in a state of enthusiastic muddle.

In this romantic confusion Harold Stearns sounded a sour note. The thing for a young American to do, he had said, was to get the hell out of his brazen country. Stearns sailed for the Café du Dôme on July 4, 1921, to join the expatriates. At the end of that July, and less advertised, my wife and I sailed on the *SS Chicago** to spend a year in Europe, living on our savings from a year of school teaching and profiting by the advantageous exchange-rates for the dollar.

I had no definite plans. Reading, thinking, traveling, the writing of a few essays; self-education perhaps sums up the activities in view. Having been in rapid succession a liberal, a socialist, a supporter of the Soviets, I had called myself for a couple of years a philosophical anarchist and had written for *Freedom*, an underground sheet published at the Ferrer colony in Stelton, New Jersey. Anarchism was an emotional choice: I waived the question of practicality. The

---

* *SS Chicago* was the Compagnie Générale Transatlantique steamship that transported John Dos Passos to ambulance service in 1917 and appears in his novel *1919*.

vision of Kropotkin would prove practical in the washing, I told myself. In literature my taste was voraciously catholic: I ranged from George Moore to Blaise Pascal. Among living writers in my country Waldo Frank was most appealing, and *Our America* I regarded as the gospel of the oncoming generation. I had defended it against the aspersions of an antisemitic editor.* *The Dark Mother* I had reviewed appreciatively, and I now thought of writing a brochure about Frank's work. Looking back, it seems I had ambition without a clear goal and a vague sense of dissatisfaction with current American writing without a fixed viewpoint to give meaning to my dissatisfaction.

After a delightful summer at Plougasnou near St. Jean-du-Doight, a spot in Britanny recommended by Van Wyck Brooks, I went back to Paris and before long encountered Man Ray whom I had known in New York. Man Ray introduced me to Tristan Tzara, and I spent an evening of halting conversation with the founder of Dada in the simplest French; our pantomime said we were amiably disposed toward each other. Tzara wanted to know if I would write something for him.

Nothing easier. I had picked up Dada literature in New York, had enjoyed Man Ray's New York *Dada* magazine, had read Picabia's *Pensées sans langage*. In the Hotel des Mines the next day I dashed off three Dada "poems," making use of multiplication tables and the mention of things tabooed and being properly idiotic. They were at once accepted by Tzara and despatched hither and yon over Europe for translation; the only translation I saw was in *Ma*, a Hungarian activist review. Of course, I attached no importance to this little stunt, but Dadaism as a movement continued to interest and puzzle me.

Late that fall I picked up at the American Express a note signed with a name then unknown to the literary world but known to me. The note informed me that Matthew Josephson was in Paris and would like to meet me. For two years Hart Crane had spoken now and then of Matthew Josephson. Crane had come to me one day in 1919 when I was working for the very short-lived *Modernist* and said that he had met a real poet, someone at Columbia, a deep student of modern French verse, a very strict judge, and so on. Crane was excited. The world of artists for him then was wonderland, as it was for me. The unicorns we heard about! I formed the impression that the "real poet" Crane was advertising was of aristocratic bearing and most exacting taste. I looked forward

* Hervey White, editor of *Plowshare*.

to seeing this brilliant personage break into print, but it seemed from Crane's letters that Josephson—for this unicorn was he—was disdainful of public print. Crane had asked me to look him up on his arrival in Paris, but Josephson got in his invitation first; I answered at once and very soon we did indeed meet. I was prepared to be bowled over, thanks to Crane's high opinion of him, an opinion later drastically revised by Crane.

I met a rather stiff young man, narrow in his interests, brittle in his thinking, and at moments charmingly pompous in speech. A certain pathos in his character was appealing. I looked at his verse. It impressed me without exciting me. I talked with him. He seemed to have escaped the muddle and ferment of 1916 to 1921 by excluding the elements of the muddle. He had no interest in liberalism, no interest in Brooks and the social approach to literature, no interest in philosophy, no interest so far as I could see in most of the topics of civilized conversation. Of a few poets, however, he condescended to speak: T. S. Eliot was one. And he knew personally two young writers whose work in the *Dial* I had followed with keen pleasure: Kenneth Burke and Malcolm Cowley. (It is amusing to remember that through my good gossip Crane I had also heard of Burke's "genius" before he had published, the herald being a Greenwich Village novelist, Floyd Dell, who had praised Burke's manuscripts to the *Little Review* editors; they in turn passed the word to Crane. An amusing recollection because of the subsequent feud between the novelist on one side and Burke-Cowley on the other.)

One afternoon Josephson and I were at the Rotonde when Tzara came in. I introduced Josephson, who had shrugged at Dada heretofore, and a conversation in French ensued far more voluble than I could join in. When we left, Josephson informed me sagely that there was nothing to Dada, it was *blague*. I had my reservations about this as well as about any contrary statement, but within a few weeks Josephson had no reservations; he reversed his first stand and swallowed Dada, calipash and calipee. I was working in a scholastic direction, trying to formulate more clearly a literary aesthetics. My preparation had been random—Spingarn's essays, Clive Bell's *Art*, Willard Huntington Wright's *The Creative Will*, Waldo Frank's obiter dicta in his Vieux-Colombier monograph, an idea here and there in the magazines—but I set to work with a wish to solidify my knowledge and to perfect an aesthetic approach to reading.

Josephson yearned to edit a magazine. I confessed to a similar yearning, apparently fixed in my nature and thus far fated to receive small gratification. At the time I was playing around on the board of editors of *Gargoyle*, which Arthur Moss was running in Montparnasse, and Josephson sought entree to its pages through me. Moss balked a little at his stuff but my recommendation carried the day, and Josephson at last was a two-times published author!* He continued to discuss literature. I enjoyed his lofty judgments pompously delivered. "Waldo Frank, Paul Rosenfeld, Louis Untermeyer and James Oppenheim," he would say, "have done the most harm to American literature." I would agree that three of his four selections were poor writers, making exception for Waldo Frank—though I wish now at this very late date to say that I have come to regard Louis Untermeyer as a remarkable agent for the good of American letters and feel like doing public penance for my cracks at him in *Secession*.

Periodicals from the states were regularly sent me. One week the literary review of the New York *Evening Post*, then edited by Dr. Canby, carried an article by Malcolm Cowley which was to bring to a sharp focus my idea of a new magazine. Called "This Youngest Generation," the article discussed certain writers under twenty-five—Kenneth Burke, E. E. Cummings, Dos Passos, Foster Damon, and Slater Brown—and remarked their divergence in aim and temper from their elders. I admired the work of these, except for Slater Brown whose brief contributions to the *Dial* had made no impression on me; I agreed with Cowley's contention that they were working at a tangent from the Mencken-Anderson-Cabell-Brooks-Dreiser literary swirl. The point was that the force of these youngsters was diffused into the corners of various magazines, and it seemed to me that it would be a good thing to concentrate the new impulses in a single review—a *tendenz* review, in short.

If printing costs were low in Vienna, my next place for an extended stay, why not start a small magazine for writers like Cowley, Burke, Cummings, Damon, Brown, Josephson, Crane, Frank, W. C. Williams, Wallace Stevens, Mark Turbyfill, Yvor Winters, Marianne Moore, Donald B. Clark, and give some showing besides to Dada writers like Aragon and Tzara? The idea was thrilling.

I showed Cowley's article to Josephson. He was interested, but remarked lugubriously: "I'm the only one of the crowd he didn't name." I told him I thought of launching a magazine in Vienna. He was very much interested, even

* He had earlier contributed to *Poetry*.

helpful. He would contribute, he would translate for me. I sent out a letter of invitation to prospective contributors.

Leaving Paris for Vienna toward the end of January, 1922, I decided to make stops on the way—the first at Dijon to pick up a copy of *Ulysses* fresh from the Darantière Imprimerie, the second at Rome to interview Harold Loeb, the editor-publisher of *Broom*. News had reached Paris that Alfred Kreymborg had resigned from *Broom*, and I had written Loeb to offer my editorial services. Loeb and his unofficial assistant, Kathleen Cannell, entertained my wife and me at a night club, but he was mystifying about the subject of my letter. He made no reference to it, and I was left to guess that he was not interested. He did, however, accept for *Broom* an essay I had submitted, "The Limbo of American Literature," and commissioned me to translate from the French a little treatise on modern poetry by Jean Epstein. I praised young writers to him, especially Josephson, who later got a job on *Broom*'s staff. I then went on to Florence, Venice, and, at last, Vienna, where I found manuscripts awaiting me. On investigation I found that the printing of a 24-page magazine with covers would cost 140,000 kronen or only 20 dollars! The dream of a little magazine was realizable.

But what to name the project that was coming to life? After a visit to the Secession Art Gallery in Vienna, I thought why not call the magazine *Secession*? There had been no use of the name in home literary circles for some time: it was fresh and expressive. So I sent out an announcement, reading in part:

Secession is an organ for the youngest generation of American writers who are moving away from the main body of intelligent writing in the United States since 1910. They are defining a new position from which to assault the last decade and to launch the next. "Form, simplification, strangeness, respect for literature as an art with traditions, abstractness . . . these are the catchwords that are repeated most often among the younger writers."—Malcolm Cowley. *Secession* aims to be the first gun for this youngest generation. It will publish stories, poems, criticism, insults and vituperations by Slater Brown, Kenneth Burke, Donald B. Clark, Malcolm Cowley, Hart Crane, E. E. Cummings, Matthew Josephson, Marianne Moore, Wallace Stevens, and by certain allied Frenchmen, Guillaume Apollinaire, Louis Aragon, André Breton, Paul Eluard, Phillippe Soupault and Tristan Tzara. It will, in its early numbers, expose the private correspondence, hidden sins and secret history of its American contemporaries, the *Dial, Little Review, Broom, Poetry*, et cetera. It already notes in current literature very much that demands hilarious comment.

Mars was certainly present at the birth of *Secession*. In fact, he was involved. The review was to be intransigent, aggressive, unmuzzled. The contributors were to handle everybody, including each other, without kid gloves. But I did not see Momus, "holding both his sides," shaking behind Mars. I walked hours along the muddy pavements of war-desolated Vienna, framing my policy. I was resolved that the magazine should strike a definite note and that there should be no hasty improvisation of policy from issue to issue. I was very serious. I felt that the review would make a little history, and in fact it did.

In March of 1922 the first number was printed by Julius Lichtner, Vienna VIII. It contained a poem Cowley had sent me—"Day Coach," the best thing in the issue, and one of Cowley's finest efforts; he is at his best when handling themes rooted in the soil of western Pennsylvania. The issue included translations from Aragon and Tzara, verse by Josephson, and an erratic, mildly interesting article, supposedly on Apollinaire but mostly on the young Dadaists by Will Bray (Josephson's pen name). There was also an exposé of the *Dial* by myself and an editorial article, "Bow to the Adventurous," which I wrote. The exposé of the *Dial* centered on its aimless catholicity, its ludicrous choice of Sherwood Anderson for its annual award, and its vulgarization. "The existence of this *Yale-Review*-in-a-Harvard-blazer is one of the bitter necessities calling for *Secession*." In "Bow to the Adventurous" there was a discussion of subject matter and form, which concluded by saying, "*Secession* exists for those writers who are preoccupied with researches for new forms." *Secession* pledged itself to continue for two years. "Beyond a two-year span, observation shows, the vitality of most reviews is lowered and their contribution, accomplished becomes repetitious and unnecessary. *Secession* will take care to avoid moribundity."

I had a little clash with Josephson, through the mail, after the first issue appeared. He and his Dada friends did not like the slant of my editorializing, and he was irritated by the return of his story "Peep-Peep-Parrish"; he had written several stories that winter that I liked but "Peep-Peep-Parrish" I regarded as tripe.

The material for the second number shaped up better. It was a thrilling morning when "The Book of Yul" arrived from Kenneth Burke and I immersed myself in the coolness and distances of its design. (Burke afterwards told me how he had come to play "long shots" consistently throughout this extraordinary tale.) Four poems came from Cummings:

> make me a child, stout hurdysturdygurdyman
> waiter, make me a child. So this is Paris.
> i will sit in the corner and drink thinks and think drinks,
> in memory of the Grand and Old days:
> of Amy Sandburg
> of Algernon Carl Swinburned.

Cowley sent in the poems entitled (in *Blue Juniata*) "A Solemn Music" and "Two Swans," both astonishingly perfected. From Josephson came a translation of Tzara and a short story, "The Oblate." And for a filler there was a bit of humor by Slater Brown. In this number I analyzed the policies of the *Little Review* and *Broom*—and distinguished the editorial policies of *Secession* from those of the other two reviews. *Secession*'s policy would argue that "an artist of acknowledged reputation has generally made his contribution. He will have far less chance with *Secession* than the unknown pathbreaking artist." Unlike *Dial* and *Little Review* and *Broom*, *Secession* would represent more fully the pathbreaking artist, and to that end, I announced, "the Directorate of *Secession* will be reorganized for the next issue."

This announcement requires a little explanation. The response to my original invitation had proved that there were seven or eight writers of the type I desired who would support *Secession* with their manuscripts, and that was all the literary support a little magazine needed. But I was faced with a practical problem. I could not pay more than twenty-five dollars for printing an issue; therefore I could not afford to print in America. Since I was leaving Europe for home and needed a friend in Europe to look after the printing, I thought why not Josephson? I had reservations about his work, but approved of it within its narrow scope. He was eager since he had no other outlet for what he wrote, and he had invested a good deal of energy in helping launch the enterprise. Why not invite him to be coeditor? This would solve the practical problem for the year or so he expected to remain in Europe. Still I wondered how we would get along on policy. If I ran *Secession* alone, it would inevitably conform to the limitations of my personality. With Josephson as coeditor, a deadlock was possible. But with a third editor, there would then be possible a majority decision on points of policy, and three editors could fairly claim to be representative of the small group of the "youngest generation." I would ask Kenneth Burke to join the board.

Josephson was of course delighted to become an editor and moved to the Tyrol for the summer and his labors in producing the third number. I told him to take sole editorial responsibility for this number and to insert a note saying he had done so. Meanwhile I sailed for America and went almost directly from the pier to Burke's farm at Andover, New Jersey.

Our greetings as I descended from the train were awkward. A short, hard-muscled man in a flannel shirt shook hands with me. I peered intently at a freight car on the siding and said, "Not much like Paris." Burke agreed glumly that it wasn't. We walked three miles to his house and I knew by then that I had met one of the best talkers in America on the art of letters, a man for whom writing was a passion, if not an obsession. My debt to him for extraordinarily sharp perceptions of the formal and stylistic aspects of literature had begun. We talked until nearly two in the morning. I had sized Burke up as a night-hawk. This man, I thought, stays up most of the night and sleeps in the quiet country until eleven. He was thinking: my guest is a city nighthawk not adjusted to the rural habit of early sleeping and early rising. We soon discovered that each of us had kept the other up for hours. About six the next morning Burke's delightful small daughter awoke us. We talked all day; and when I left, Burke had agreed to join *Secession*'s board, beginning with the fourth number.

The third number of *Secession* (August, 1922) came over, flying the names of Munson and Josephson as editors. But there was no announcement that Josephson was solely responsible for the issue. On the whole, it was a lively one. The Dada representation was a little heavier—Soupault and Arp; there was a slight uncollected poem by Cowley, Kenneth Burke's "First Pastoral," a poem by W. C. Williams, and, to lead the issue, a story by Waldo Frank. These contributions maintained the pace the first two issues had set. In the back Josephson had made passes with a knife at Mr. Blunderbuss (Paul Rosenfeld) and at *Vanity Fair*. There was, however, one big mistake in the issue—Josephson's inclusion of his rejected story, "Peep-Peep-Parrish," an adaptation, already done a score of times, of the "movie-chase" to the short story. It didn't seem sporting of him to slip it in, but I set down its inclusion not to malice but to overzealousness for getting into print by one who had seldom been published. Anyway, I mused, from now on such things would not happen.

With Burke on the board, manuscripts would be voted on by three editors, and two votes were required for acceptance. This applied to the editors' own offerings. The editor offering a piece voted for it by that action; he needed only the vote of one other editor to insure its acceptance. This arrangement undoubtedly irked Josephson. Burke and I, consulting together in America, held the balance of editorial power. He, in Berlin, was supposed only to receive manuscripts from European contributors and to send them, together with his own writings, to us for decision—indicating of course his approval of what he sent over. It soon became clear how little he respected this arrangement with his colleagues.

To anticipate the story by a half year or so, the stir that *Secession* made was surprising. I do not mean that literary America became intensely conscious of the little venture, but the effect was out of proportion to the magazine's size and circulation. Articles about *Secession* were written by Edith Sitwell (*New Age*), Louis Untermeyer (*New Republic*), and Van Wyck Brooks (*Freeman*). Editorial comment—sometimes twice or thrice repeated—poured on us from *Little Review*, *Dial*, *Criterion*, *Broom*, *Nation*, *Double-Dealer*, the New York *Times*, and others. Our subscription list numbered exactly fifty and contained some distinguished names: Alfred Stieglitz (the founder of the Photo-Secession Gallery liked our name), Ezra Pound (his letter was signed "Your Affectionate Grandfather"), Amy Lowell, Alice Corbin, Alyse Gregory, Mitchell Kennerley, Melville Cane, Kenneth Macgowan, Hansell Baugh. I made out an exchange list of about fifty periodicals, American and foreign, and a "free list" of about one hundred well-known literary people. It was for the free list that *Secession* was edited. We wanted to have some audience in view, and so we picked our audience instead of waiting for it to find us. The shops took about one hundred fifty copies for sale. Somehow each printing of five hundred was exhausted, and I had only one complete set for my personal library.*

After number three, I was invited by Norman Fitts, editor of *S4N*, to write

---

* That set, the *Secession* correspondence file, and a scrapbook of clippings were lost in an auction sale illegally held by a storage warehouse about 1954. The eight numbers of *Secession* were reprinted in 1967 by the Kraus Reprint Corporation.

a manifesto-article, and I contributed "The Mechanics for a Literary 'Secession' " to the November, 1922, issue of *S4N*. "I begin with a general call to writers to secede," I declaimed, stating that several requisites for a literary secession had been established. First, I said, "We have something from which to secede. The last decade has seen a literary milieu created in America. . . . The act of Ezra Pound in 1908 need not be repeated. The young American can now function in his home milieu. If he doesn't like it, he has another and less distorting alternative than revolt into exile: he can secede." Among the "bitter necessities demanding secession," I suggested, were the "aesthetic sterility of the present directions of American letters . . . the general flabbiness of American criticism and the negative attitude towards modern life."

"The last requisite is a nucleus of writers who are ripe for a secession. And this nucleus, I believe, our youngest generation, the chaps from twenty to twenty-six or so, provide." I proceeded to name them. "One of the distinguishing marks of 'secessionist' writing is its cerebral quality, manifested particularly by Kenneth Burke and Malcolm Cowley." William Carlos Williams ("an older poet with a strong following among the young men") and E. E. Cummings were cited for "simplification," one of Cowley's catchwords for "this youngest generation." The example for "strangeness"—another catchword—was Matthew Josephson, who, I said, "deliberately negates logic with his intellect and becomes an intellectual freebooter." I went on to remark the respect of these young writers "for literature as an art with traditions. That is to say, the youngest writers go back of Shaw and Ibsen. Their favorite sourcebooks are Elizabethan, and their principal foreign influence is French in two opposed tendencies—one from de Gourmont, the other from Apollinaire and the Dadaists." And finally there was abstractness, the concomitant of form."

Speaking of Waldo Frank and a new primitiveness, I said, "Frank, more instinctive and emotional though still very intelligent, locates on the fringes of the *Secession* group." And there was Cummings' championship of the American language to be reckoned with. "It is for this group and kindred writers like Slater Brown, Hart Crane and Foster Damon that I founded *Secession*."

About the time of this manifesto in *S4N*, Amy Lowell came to the Hotel Belmont and summoned Burke and me for an audience at five in the afternoon. We waited in the sittingroom of her suite, at first standing by the windows and discussing architecture. After half an hour we sat down. A quarter of an hour later Miss Lowell's companion swept in and offered us Amy's cigars. We understood Miss Lowell was getting up for her day (which was night) in the next room. We finished the first cigars, waited some more, and started second cigars. At half past six Miss Lowell majestically entered and sat in a high capacious chair, her delicately modeled hand holding one of the famous cigars. She ordered Burke, a short man, to sit at her feet on a tiny stool. I was at her feet too, in a slightly higher chair.

She began imperiously. "The trouble with you young men is that you are too critical. You can't decide whether to be poets or critics. Look at Malcolm Cowley." A torrent of hearty defense opened out, for under the guise of dogmatic attack it was defense, as Miss Lowell's printed remarks on *Secession* later revealed. I watched Burke squirm on his footstool, his eyes blaze in an argument, his words come fast. But Amy would not let him cut in. She was reducing us to schoolboys, not arguing. Abruptly she closed the audience. Her breakfast was arriving. Burke and I walked over to the West 42nd Street ferry, and I heard another torrential lecture. Vehemently Burke poured out all the things Miss Lowell had choked in his vocal chords.

One Friday afternoon, the day of the week that William Carlos Williams took off from his busy medical practice, Burke arranged for a meeting, and the three of us rode about in Dr. Williams' car, finally stopping at the Fountain Room of the Hotel Pennsylvania for further talk. Williams, whose head was a dice-box rattling with ideas and whose manner was far more genial than his intransigent prose, was curious about the personalities of *Secession*'s contributors. The majority of them had married young, and Burke was already a landowner and twice a father. Kenneth expressed the belief that a man ought to settle down at twenty-five and cut loose at forty. Williams commented on this tendency to early marriage, and Burke produced a sudden generalization. "The young writers of the 'nineties," he said, "were bachelors and went in for intoxication in their works. Young writers of today are married and strive for solidity in their writing."

(But taking a retrospective view of those days and using *Secession*'s history as a microtome for determining their quality, I will venture the remark that if the word for the Yellow Nineties is pretty *infantilism*, the word for the Twenties is arrogant *juvenility*. Perhaps that is why I cannot, in the manner of several chroniclers of the early jazz age, review my immersion in it with romantic regret over time's passing. The period was something to be outgrown.)

Numbers four and seven I regard as *Secession*'s best. Number four listed a cover design by William Sommer, a Cleveland painter "discovered" by Hart Crane; five poems by Richard Ashton; "In Quest of Olympus," a story by Kenneth Burke; "Last Looks at the Lilacs" by Wallace Stevens; "Poster," a poem by Hart Crane; "The Hothouse Plant," a poem by William Carlos Williams; "A Garden Party," a story by Slater Brown; Correspondence; Note on "Der Sturm"; and Book Reviews. In reply to a correspondent I had the chance to reaffirm our policy. "[*Secession*] is, in essence, a prompt deviation into immediate aesthetic concerns."

There was an abortive feature of number four—a mutilated poem that was blacked out in all but a very few copies—that nevertheless received considerable publicity in subsequent accounts of *Secession*. A contributor* using the pseudonym of Richard Ashton had submitted six poems, some in polyphonic prose. Burke and I had accepted them, and they were duly mailed to Josephson in Berlin for inclusion in number four. A wail of dissent came back; but outvoted as Josephson was, what could the dissenting editor do? We saw what he could do when copies arrived from Berlin—a petty piece of sabotage at the expense of a helpless contributor. The first eighteen lines of a twenty-line poem had been deleted, and the last two lines had been printed as if they were the entire poem. The effect was silly. This aborted poem, however, did not get into circulation; it was blacked out in all copies distributed in America, and the table of contents was corrected to read "Five Poems" by Richard Ashton.

Josephson's brief editorial link with *Secession* stopped after this malicious prank. The severance was scarcely a blow to him, for he had recently joined the staff of *Broom*; and *Broom* was now out to steal *Secession*'s thunder. Nor did Josephson have to regret that he had invested any money in *Secession*. Although he had made the grand gesture of paying for number four from his own pocket, accepting the gratitude of the impecunious New York editors, the gesture had been only that. Not Josephson but poor Julius Lichtner, the Vienna printer, was the one who was paying for number four. Josephson had simply taken the money I sent him to pay the printing cost of number three and paid it instead to the Berlin printer of number four, adding a mere two dollars and a quarter from his own pocket.

* Donald B. Clark. When a graduate student at Harvard, Clark had been editor of a magazine, *Youth—Poetry of Today*, and a protégé of Amy Lowell in writing polyphonic prose. He had also contributed to the *Dial*.

After Josephson's dismissal, Burke and I carried on against unforeseen difficulties that added up to a virtual hijacking of our magazine in numbers five and six. This phase of *Secession*'s story has been written about in several books, but the inside facts have never been divulged by those who know them and have never been communicated to me, the intended victim of the hijacking. One cannot learn them, for example, in the chapter on *Secession* in the Hoffman-Allen-Ulrich history and bibliography, *The Little Magazine*. Nor can one get the whole story from *The Way It Was* by Harold Loeb, *Life Among the Surrealists* by Matthew Josephson, and *Exile's Return* by Malcolm Cowley. I shall not clutter this narrative with corrections of earlier errors, but simply strip the story of numbers five through eight of *Secession* down to the essential and revelant facts.

Burke and I often lunched in a cheap upstairs Italian restaurant on Lower Sixth Avenue, sometimes with Slater Brown, the "B." of Cummings' *Enormous Room*, sometimes with Glenway Wescott, effervescing with anecdotes, ideas and opinions, a brilliant describer of people and scenes. At one of these luncheons Burke urged on us the criticism of Paul Elmer More, whose most recent book he had reviewed for the *Dial*. More had not worked out his aesthetic, according to Burke, but he had praise for More's dualism, which he defined as "unity through a balance of conflicting parts," an idea later imbedded in the story "Prince Llan." Sometimes we lunched with a very Bostonian chap, John Brooks Wheelwright.

Wheelwright, I believe, had set out to be a divinity student, had switched and left Harvard, and was now leading a dilettante's life. A friend of Damon, Hillyer, and Cowley, he subsequently became a student of architecture and an eccentric leftist. But at this period he wrote some verse and prose (neither very well, I thought) and was editing *Eight More Harvard Poets*. He liked Burke, but he and I were not much interested in each other. For some reason, however, Wheelwright was very much interested in *Secession*: he had even defended the magazine against Brooks in a letter to the *Freeman*.

Wheelwright was going to Italy and offered to supervise the printing of future numbers in that country. Not only that; he would foot the printer's bills too. His offer was immediately accepted. It seemed a godsend, for the "resignation" of Josephson had left us with no agent in Europe. So Burke and I made up a packet of manuscripts for the fifth number; it included the first essay on Cummings to be written, a job of mine; and off went Wheelwright in the spring of 1923.

Ah, yewth, yewth! We fledgling writers were more adept in sizing up books than in sizing up people. If we liked a man in his literary capacity, we didn't inquire too deeply into his other capacities—or incapacities. We were trusting and uncritical of the practical aptitudes of our friends. It never occurred to Burke or me to be suspicious of Wheelwright's offer; we never wondered *why* he should make it or guessed at his motive. Nor did we ask if he had ever learned how to produce a magazine from manuscript to shipment to the point of distribution.

Wheelwright had earlier played a practical joke on Kenneth Burke that should have raised some doubts about him. Burke commuted from his farm fifty-five miles outside New York to the *Dial* office on West 13th Street where he was employed as a junior editor. The salary was small and Burke had to watch expenses carefully. Wheelwright, in contrast, was very much a young gentleman of leisure, apparently well-heeled, and free of the family responsibilities that Burke had already assumed. It was important to Burke to catch the morning train at the railroad station three miles from his farmhouse, whereas it made no matter to Wheelwright if he missed it and did not get back to New York until mid-afternoon from a weekend visit to Burke's farm.

Burke's trip to New York began with pedaling his bicycle three miles to the nearest railroad station. When he had a guest returning to the city, the custom was to alternate bicycling and walking to the station. The guest would start off on the bicycle, pedal for about three-quarters of a mile, drop the bicycle by the roadside, and proceed on foot. Burke would have followed at a brisk pace, pick up the bicycle when he reached it, and ride the second three-quarters of a mile. Thus guest and host would alternate until each had covered the three miles in much less time than walking alone would take. It appealed to Wheelwright's "rich man's sense of humor" to set off on the bicycle and ride all the way to the station. Burke followed on foot, growing more and more amazed to find no bicycle waiting for him, and more and more anxious about catching his train. Finally he broke into a trot to get to the station a couple of minutes before the train. Wheelwright thought the affair quite funny.

Wheelwright was surely no proofreader, nor had he any conception of the mechanical work of getting out a magazine. For a long time I was sure that he had done his best. He put his money into three issues of *Secession*. And I was not unappreciative of the time and trouble he expended on these issues, even though he never wrote me about his progress with them. But now, as I return to these fledgling years of the *Secession* writers, I wonder if Wheelwright—or "Wheelswrong," as Cummings named him when he saw the typographical carnage in number five—really had good will toward "the bosses in New York," as he called Burke and Munson. It all depends on what happened at Giverny, France, where Monet used to paint and where several Dadaists established a temporary base in 1923. On his way to Italy, Wheelwright stopped at Giverny to meet Josephson, who was sore at *Secession*, and Cowley, who took Josephson's part without hearing the other side. What plot was cooked up by the three has never been disclosed or confessed, but what happened was the virtual hijacking of *Secession* by Wheelwright and Cowley. The names of Burke and Munson were listed as editors but the following note was appended to the masthead in number five: "Material for Nos. 5 and 6 was accepted and rejected with the advice of Malcom [*sic*] Cowley. It was printed under my direction, with the kind assistance of Mr. Richard Basset and Miss Susan Street.—J. B. Wheelwright."

The hijacking was not obvious in number five (misprinted as number six) but the wretched proofreading required hours of correction by pen before the issue could be distributed. Most of the contents had been chosen in New York or would have been accepted there. A poem by Mark Turbyfill led the issue, followed by "Syrinx," my essay on the prose and poetry of E. E. Cummings.* Number five also presented four poems by Cummings, a poem by Marianne Moore, and "Old Melodies" by Malcolm Cowley. But "Wheelswrong" took over the department of editorial comment and continued Josephson's feud with *Secession*. He devoted the department to the mutilated poem by Richard Ashton that had never appeared in number four. "The Jilted Moon" was now printed in full, all 20 lines, but it was preceded and followed by nasty commentary that was intended to insult our contributor.

Number six, which was shipped to New York simultaneously with number five, was entirely a Wheelwright-Cowley job, and the poorest of the eight numbers. This time Hart Crane was the chief victim of the Josephson-Cowley-Wheelwright imbroglio. Burke and I had sent over the complete text of "For the Marriage of Faustus and Helen," Crane's first major poem, which had already suffered editorial incomprehension and dismemberment in *Broom*. But when *Secession* number six reached New York Burke and I were shocked to find that "For the Marriage of Faustus and Helen" had again been dismembered and printed incompletely. Philip Horton has told of Crane's disappoint-

---

* Reprinted in *E. E. Cummings and the Critics* (1962).

ment in his biography of the poet. "The entire second part had been omitted, as well as single lines here and there, and appalling typographical errors had been made. . . . Crane was violently outraged. 'Why don't you wire the consulate in Florence,' he wrote Munson, 'to stop W. from any further rape of S.' "

There was nothing for it but to strike out the poem's title on the contents page and to excise with a razor blade pages 1 through 4 of the 32-page issue. This left a very weak number. The dullest of Dada stories surely must be "The Crimson Emerald," an imitative story by Robert Coats (as Wheelwright spelled "Coates"); and Wheelwright's own poem about Christ, "Unpublished Portions of 'Q,' " came close to "The Crimson Emerald" for tedium. Better stuff was "Fantasia in a Restaurant" by S. Foster Damon and "Into That Rarer Ether" by Malcolm Cowley; but the unsettled tone of the issue dropped in its back pages to bickering with a *Vanity Fair* contributor by J. B. W. A harmless misprint in J. B. W.'s "Comment" was intended to be turned into an obscene retort, but "Wheelswrong" messed up even his errata notice and simply compounded confusion for the reader.

A third shipment now came from Florence that was the climax of Wheelwright's eccentricity. We had sent him a short treatise by Yvor Winters on "the mechanics of the poetic image." This, Wheelwright decided to print as a pamphlet instead of a magazine, and we unpacked a true "whatizzit" after customs released the shipment. The cover bore no date or number, and "Secession" was in jumbled type. No editors or address were given. On page one the heading "Number Eight" was mysteriously superscribed. Misprints abounded so that it was necessary to run off a mimeographed list of errata for insertion in the mailing. And, of course, the correct spelling of Winters' first name was unacceptable to Wheelwright. "Yvor" in the script we sent to him was changed to "Ivor" on the cover and end-page of the pamphlet. Wheelwright printed "Number Eight" on page one but there had been no number seven of *Secession*. I determined to bring out a seventh number as soon as I could and to hold off the Winters treatise until *Secession*'s allotted two years were up, and then release it as the final number eight.

At the same time that *Secession* was being hijacked, it was also subjected to hostile actions by the tiny incipient American Dada movement. The peanut politics practiced by the would-be American Dadaists made my colleague Kenneth Burke uncomfortable, coming on top of his regret over the hijacking; and I am sure that he was relieved when I suggested that he would not hurt me if he resigned. I was relieved too when he resigned, because I now wanted to involve *Secession* in a philosophy of letters as well as in aesthetics, and Burke might not have agreed with the direction I wanted to take. Assuming skill as the first requirement, I had been vitally interested in the question of literary significance. "All deep art," I had observed in my monograph on Waldo Frank, published in 1923, "spreads beyond precision into mystery." Such questions as the following had grown more acute as I thought about *Secession*'s policy. Since skill in writing produces calculated effects upon the reader, by what criterion shall these effects be judged? What really is the aim of literary skill? What mark should literature wish to make on life? In the fall of 1923 I was groping my way from aestheticism to a philosophy of letters, from the workshop to the world, and I felt I was beginning to see life and letters by a stronger light.

I wrote about this turning of *Secession*'s course from experimental aestheticism to a kind of Stieglitz-Frank mysticism in a letter to Alfred Stieglitz, November 24, 1923.

Word from you was very welcome. . . . The fact that you liked my Cummings essay is a corroboration that means something to me.

My health has been seriously threatened this fall and I have been obliged to spend a good many weeks in the country, first with Toomer at Ellenville and later with [William Murrell] Fisher, whom I know you remember from "291" days, at Woodstock. During the fall many things have happened to *Secession*. Our agent in Florence, Jack Wheelwright, botched the last two numbers horribly, Burke has resigned as a purely literary move (his probity is unimpeachable and our friendship continues strongly), Cowley and Josephson have become active and venomous enemies. I have gained the following knowledge and I prize it highly. I know that Burke and Cowley are weak, not as artists, but weak in their morale. They are not drastic. Also I have gained complete severance from a thorough fake (Josephson) and complete control of *Secession*. I shall henceforth publish it in America and drive it in a direction contained in the work of [Waldo] Frank, [Jean] Toomer, [Hart] Crane and [Gorham] Munson. I have had the bitter experience of purifying my motives, taking a clear and inflexible stand, and of having this attitude met by something not quite to the point. . . . In the crises I have gone through the spectacle of your integrity has been a great help to me.

I am going back to New York very soon, some fifteen pounds heavier than when I left and in fairly good shape. . . . I hope to see you this winter, to see what you and [Georgia] O'Keeffe have been doing at Lake George, and to talk over several matters with you. . . . I want to be clarified myself. The thing I feel is this: that in your photography, in Crane's poetry, in Toomer's work and in Frank's work there is a FORCE that is pure and of the utmost significance. I think that this FORCE will dominate the future and that those who manifest it should stand back to back. Quite humbly, I wish to prepare myself to cooperate. . . .

I have just received a very stimulating letter from Leo Stein about my book on Frank . . . a record of what my book can do against the grain of an opposing temperament.

I was very proud of two contributions I had in hand for number seven: Hart Crane's triad of poems which was titled "For the Marriage of Faustus and Helen" and Waldo Frank's manifesto, "For a Declaration of War." It is incredible that the *Dial* had declined "Faustus and Helen" to whom it was first offered. Then *Broom* had failed to see any relationship of the first and third parts to the second part, which it published as a separate independent poem. Next, *Secession* had had to excise the botched presentation of "Faustus and Helen" in the Wheelwright-edited September, 1923, number. Now at last in the projected number seven Crane's great poem would be published in entirety and without corruption of its glorious text.

Frank's "For a Declaration of War," to be published later in *Salvos* (1924), was a prospectus of the critical position he would take and elaborate upon in *The Rediscovery of America* (1929). Frank proclaimed that the old culture of the Western world was disintegrating. He listed some sixteen "basal assumptions," which he said were undergoing destruction. "The old spiritual body is breaking up. Ere we can be whole and hale again, we must create a new spiritual body. And that means birth." Frank then denounced the "tenet of self-defense" that "art must be three dimensional, and must remain the presentative of three dimensional consciousness." "Upon the outworn bonds of a glorious but dying culture, there is War."

In conclusion, Frank proclaimed fourteen propositions of the new culture. The essence of those propositions can perhaps be gleaned from the following examples. "Art," said Frank, "by the elements of its creation, brings into the consciousness of mind quantities and values of life which mind alone is unable to perceive or control." Further, Frank suggested, "The noblest function of art is, then, not to subserve the intellectually accepted forms of life; but to conquer new forms of life and to bring them within the reach of intellect. Art is the language which expresses vision of being that has not been conventionalized into simple words and concepts." And the final proposition offered, "In periods of basic cultural transition, therefore, the criticism which does not start out from metaphysics and a true understanding of the religious experience . . . is idle, irrelevant, impotent and anti-social."

"For the Marriage of Faustus and Helen" and "For a Declaration of War" were, I felt, prophetic examples of that FORCE about which I had written Alfred Stieglitz. To go with them in number seven I had three fine imagist poems by Yvor Winters and another experimental story by Kenneth Burke. I regretted I had nothing from Jean Toomer.

There was no problem about getting desirable manuscripts to fill the issue; there never is. But there was a problem about the funds to produce the next number; there always is. Thanks to the favorable rate of exchange for the dollar in Austria and Germany (and to Josephson's failure to pay the printer of number three), the total printing costs of numbers one through four had not exceeded $75. The cost of printing numbers five, six, and eight in Italy was never told me, but was presumably met by Wheelwright. But the estimate for printing number seven in New York was $85! There was nothing in my bank account to meet this staggering figure.

Nevertheless, encouraged by the willingness of a sympathetic printer to extend credit, I went recklessly ahead. That printer was Maurice Bernstien who printed catalogs and book jackets for Boni and Liveright. Bernstien, a book and music lover, was to become some years later the operating head of Horace Liveright, Inc., when it fell on evil days. I think he was prepared to be the angel of *Secession* in case I did not pay him—but in time I paid him in full.

I rounded out the issue with an attack on the book review policy of the *New Republic*, a review of Josephson's *Galimathias* ("one is depressed by an emptiness in back of the shrillest exclamations"), and a brief rejoinder to Ernest Boyd's "Aesthete: Model 1924." (I recommended the *American Mercury* to liberated adolescents, the middle or muddle generation, and "blockheads who think that Masters is a great poet.")

In April, 1924, I released number eight, "The Testament of a Stone," by Yvor Winters, which I then regarded as the best theoretical defense of imagism

I had encountered. Soon afterward I mailed to the press, our subscribers, and our free list a mimeographed statement called "Post Mortem" which read in part:

> *Secession* was . . . a trial balloon cut loose for a short voyage and manned by a green crew. That it turned out to be no ordinary experiment is attested by the observers who wrote about it. . . . The stories of Kenneth Burke in which an important theory of fiction is worked to unprecedented discoveries: several poems by Malcolm Cowley which are assured of preservation in anthologies: the fierce satiric poetry of Cummings: "Faustus and Helen" by Hart Crane: the verse doctrine of Yvor Winters: a manifesto by Waldo Frank . . . these are some of the claims of *Secession* to distinction. . . . *Secession* will perhaps be known as the magazine that introduced the twenties.

American Dada Flop

A name illustrious in avant-garde circles was that of Man Ray—painter, photographer, film maker, infrequent lecturer, and very occasional writer. I had come to Man Ray's tiny room on West 8th Street in December of 1920, and he had photographed me in a blue Russian blouse my mother-in-law had made. "My first sitter!" Man Ray told me many years later. "And do you remember what you charged?" I asked. The famous photographer did not. "Ten dollars." He sounded disgusted by the low price, even though, at the start of his photography, he often made portraits for nothing. But they were portraits of the great like James Joyce and Gertrude Stein, whereas I was an unknown, the first unknown to beat a path to his studio. At that sitting Man Ray had indicated his esthetic of the camera.

"The photographs of Stieglitz," he said, "are perfect—too perfect. I am interested in the flaws, the accidents, the defects in a picture. One could develop from an imperfection, grow an art from a shortcoming. One would exploit the defect—make it greater—and beautiful." Not verbatim, but as close to his expression of a point of departure as memory will take me. He was saying, I thought at the sitting, that Stieglitz was a classical photographer whereas he, Man Ray, would make a romantic departure in the new medium.

Even before he went to Paris, Man Ray was a Dadaist. A friend of Marcel

Duchamp, he had joined in the production of a single-issue magazine called *New York Dada.* He reached Paris on July 14, 1921. "Duchamp," Man Ray tells us in his autobiography, *Self Portrait,* "met me at the station—he had reserved a room in a hotel in quiet, residential Passy, that had just been vacated by Tristan Tzara. . . . Late in the afternoon Duchamp took me to a café in the boulevards where the young writers of the Dada movement met regularly before dinner. . . . I felt at ease with these strangers who seemed to accept me as one of themselves." Breton, Eluard, Soupault, Rigaud were there. And "Louis Aragon, writer and poet [who] bore himself with assurance and a certain arrogance."

Man Ray has written fascinating reminiscences of his membership in the Dada and Surrealist movements in which he was an equal among equals. But he has only this to say of two young American protégés of Louis Aragon: "Matthew Josephson and Malcolm Cowley, eager to absorb the Paris atmosphere but prudently keeping a foot on American shores." Thus quietly Man Ray ignores the American Dada fiasco, for Josephson and Cowley, self-proclaimed Dadaists, were to return to America in 1923 and attempt to start an American Dada movement. Man Ray stayed abroad permanently, except for the World War II years, and participated fully in the European movements of Dada and Surrealism.

Cowley had by 1923 abandoned his influential article "This Youngest Generation," which had inspired the founding of *Secession.* In *Exile's Return* he tells how he drifted away from the attitude and interests of this article into a state of bedazzlement with Dadaism: "at least it was young and adventurous, and human"—certainly a fledgling sentiment.

It used to be my opinion that a chronological analysis of *Blue Juniata* would show that Cowley had written his best verse before 1923, some as early as 1918 in *Youth: Poetry of Today,* edited by Donald B. Clark (Richard Ashton), and in *Pagan,* edited by Joseph Kling. Cowley had also been writing reviews for *Dial* that showed the makings of an able neoclassicist, and at Montpellier he was preparing a study of Racine. Up to 1923, Cowley was, critically and poetically, one of the literary fledglings most likely to mature into a true man of letters. But then occurred a detour. He went up to Paris from Montpellier, met the Dadaists, moved on to Giverny, and was dazzled to the point of gaping a good western Pennsylvanian gape. Such insouciance, such dash, such engaging absurdity these Frenchmen displayed; and they were perfectly willing to take up any young American who admired them—as I knew from my stay in Paris. Cowley was swept away. He too would revolt against literature.

Cowley could write Dada, but never, I ventured to say at the time, was there a temperament less suited to act Dada. He was pen-clever but not speech-clever. When I met him, I saw a man of medium build with a heavy countenance, "the brow of Moby Dick beating through a smoke-fog," in Hart Crane's phrase. Cowley was slow in speech, a little countrified, apparently phlegmatic; a plodder, one would wrongly guess. Despite this slow temperament he yearned to cut a dash as a Dadaist, to be brilliantly unexpected like Apollinaire, to be infectiously droll like Tzara. Of course, in those days he wasn't a *New Republic* liberal; that was the last thing he would have dreamed of being.

In Giverny, Cowley made contact with Josephson, a friend of several years standing, and now an editor of *Broom*. Josephson was intent on converting *Broom* into a Dadaist magazine, and Cowley joined forces with him. *Broom* had been the idea of Harold Loeb, a relative of the powerful banking Loebs and the copper magnates the Guggenheims. But Harold was neither as rich nor as powerful as the Guggenheims and the other Loebs. He seems to have lacked self-confidence, and he was often distrustful of other people. He was drawn toward the artistic life, invested in a bookshop, yearned to become a writer—and one day decided to start a magazine on a capital insufficient for a venture of any magnitude. He chose for an associate Alfred Kreymborg who had a good avant-garde reputation and immediately attracted artists and writers to the new magazine, which was published in Rome in November, 1921. But the association of Loeb and Kreymborg lasted only a few months.

As we can learn from Loeb's history of *Broom*, recounted in *The Way It Was*, Loeb's associates did not last long in their posts. And Loeb himself supplied whatever editorial direction *Broom* received, however weak it might have been. Alfred Kreymborg was bought out by Loeb for five hundred dollars; Dorothy Kreymborg, of course, left with him. (They had been preceded by a staff secretary, a New York book shop girl called Lorraine in Loeb's memoir, who had not even stayed employed until *Broom* started in Rome.)

The Italian editor, Giuseppe Prezzolini, and the secretary, Rendo Rendi, soon followed the Kreymborgs. The New York office manager, Nathaniel Shaw, was dismissed after *Broom* III came off the press. And so *Broom* continued to sweep out its staff in a rapid turnover of personnel, as a business manager might say.

Associate editors were Edward Storer and, later, Matthew Josephson. Lola Ridge, assisted by Kay Boyle, ran the New York office for a few months. Throughout, behind the scenes, a woman friend, Kathleen Cannell, appears to have participated in Loeb's editorial policy. Finally, a kind of editorial committee consisting of Malcolm Cowley, Slater Brown, Harold Loeb, and Matthew Josephson, with the last acting as the executive, took over *Broom*, which thereupon moved to New York in the spring of 1923. Loeb himself played only a small part in this last or Dada phase of *Broom*.

Inefficiency is the mark of the business management of most "little magazines," but none has exceeded the record of inefficiency Loeb has painstakingly set down for *Broom* in *The Way It Was*—and with nary a smile, too, though parts of the record are funny. Inefficiency hurt even the handling of editorial correspondence with authors. Loeb has told us of the annoying correspondence between Gordon Craig and Alfred Kreymborg, which aroused his suspicion that the artists were manipulating the business man (himself). In his obsession with the trivial, he also records the breach of editorial manners committed by his associate editor Josephson after Loeb himself had rejected on the ground of its length a manuscript I had submitted. Loeb was correct in his handling of the rejection, but he had in such matters no control over his staff. His associate editor proceeded to rub in the rejection with a long, uncalled-for letter of insolent criticism, and then refused to show his boss either my rejoinder to his bad manners or a copy of his offensive letter. As Loeb writes, this was truly "an absurd conflict with Gorham Munson that should have been avoided" and would have been on a well-run magazine—"and was," Loeb ruefully adds, "to be more damaging in its side effects than any of us foresaw." Loeb here exaggerates the incident, which of course made for bad feeling but was not central to my conflict with Josephson over *Secession* and had no side effects that I know of.

Malcolm Cowley has told us in *Exile's Return* that he was a disciple of Louis Aragon in the spring of 1923. Under Aragon's influence he became "a Dadaist in spite of myself, was adopting many of the Dada standards, and was even preparing to put them into action." Much earlier, Josephson had been captivated by Aragon who laid out a reading program for him; he had been a diligent translator of the works of the leading Dadaists, had frequented their meetings and written about their "shock treatment for a crazed humanity." Cowley and Josephson with *Broom* in their hands now dreamed "of reproducing in New York the conditions that had seemed so congenial to us abroad"—Cowley's words—

181

"and of continuing to appreciate and praise the picturesque qualities of the Machine Age and the New Economic Era while living under their shadow."

Very soon, however, they were complaining to their colleague in Europe, Harold Loeb, that America was stony soil for the seeds of their Dadaism. Josephson wrote that "the 'group' which is roughly associated with *Broom* is in a remarkably sterile mood. . . . Especially discouraged by Burke's apathy." And again: "The absence of any real cooperation (outside of Nagle, Brown) on the part of the younger generation is highly discouraging." Cowley complained that "the people I meet in New York seem to have lost all capacity for indignation, and are content to accept the unimportance of their lot or to solace themselves with piddling drunks."

Burke's discomfort at this time was indeed quite visible. As he read Cowley's exhortations to go Dada, it seemed as though he were watching a literary suicide; he was searching for a principle of permanence in letters and his friend was telling him that there was only change—the dictum of a twenty-five year old. As for Josephson, Burke dubbed him a "Dada Austin Dobson."

But can we now blame the younger generation for not taking fire from the "significant gestures" of the two American Dadaists? The first "significant gesture" we heard about was the book burning and micturating party at Cowley's house in Giverny. This had been a private "significant gesture" and the underground account of it was only partly true. Gossip had put Josephson at the scene but this was denied years later. Cowley was said to have burned his set of Racine on whom he had been writing a thesis. This was also denied a few years later. The New York reaction to the grapevine story was that the party had been a pretty silly and insignificant gesture.

Ten or twelve years later Cowley attempted to overcome for the historian the New York impression of insignificance. He tried to pump a little significance into the party by crediting himself with a speech against book fetishism. "We all have that weakness and should take violent steps to overcome it." Whereupon he had set fire to "an assortment of bad review books and French university texts." Harold Loeb, however, who was present, failed to report the alleged substantiality of the Cowley gesture. "The more wine we drank, the duller the conversation got," he reported. Then he heard Cowley shouting: "Too much *merde*, too much junk. Words aren't enough." He watched closely "to make certain no *Broom*s went into the holocaust." Later "the soft night smelled of urine and burning paper."

182

Horace Gregory was one of the young writers of 1923 who was unaroused by American Dada. Reviewing Loeb's book in 1959, Gregory asked: "What group of young Americans today would set fire to books written by their betters in an open fireplace? Yet that is one of the incidents that Loeb records. It is not a pretty scene, nor a courageous one, but there it is—and it all seems very long ago."

Nor does the scene of Cowley at the Rotonde punching the proprietor—it also seems very long ago—look either pretty or courageous. This was a public "significant gesture" in Paris, which was vaguely relayed to New York via transatlantic grapevine and seemed pretty insignificant on arrival. Ten years later Cowley blew up the story into quite an affair. In the eyes of the French Dadaists, he claimed, he had performed an act to which all the favorite Dada catchwords could be applied. "I had been *disinterested*. I had committed an *indiscretion*, acted with *violence* and *disdain* for the law, performed an *arbitrary* and *significant* gesture, uttered a manifesto: in their opinion I had shown *courage*." But the young American writers couldn't read all of this into a common little brawl. All we knew was that Cowley was one of a group of a dozen who had been drinking on Bastille Day and went to the Rotonde looking for trouble. Cowley had darted out and struck the proprietor a glancing blow. "It could be," Loeb has remarked, "that Malcolm wanted to show his friend Aragon that Americans, too, were capable of gesturing significantly at the risk of limb." Cowley was rushed away but came back later and yelled foul words at the proprietor, whereupon Cowley was arrested. "So what?" was the bored New York reaction, causing Cowley to complain a couple of months later that "the situation could be less discouraging if anybody retained the capacity for indignation."

Perhaps it was the lack of style in such incidents as the book burning and the café disturbance that left the young Americans, whom *Broom* wished to rally, so apathetic toward the incitements of Cowley, Brown, Loeb, and Josephson. Aragon had told Josephson that the literature of Dadaism "was to be *action*, action designed to subvert men's minds by laughter and ridicule, by generating a mood of disgust everywhere." It is to be noted that the actions of Dadaists like Soupault and Aragon were carried out with style but style could hardly be said to characterize the next "significant gesture," this one attempted by Josephson.

The Josephson gesture was the aftermath of the unity meeting Cowley called for the purpose of mounting a Dada attack on the New York literary scene—on the establishment, as we would have said in the sixties. I received an urgent invitation from Cowley to attend this meeting and noticed that it suggested no idea, no attitude, no principle on which young writers could rally. Were *les jeunes* expected to form a clique or a côterie for self-advancement? I replied that it wasn't practicable to interrupt my convalescent regimen at Woodstock by a New York trip. Cowley thereupon solicited a statement to read at the meeting. I was naive enough to comply.

Cowley has written much about the manner of the statement I sent but very little about its matter. The statement was aimed to produce a showdown—first, on the fit personnel of an attacking party in American letters, and second, on an issue for fighting the existing order (or establishment). As to the first, I could not see how a group could effectively attack a ruling group so long as it tolerated within its ranks the very kind of weakness it proposed to castigate. I had come to regard Josephson as a literary opportunist, an example of last minutism, a kind of stage player of the arts, to adapt a phrase of Nietzsche. I emphasized these things and called him an intellectual faker—fighting words, they turned out to be. I therefore declined to participate in any group containing so vulnerable a member. In the second place, I declared that some conscious life-attitude was necessary. I borrowed a phrase from Middleton Murry to name what was needed: "the passionate apprehension of life." In brief, the position taken was that life can once more become highly significant, and contemporary literature has a role to fulfill in bringing back significance to life.

This statement, Cowley says without reproducing any passage to support his assertion, was written in a grotesquely bad style, and this bad style caused him to give a burlesque reading of it. Josephson, however, has testified differently; writing to Loeb after the "unity" meeting, he mentioned "a long letter from Munson (unusually well written for him)." But my statement failed completely to produce a showdown on the twin questions of a fit personnel and a fit attitude for a party of assault on the literary establishment of the day. The dinner party, as Cowley has described it, behaved more like an outraged clique than a group of young writers "come together for ten minutes in the cause of literature."

Why my independent position should have caused so much fury and disheartenment and been blamed for ruining the prospects of the *Broom* clique still confounds me many years afterward. I was one writer, content perfectly to go my way. They were about a dozen writers, talented and lively. What prevented them from proceeding in their way, ignoring me completely? Why should my firm stand have spoiled the party?

Cowley's account in *Exile's Return* of what he calls "the disastrous meeting in Prince Street" does not answer these questions. He bypasses them when he says "we should have realized that there was no chance of imposing our ideas on others when we couldn't agree among ourselves, or even preserve the decorum customary in an Italian speakeasy."

Josephson's reaction was adolescent. He was pained and angry and traveled a hundred miles to attempt a "significant gesture" in retaliation. One cannot say, however, that a thin skin alone explains his violent reaction. The reader should recall that one of the ingredients of Dadaism was a cult of action. Not action in the world of affairs, such as Sidney, Raleigh, Swift, Burke, and many another writer has displayed, but petty action—direct insults, vaudeville behavior, fisticuffs, and the like—was extolled by the Dadaists. In a single illustration, the idea of the cult was that if a man wrote a review of you which you resented, you didn't meet him with literary weapons; you went forth and wrecked his office, as Aragon had once done. The physical retort to the intellectual rebuff—that was its essence; and it appeared to be an attractive cult to Cowley and Josephson. But at least one should be a herculean fellow to carry it out.

Momus was on hand the afternoon Josephson came to William Murrell Fisher's cabin in the woods and shouted for battle. He was enraged and aggressive, in no mood for reason. However, he wasn't fearsome: slightly built, he looked anything but formidable. It's stretching a bit to call what ensued a "fight." Rather it was a scene in the theater of the absurd (or would have been had that theater then been born). Josephson was ignorant of boxing as well as unathletic in build. The encounter was more nearly a scuffle than a fight. Its high point—or better, the low point since it occurred on the ground—was reached when the Dadaist lay supine under the rump of the Secessionist, his body writhing beneath the weight of a convalescent who had been on a building-up diet for six weeks, his arms pinioned by the knees of his critic, the dampness of the ground chilling his temper. "Let me up" was the manifesto of this upsetting moment in the history of American Dadaism when instead of Dada attaining to its apex, the movement's chief was thrown struggling beneath the podex of the opposition.

At the time there was no publicity about this farcical incident that ended harmlessly in a state of breathlessness.* A long time afterward the scuffle has been extensively and injudiciously publicized by Cowley, Loeb, and Josephson in their books on the exiles of the *Broom*-Dada years. Had there been no publicity, I would not have ridiculed my Dadaist opponent's earnest effort to live up to a schoolboy's idea of honor. I would have preferred to leave this "significant gesture," so lacking in significance and in style, in a limbo of private anecdote. But perhaps this picture of "Secessionist sitting on chest of Dadaist" deserves hanging after all, as the most Dada incident in the very brief history of American Dadaism.

As I have said, there was no publicity about Josephson's Woodstock mission, but there was a teapot-tempest of damaging publicity about the next and final "insignificant gesture" of the American Dadaists. Burton Rascoe in "The Bookman's Day Book" buried the *Broom*-Dada movement under columns of derision.

In January, 1924, appeared the first number of the *American Mercury*, edited by H. L. Mencken and George Jean Nathan. It featured an imaginary portrait of a literary type, "Aesthete: Model 1924," by journalist Ernest Boyd. Hoping that Boyd was portraying the aesthete of the *Secession* group, which could mean valuable publicity for our review, even if the portrait was satirical, I got the magazine at once and raced through the Boyd piece. I was disappointed, for the piece was entirely imaginary and related to no writer and no review that I could identify. No research had gone into "Aesthete: Model 1924" and the satire of the imaginary figment was faint indeed. The portrait was hack work and unworthy of notice.

In a few days, however, I was amazed to learn that the American Dadaists—both of them, with two or three friends assisting—were trying to raise a stink over Boyd's feeble portrait. They were claiming to be the objects of Boyd's satire and brashly identified themselves with the foppish, effeminate young man he was supposed to have in mind. They were harassing him with telephone calls and threatening violence upon his person. This seemed to me merely a foolish attempt to gain notoriety, and it struck me as a bad tactical mistake. Notoriety they won, for the journalist Burton Rascoe immediately published a jeering ac-

---

* Fisher intervened and led out-of-breath Dadaist away. "Who do you think won?" asked Josephson. "Neither of you," Fisher told him and added: "The worst fight I ever saw."

count of their harassment of Boyd, and the public bought out the *American Mercury* and demanded a second printing. The "stink" was fine for the sales of the *American Mercury* and fine for the market of Ernest Boyd who unexpectedly found himself hailed as a hero and besought for articles on Greenwich Village, art magazines, and the younger generation. He professed to have had no prior knowledge of the "aesthetes" who were protesting his imaginary portrait, and he may easily be believed. For this Irish exile with the brown beard and brown dinner jacket was incurious about the American literary scene; he had lost the emotional vigor of his Dublin days when he wrote for Orage's *New Age*. He was, in fact, two-thirds exhausted in his literary life—a state of being I described in some cruel lines a few years after the American Dadaists had restored Boyd's prestige:

> This mind has ticked itself away,
> Emotion too has had its day;
> Yet do not think he is a ghost,
> He sprouts a beard as brown as toast.

That was all the response needed to Boyd's provocation but instead the Dadaists overreacted. "My *disinterestedness* was interpreted," Cowley complained, "as a meddlesome effort to push myself forward, to break the front page. My *significant gesture* was a silly touchiness, an offense taken where none had been intended. My manifestation was a flop." True, true—American Dadaism had been petty and spiteful, and now it was expiring in abuse of a minor literary journalist who had been almost unaware of its existence.

In the end *Broom* died without a death-struggle. In its penultimate number the editors had published a moralistic pulp magazine fantasy that today would be called a ripe, rank specimen of *camp*, "so bad that it was good," and this worthless piece of *camp* is conjectured to have alerted the post office censor in New York to examine the next and, as it turned out, ultimate number of *Broom*. Therein the censor discovered "Prince Llan: An Ethical Masque" by Kenneth Burke, which was certainly caviar to the general, but contained a couple of references to female anatomy that it is guessed were intelligible to the censor and in his judgment objectionable. *Broom* was suppressed under Section 480 of the Postal Laws which prohibited the mailing of contraceptives and obscene matter. Fifteen hundred copies were dumped back at *Broom*'s address, and the editors meekly destroyed them.

Here at last *Broom* had a case, a strong one. Here at last was the time and the occasion for a powerful significant gesture. "Prince Llan" was a story of distinction. The pretexts for censoring it were unusually weak and probably could not have survived exposure in court. Publicity for *Broom* in fighting a censorship would have been favorable, and the magazine could have gained important support. Margaret Anderson and Jane Heap had fought valiantly against the censorship of the *Little Review*. *Broom* could hardly do less. Yet it did nothing.

"We were tired and beaten," wrote Cowley. "We began to see how hopeless was the affair." And Josephson, "The editors, battle-weary and dead broke, were unable to take advantage" of this situation. They quit.

This comedy of exiles ended in impotence. Quickly and easily the two leading players abandoned their roles. Cowley ably practiced journalism and became the best literary journalist of his generation. Josephson turned to biography and wrote a eulogistic life of Zola. Naturalism was the polar opposite of Dadaism, and espousal of naturalism presented a much better opportunity for a young writer.

CHAPTER 12

"On Perilous Seas Forlorn"
The Untold Story of Hart Crane

Part One: Ecstatic Illuminations

My acquaintance with Hart Crane began with a poem. In the fall of 1918, I haunted Greenwich Village and never failed to buy each month the little magazines being published there. It was in the *Pagan Anthology* that I encountered "October-November" and liked it very much. I was enchanted by its closing lines:

> Then the moon
> In a mad orange flare
> Floods the grape-hung night.

I have continued to like this poem more than its author did, for Crane did not include it in *White Buildings*, his first book.

I think I know why he excluded "October-November." The poem was in free verse; and Crane, fired by the Elizabethans, had matured into a master of blank verse. The poem was impressionistic and imagistic; it lacked the complexity of metaphor that was to make Crane's later poems difficult for many reviewers. Perhaps he felt that the poem was in doubtful taste. It was not "hard-edge" imagism. Rather it was a romantic, violent, gorgeous swirl of Indian-summer colors. It was, indeed, almost gaudy imagism. And yet to this hour I like this little exercise. Every time I read it, I remember the thrill of my first reading that made me note the poet's name.

2.

My friendship with Hart Crane began one morning about the middle of March, 1919, in the Pagan Book Shop on West 8th Street. I had taken a room in one of the old Rhinelander houses on West 11th Street. At about this time Joe Kling moved the *Pagan* from the Rand School building on 15th Street to a location a few doors from the already-famous Washington Square Book Shop and opened there a rival book shop. Kling took me on as a sort of unpaid volunteer clerk and also appointed me an associate editor of the *Pagan*, thus linking me to Hart Crane who was already an associate editor.

Kling and I were "minding the store" on the morning I have mentioned when a young man came briskly in. He and Kling began at once to shout. Kling stopped to introduce me to an obvious midwesterner, and I became alert at the name of Hart Crane. Then the good-natured shouting was resumed.

Hart Crane did not look like a poet. A slim, brown-haired, brown-eyed fellow, he could have been an energetic young businessman. His voice was midwestern, vigorous, almost harsh. The general effect of his personality was masculine.

Suddenly he and Kling broke off their shouting, and Crane turned to me. "Munson, why don't we have dinner together some time?" Surprised by this abrupt proposal, I replied, "Why not tonight?" And for that night it was arranged. I was to call at 307 West 70th Street where Crane shared rooms with a young history instructor, Alexander Baltzly, and we would dine in a bourgeois restaurant near 72nd Street and Broadway.

Crane took the lead in our conversation that night. We discussed the *Pagan* but quickly confessed to liking the *Little Review* much better. Joyce's *Ulysses* had begun to appear serially in the *Little Review*, and we both admired that revolutionary work. From the start I looked up to Crane. He was much better read in the new poets like Ezra Pound than I was, and I was especially impressed by his acceptance in the *Little Review*; "In Shadow" had appeared in the December, 1917, issue of this review whose masthead slogan was "Making No Compromise with the Public Taste." My great enthusiasm at this time was the poetry of William Vaughn Moody; I had thought of writing a study of his plays and poetry. Hart told me that he had met the widow of Moody and she had shown interest in his poetry.

I learned at this first dinner that Hart had only the vaguest plans for entering college. He had spent about three years at high school and had received some tutoring since, most beneficially in French. But it did not occur to me to size him up as incompletely educated. His deficiencies in education would become painfully apparent to me when he attempted to make a myth of the American past in *The Bridge*, but at the beginning I was dazzled by the *literary* education he was giving himself. His private "college" was the *Little Review*, which he read from cover to cover, advertisements included. The head teacher in the *Little Review* was Ezra Pound, and Hart was quick to take the courses of reading that Pound recommended.

3.

In the next seven months Hart and I met frequently, forming a firm friendship that was not to weaken for five years. He left New York in November, 1919, and we soon began the correspondence that has been a rich quarry for his biographers. In all, I received 129 letters from him, of which 123 were acquired by the Ohio State University Library; the remaining 6, more intimate than the others, have been lost. Literary nationalism was the fairly steady keynote of the many conversations Hart and I had in the spring and summer of 1919. We did not compare family trees, but if we had, we would have been delighted with the discovery that both of us came from old Connecticut Yankee stock. Both the Cranes and the Harts had migrated to Ohio in the early nineteenth century and prospered there. The boy Harold Hart Crane had grown up loving the countryside of the fertile Mahoning Valley and soaking up impressions of the town of Warren situated northwest of Youngstown. Soon after I met him Hart was to give fervent praise to Sherwood Anderson for his tales of Winesburg, Ohio.

Literary nationalism which had been excitingly expressed in the *Seven Arts* was vibrant in the air. To the October, 1916, issue of the *Pagan* a short letter from H. H. C. of Cleveland had been contributed; Hart had said: "I am interested in your magazine as a new and distinctive chord in the present American Renaissance of literature." This "American Renaissance," which we saw exemplified in the new poets like Masters, Sandburg, Lindsay, Frost, and the contributors to *Others*, was the staple of our conversation.

When *Dial* was transformed in 1920 from a fortnightly with political interests to a monthly magazine of the arts with an international policy, Hart was,

191

so to speak, graduated from the *Little Review* "college." He went on to the *Dial* as though to a "university." But though he read widely and deeply in the moderns—English, American and French—and in the Elizabethans, his study of American history and culture was never more than superficial. And this was to handicap him in his ambition to write an American epic.

4.

Hart had received his accolade in December, 1917, when Margaret Anderson accepted "In Shadow" and saluted him: "Dear Hart Crane, poet!!" He would appear in this magazine that published Yeats, Pound, and Eliot. This, however, was not full recognition. *Little Review* was truly a little magazine, with a small circulation. And it did not pay its contributors. Payment in prestige was exhilarating; but cash payment, however small, meant real recognition of merit.

Early in November, 1919, just before he left New York for Cleveland, Hart wrote, "I am beginning something in an entirely new vein." He was stalled in the writing of "My Grandmother's Love Letters" after a few weeks: "I have a good beginning. . . . If I cannot carry it further, I may simply add a few finishing lines and leave it simply as a mood touched upon." But he persisted, and by mid-December he was sending copies of the completed poem to friends. He must have submitted "My Grandmother's Love Letters" to the *Dial* in January, 1920, after a refusal from the *Little Review*. In early February he wrote exultantly to a friend: " 'My Grandmother's Love Letters' tempted The Dial to part with ten dollars, my first 'litry' money."

The poem appeared in the *Dial* for April, 1920. "I cut it in several places, which improved it, I am sure," Crane explained. He was very proud of it. "It's the only thing I've done that satisfies me at all now."

It still satisfied him in 1926 when he included "My Grandmother's Love Letters" in *White Buildings*. The poem was a fine achievement in free verse; its beautifully modulated cadences, its gentle assonance, its occasional resort to subtle play of end-rhyme and internal rhyme—all were evidence of Eliot's dictum that no *vers* is *libre* to the man who does a good job. Now Crane was fully recognized: published in a big magazine with a broader circulation than the little magazines he had heretofore appeared in, and paid besides, the final seal of recognition. Yet he wondered whether he could "ever equal it in the future."

5.

Crane need not have worried about his ability to write new poems on the level of "My Grandmother's Love Letters." Brom Weber, the second of Crane's biographers, said of the early poems "that there can be no doubt about the truth of Gorham Munson's statement in *Destinations* (1928) that 'at sixteen he was writing on a level that Amy Lowell never rose from.' " Now Crane had ascended for good to a higher level in which he was strongly influenced by the symbolist movement in French poetry. Then, in February, 1921, he made a leap to a still higher level when he wrote "Black Tambourine." When he sent me the first draft he said this poem was "something definitely my own." He correctly felt that he had absorbed his influences and welded the diverse elements of his personality into a distinctively individual poem. Nine months after he wrote it, Crane said that this poem "becomes to my mind a kind of diminutive model of ambition, simply pointing a direction."

"A Baudelairesque thing," Crane called "Black Tambourine," and he explained that "the value of the poem is only, to me, in what a painter would call its 'tactile' quality—an entirely aesthetic feature." And indeed this poem does have the hard, classical finish of the Baudelairean line: "Gnats toss in the shadow of a bottle / And a roach spans a crevice in the floor . . . And, in Africa, a carcass quick with flies."

Of course, there was more to "Black Tambourine" than a Baudelairesque surface, as Crane well realized. Nearly a year after its composition, he wrote Sherwood Anderson, "what I want to get is . . . an 'interior' form, a form that is so thorough and intense as to dye the words themselves with a peculiarity of meaning, slightly different maybe from the ordinary definition of them separate from the poem. If you remember my 'Black Tambourine' you will perhaps agree with me that I have at least accomplished this idea once."

Let me try to bring out the "peculiarity of meaning" of "Black Tambourine." Although the poem is about the Negro in white America, it avoids being political or sociological or propagandistic; it is a purely poetic treatment of incontestable facts. The interests of a black man in the social limbo ("cellar") of white America make a belated indictment of the world's prejudice against his color. He dwells in squalor.

The second stanza is an ironic allusion to Aesop, the fabulist, who was reputed to have been a slave of Samos about 600 B.C., but who may never have existed and whose grave is unknown. Nevertheless his wisdom has survived and his name has persisted in "mingling incantations on the air."

Crane's forlorn black man, misrepresented and unaccepted, wanders in a sociological midkingdom that lies between the present (the minstrel show image of the Negro—black tambourine) and the historical past (primitive African origin—fly-infested "carcass"). "The poem," Crane told me, "is a description and bundle of insinuations, suggestions bearing on the Negro's place somewhere between man and beast. . . . My only declaration in it is that I find the Negro (in the popular mind) sentimentally or brutally 'placed' in this midkingdom."

It was during these years of 1918 to 1921 that Crane formed his conception of the artist in twentieth-century Western society. Although he had read and been deeply affected by James Joyce's *Portrait of the Artist as a Young Man*, the French symbolist poets to whom Arthur Symons introduced him in *The Symbolist Movement in Literature* exceeded the influence exerted by the Joyce novel. Crane was introduced to the great symbolist poets by several sources—Pound, Eliot, *Dial, Little Review*. His writing was markedly affected by Baudelaire, Corbière, Laforgue, Verlaine, Mallarmé, and above all, Rimbaud. But there was more than a literary effect from these encounters; there was a deep effect upon his life as well.

The lives of these French poets had usually been short. Baudelaire had died, paralyzed and speechless, at forty-six; Tristan Corbière had lived only thirty years; Verlaine had died at fifty-two; Laforgue died of consumption at twenty-seven; Rimbaud died after an amputation at thirty-seven; the longest lived and most orderly had been Mallarmé, but he lived only fifty-six years. Usually, too, these French poets had been bohemian rebels. They had rebelled against bourgeois industrial society and found refuge in the Latin Quarter. Except for Mallarmé, they had all known poverty and disease. They had suffered from alcoholism; homosexuality had attracted some; they were social deviants as well. Violent disorder was the symptom of their bohemian lives.

Crane aspired to play the role of poet; he scarcely ever wavered, and then only a little, in his resistance to his father's efforts to force him into being a businessman who wrote poetry on the side. The French symbolist poets served as no less than a magnetization of his personality with its own dreams of becoming a poet. He, too, would lead an unconventional Latin Quarter life; he would pay the price of poverty and disorder; he would accept his sexual deviation and wild dissipation. In short, he would identify his life-role with their role-playing. (In advanced stages of drunkenness, Crane sometimes shouted, "I am Rimbaud.")

I do not mean to imply that Crane's image of the poet was reached by deliberate thought and imagination. He was simply captivated by the example of the symbolists, as Arthur Symons had been. It was a magnetization of his aspiration. Unfortunately it was a magnetization of several neurotic tendencies Crane already had, which would in time produce disaster.

6.

Crane's next milestone was the triadic poem "For the Marriage of Faustus and Helen," composed between April, 1922, and February, 1923. It is the highest peak he scaled in his poetry, equalled but not transcended in a few other poems, and sufficient by itself to make permanent Crane's high place in the American slope *ad Parnassum*.

Crane's poem began as a vaguely conceived triad, broke into separate poems, and finally fused into one triadic composition. Part I, he said, was Meditation, Evocation, Love, Beauty. "So I found Helen sitting in a street car." Part II was Dance, Humor, Satisfaction. "The Dionysian revels of her court and her seduction were transferred to a Metropolitan roof-garden with a jazz orchestra." Part III was Tragedy, War Resume, Ecstasy, Final Declaration. "The katharsis of the Fall of Troy I saw approximated in the recent world war."

It will be seen that there is no natural or profound logic giving structure to the three parts. Architecturally, the poem is too simple and weak. But it is unified in the "Final Declaration":

> Distinctly praise the years, whose volatile
> Blamed bleeding hands extend and thresh the height
> The imagination spans beyond despair,
> Outpacing bargain, vocable and prayer.

For Crane did succeed in his expressed aim, which was to write a poem of affirmation against the negativism, as he conceived it, of T. S. Eliot's *The Waste Land*, which had appeared while Crane was struggling to fuse his three poems into one.

Better than his list of abstractions for describing "For the Marriage of Faustus and Helen" was Crane's statement about its composition: "I found that I was really building a bridge between the so-called classic experience and many divergent realities of our seething confused chaos of today, which has no formulated mythology yet for classic reference or for religious exploitation."

Crane's symbols have little traditional content. Helen, he said, is "the symbol of the abstract 'sense of beauty'—Faustus the symbol of myself, the poetic or imaginative man of all times." Crane's Helen is neither the Helen of Greek legend nor the Helen of Marlowe. She is a Platonic Helen, "the symbol," as he had declared, "of the abstract 'sense of beauty.' " Similarly, Crane's Faustus has little, if any, connection with the historical Dr. Johann Faust, that strange savant and hypnotic personality who died about 1541, or with Goethe's Faust. Nor does he resemble Marlowe's Faustus, the doctor of knowledge and magic. Crane departs from the traditional Faustus and makes him simply "the symbol of myself, the poetic or imaginative man of all times."

It is important to consider just what Crane's conception of "the poetic or imaginative man of all times" was. It was different from that French-poet-magnetization of his role that I have already alluded to. The conception was derived from a book that Horton and Weber both concede had profoundly influenced Crane—*Tertium Organum* by P. D. Ouspensky. Crane's intention in "For the Marriage of Faustus and Helen" and later in *The Bridge* cannot be grasped without pursuing this Ouspenskian link.

Crane had read and marked in his copy of *Tertium Organum*:

> The content of emotional feelings, even the simplest—to say nothing of the complex—can never be wholly confined to concepts or ideas, and therefore can never be correctly or exactly expressed in words. Words can only allude to it, point to it. The interpretation of emotional feelings and *emotional understanding* is the problem of *art*. In combinations of words, in their meaning, their rhythm, their music—the combination of meaning, rhythm and music; in sounds, colors, lines, forms—men are creating a new world, and are attempting therein to express and transmit that which they feel, but which they are unable to express and transmit simply in words, i.e., in concepts. The emotional tones of life, i.e., of "feelings," are best transmitted by music, but it cannot express concepts, i.e., thought. Poetry endeavors to express both music and thought together. The combination of feeling and thought of high tension leads to a higher form of psychic life. Thus in art we have already the first experiments in *a language of the future*. Art anticipates a psychic evolution and divines its future forms.

Another passage in *Tertium Organum* that will enrich one's understanding of the Faustus figure in Crane's poem asserts:

> The phenomenal world is merely a means for the artist—just as colors are for the painter, and sounds for the musician—a means for the understanding of the noumenal world and for the expression of that understanding. At the present stage of our development we possess nothing so powerful, as an instrument of knowledge of the world of causes, as art. . . . Only that fine apparatus which is called *the soul of an artist* can understand and feel the reflection of the noumenon in the phenomenon. In art it is necessary to study "occultism"— the hidden side of life. The artist must be a clairvoyant: he must see that which others do not see: he must be a magician: must possess the power to make others see that which they do not themselves see, but which he does see.

I can personally testify that Hart thrilled in his consent to the statement that the artist must be a "clairvoyant" and a "magician." He once read aloud to me this passage and demanded my subscription to it. I do not exaggerate the effect that *Tertium Organum* had upon his poetic development. Understanding Crane's Faustus as an Ouspenskian "poetic or imaginative man of all times" seeking to marry Helen, "the symbol of the abstract 'sense of beauty,' " seems entirely reasonable when we read what Ouspensky wrote about the search for beauty— another passage that Hart read aloud to me in 1923.

> Art serves *beauty*, i.e., emotional knowledge of its own kind. Art discovers beauty in everything, and compels man to feel it and therefore to *know*. Art is a powerful instrument of knowledge of the noumenal world: mysterious depths, each one more amazing than the last, open to the vision of man when he holds in his hands this magical key. But let him *only think* that this mystery is not for knowledge but for pleasure in it, and all the charm disappears at once. Just as soon as art begins to take delight in that beauty which is already *found*, instead of the *search for new beauty* an arrestment occurs and art becomes a superfluous estheticism, encompassing man's vision like a wall. The aim of art is *the search for beauty*, just as the aim of religion is the search for God and truth. And exactly as art stops, so religion stops also as soon as it ceases *to search* for God and truth, thinking it has found them.

Ouspensky's dictum on art and cosmic consciousness—"Art in its highest manifestation is a path to cosmic consciousness" was something Hart Crane believed and wanted to believe. "For the Marriage of Faustus and Helen" was a harbinger of *The Bridge*, and Crane's remark that he found during the ten-month travail of composing it "that I was really building a bridge between the so-called classic experience and many divergent realities of our seething confused chaos of today" should be pondered. Weber has noted that in *Tertium Organum* Crane found an excerpt from Max Muller's *Theosophy* which stated that "the founders of the religions of the world have all been bridge-builders." Ouspensky himself declared that "religion is the bridge between the *Visible* and the *Invisible*, between *Finite* and *Infinite*." Weber's insight is apt when he comments that "in the light of the role which Ouspensky has assigned to poets and all artists, it is not inconceivable that they too are 'bridge-builders' in their work, and that Crane's conception of *The Bridge* may have been stimulated by this interpretation."

The key to the meaning of "For the Marriage of Faustus and Helen" is to be found in the lines interjected between the second and third stanzas of Part I:

> *There is the world dimensional for those untwisted by the love of things irreconcilable . . .*

The mind in the world of three dimensions has been limited by its subjective conventions. It has shown itself

> Too much the baked and labeled dough
> Divided by accepted multitudes.

Nevertheless in our tridimensional world, unquestioned by most people, for some there are intimations of a world of higher dimensions. In some irregular way the poet escapes the Kantian limitations of our world:

> And yet, suppose some evening I forgot
> The fare and transfer, yet got by that way
> Without recall . . .

He then, in his search for beauty, might encounter Helen, in a street car, "half-riant before the jerky window frame." He pledges devotion to her:

> Accept a lone eye riveted to your plane,
> Bent axle of devotion along companion ways
> That beat, continuous, to hourless days—
> One inconspicuous, glowing orb of praise.

198

I happened to be visiting Hart in the "tower room" of his Cleveland home when he wrote these four lines that conclude Part I. The lines were inspired by a drawing of him made by William Lescaze. In the drawing the right eye is fully developed while the left eye is merely suggested. A line slanting across the forehead gives a curious turning effect to the face, which indeed suggests that the "lone eye" is an axle. What Hart especially liked about the Lescaze drawing was the prominence of the right eye, for he had read in *Tertium Organum* an assertion by Boehme that the right eye of a mystic was more seeing than the left; Boehme called it "the eye of eternity." In Part I, then, Faustus proffers to Helen "the eye of eternity."

Part II is Dionysian. Weber has well observed "that Nietzsche's aesthetic and philosophical ideas, particularly as expressed in *The Birth of Tragedy*, received an opportunity to display themselves concretely in Crane's career. . . . It is even possible that Nietzsche's call for "a rising generation . . . with bold vision . . . to desire a new art, the art of metaphysical comfort . . . to claim it as Helen, and exclaim with Faust in *The Birth of Tragedy* contributed to the genesis of 'Faustus and Helen.' " In passing, we may note that there was a degree of congruity between the doctrine of Nietzsche and the doctrine of Ouspensky. Nietzsche's Zarathustra declared that "what is great in man is that he is a bridge and not a goal"—a declaration that Crane may well have found a reinforcer of his master-metaphor.

Part III is in the affirmative spirit that one may find aroused by a reading of *Tertium Organum*. That work emphasizes the potentialities of man for greatness; it affirms the possibility of states of expanded consciousness and greater knowledge of the universe. While he was finishing Part III, Hart wrote me, "I feel that Eliot ignores certain spiritual events and possibilities as real and powerful now as, say, in the time of Blake." Ouspensky had shown Crane the "spiritual events and possibilities" that Eliot had ignored in the pessimistic visions of *The Waste Land*. In reply Crane wrote:

> Delve upward for the new and scattered wine,
> O brother-thief of time, that we recall.
> Laugh out the meager penance of their days
> Who dare not share with us the breath released,
> The substance drilled and spent beyond repair
> For golden, or the shadow of gold hair.

199

And now a word about the "Munson influence" which critics have discerned in the vocabulary and idiom and attitude toward the machine of "For the Marriage of Faustus and Helen." When I visited Hart in July of 1922 I brought with me the first draft of my monograph on Waldo Frank. Hart was impressed by a section I had written on man, nature, and the machine.

I had said that "hitherto, there have been two factors in culture, man and nature. The great cultures have attempted to adjust man's spiritual life to nature. . . . And the resultant poise achieved has been expressed in great, profound and lofty works of art. . . . But," I went on to say, "from the time of Rousseau onward we have had an art of maladjustment. . . . It is apparent that something has upset our old equilibrium, that an alien factor is disrupting man and nature. And that factor, it is now clear, is Machinery."

I then gave examples of the alterations in "the inner texture and quality of human life" that mechanization had wrought over the last two hundred years. And I went on to suggest that "culture must now work out a harmony among three factors, man, nature and Machinery, that the former definition of art must be amended to read 'nature and Machinery seen through a temperament' or, to revise a newer definition, 'a temperament revealed by laws of nature and Machinery,' that we must, in short, bring the Machine into the scope of the human spirit. We must make the Machine our fraternal genius." In conclusion, I averred that we, "by the chronological accident of our birth, [had been] chosen to create the simple forms, the folk-tales and folk-music, the preliminary art that our descendants may utilize in the vast struggle to put positive and glowing spiritual content into Machinery."

I was surprised by the serious way Hart took this theory, for only a year before, in writing on Sherwood Anderson, he had denounced the machine, "the monster that is upon us all." Now he made a *volte-face* and within a few months declared that he felt "quite fit to become a suitable Pindar for the dawn of the machine age, so-called."

He at once applied the theory to the technical problems of Part III of "For the Marriage of Faustus and Helen." The application gave us such lines as

> We even,
> Who drove speediest destruction
> In corymbulous formations of mechanics—

But he did not go as far in his reconciliation with the machine as his first impulse. About the last section, he wrote me, "I think I shall not attempt to make it the paragon of SPEED that I thought of. I think it needs more sheer weight than such a motive would provide." And again: "And as for the third part, I am interested enough in the aeroplane, war-speed idea but I think it would be better developed under a different sky."

Still he wrote lines of exhilarated modernity like the following in Part III:

> We know, eternal gunman, our flesh remembers
> The tensile boughs, the nimble blue plateaus,
> The mounted, yielding cities of the air!

Later, when he came to write the Cape Hatteras section of *The Bridge*, Hart still held to the view I had sketched in my study of Waldo Frank. By then I had dropped and almost forgotten this truly half-baked theory of mine. It had been derivative from European machine-worship in the first place; it was certainly shallow in conception; and it was oversimplified in exposition. Looking back, I am embarrassed by the serious regard Hart had for it, and I find it hard to believe that it actually inspired a series of articles by C. M. Grieve in the *New Age* (London) on the challenge to poets of the machine age. It can be fairly said, however, that this "Munson influence" did Crane no harm in his poetic development, but rather led to an enrichment of his technical resources.

7.

There are three kinds of influence that affect the education of human beings according to P. D. Ouspensky. We all experience the first kind, which Ouspensky named A Influences. A Influences are created by life as we know it and are felt in ordinary life. Examples of A Influences are the desire for worldly goods and riches, interest in health and personal safety, the driving-force of vanity and pride, the yearning for security, the desire for social position, and so on.

The second kind of influence, those not directly related to life experiences, Ouspensky called B Influences. These less-common influences originate in states of consciousness that are not usually achieved by human beings. They reach us through religion, art and literature, and philosophy. But often they are diluted or distorted in transmission. B Influences reached Crane in his reading, and his biographers have given a good account of them.

Philip Horton tells of the schoolboy reading and writing in his tower room. "Among his books . . . were more important than all others, the *Dialogues* [of

Plato], where he read of that clear and radiant progression from the beauties of earth upwards to that other beauty, from all fair notions to the notion of absolute beauty and the final revelation of the very essence of beauty. He read, too, of the necessity of madness in a true poet, and this he thought true enough to underscore doubly with red ink." In his eighteenth year Hart's mother gave him the works of William Blake; and he read avidly in them, feeling, as Weber says, a profound fascination that lasted for years. Crane's reading of Nietzsche also counts as a B Influence. Weber has seen that "to Friedrich Nietzsche must unquestionably be assigned a considerable share in the development of Hart Crane. . . . Crane's faith in myth, his desire to transmute music into his poetry, his disregard for cause and effect logic, his affirmation of life's joy coupled with an affirmation of suffering and tragedy, his belief in metaphysical inquiry as the artist's task—the entire Dionysian complex of dance, ecstasy, and triumph of the will which Nietzsche portrayed formed the backbone of Crane's life." Plato, Blake, Nietzsche—three powerful B Influences in Crane's development. But the most potent B Influence to nourish the growing poet was Ouspensky.

Crane probably first read *Tertium Organum* in the spring of 1920 in Akron, before the book was favorably reviewed in the *Dial* by W. C. Blum (James Sibley Watson, Jr.). Crane would have been impressed by this review, because Blum had previously captured his admiration by his essay on Rimbaud and translation of *A Season in Hell* in the *Dial*. But through a chance combination of circumstances, related in detail by Weber, Crane likely read *Tertium Organum* even before Blum reviewed it.

By the time (about June 18, 1922) Hart wrote his letter about his anesthetic revelation of the winter of 1921/1922, he had thoroughly immersed himself in the B Influence of Ouspensky. Weber has noted that what the "objective voice" tells Crane is straight from the pages of *Tertium Organum*. And Horton has made the case for the importance of this letter in determining whether or not Crane actually experienced the state of mystical illumination. Here is a portion of this often-quoted letter.

> At times, dear Gorham, I feel an enormous power in me—that seems almost supernatural. . . . Did I tell you of that thrilling experience this last winter in the dentist's chair when under the influence of ether and *amnesia* my mind spiralled to a kind of seventh heaven of consciousness and egoistic dance among the seven spheres—and something like an objective voice kept saying to me—"You have

the higher consciousness—you have the higher consciousness. This is something very few have. This is what is called genius." A happiness, ecstatic such as I have known only twice in "inspirations" came over me. I felt the two worlds. And at once. As the bore bit into my tooth I was able to follow its every revolution as detached as a spectator at a funeral. O Gorham, I have known moments in eternity. I tell you this as one who is a brother. I want you know me as I feel myself to be sometimes. . . . But since this adventure in the dentist's chair, I feel a new confidence in myself. At least I had none of the ordinary hallucinations common to this operation. Even that means something.

There is only one reference to *Tertium Organum* in Hart's voluminous correspondence, and it is a guarded one. Writing to Allen Tate (February 15, 1923), Hart somewhat defensively recommended Waldo Frank's *City Block* and declared that "Frank has the real mystic's vision." He immediately added: "I have also enjoyed reading Ouspensky's *Tertium Organum* lately. Its corroboration of several experiences in consciousness I have had gave it particular interest." But in an age when positivism is the ruling philosophy, it is not unusual for the mystically inclined to be defensive and guarded or even secretive in avowing their interests until they have tested the attitudes of their friends.

A few weeks after writing Tate, Hart came to New York and stayed a number of weeks in my Greenwich Village apartment. He brought very few books. The only one I remember was *Tertium Organum*, and perhaps there were no others. During his visit he was insistent that I read Ouspensky, and I was resistant. I had a prejudice against books of the sort I fancied *Tertium Organum* to be, and my prejudice was not reduced by the many interruptions Hart made in my book reviewing with pleas that I listen to this or that exciting passage. Finally, I promised that I would read the great book in the summer. Which I did. And was put on a new course in life.

Not until several years later did I realize what was occurring in Hart's personality that spring of 1923. B Influences had been accumulating, and their results had been taking a settled and definite form in his personality. This crystallization of the B Influences was evident during the whole of the coming year, from the spring of 1923 to the spring of 1924 when an altogether different influence, unforeseen and astonishing, appeared in New York. A *magnetic center*, which may be defined as a compact mass of memories of B Influences that attract a man in a certain direction, had begun to form in Hart. Such a magnetic center, or complex of interests, can guide and to a degree control the direction of a man's life.

In this crystallizing of the results of B Influences upon Crane, two writers—Rimbaud and Dostoyevsky—had played considerable parts. With intense excitement Crane had read about Rimbaud in the *Dial* in 1920 and how "the poet makes himself a visionary by a long, immense and reasoned derangement of all the senses." He had learned that Rimbaud strove to get beyond nature, beyond the visible and sensible world to the reality which is one and unifying. There was much in Rimbaud's doctrine that was dangerous to Crane—for one thing, it sanctioned his tendency to alcoholism—but he was fascinated by the aim of Rimbaud to become, in Wallace Fowlie's words, "the seer, the one who knows because he had traversed all knowable experience and come face to face with the unknown."

As for Dostoyevsky, Crane wrote on November 9, 1920, "he does give one more life than my mundane world supplies,—and stimulates." After reading *The Brothers Karamazov*, he wrote: "Dostoyevsky seems to me to represent the nearest type to the 'return of Christ' that there is record of,—I think the greatest of novelists." Then he read "a very fine biography and estimate and analysis by J. Middleton Murry," which brought out the full mystical import of Dostoyevsky. Murry maintained that there were two time-worlds in Dostoyevsky's fiction: his great major characters lived in a timeless world of eternity, whereas the majority of Dostoyevsky's characters lived in conventional time. To Crane, puzzling over the nature of time in *Tertium Organum*, Murry's interpretation was heady speculation.

One may find a metaphor for the magnetic center that has as much validity as the metaphors of Freudian psychology—a metaphor, that is, of usefulness in understanding individual psychology even though it is unscientific in a descriptive sense. Those who have acquired a magnetic center are men on a quest for hidden knowledge. Restlessly, they read esoteric literature; they travel abroad in search of teachers; they test schools of philosophy and religion for enlightenment. Always they are dissatisfied and always they are expectant of discovery of new-old keys to a greater knowledge of life.

8.

Early in 1923, Crane was possessed by a grand conception of what would be *The Bridge*; he wrote that his ruminations on the new poem were becoming more like seizures, "cogitations and cerebral excitements." On February 18, he wrote me that "I am too much interested in this *Bridge* thing lately to write letters, ads or anything. It is just beginning to take the least outline,—and the more outline the conception of the thing takes,—the more its final difficulties appall me. All this preliminary thought has to result, of course, in some channel forms or mould into which I throw myself at white heat. Very roughly, it concerns a mystical synthesis of 'America.' "

Crane explained:

> The initial impulses of "our people" will have to be gathered up toward the climax of the bridge, symbol of our constructive future, our unique identity, in which is included also our scientific hopes and achievements of the future. The mystic portent of all this is already flocking through my mind (when I say this I should say "the mystic possibilities," but that is all that's worth announcing, anyway) but the actual statement of the thing, the marshalling of the forces, will take me months, at best; and I may have to give it up entirely before that; it may be too impossible an ambition. But if I do succeed, such a waving of banners, such ascent of towers, such dancing, etc., will never before have been put down on paper!

By the "mystic possibilities" of the new poem, I understood Hart to mean— and I had reason to so understand him—that the bridge would symbolize a passage from our present waking state of consciousness to a higher consciousness, a crossing-over from the human condition of duality and tridimensionality to the normal condition of ecstasy of an expanded and higher consciousness. The ultimate meaning of *The Bridge* would be Ouspenskian to an even greater degree than the ultimate meaning of "For the Marriage of Faustus and Helen" had been. In a short time Hart and I would take some phrases from Waldo Frank and speak of *The Bridge* as a transition (crossing-over) from "an old slope of consciousness" to "a new slope of consciousness," the new slope having the characteristics of the Ouspenskian model of the universe.

While Hart was staying in my apartment in April of 1923, the abstract bridge of the new grand enterprise became a concrete bridge with a name and material abutments on real shores. Hart had been exploring Lower Manhattan one afternoon and returned in a state of intense excitement. He had come upon Brooklyn Bridge and had walked across it. He had been smitten at once by the singing strength of this structure, and from this moment of rapture the bridge of his poem became his mythopoetic Brooklyn Bridge.

205

Shortly before his rapturous walk across Brooklyn Bridge, Hart had met Waldo Frank who joined the B Influences playing upon his development. When he read my monograph on Frank,* Hart sent a typescript of "For the Marriage of Faustus and Helen" to Frank, and Frank's sensitive reception of the poem immediately won over the poet.**

Another B Influence acting on Hart in the gestation period of *The Bridge* came from Alfred Stieglitz. Seeing Stieglitz's photographs in April, 1923, Hart felt immediately a kinship with the great photographer and self-made mystic. "That moment was a tremendous one in my life," he wrote Stieglitz, "because I was able to share all the truth toward which I was working in my own medium, poetry, with another man who had manifestly taken many steps in that same direction in *his* work." Ten weeks later he wrote Stieglitz: "I feel you as entering very strongly into certain developments in *The Bridge*. May I say it, and not seem absurd, that you are the first, or rather the purest living indice of a new order on consciousness that I have met? We are accomplices in many ways that we don't yet fully understand. 'What is now proved was once only imagined,' said Blake." Hart is here manifesting the trait of a man with a magnetic center; he is in search of men who have risen to the "new order of consciousness." His course has been set in a certain direction.

Hart recognized another companion in his search for the miraculous in Jean Toomer, a writer of poems, stories, and sketches of Negro life that had been collected in *Cane*, with an introduction by Waldo Frank. Toomer had undergone the training in "the conscious control of the body" prescribed by F. Matthias Alexander and was quite convinced that in a disruptive age the first duty of an artist was to unify himself. Speaking of his friends—Waldo Frank, Frank's erstwhile protégé Jean Toomer, progressive educator Margaret Naumburg, and Gorham Munson—Hart wrote warmly to Alfred Stieglitz on October 26, 1923: "Isn't this little handful of us fighting though?" Hart actually thought in his innocence of the mystical disciplines that we were all progressing toward the "higher consciousness." Thus, on January 9, 1924, he noted:

---

    * "I am interested in Frank and thank you for putting me out of prejudice."—Hart Crane to Gorham Munson in a letter in September (?), 1923.

    ** "Frank has done me a world of good by his last letter (which promised another soon including further points of 'F and H.') . . . He gripped the mystical content of the poem so thoroughly that I despair of ever finding a more satisfying enthusiasm."—Hart Crane to Gorham Munson, March 2, 1923.

Jean's [Toomer] new hygiene for himself is very interesting to me. He seems
to be able to keep himself solid and undismayed. Certain organic changes are
occurring in us all, I think, but I believe that his is more steady and direct than
I have been permitted. My approach to words is still in substratum of some new
development—the same as it was when we talked last together—and perhaps
merely a chaotic lapse into confusion for all I dare say yet. I feel Stein and
E. E. C. [Cummings] are active agents in it. . . . I am very dissatisfied with both
these interesting people.

Hart's feeling of the birth-symptoms of "a new order of consciousness" was,
of course, an illusion. We were innocents in those days and quite unknowing
of where we were going. We were definitely not members of the "lost generation," as it would soon be named, but rather were alive with premonitions and
expectancies of a revival in American letters. "Our America" of Waldo Frank's
prophecy would come into being. We did not dream that our "handful"—with
the exception of Stieglitz—was set on a collision course with a strange force
that rarely appears in public history but would come to the surface of American
life in the spring of 1924.

9.

What collided with us was a C Influence. A Influences, it should be remembered, are comparatively unconscious influences created by the life of men in
the ordinary state of waking consciousness. B Influences are conscious in origin
but unconscious in action. They originate in states of consciousness "outside
life" but are refracted and distorted and diluted as they pass through literature,
religion, and philosophy to modern man. C Influences are also conscious in origin, but they differ from B Influences in being conscious in action too. A C
Influence takes the form of a *school*. A C Influence is exercised only by direct
contact of master with disciple. Its methods are direct instruction and demonstration; its teaching is oral and dramatic.

The knowledge of the school is traditionally called hidden knowledge, and
the schools are seldom part of man's public history. In American history, for
example, there is no trace of a C Influence until 1924. A man like Henry David
Thoreau, who fed on B Influences and developed a powerful magnetic center,
never, for all that he traveled much in Concord, encountered a C Influence—
and never had the remotest chance of initiation into a school. Yet we know that

there were C Influences acting in Europe between 1000 A.D. and 1400 A.D. One school consisted of the mysterious builders of the Gothic cathedrals, and Mont St. Michel and Notre Dame de Paris are monuments of their emergence into public history.

The C Influence that astounded New Yorkers in 1924 and increased their awareness of more distant and broader horizons of life was the Institute for the Harmonious Development of Man, which had been founded in 1921 at Fontainebleau by a Caucasian Greek named G. I. Gurdjieff.

10.

At this point, several questions about the later years of Hart's brief life should be raised. Why was *The Bridge* never completed? Why was *The Bridge* a failure in meaning, form, and style in the judgment of some of the most acute critics of Crane's own generation? Why did Crane himself come to doubt the value of *The Bridge* and lose faith in it and in himself? Why did he write so little in the last five years of his too-short life?

Completely satisfying answers are impossible to attain. One may, however, shed some light on Crane's loss of power if one studies his contact with the Gurdjieff school and his recoil from it as though shocked by a high-voltage current. For that reason it seems worthwhile to review the scanty material on Hart's collision with the Gurdjieff school and his subsequent aversion.

Hart was in a high state of excitement one morning in January, 1924, when he rang my doorbell on West 11th Street. He had called to give me the news he had just heard from Jane Heap, associate editor of *Little Review*. "Gurdjieff is coming!" he burst out. "He is the master Ouspensky found." Lest I think that Gurdjieff might be a Tagore-like mystic, Hart emphatically assured me: "Gurdjieff is solid." On February 2 Hart attended a Gurdjieff demonstration at the Neighborhood Playhouse on Grand Street. Elizabeth Delza and I were invited to this same demonstration and were sleepless for hours afterwards, such was its awakening effect upon us.

The demonstration was introduced by A. R. Orage, for many years editor of *New Age* (London), who said that "sacred dances and posture and movements in series have always been one of the vital subjects taught in esoteric schools in the East. They have a double aim: to convey a certain kind of knowledge, and to be a means for acquiring an harmonious state of being. The farthest limits of one's endurance are reached through the combination of non-natural and non-habitual movements, and by perfecting them a new quality of sensing is obtained, a new quality of concentration and attention and a new direction of the mind—all for a certain definite aim. . . . In ancient times the dance was a branch of real art, and served the purposes of higher knowledge and religion."

Among the dances performed were two sets of six "obligatory exercises," the Initiation of a Priestess, several Dervish dances, a pilgrimage movement called "measuring the way by one's length," several women's dances, the Big Seven dance, the "stop exercise," and a number of folk and manual labor dances. Part of the program was devoted to "tricks," "half-tricks," and "real supernatural phenomena," but only the "tricks" and "half-tricks" were shown and partly explained. Most members of the audience were lifted out of their usual art-experiences, and there was a great desire to follow up this first impact of the Gurdjieff school.

The next day Hart wrote his mother:

> Last night I was invited to witness some astonishing dances and psychic feats performed by a group of pupils belonging to the new famous mystic monastery founded by Gurdjieff near Versailles (Paris), that is giving some private demonstrations of their training methods in New York now. You have to have a written invitation, and after that there is no charge. I can't possibly begin to describe the details of this single demonstration, but it was very, very interesting— and things were done by amateurs which would stump the Russian ballet, I'm sure. Georgette LeBlanc,* former wife of Maeterlinck, was seated next to me (she brought them over here, or was instrumental in it, I think) with Margaret Anderson, whom I haven't seen since she got back from Paris in November. Georgette had on the gold wig which the enclosed picture will show you, and was certainly the most extraordinary looking person I've ever seen; beautiful, but in a rather hideous way.

On the same day that he wrote his mother that the Gurdjieff private demonstration was "very, very interesting," Hart was making an extraordinary contradiction of this report. I had anticipated that he would tell me that he had

---

* Georgette LeBlanc became a pupil of Gurdjieff and wrote a book, *The Courage Machine*, about her experiences.

been transported. Instead he quite dashed my own enthusiasm. He hadn't cared much for the show. He was unenthusiastic about Gurdjieff. He had little to say and quickly dropped the topic. I learned that he had drunk heavily before he saw the demonstration and that he had attended it with a Greenwich Villager, Susan Jenkins, who was connected with the Provincetown Playhouse. His companion had scoffed at the dances (there were people who thought the dancers were hypnotized and joyless). Hart, for all the intensity of his poetry, was highly affectible by the attitudes and opinions of his friends, and I suspected that he had been scoffed into a scoffing mood himself as the demonstration proceeded. Still he wrote his mother that "things were done by amateurs which would stump the Russian ballet." But I did not know this until thirty years later.

A few evenings later I went with Hart to a meeting at the apartment of Margaret Anderson and Jane Heap. About twenty of the intelligentsia were there to hear A. R. Orage tell about the Institute for the Harmonious Development of Man. I knew many by reputation but remember seeing there only Henry McBride, the art reporter (he refused to be called a critic), and Edna Kenton, who had been on the advisory board of *Seven Arts*. Orage talked about psychology but only incidentally about art, which disappointed this art group. Hart was silent throughout the meeting and expressed no views afterward.

I began to read Orage's causeries, *Readers and Writers*, which had been praised by judicious reviewers, and thought to turn the tables on Hart by reading aloud to him brief passages that showed great insight into mysticism—just as Hart had once read bits of *Tertium Organum* for me to admire. I gave him Orage on Plotinus and received only a grudging assent to its truth. It was plain that Hart had not been hooked by those fishers of men, Gurdjieff and Orage. Several of his friends had—Jean Toomer, Margaret Naumburg, Elizabeth Delza, and I— and were attending meetings and talks by Gurdjieff at the Rosetta O'Neill Studio. But Hart stayed away and seemed to be waiting for our infatuation to run its course and disappear.

That summer Jean Toomer went to the Institute at Fontainebleau. Hart thought wistfully of the little "handful" of friends he had written about to Stieglitz before the advent of Gurdjieff, and wrote me on July 9, 1924, about an evening he had lately spent at my apartment. "I admit to a gratifying sense of excitement when I left that recalled some of the earlier Munson-Burke-Toomer-etc. engagements that took place before the grand dissolution, birth control, re-swaddling and neo-synthesizing, grandma confusion movement (of which I am probably the most salient example) began." This was a feeble attempt to exorcize the Gurdjieff shock by humor.

In the fall Orage, back from the Institute at Fontainebleau where Gurdjieff had suffered a nearly fatal accident, called an open meeting at the Finch School. I invited Hart to attend and he sat blankly through the talk. It was his last exposure to Gurdjieff's ideas, and I must add that it was unresentfully endured.

Two and a half years later Hart was bursting with puerile resentment in a letter to Allen Tate. "Your comments on Gorham's shrine and gland-totemism," Hart said, "convince me that Orage talked as vaguely and arbitrarily in your presence as he did in mine on a similar occasion. Some great boob ought to be hired as a kind of heckler and suddenly burst out in one of those meetings held each year to attract converts,—'come on now, do your stuff—there's millions waiting!' Or some such democratic phrase." What had happened between the fall of 1924 and January of 1927 to change Hart's mild negativism to resentment may be partly explained by his exasperation that the Gurdjieff shock wouldn't go away. Even his friend Waldo Frank had attended an Orage group for a year; and although he had dropped out, he had nonetheless borrowed some ideas from it.

In May of 1927 Hart was exploding to Yvor Winters: "You need a good drubbing for all your recent easy talk about 'the complete man,' the poet and his ethical place in society, etc." He went on to say:

The image of "the complete man" is a good idealistic antidote for the hysteria for specialization that inhabits the modern world. And I strongly second your wish for some definite ethical order. Munson, however, and a number of my other friends, not so long ago, being stricken with the same urge, and feeling that something must be done about it—rushed into the portals of the famous Gurdjieff institute and have since put themselves through all sorts of Hindu antics, songs, dances, incantations, psychic sessions, etc., [Hart's Sunday supplement version of the Orage groups] so that now presumably the left lobes of their brains and their right lobes respectively function (M's favorite word) in perfect unison. I spent hours at the typewriter trying to explain to certain of these urgent people why I could not enthuse about their methods; it was all to no avail, as I was told that the "complete man" had a different logic than mine, and further that there was no way of gaining or understanding this logic without first submitting yourself to the necessary training. I was finally left to roll in the gutter of my ancient predispositions and suffered to receive a good deal of unnecessary pity for my obstinacy. Some of them . . . have ceased writing altogether.

If all those papers of explanation (letters?) ever come to light, they will provide most valuable clues to an understanding of Hart's retreat from the Gurdjieff encounter to which *Tertium Organum* had led him. But do these papers exist? Were "hours at the typewriter" ever spent in writing them? I never heard of any of Hart's friends receiving them, and certainly the answers Hart alleges he received do not sound like Gurdjieffian answers. Rather they sound like Hart's garbled recollection of some things Ouspensky said in *Tertium Organum*, a pre-Gurdjieffian book, about the logic of superman. Most mystifying of all is the reference to some of these friends having stopped writing.* The whole passage is probably an argument and rebuttal solely carried on in Hart's mind.

In *The Letters of Hart Crane* there is only one more reference, an oblique one, to the Gurdjieff system. In a letter to Allen Tate (July 13, 1930) about Tate's review of *The Bridge*, Hart digressed to say that "[Genevieve] Taggard, like Winters, isn't looking for poetry any more. Like Munson, they are both in pursuit of some cure-all."

Did Crane repudiate the mystical vision that had inspired him in 1922 to 1924? Did a decline of faith in *The Bridge* and in his powers ("an enormous power . . . that seems almost supernatural," he had called it in 1922) take place in the years of his retreat from contact with the Gurdjieff school? That is the question we will address next.

Part Two: The Bridge

Writing about Hart Crane in the fall of 1923, Brom Weber observes that "the pattern of Crane's life was cooling into finality." Two friends who were deeply concerned about Hart's repetitive behavior at this time were Waldo Frank and I. It seemed to us that he was wasting extravagantly his gifts and was writing so few poems because he lacked any kind of discipline. We discussed his future. Would psychoanalysis help him as a poet? We decided that analysts did

* Certainly not Jean Toomer. Toomer published short stories in *Little Review*, *Dial*, and *American Caravan*. He wrote essays, a play, and a book of aphorisms during his first five years in the Gurdjieff work.

not understand the problems of a creative person like Hart. Their therapy, even if Hart could be induced to undergo it—which was doubtful—would be ineffective in developing his creative powers. Love then? Yes, but not from the attachments Hart seemed to prefer. He preferred the rougher types—men he found on park benches—to the sensitive polished types like a certain young novelist we knew. Finally a solution occurred to Waldo but, alas, a highly impracticable one. "If Hart would only fall in love with an older disciplined homosexual, someone like André Gide, whom he would enormously respect as well as love, then he would probably acquire discipline by contact."

Hart was also being defeated in the economic struggle. The advantage he seemed to have had in being the son of a rich candy manufacturer was no advantage at all. His father wanted him to enter the candy industry and write poetry as an avocation. But Hart could not—like Wallace Stevens in insurance, T. S. Eliot in banking, or William Carlos Williams in medicine—adjudicate between the claims of poetry and the need to earn a livelihood. Hart was an emotional type; his practical side was weak, and his intellect was ordinary. Thus structured with an overwhelming emotional bias, he was able to get jobs but unable to keep them. Often he resigned. Always he rationalized his one-sided nature into a virtue—he was a poet and should not have to serve King Admetus when Apollo was his lord. And so he revolted against the prospect of a partnership in his father's company, and he resigned from a position in the leading advertising agency in America.

From then on Hart evaded the issue of earning a living. His friends and parents helped him, but not very much. When desperate, he took some sort of a job but it did not last. He found a patron in Otto Kahn for a couple of years. He received a small legacy. He was given a Guggenheim Fellowship in Mexico. But always he remained type-bound and was irascible when preached to by exponents of the complete man like Yvor Winters. Of course this man of psychological disharmony, of discord between practical living and poetic living, found unappealing any school with a title like the Institute for the Harmonious Development of Man.

At the time when Hart, acting on bad advice from two of his friends, left the J. Walter Thompson Agency, he was on the way to becoming the alcoholic he subsequently became. "Be drunk, always. With wine, with poetry, or virtue, as you please. But be drunk," Baudelaire had written; and Hart had responded with Dionysian fervor. Alcohol, as a chemical means to the liberation of emotion, had initially worked very well as a stimulant to conceiving and writing poems. Hart probably felt that he had come upon Rimbaud's secret of the derangement of the senses. But with continued use and ultimately continual use, the stimulant changed into a narcotic. Crane drunk eventually made one think less of Poet Drunk and more of Everyman Besotted. He became insulting and violent, self-destructive, a victim of hangovers and hysterical attacks, and in his cups a frequent betrayer of his ideals.

Then there was the acceleration of his homosexuality from occasional affairs to frequent and random gratifications of lust. His friends did not think that his homosexuality was congenital;* rather they were inclined toward a Freudian interpretation. Hart suffered from the curse of sundered parentage and had been, we believed, caught in an Oedipal situation. No one thought of curing him. But we did believe that a balanced view of his father and mother would help him to be more stable. Something like this was attempted by the two friends mentioned above who advised him to quit the best job he had ever had. The improvement was quick—but only temporary.

Such was the pattern of Hart's behavior—jobless and dependent, alcoholic, and homosexual—when he was attracted to the Gurdjieff demonstration at the Neighborhood Playhouse and repelled by something he felt there.

What repelled him? Horton has guessed that "it was the insistence upon discipline, above all, that prejudiced Crane against the [Gurdjieff visitation]." This is correct. Crane was not declining a therapeutic challenge when he turned away, for Gurdjieff did not offer a therapy. Gurdjieff did not propose the reform of one's "vices" or adjustment to one's environment. What Crane felt was an immediate threat to his illusions. He believed that he already had a higher mystical consciousness ("You have the higher consciousness" he had heard in anesthetic revelation); he believed in the primacy of poetry for advance into the higher consciousness realm; he believed that he was on the path to a new order of consciousness. Now he was told—forcefully, even shockingly—that he was a strictly determined being, an irrational machine, with no ability to do. And he was told that he could not develop into the free being he fancied he already was unless he acquired a discipline of self-knowledge and self-development and worked with all his strength to gain freedom.

Discipline suggests a price to be paid. The passivity and inertia of one's psy-

---

* "An extreme example of the *unwilling* homosexual."—Allen Tate.

chology resist discipline. There is the fear of losing the life one has. Man is strangely attached to his weaknesses. Sometimes he would like to grow out of them, but not at the price of hard struggle against them. In a crisis of life-change men find that they love their suffering and are fearful of the vista of a new life.

It is possible that Crane's magnetic center was neither large enough nor strong enough to help him absorb the Gurdjieff teaching, which was so different from the A and B Influences that had heretofore nourished him. He became critical before he could know anything of the Gurdjieff "fourth way." When he saw the first difficulties of the "fourth way," he immediately withdrew. He turned back from Gurdjieff, and his life was arrested at that point. "Crane had achieved the highest level of social and emotional maturity which he would ever reach." This is Brom Weber's judgment on Crane at the close of 1923, one month before Gurdjieff visited New York.

2.

I have been suggesting that the impact of Gurdjieff produced a crisis in Hart's life. It is doubtful, however, that he was aware of being in crisis—at least not for a year. He probably rationalized that he and his friends had been hit by a divisive influence that was merely temporary. In a few months the Gurdjieff group would return to France; the sensation would die away; the happy days of personal unguided groping toward the light would be resumed. He was dismayed to find that in the fall of 1924 several large study groups had been formed in New York by A. R. Orage, Gurdjieff's representative, and in these groups were many people Hart respected. The visit of Gurdjieff had sent down roots that began to spread.

In some ways the year from spring of 1924 to spring of 1925 was to be a good year for Crane. He got a job that paid the rent and restaurant checks. He enjoyed and suffered the deepest and finest love affair of his whole life. He confided that it was the first relationship with a man in which he had experienced more than sensual gratification; this, he said, was real love—and we can believe him.* Although he had said something similar during an earlier affair, he had never written anything about it, or his other affairs, that had the purity and

---

* See Crane's letter to Waldo Frank, dated April 21, 1924, beginning: "For many days, now, I have gone about quite dumb with something for which 'happiness' must be too mild a term."

intensity of his Voyages poems. "Voyages II," written a few months after Gurdjieff's visit, was called by Yvor Winters "one of the most powerful and one of the most nearly perfect poems of the last two hundred years." Hart was quite conscious when he showed me "Voyages II"—with what pride! — that he was at the very flood of his powers.

And yet things were not as they had been before, not as they had been when he was writing "For the Marriage of Faustus and Helen" and learning the truth of Ben Jonson's dictum: "Who casts to write a living line, must sweat." A seed of doubt had entered into his poetic constitution, and it was to grow until in 1929 it would almost choke his genius.

Hart's friends in the Orage group tried not to show that any alteration in their regard for him had taken place. Friendships continued on the surface as if no new critical light had been flashed on literature. And yet Hart could not help but feel that his friends were drawing away. They had less time for him. They had new absorbing interests that they did not talk about. Somehow, while they liked his new poems very much, there was a reserve, he felt, in their liking, as though he were being judged in a new perspective and by a higher standard than before.* This was baffling. "They have become hermetically sealed souls to my eyesight," he wrote to Winters a few years later, "and I am really not able to offer judgment."

At this point in the untold story of Hart Crane, examination of a poem he wrote in October of 1925 will yield biographical keys to an understanding of his growing sense of entrapment. This creative year—the year of his affair with E. O. and the writing of five of the six Voyages poems—was also the year in which the feeling grew in Hart of being "caught like a rat in a trap." One of a small group of visionary lyrics, "Wine Menagerie" has been overpraised. I cannot agree with R. W. B. Lewis that it is one of Crane's "most consummate lyrics"; and in declining the poem for *Criterion*, T. S. Eliot evidently found it less than consummate. Marianne Moore's dissatisfaction with the draft submitted

---

* At the first luncheon I had with A. R. Orage, I "put my cards on the table" as I thought, by volunteering that I had never had any "mystical" experiences, meaning that I had never had any revelations of the sort claimed by Crane and Waldo Frank (*S4N*, Issues 30–31) and attributed by Middleton Murry to Dostoyevsky. "You are lucky," Orage said. He explained that such experiences were pathological: "Peeping-Tom glimpses of the universe through a smutted window-pane." The first thing to do, Orage said, was "to clean the window-pane." Naturally this affected the earlier "rating" I had given Hart's "mysticism."

to her led her to cut a 49-line poem to 18 lines, some of them revised, and to entitle the short version "Again." Miss Moore's editorial presumption in revising "Wine Menagerie" has been properly censured. It has not been noted that she moulded out of Crane's incompletely formed poem a genuine poem that is quite interesting in itself—only it wasn't Crane's poem. She did more than take all the wine out of the menagerie, as Kenneth Burke wryly observed. She banished the menagerie too.

The setting of "Wine Menagerie" is a cozy speakeasy on a snowy day in a metropolis like New York. As the poet is drinking himself into a visionary state, his mind becomes a collection of wild animals. The lying reality of everyday is transcended. "Between black tusks the roses shine!" and a vision comes of—

> New thresholds, new anatomies! Wine talons
> Build freedom up about me and distil
> This competence—to travel in a tear
> Sparkling alone, within another's will.

But the everyday world is not really transcended. "Ruddy, the tooth implicit of the world / has followed you." The poet's capability for a state of higher consciousness lessens and he is betrayed. He must leave the "wine menagerie" and walk away.

> "Rise from the dates and crumbs. And walk away,
> Stepping over Holofernes' shins—
> . . . .
> "—And fold your exile on your back again;
> Petrushka's valentine pivots on its pin."

There is the possibility that if he accepts the necessary solitude of his poetic mission, he may regain his heightened vision—but this possibility is only implied and not excitatory.

The incident of Marianne Moore's alteration of "Wine Menagerie" reveals a pattern that was to be repeated again and again in the last six years of Crane's life. It begins with a compromise. Crane needed money so badly that he accepted twenty dollars from the *Dial* for Marianne Moore's remodeled poem, "Again"—"a unique instance of Crane's yielding poetic integrity for a material consideration," R. W. B. Lewis notes. As time went on, Crane was to make other compromises of his critical and even personal integrity. Trapped in his compromise, Crane would violently appeal to one or another of his friends. This

217

time he went to the house of Matthew Josephson and wept over the injustice Marianne Moore had inflicted. Josephson undertook to intervene in his behalf, officiously offering to buy the poem back from *Dial*. Whereupon Crane disclaimed all responsibility for Josephson's impertinent intervention and refused to go back on his word to Miss Moore, who now castigated Josephson for impudent meddling. A mess all around.

And there were other equally messy compromises—including those involved in Crane's effort to play both sides of the fence during the *Broom* vs. Munson conflict discussed in Chapter 11. Horton has discussed the dualism in Crane that caused him so much grief, the "desire for affection and the fear of betrayal" that "gradually became one of the irreconcilables that distorted his life."

I think he felt "trapped like a rat" because of the weakness generated in him by this affection-fear duality. He was repudiating that growing-end of his personality that he called his "mysticism." He could not have been happy in an atmosphere of attacks and counterattacks, let alone the downright feuding he was exposed to. As he crossed from side to side, he compromised his own views. He was loyal to neither side. He carried tales, and he probably hated himself for denouncing each side to the other. But it was worst of all for him when he began to repudiate his own critical direction under pressure from the anti-mystical *Broom* writers. Simultaneously he began to reject the direction of the magnetic center that Ouspensky had crystallized in him.

Magnetic centers do not survive the shock of an encounter with Influence C. If the person meeting a school enters upon its work, the school takes the place of his magnetic center. If he does not enter the school's work—if he averts his course in life from the school—then his magnetic center begins to dissolve. This happened with Crane. The image of the poet he derived from Rimbaud and the Symbolists took over. His magnetization by these poets' lives from now on had precedence over the B Influences (Nietzsche, Blake, Ouspensky, *et al.*) that had led him to the C Influence of Gurdjieff. He began to doubt the vision of *The Bridge*.

3.

The change in what may be called Crane's poetics that took place in 1924–25 is perhaps best discerned in a private paper, "General Aims and Theories," which he prepared for Eugene O'Neill as an aid for writing a foreword a publisher had requested of O'Neill. It is a somewhat cloudy piece of writing, often imprecise in wording and undiscriminating in references. A sentence like "the great mythologies of the past (including the Church) are deprived of enough facade to even launch raillery against" illustrates the untidy thinking of the piece. And yet it is possible to loosely define Crane's position in 1925.

What is most significant is the disappearance of Ouspensky in the statement of general aims and theories. In recoiling from Ouspensky's master, Crane seems to have impulsively swept Ouspensky's ideas out of his mind. He replaces Ouspensky with Walt Whitman and Hegel's absolute idealism.

In *Our America*, Waldo Frank had presented Walt Whitman as the prophet of a new order in America, and we now find Crane stating his Whitmanism in a paragraph I shall quote in full. This is not Ouspenskian talk but Whitmanesque talk. "I am concerned with the future of America, but not because I think that America has any so-called par value as a state or as a group of people. . . . It is only because I feel persuaded that here are destined to be discovered certain as yet undefined spiritual quantities, perhaps a new hierarchy of faith not to be developed so completely elsewhere. And in this process I like to feel myself as a potential factor; certainly I must speak in its terms and what discoveries I may make are situated in its experience."

But the core of "General Aims and Theories" is Crane's version of the absolute idealism of Hegel. I do not know where Crane picked up his Hegelianism; he may have read Hegel, but more likely he found Hegelian ideas somewhere in the course of his unsystematic reading and reworded them as follows:

It is my hope to go *through* the combined materials of the poem, using our "real" world somewhat as a spring-board, and to give the poem *as a whole* an orbit or predetermined direction of its own. I would like to establish it as free from my own personality as from any chance evaluation on the reader's part. (This is, of course, an impossibility, but it is a characteristic worth mentioning.) Such a poem is at least a stab at a truth, and to such an extent may be differentiated from other kinds of poetry and called "absolute." Its evocation will not be toward decoration or amusement, but rather toward a state of consciousness, an "innocence" (Blake) or absolute beauty. In this condition there may be discoverable under new forms certain spiritual illuminations, shining with a morality essentialized from experience directly, and not from previous precepts or preconceptions. It is as though a poem gave the reader as he left it a single, new *word*, never before spoken and impossible to actually enunciate, but self-evident as an active principle in the reader's consciousness henceforward.

In brief, Crane in 1925 defined himself as a twentieth-century metaphysical poet, one who was "interested in the *causes* (metaphysical) of his materials, their emotional derivations or their utmost spiritual consequences."

4.

At the end of spring of 1925 Hart, exclaiming that he was "caught like a rat in a trap," resigned from his job at Sweet's Catalogues and went to stay with friends at Paterson, New York. He had by now enough poems—about thirty— to make the customary slim volume of the new poet, and he was offering it to publishers—and getting rejections. Toward the end of the year he applied to the international banker and art patron Otto Kahn for a grant.

I cannot recall whether it was I or someone else who suggested that Hart make application to Kahn. Waldo Frank had told me of Kahn's frequent acts of patronage of artists and had suggested that I apply for aid. But I had a managing editorship of a popular magazine and did not want to resign and reduce my income to the probable size of a grant. I had passed on the word about Kahn to a painter, Ernest Fiene, who applied and was extended a check for two thousand dollars. But even as Kahn was extending the check, he made a condition that a certain gallery (Daniel) should handle Fiene's sales. "I am sorry," said Fiene courageously, for he desperately needed support; "but if that is the condition, I must decline," and the check stopped in midair. I could very well have told Hart about the Fiene application. I'm inclined to believe I did, but I cannot swear to it.

When it came Hart's turn to be interviewed by Kahn, the banker told him that he had the greatest respect for the judgment of Waldo Frank and Eugene O'Neill, who had sponsored Crane, and he attached no conditions whatever to his grant. Crane sped out to Paterson and resumed work on *The Bridge*.

Now seemed a good moment to write an essay on Hart. He had surpassed his earlier poems in Voyages II, III, IV, V, VI, and he had a book ready for publication. He was beginning serious work on the biggest project of his career, *The Bridge*, which might take a year or two to complete. In December of

1925 I labored over the first essay to be written about Hart and began to submit it soon afterwards—without success. I sent a copy of "Hart Crane: Young Titan in the Sacred Wood" to Hart, whose reaction has been reproduced and commented upon several times without giving a fair summary of what was said in the essay.

My essay began by disposing of the "superficial legend that [Maxwell Bodenheim] is a 'contemporary Rimbaud.' " Hart Crane, I declared, is the writer of "a totally different and higher order of poetry." The energy of his poetry I called "that intense, Dionysian, dancing, exalted energy that by sheer pressure lifts him to heights unattainable by less titanic poets." This judgment that Crane was a Dionysian in the Nietzschean sense is one I would press today. The essay went on to call Crane a prodigy, which took real courage to say in 1925, when Crane's poems were still receiving far more rejections than acceptances. "Of the poems he has composed there are perhaps twenty that [Crane] cares most about saving. But those twenty should not be lost to American letters." The central point of my essay was the statement that Crane's "poems are ecstatic illuminations, the tensile expansions of his psychology."

With all of this the subject of my essay was quite naturally in agreement. It was the second half of the essay, in which I discussed the obscurity of his poetry, that caused Crane to react in disagreement—over-react, as I shall soon claim.

I contended that Hart's obscurity could be traced to "a highly specialized subjectivity and to 'metaphysical' guessing." I said bluntly that "he doesn't know enough." In America, I said, "he has breathed an uncritical atmosphere; he has dined on meager ideas; he has been stranded in an arid region so far as currents of fresh, intelligent and alive thought go." He feels free, I charged, to invest his subject matter "with private feelings and associations and magnifications." In short, he "is a 'mystic' on the loose."

> There is no system, but only this: a doubt of the truth of the appearances which the world shows us, and intuitions of higher dimensions, of the dimensional character of time in particular, of hidden forces, of an ultimate "circuit calm of one vast coil". . . . Just as the symbol and its overtones are the heart of his technique, so are his intuitions at the heart of his meaning.
>
> But we know that intuitions, while valuable, are allied to guessing. We know that intuitions may be mistaken or even diseased. We know that something must

221

be added to them—and that is certitude—to make them knowledge . . . the risk
Hart Crane is taking . . . the risk any gifted inspired and possessed writer takes.
The risk of bringing back a distorted and poorly glimpsed vision. What is more,
such intuitions and ecstasies and visions are very hard to scrutinize with detachment. One writes, in fact, too spontaneously about them: one is sometimes identified with them and sometimes outside, but always carried *blindly* along with them.

Then came a paragraph that especially offended Hart. "Crane cannot maintain his feelings on this plane [of higher emotion]. He drops off until fortune
gives him another ecstasy after which in turn he slumps. That, I take it, accounts for a tendency in his writing to oscillate between a description of his
personal wretchedness and the moments of supernal beauty he experiences."
The conclusion of the essay, then:

> To be divinely mad is to be a titan, storming upward by sheer energy toward
> a heaven that is intuited but not known. But, on the other hand, there is divine
> sanity with Plato, a philosopher who it is often said wrote like a poet, as its ex-
> emplar. Divine sanity places the emphasis upon procedure, upon the perfection
> of the individual for knowing, upon the organization of what the individual knows,
> upon the steady viewing of wholes. And if Plato was not a god, at least he was
> godlike in his objectivity and impartiality, at least the emotions he felt sprang
> from the contemplation of what can more plausibly be considered knowledge
> than speculations. A genuine metaphysical poetry will originate in our era when
> an individual poet is stirred by large and true *facts*, and until then we shall have
> but lyrical pyrotechnics in the void of man's ignorance.
>
> From this point of view, great poetry is an addition to wisdom, since it springs
> from wisdom. Whereas most poetry, including Crane's, is on the terrestrial side
> of knowledge and hence short of wisdom, since the latter is but the *realization* of
> knowledge.

It should be evident from this abridgment of my essay that it was concerned
with what AE has called "the important thing about a poet [which] is finally
this: 'Out of how deep a life does he speak.' " Crane's "poems are ecstatic illuminations," I had declared; and somewhat tentatively I had concluded that
Crane on a few occasions—as in Voyages III (I should have cited Voyages II
as well)—spoke out of an emotional source purer and higher than the familiar
sources of poetry. In his reply to my criticism, Hart paid no attention to this

speculation, which I regarded as the most important conjecture in the essay. "And yet," I had mused, "there is something more about the quality of Crane's emotions that causes wonder and speculation. I do not dare to say what it is, but it is as though Crane accidentally tapped some potential reservoir of emotions, purer and higher than those with which we are ordinarily familiar. We are ignorant as to just what the frame of human psychology includes as potentials, and it may be that emotions of another order, dormant in most of us, somehow break through into activity in certain poetry and produce a rare literary experience."

Crane's reply to this essay is of great significance in the untold story of his collision with a C Influence and his subsequent crack-up. He had requested an advance look at the essay, saying that "there may possibly arise (between ourselves) certain questions of direction, aims, intentions, which I may feel are erroneously ascribed to me." Having read the essay, Hart defended himself in "my rummy conversation last Monday" which gave "but a poor explanation of my several theoretical differences of opinion with you on the function of poetry, its particular province of activity, etc." He tried again in a long letter that bears some evidence of his having consulted with Allen Tate. This letter shows that Crane had entered on that period of confusion about his "general aims and theories" (so recently set down for Eugene O'Neill) that was to last until his death six years later. At the time Crane wrote his defensive letter, he was realizing "only too keenly," as Horton has noted, "the discrepancy between his own philosophical affirmations and the negative skepticism of his contemporaries" (Cowley, Slater Brown, Tate and others of the Paterson group). "Whenever Crane and the Tates and Browns spent an evening together," Horton has written, "the conversation inevitably turned to the question of the modern poet's dilemma, and they discussed in the terms of T. S. Eliot's poetry and criticism the lack of an adequate faith or hierarchy of values in society, its spiritual drought and intellectual dessication." He had turned to me for relief from this "continued spiritual suffocation" and had written: "But in the face of such a stern conviction of death on the part of the only group of people whose verbal sophistication is likely to take an interest in a style such as mine,—what can I expect? . . . I shall at least continue to grip with the problem without relaxing into the easy acceptance (in the name of 'elegance, nostalgia, wit, splenetic splendor') of death which I see most of my friends doing. O the admired beauty of a casuistical mentality! It is finally content with twelve hours' sleep a day and archaeology." After writing this to me Hart received from me the essay, "Hart Crane: Young Titan in the Sacred Wood," wherein he confronted a comparison of "divine madness" with "divine sanity." And the essay was, in fact, founded on the distinction between the two categories of art, subjective and objective—unconscious and conscious. I trusted that the discerning would see that I was comparing the modern subjective artist with the objective artist, the Titanic "divine madness" with the Olympian's "divine sanity."

Crane searched for a "Gurdjieffian point of view" or "Gurdjieffian content" in the essay. But never having studied the teaching, he was, of course, unable to recognize the unlabeled "Gurdjieffian element." Failing to realize that the essay centered on the psychology of the poet, Crane assumed wrongly that the essay prescribed for the poetry "man's relationship to a hypothetical god," "ethical morality or moral classification," "subordination to philosophy." The result of his misreading was a question-begging reply.

Crane first attempted to escape from the responsibilities of the metaphysical poet. Weber was keen enough to note this and said flatly that "first, [Crane] disputed Munson's assertion that he had ever attempted to be a metaphysical poet." Examining Crane's error, Weber concluded that "Crane was literally attempting to skip out from under Munson's charge that he could not be a metaphysical poet without acquiring more knowledge." In dodging thus, Crane became confused about his "general aims and theories," for there can be no doubt that up to then he had both considered himself and had been a metaphysical poet.

In the second place, Crane was indignant about what he regarded as "personal" criticism. My specifying the fitfulness of inspiration of the subjective artist struck too near home. Ecstasy is not within the control of the subjective artist, and creation just happens with him rather than being willed. Two years later, when the essay appeared as a chapter in *Destinations*, Hart moderated his indignation. "As for Hart Crane," he confessed, "I know him too well to disagree on as many points as I once did . . . when I first read the essay."

In the third place, Crane begged the question about "knowledge." "As Allen said, what exactly do you mean by 'knowledge'? " I could have replied: "I mean by 'knowledge' what you and I understood when we read that book you insisted I should read—*Tertium Organum*. Here is what we pondered on: 'Man realizes his existence and the existence of the world, a part of which he is. His relation to himself and to the world is called knowledge. The expansion and deepening of his *relation* to himself and to the world is the expansion of knowledge.' " (Italics added.)

I did not make this reply, because there was nothing esoteric in the nature of the knowledge I desiderated for the metaphysical poet. I was, in fact, taking the term over from T. S. Eliot where Crane and Tate had experienced no trouble in understanding it. Eliot, quoting Arnold to the effect that "the English poetry of the first quarter of this century, with plenty of energy, plenty of creative force, did not know enough," had remarked that Arnold's observation "will probably be as true of the first quarter of the twentieth century as it was of the nineteenth." A further clue to the meaning of "knowledge" in my essay was offered by a second quotation from Arnold: "In the Greece of Pindar and Sophocles, in the England of Shakespeare, the poet lived in a current of ideas in the highest degree animating and nourishing to the creative power."

I felt that Crane, in staying away from the Orage-Gurdjieff study groups in New York, was remaining outside "a current of ideas in the highest degree animating and nourishing to the creative power." He was, I asserted, "stranded in an arid region so far as currents of fresh, intelligent and alive thought go." The C Influence provided "the true basis for the creative power's exercise." But Crane had reacted against the C Influence and was now over-reacting to an essay that he suspected was colored by the C Influence. His over-reaction carried him into a permanent mood of confusion and doubt. It began what Brom Weber has called "the collapse of the myth."

5.

I was a close friend of Hart Crane during the best years of his life—1919 to 1925. The next seven years, except for a great burst of composing sections of *The Bridge* in the summer of 1926, were mainly sterile. He forced himself to write another section and three songs for *The Bridge* in 1929, and there were a few scattered poems along the way, and at the very end came the overpraised "Broken Tower," but most of the time he was impotent to create even slight poems.

It was a time of growing distance between Hart and me. We never had a violent break, as happened with so many friends of Hart in the tormented last years of his life. But a break was avoided only because we seldom saw each other—not more than five times—after Hart returned from the Isle of Pines in 1926. I came to look upon our friendship in the past tense, as was revealed in the wording of the dedication of my short biography of Robert Frost in 1927. That dedication read as follows:

To

HART CRANE

in memory of many
enthusiastic con-
versations about
poetry

When I read about the mad years of Hart, I feel that I am reading about a stranger. The roots of alcoholism, debauchery, violence, hallucination, and self-destruction were in the Hart Crane I knew. But what a monstrous growth choked the poet in him and doomed him to suicide. Cowley, who knew him well during the years of his disintegration, has given a charitable description of Crane's last year. "When I heard the full story of his year in Mexico," and Cowley might well have included the last three years, "it seemed to me not so much the adventures of a living poet as the pathology and symptomatology of a fatal disease."

Crane's magnetic center had been fragmented on collision with the Gurdjieff school. In June of 1926 he confided to Waldo Frank that one does not "build out of an emptied vision." He confessed that the meaning of his original conception for *The Bridge* had been lost. "Emotionally I should like to write *The Bridge*; intellectually judged the whole theme and project seems more and more absurd. A fear of personal impotence in this matter wouldn't affect me half so much as the convictions that arise from other sources. . . . I had what I thought were authentic materials that would have been a pleasurable-agony of wrestling, eventually or not in perfection—at least being worthy of the most supreme efforts I could muster."

But the support for these materials that Crane had found in Ouspensky was not forthcoming from the coterie of young writers who now surrounded him. The best critic of these, Allen Tate, though perceptive of romantic strength and verbal mastery in Crane, was skeptical of the possibility of a poetic myth in the static America of the 1920s and disapproved of the bridge enterprise. Crane read Whitehead and I. A. Richards, but from neither did he receive the shock, the impetus to development, that Ouspensky had once given him.

Crane went on to comment to Frank on the worthlessness of present-day America, reflecting perhaps some of Allen Tate's view of its unsuitability for the making of a myth.

> The form of my poem rises out of a past that so overwhelms the present with its worth and vision that I'm at a loss to explain my delusion that there exist any real links between that past and a future destiny worthy of it. The "destiny" is long since completed, perhaps the little last section of my poem is a hangover echo of it—but it hangs suspended somewhere in ether like an Absalom by his hair. The bridge as a symbol today has no significance beyond an economical approach to shorter hours, quicker lunches, behaviorism and toothpicks. And inasmuch as the bridge is a symbol of all such poetry as I am interested in writing it is my present fancy that a year from now I'll be more contented working in an office than before. . . . If only America were half as worthy today to be spoken of as Whitman spoke of it fifty years ago there might be something for me to say—not that Whitman received or required any tangible proof of his intimations, but that time has shown how increasingly lonely and ineffectual his confidence stands.

It seemed unlikely in 1926 that *The Bridge* would ever be composed; and yet by July 24 the barriers had broken. He wrote the "Proem: To Brooklyn Bridge" and sent it with an exultant "Hail Brother!" to Waldo Frank. "I feel an absolute music in the air again, and some tremendous rondure floating somewhere." For five weeks "my plans are soaring again, the conception swells." More than half of *The Bridge* was written in this long-delayed burst of creation. And then distrust of his materials and distrust of himself plunged his curve of hope down again. "I seem to be going through an extremely distrustful mood in regard to most of my work lately," he wrote Allen Tate in January of 1927.

In March of 1928 he cried out to Waldo Frank, the "dear repository of my faith," that "God knows, some kind of substantial synthesis of opinion is needed before I can feel confident in writing about anything but my shoestrings." And in April, writing to me, he blamed the age for his paralysis of doubt. "The spiritual disintegration of our period becomes more painful to me every day, so much so that I now find myself baulked by doubt as to the validity of practically every metaphor I coin."

There were no fluctuations in his spirit. "I haven't had a creative thought

227

for so long that I feel quite lost and *spurlos versenkt*," he told one of his oldest friends on October 23, 1928. And to Isidor Schneider on May 1, 1929, he wrote, "I haven't so far completed so much as one additional section to *The Bridge*. It's coming out this fall in Paris, regardless. ———If it eventuates that I have the wit or inspiration to add to it later—such additions can be incorporated in some later edition." That, of course, he never did.

6.

The consensus of the critics is that *The Bridge* was a failure. L. S. Dembo, in summarizing the charges of Crane's detractors, includes the charge that "a loss of faith in his subject which occurred during the writing of the poem destroyed whatever logic there may have been in the original plan." According to Dembo, "*The Bridge* has been considered an abortive attempt to establish an American myth and a failure in meaning, form, and style."

It seems to me that too little emphasis has been placed on the fact, confessed by Crane, that *The Bridge* was never finished. It was begun from both ends, but there were gaps that were never spanned. At least two projected sections were never written. Lamely, Crane explained to friends that he was letting the Crosbys publish the unfinished *Bridge* because he could always finish it later. But he made no effort to connect the sections he had already written and to add new ones. There was no final effort to unify the poem into an epic.

The lack of unification of conception, theme, and development is the second major shortcoming of the poem to emphasize. Weber is right: "nothing useful can be accomplished, therefore, in persisting in the consideration of *The Bridge* as a unified poem." L. S. Dembo has persisted longer than most, but only by unnaturally forcing the construction and by accepting illogical symbolism. But even Dembo declares that "as a quest, *The Bridge* is actually a romantic lyric given epic implications." Here again Weber is right: "*The Bridge* is a collection of individual lyrics of varying quality." And indeed there is much to be said for Weber's division of *The Bridge* into four main groups of poems rather than the nine sections set up by Crane.

It is best, therefore, to give up the attempt to read *The Bridge* as an epic of the modern consciousness, the Myth of America, and instead to read its parts as individual poems separable from the original epic design. Read this way, it is difficult to deny greatness to "Proem: To Brooklyn Bridge" and "Atlantis"—the two parts that are devoted to the mystical portent of Brooklyn Bridge. And to these should be added "Ave Maria," a poetic flight soaring from Columbus' journal. It is possible that these three poems, and especially "Proem," tapped that potential reservoir of emotions of a higher order that I had spoken of in my 1925 essay on Hart Crane, the young titan.

7.

On the ship taking him to Vera Cruz in April of 1931, Crane "had better than usual luck by meeting on the second day out the great Dr. Hans Zinsser, of Harvard, who was probably the world's greatest bacteriologist." Crane lauded his new friend—and borrowed money from him. "And what a man besides!" he exclaimed after reaching Mexico City in Zinsser's company. "He arrived along with me last night with letters from the state and war departments and a half a dozen rats in the hold loaded with deadly typhus. He is to conduct some local experiments and then return to Harvard in two weeks. . . . Zinsser, a product of Heidelberg, the Sorbonne, Pasteur Institute and other places besides American Universities, knows and has more interesting ideas about literature than almost anyone I have ever met. What conversations we had!— He's about 51, bandy legged from riding fast horses, looks about 40 at most, writes damn good poetry (which he claims he'd rather do than excel as he does in the scientific world) and in carelessness and largesse is a thoroughbred."

Some time after getting settled in Mexico, Crane wrote a prose poem, "Havana Rose," about Zinsser and the stop at Vera Cruz enroute to Mexico City. "Havana Rose" is a moment of lucidity in the lurid confusion of Crane's last year; it contains, it seems to me, the key to Crane's tragic untold story.

Havana Rose

Let us strip the desk for action—now we have a house in Mexico . . . That night in Vera Cruz—verily for me "the True Cross"—let us remember the Doctor and my thoughts, my humble, fond remembrances of the great bacteriologist . . . The wind, that night, the clamour of incessant shutters, doors, and the watchman tiptoeing the successive patio balconies trundling with a typical pistol—trying to muffle doors—and the pharos shine—the mid-wind midnight stroke of it, its milklike regularity above my bath partition through the lofty, dusty glass—Cortez—Cortez—his crumbled palace in the square—the typhus in the trap, the Doctor's rat trap. Where? Somewhere in Vera Cruz—to bring—to take—to mix—to ransom—to deduct—to cure. . . .

The rats played ring around the rosy (in their basement basinette)—the Doctor supposedly slept, supposedly in #35—thus in my wakeful watches at least—the lighthouse flashed. . . . whirled. . . . delayed, and struck—*again, again.* Only the Mayans surely slept—whose references to typhus and whose records spurred the Doctor into something nigh those metaphysics that are typhoid plus and engaged him once before to death's beyond and back again,—antagonistic wills—into immunity. Tact, horsemanship, courage, were germicides to him. . . .

Poets may not be doctors, but doctors are rare poets when roses leap like rats—and too, when rats make rose nozzles of pink death around white teeth. . . .

And during the wait over dinner at La Diana, the doctor had said—who was American also—"You cannot heed the negative, so might go on to undeserved doom . . . must therefore loose yourself within a pattern's mastery that you can conceive, that you can yield to—by which also you win and gain mastery and happiness which is your own from birth."

There had been an exciting growth in the period when the vision of *The Bridge* intoxicated Crane; then came the crisis of 1924–25; and the entrapment ("Or perhaps I've made too many affable compromises"—Crane in 1931); and finally the decline and the destruction of his genius. In his last days he kept referring to himself as a "rat in a trap."

In "A Poet's Suicide and Some Reflections," in the *New English Weekly* (June 23, 1932), I described the suicide act.

A few seconds before noon on April 27 Hart Crane, wearing an overcoat over pajamas, came up on deck on the Ward liner "Orizaba," then about three hundred miles north of Havana. He had just visited a friend's cabin and said goodbye, but not in a way to foretell his next and last action. As the whistle blew he discarded the overcoat and dropped over the stern. . . . The person* who described his death to me saw Crane drop—not dive or leap—overboard, but he was some distance away, and when he had run back to the stern Crane was not visible. His opinion is that Crane was sucked back under the ship and killed by

* The painter Stefan Hirsch.

the churning propeller. The ship, of course, stopped and lowered a boat, fruit-lessly. The captain is reported as believing that a shark devoured the poet. Such was the extinguishing, at the age of thirty-three, of the rich promise contained in Hart Crane.

What happened on the road from the time when Crane wrote, "I feel an enor-mous power in me—that seems almost supernatural," and those last days in Mexico when he said, "I'm just a careening idiot, with a talent for humor at times, and for insult and desecration at others"? What happened is the hitherto untold story of Hart Crane, and I have written here a brief for a certain way of telling it. But I must add that this is a story that perhaps will never be con-vincingly told—with the whole truth hidden from both Crane and his friends.

CHAPTER 13

Chaplinesque

In the fall of 1923 one could walk about Greenwich Village and find a good unfurnished apartment for rent within a few hours. I took a small one on West 11th Street and moved in on October 1. On the fourth night after, at about half past ten, the bell rang insistently; but I had gone to bed and did not answer. My wife and I were still not completely unpacked, and the apartment was cluttered with unopened boxes. Besides, we had had a tiring day. We weren't receiving.

The next morning I found that my stock with the landlord's family on the first floor was high. From a young Paganelli I learned, when I went down for the mail, that it was Charlie Chaplin who had called the previous evening. In my mailbox I found a note from Waldo Frank explaining the call. Frank invited me to follow him and Hart Crane and Charlie Chaplin over to Paul Rosenfeld's apartment, which Frank had borrowed for a month. But even though the three of them had talked until dawn, as Hart told me later in the day, I had, of course, picked up the note several hours too late to join even the tailend of the conversation.

In *My Autobiography* Chaplin tells the story of the evening I didn't meet him, though he naturally leaves out that fact. He also misdates the evening. Chaplin begins the account by saying, "I came to know Waldo Frank through . . . *Our America*. . . . Waldo was the first to write seriously about me. So, naturally, we became very good friends." Waldo had indeed hailed Chaplin in 1919 as "our most significant and most authentic dramatic figure." Waldo had made this judgment after seeing such early films as *The Immigrant*, *A Dog's Life*, and

Shoulder Arms, which did contain scenes of acting greatness. In *The Immigrant* it was card-playing of marvelous dexterity; in *A Dog's Life* it was a wonderful pantomime with hands; in *Shoulder Arms* it was Charlie disguised as a tree that is unsurpassed comedy. Nevertheless Frank's judgment was bold in 1919, as we recall that Chaplin had not yet produced *The Kid* and the great tragicomic films of the 1920s.*

I had heard of Chaplin's sympathetic interest in the intelligentsia who were speaking out against reaction in the early postwar years. In 1919 I had been engaged at no salary as an assistant editor of a new radical magazine, *Modernist*. The initial task of this publication was to raise money to print its first issue, and Chaplin had been appealed to. I remember the excitement the impecunious staff felt on the day Chaplin subscribed for a ten-dollar share of "stock." So it was true, what we had heard—Chaplin was a friend of Frank Harris and Max Eastman.

Not only had 1920 seen remarkable literary achievements—*This Side of Paradise, Main Street, Beyond the Horizon, Emperor Jones*, "Hugh Selwyn Mauberly," and *The Sacred Wood*—it was also in that great opening year of the new decade that *The Kid* appeared. Hart Crane saw it in Cleveland the following year and wrote me about it in Paris. "I must tell you that my greatest dramatic treat . . . was recently enjoyed when Charlie Chaplin's *The Kid* was shown here. Comedy, I may say, has never reached a higher level in this country before. We have (I cannot be too sure of this for my own satisfaction) in Chaplin a dramatic genius that truly approaches the fabulous sort. I could write pages on the overtones and brilliant subtleties of this picture, for which nobody but Chaplin can be responsible as he wrote it, directed it,—and I am quite sure had much to do with the settings which are unusually fine."

With this letter came lines of a poem, "Chaplinesque," inspired by *The Kid*. "My poem," Hart said, "is a sympathetic attempt to put in words some of the Chaplin pantomime, so beautiful, and so full of eloquence, and so modern." Before I could answer, another letter came from Hart. "Here you are with the rest of the Chaplin poem. I know not if you will like it,—but to me it has a real appeal. I have made that 'infinitely gentle, infinitely suffering thing' of Eliot's

* Frank had quickly corrected his first impression in 1917 that "Charles Chaplin is an extremely brilliant clown, but he is also an unhealthy one." In 1924, Frank said "Mr. Chaplin is far from unhealthy. His art indeed is a symbol of health in a completely morbid world."

into the symbol of the kitten. I feel that, from my standpoint, the pantomime of Charlie represents fairly well the futile gesture of the poet in U.S.A. today, perhaps elsewhere too. And yet the heart lives on."

Apparently I sent Hart a reaction to "Chaplinesque," but I cannot recall what it was. Hart's friends instinctively saved his letters, but he does not seem to have been a letter-saver at all. Or did he destroy the accumulated correspondence from his friends in one of his drunken rages? Whatever the reason, virtually all originals of letters to him have been lost, and I did not make carbon copies of mine. So I find Hart replying to an unrecallable reaction of mine:

> As you did not "get" my idiom in "Chaplinesque," I feel rather like doing my best to explain myself. I am moved to put Chaplin with the poets (of today); hence the "we." In other words, he especially in *The Kid*, made me feel myself, as a poet, as being "in the same boat" with him. Poetry, the human feelings, "the kitten," is so crowded out of the humdrum, rushing, mechanical scramble of to-day that the man who would preserve them must duck and camouflage for dear life to keep them or keep himself from annihilation. I have since learned that I am by no means alone in seeing these things in the buffooneries of the tragedian, Chaplin, (if you want to read the opinions of the London and Paris presses, see *Literary Digest*, Oct. 8th) and in the poem I have tried to express these "social sympathies" in words corresponding somewhat to the antics of the actor. I may have failed, as only a small number of those I have shown it to have responded with any clear answer,—but on the other hand, I realize that the audience for my work will always be quite small. I freely admit to a liking for the thing, myself.

Apparently I stood my ground, for in his next letter Hart wrote that "I can't blame you for not seeing as much in 'Chaplinesque' as myself because I realize that the technic of the thing is virtuosic. . . . Chaplin may be a sentimentalist, after all, but he carries the theme with such power and universal portent that sentimentality is made to transcend itself. . . . It is because I feel that I have captured the arrested climaxes and evasive victories of his gestures in words, somehow, that I like the poem as much as anything I have done . . . I was much surprised that Sherwood Anderson should like it, who is not prone to care for complicated expressions."

I was able to do something practical for Hart: I secured publication for "Chaplinesque." Arthur Moss, who had edited a Latin Quarter magazine in New York, was then publishing *Gargoyle*, an American expatriates' magazine in Paris' Latin Quarter. He had made me a contributing editor, and I promptly did him the very good turn of offering "Chaplinesque." Hart was pleased. Extravagantly, he wrote me on Christmas Day of 1921, "note of the seventh announcing my presence on the boulevards (in Chaplinesque attire) provided me with rich materials for a kind of Christmas tree, at least as thrilling as any of remotest childhood memories."

"We became very good friends," Chaplin writes of himself and Waldo Frank, while referring to those years when he was making such films as *Sunnyside*, *The Kid*, and *The Pilgrim*. Frank has told of incidents in their friendship in "Funny-Legs," his *New Yorker* profile of Chaplin, which he signed Search-Light, pointedly hyphenated. Frank, it probably needs recalling, was one of the first regular contributors of profiles to the *New Yorker*; he published twenty in one year. But the form was then primitive—brief, a mere elaboration of the seventeenth-century Character that English writers took over from Theocritus. The chief incident Frank narrated in "Funny-Legs"—one not mentioned in *My Autobiography*—was the visit to the Cirque Medrano which Frank, Jacques Copeau, and Charles Chaplin made in 1920.

> When Chaplin, flanked by his friends, slipped into his seat in the first ringside row, the brothers Fratellini were cavorting in the sawdust. They had the funnel-shaped house focussed on themselves. It was hard to say if anyone had remarked Chaplin's entrance.
>
> But the Fratellini act was the signal for intermission. The high-tiered human monster, suddenly shouting *Charlot!* with a thousand throats, avalanched down upon a single spot at the arena rail, where a little man in a dapper dinner coat sat blinking. He was engulfed, and lost. A score of gendarmes broke into the delirious maze of men and women, pressing on Chaplin as if they were hungry to devour him. The police formed a phalanx about him and he was shuttled out into the Place Pigalle.
>
> But the cry *Chalot!* had got there first. The square, the boulevards that lead to it, turned into a magnetized mob; thousands came pouring, pushing, shouting. Men touched him; women tried to kiss him. At last, with his London-tailored garments reduced to a state of a rummage sale in the Bronx, Charlie was swept into a strategic taxi.

There was a minuscule "magnetized mob" following Chaplin on that early October night in 1923 when Waldo Frank brought him to my door. Frank had taken Chaplin to dinner in Greenwich Village and had proposed that they pick up a couple of his young friends—Hart and me—after dinner. So Frank and Chaplin had climbed one flight at 45 Grove Street and rapped on the door of Crane's one-room apartment. Crane was in pyjamas and playing his Victrola.

"I opened and in walked Waldo Frank," Hart wrote his mother the next day; "— behind him came a most pleasant-looking, twinkling little man in a black derby—'Let me introduce you to Mr. Charles Chaplin,' said Waldo."

"I was so surprised that I acted natural," Hart told me in a gusty recital of the meeting. To his mother he wrote: "Well!—I was quickly urged out of my nightclothes and the three of us walked arm in arm over to where Waldo is staying. . . . All the way we were trailed by enthusiastic youngsters. People seem to spot Charlie in the darkness. He is so very gracious that he never discourages anything but rude advances."

On the way they stopped at 144 West 11th Street to rout me out. The crowd that had followed them from Grove Street shouted advice to Chaplin as he waited on the steps. "Don't go in there, Charlie. That's a bad house." The small commotion drew the landlord's son, a young lawyer, to open the front door. He was bowled over by confronting Charles Chaplin. Since I appeared not to be at home, the little procession moved off in the direction of Union Square.

The all-night conversation of the poet, the novelist, and the mime ought to have been extraordinary, for each was an extraordinary man of the Twenties. Hart Crane had already won the plaudits of judicious watchers for new talents among the poets. Waldo Frank had assaulted the Genteel Tradition in American life and prophesied in *Our America* the coming of poets like Crane who would celebrate a Whitmanian vision. And there was Charles Chaplin, the gay circumventer of the Genteel Tradition who was playing with the ideas for his next great film, *The Gold Rush*.

In the Keystone comedies, Chaplin had been a great genius of *commedia dell' arte*. We knew that he ranked with the great clowns of history, with Deburau of France, praised by Baudelaire, and Grimaldi of England, praised by Coleridge and Leigh Hunt. But his creation had been greater than any of theirs. Chaplin had not played himself, but he had created and played Charlot, "the little tramp." To Harlequin and Columbine and Pierrot and Pantaloon and Robin Goodfellow he added Charlot, and Charlot won the heart of the whole world.

Charlot was born in 1914 when Mack Sennett made the one-reel *Kid Auto Races at Venice*. Chaplin has told us that he had no idea of the character until he had improvised the dress and make-up and strutted forth, swinging a rattan cane. Then he felt the character and explained: "This fellow is many-sided, a tramp, a gentleman, a poet, a dreamer, a lonely fellow, always hopeful of romance and adventure. . . . However, he is not above picking up cigarette butts or robbing a baby of its candy. And, of course, if the occasion warrants it, he will kick a lady in the rear—but only in extreme anger!"

Hart wrote his mother: "I can't begin to tell you what an evening, night and *morning* it was." But he was scarcely coherent the next day when he exclaimed to me over the joys of meeting Chaplin. He even gave me the strong impression that he had fallen in love. Hart's letter to his mother went on to say:

> Among other things Charlie told us his plans (and the story of it) for his next great film [*The Gold Rush*]. He has a five acre studio all his own now in Berkeley, and is here in New York at present to see that the first film he has produced in it gets over profitably. He doesn't act in it. But he wrote the story, directed and produced it entirely himself. It's running now for just a week or so more at the "Lyric" theatre to box prices. Then it will be released all over the country. *A Woman of Paris* it's called. . . .
>
> Our talk was very intimate—Charlie told us the complete Pola Negri story—which "romance" is now ended. And there were other things about his life, his hopes and spiritual desires which were very fine & interesting. He has been through so much, is very lonely (says Hollywood hasn't a dozen people he enjoys talking to or who understand his work) and yet is so radiant and healthy, wistful, gay and *young*. He is 35, but half his head is already grey. You cannot imagine a more perfect and natural gentleman. . . . Stories (marvellous ones he knows!) told with such subtle mimicry that you rolled on the floor. Such graceful wit, too—O that man has a mind. . . . I am very happy in the intense clarity of spirit that a man like Chaplin gives one if he is honest enough to receive it.

Such was Hart's report twelve hours after the meeting. Forty-one years later Charles Chaplin published his recollections of that evening which he inaccurately referred to as "interesting evenings [*sic*] together. . . . They were enthralling symposiums, the three of us reaching out mentally for the subtle definition of our thoughts." He remembered that Hart had a "gentle sweetness."

"We discussed the purpose of poetry," Chaplin also remembered. "I said it was a love letter to the world. 'A very small world,' said Hart ruefully. He spoke of my work as being in the tradition of the Greek comedies. I told him that

I had tried to read an English translation of Aristophanes but could never finish it." We also know from Chaplin's autobiography that Hart sent Chaplin an inscribed copy of *White Buildings*. But the inscription referred to *The Kid* only: "To Charles Chaplin in memory of *The Kid* from Hart Crane. 20 January, '28."

Waldo Frank dashed off a profile of Chaplin that was included in *Time Exposures* (1926), a collection of his *New Yorker* profiles. He had stayed in Chaplin's home in Los Angeles and had seen *The Gold Rush*; now he declared that Chaplin "has become a self-doubting, melancholy, haunted man—oscillant between gayety and despair. . . . He goes on seeking. And his quest slows his work, sicklies the pure lyricism of his art with a pale cast of thought. . . . Will there be naught at the end, but the unceasing pain of the unceasing question?" Frank even asked: "Is it all a mirage—this power and this fame of Charlie Chaplin?"

By 1929, when he wrote his prophetic book *The Re-Discovery of America*, Frank answered these questions and placed Chaplin in his scheme of "post-culture" (the cultural dissolution of the Old World) and "pre-culture" (the primitiveness of the New World). The New World liked Chaplin, because he offered "a myth of refuge within the self." But he was equally popular in the Old World for the same reason. Comedy, Frank declared, is the art of escape, and he wondered "if escape could make more loveliness than his," Chaplin's, escape. "Its motif is a sly self-preservation through a refusal of the challenge of our jungle and a retreat into a personal realm of faëry." He called Chaplin a pessimist and a defeatist.

The marvelous fact is that Chaplin created in the spirit of Nature, as Shakespeare did when he created the figure of Falstaff. Note well what Charles Chaplin, Jr., has said about his father's creation of Charlot, the Little Fellow, the Little Tramp. "With the tramp outfit came the tramp personality. It wasn't a studied character. *It was just released whole from somewhere deep within my father.* It was really my father's alter ego, the little boy who never grew up: ragged, cold, hungry, but still thumbing his nose at the world." (Italics added.) What one should be marvelling at is the genius, the creative stuff, the demiurgic force that makes Charlot have his being on equal terms with a creation of Nature. The pity is that Frank found in Charlot only "the sureness of the unreal, with beauty and love platonically present," and a feeble daring to "give a fillip—even a kick to the world." Chaplin transcends all talk of escapism.

His transcendence is revealed in his own appraisal of the tramp. "He was myself," Chaplin said in a retrospect of his life, "a comic spirit, something within me that said I must express this. I felt so free. The adventure of it. The madness. I can do any mad, crazy thing I like."

"Thanks to the nature of life," A. R. Orage once asserted while exposing the fallacy of aristocracy, "there is an insubordinate imp in each of us that prefers in the long run all the horrors of freedom to all the amenities of benevolent slavery." Charlot is that insubordinate imp in each of us who is undefeatable in his love of liberty.

Frank's last word on Chaplin was in a footnote to his "placement" of the great comic. "Rousseau is the philosopher of our epoch of death and birth: Chaplin is its poet." Which brings us back to Crane's remark years before: "I was moved to put Chaplin with poets (of today)"—hence the "we" in the first line of "Chaplinesque": "We make our meek adjustments."

We do not know how Chaplin took Frank's criticism. In 1942 I attended a dinner in New York in honor of Waldo Frank. I heard someone say excitedly: "There's Charlie Chaplin," and there he was among the diners, though not at the head table. But there is nothing about this in *My Autobiography*. Although his recollections are extensive, Chaplin drops Frank after recalling the meeting I missed in 1923. How many times I have regretted not answering the doorbell that night.

CHAPTER 14

The Classicism of Robert Frost

One night in the fall of 1926 I found a note in my mailbox that gave me a jump of excitement. I saved that note for many years but cannot reproduce it now, for it vanished with other literary effects I prized, in the aforementioned illegal sale of goods I had trustfully stored in a warehouse. It may turn up some day in a pile of rummage; but it is likely, I think, that it was destroyed as worthless at the time of the auction.

The note on a small sheet of paper—was it torn from a notebook?—was signed "Robert Frost." I do not remember whether it was penciled or penned, or if it contained any message other than a request for me to telephone its signer at Ridgely Torrence's number in the morning. I was surprised, but immediately guessed that the note had something to do with an interpretative essay on Frost I had published a year and a half earlier in the *Saturday Review of Literature*. I had heard indirectly that Frost had liked this essay. He had been to Dartmouth "barding around," and he had told a Wesleyan classmate of mine, George R. Potter, who was teaching there, that he liked my *Saturday Review* piece, because "it said something new about me." Potter had written me this praise. So I was expectant of some sign of favorable interest in me when I called the Torrence number from the pay telephone at Charles French Restaurant on Sixth Avenue, where in those days I often went for breakfast.

Frost shyly told me why he had left the note at 144 West 11th Street. John Farrar, the young editor at George H. Doran Company, a Vermonter, wanted to publish a biography of Frost. He was launching a series—the Murray Hill Biographies—and had commissioned books on Upton Sinclair, Nathaniel

Hawthorne, Edwin Arlington Robinson. Now he was looking for somebody to write on Frost. Very tactfully Frost sounded me on my willingness to undertake such a commission. He was so tentative in his approach that it would have been easy to decline the flattering suggestion. But I said at once that I would like to discuss the suggestion, and Frost invited me to dinner at the Torrence apartment on Morton Street deep in the Village.

In 1926—at this stage in my own career as a young critic—being asked by Robert Frost to write a critical biography of him was gratifying. Frost was, by this time, recognized as a preeminent American poet. His 1924 Pulitzer Prize had established him as a poet of ultimate achievement. But it had not always been so.

Frost had written poetry for twenty-five years without recognition, until Ezra Pound wrote his review of *A Boy's Will* for London and Chicago literary magazines. Published perhaps a dozen times in American magazines, Frost had had a devoted reader in Mrs. Frost; but he had been pretty often rejected for all these years, and he had been deeply hurt in his isolation. (To his dying day he never allowed the later editors of the *Atlantic Monthly* to forget that the *Atlantic* declined his poems in the 1890s.) Nor had he experienced any literary fellowship until he went to London in 1912. Of a literary milieu—of bookshops for poetry lovers, of cafés for writers, of lectures and readings, of studio teas and summer colonies, of editorial sessions and group-anthologies, of parties and Bohemia—Frost had known nothing.

Pound had immediately recognized the genuineness of Frost's poetry and introduced him—at the age of thirty-nine—to literary London; Frost who had been starving for recognition ate unforgettably of the nourishing food of corroboration of his gift. Early in June of 1913 Pound wrote to his father, saying "I'll try to get you a copy of Frost. I'm using mine at present to boom him and get his name stuck about." Pound's London review of *A Boy's Will* appeared in the *New Freewoman* on September 1, 1913, and his recognition of Frost has the air of being "dashed off." It read, in part, "Mr. Frost's book . . . has the tang of the New Hampshire woods, and it has just this utter simplicity. . . . This man has the good sense to speak naturally and to paint the thing, the thing as he sees it. . . . One reads the book for the 'tone,' which is homely, by intent, and pleasing, never doubting that it comes directly from his own life. . . . He is without sham and without affectation."

"Dashed off" it may have been, but this review did strike the keynote of the criticism of Frost during his 1913–1930 period. Norman Douglas, for example, had called *A Boy's Will*, even before Pound's review, "an image of things really heard and seen. There is a wild, racy flavor in his poems: they sound the inevitable response to nature which is the hallmark of true lyric feeling." Of *North of Boston*, Edward Thomas wrote perceptively: "It speaks, and it is poetry." Lascelles Abercrombie spelled out what Pound and Thomas had asserted about tones. "It is, in fact," Abercrombie said in his review of *North of Boston*, "poetry composed, as far as possible, in a language of things. . . . [Frost] seems trying to capture and hold within metrical patterns the very tones of speech— the rise and fall, the stressed pauses and little hurries, of spoken language." And Wilfrid Wilson Gibson joined the chorus when he declared that "Mr. Frost has turned the living speech of men and women into poetry." Thus was the first phase of the criticism of Frost opened, the phase that began with Pound's excited discovery of a new American poet.

It was, then, no peer I'd been invited to meet. And it was with some eagerness that I made my way next evening to the Torrence apartment.

I had met Ridgely Torrence several times previously at 107 Waverly Place, where he lived in the top-floor apartment his friend William Vaughn Moody had once occupied. Moody's rich widow had kept the apartment and put the Torrences in it, and I had invited myself there in 1918 to look at the amateur paintings of William Vaughn Moody that graced the walls. My memory of these is dim and my notes on them disappeared in the auction sale disaster, but I believe they were pictures of moors and the sea, bluish in tone and misty in effect. Torrence was the self-effacing poetry editor of the *New Republic*, and was recognized by a few—Colum and Robinson and Frost—as himself a fine poet.

I was greeted by tall, gentle Ridgely and by Olivia Howard Dunbar, his writing wife who was to write a book after Mrs. Moody's death in 1932 about this shining salon mistress—Harriet Moody who had encouraged Hart Crane when he was sixteen. I was then presented to the house guest. "Prohibition cocktails" appeared, and we drank them standing up. I noticed that Frost was no sipper, but downed his drink like a Vermont farmer, and we sat down to table. As might have been expected on this occasion, and as always happened in his company, Frost led the conversation and contributed the most.

What he told me was certainly flattering, but it was clearly not intended to flatter. He said that when Farrar had asked him to suggest someone to write a

Murray Hill Biography of him, he had named me because I had said something different about him and he felt I would make a critical book. He made it plain that he did not want a personal life that invaded his privacy. He wanted a biography that would be a critical account of his work, one that would observe the line between the public and the private life and would respect his reticence about his family life. He had never written me about my *Saturday Review* essay, because, he said, "I was waiting for a chance to do something to show my appreciation." That chance had come when John Farrar had asked him to nominate a biographer.

I told Frost that the restrictions he imposed on his biographer were entirely acceptable. I would much rather write a critical biography than a personal, probing, psychological study such as was coming into vogue. And so we parted early that night with the understanding that Farrar would offer me a contract.

In the summer of 1924, I had read all of Frost I could find. What started me on this thorough study of a poet whose poems I had hitherto read only sporadically was his most recent book—his fourth—*New Hampshire*. I had been surprised and delighted by the title poem, a Horatian satire in a contemporary manner. I had not expected to find a bucolic poet at play in the midst of the sophisticated literary currents of the period. But there Frost was, knowledgeable of the new literary forces, but humorous and satirical about them. "New Hampshire" was different from anything Frost had written before; and I, a modern, responded with an enthusiasm not felt for *A Boy's Will* and the other early volumes. These I had respected, but *New Hampshire* raised my appreciation of them by giving me insight into the poet's direction.

> I may as well confess myself the author
> Of several books against the world in general.

What did Frost mean by these lines, I asked; for until then Frost had been classified by Amy Lowell, Waldo Frank, and other champions of the "new poetry" as a votary of the new movement in American literature. But in "New Hampshire" Frost seemed to disassociate himself from the new wave of American writers. He took a stand against their tendencies and revolts.

I was made equally curious by Frost's reply in "New Hampshire" to "a narrow choice the age insists on." According to the poem, Frost had been commanded: "Choose you which you will be—a prude, or puke, / Mewling and puking in the public arms." "Me for the hills where I don't have to choose" was Frost's first reply, and then he said: "How about being a good Greek, for instance?" In that question I seemed to discover a key to Frost's poetic intentions, but I needed corroboration. That corroboration I received from an accident of reading that same summer.

In a conversation with Edwin Seaver about letters and the young generation, Seaver told me of the stimulation he had received from Irving Babbitt's famous course at Harvard on Rousseau and romanticism. He so far overcame the prejudice against Babbitt that I had acquired from the aspersions of H. L. Mencken and Van Wyck Brooks that I found myself carrying Seaver's copy of *Rousseau and Romanticism* home with me. Soon I was engrossed in this illuminating study of the imagination, its nature, kinds, and function; and the further I read into it, the more light it seemed to throw on the poetics of Robert Frost. Babbitt's study of the imagination gave me an explanation of why Frost went against the general drift of the world and why he wanted to be a good Greek: I saw that Frost was not a romantic poet, as some would have it, but a classical poet, as nobody seemed to be remarking.

So I wrote a paper at the end of that summer of 1924 that was intended to show that Robert Frost was a poet of humanistic temper. "The purest classical poet of America today is Robert Frost," I declared at the outset of this paper. This was the "something different," the "something new" that I had said about Frost that led him to leave a note in my mailbox a couple of years later.

I did not know at the time that Irving Babbitt and Paul Elmer More, the leaders of the New Humanism as it was to be called in the last years of the 1920s, had discovered the humanistic nature of Frost's poetry as early as 1916. Nor had I then read an essay on Frost's neighborliness by a follower of Babbitt and More, a young Amherst professor, G. R. Elliott, in which Frost's neighborliness was differentiated from humanitarianism, a romantic cult Frost despised. As Lawrance Thompson was to observe long after Elliott's essay, "the metaphor which represents the key to Frost's social outlook is the metaphor of community relationship: neighborliness." Frost felt, in Thompson's well-chosen words, that "the well-meaning pity of the humanitarians encourages the abandonment of that self-discipline and individual action which is the basic unit of social strength."

A few years later Frost was protesting vigorously against being labeled a New Humanist. He was quite right. His temper was humanistic but his poetry cannot be defined by or confined to intellectual concepts. Lawrance Thompson quite sensibly observes that "certain aspects of the Emersonian position in poetic theory proved to be closely akin to the poetic theory and practice of Robert Frost. But Emerson's aesthetic utterances were elucidated and modified into a somewhat extreme aesthetic by the 'new humanist,' whose dogmatic claims were much too rigid to attract Frost." Let it be repeated: the poet Frost would never enlist under the banner of any school of criticism, New Humanist, Neoclassical or Romantic. And a critic who insists on a label for Frost's philosophy and poetry is too much of a schoolmaster in a field where judgments should be flexible.

"There is some truth in Gorham Munson's early judgment," Malcolm Cowley says in his essay "The Case Against Mr. Frost," referring to the judgment that Frost is "the purest classical poet of America today"; and I would reassert, long after my short biography of Frost appeared, the "some truth" in its early judgment that Cowley concedes.

The most classical trait of Frost, I should say, is the high place he gives to form in his *ars poetica*. In his early conversations with me, he several times mentioned form as one of the highest literary qualities. Four years later, at one of his New School for Social Research lectures, I took down verbatim his definition of creation: "Creation has its end implicit in the beginning but not foreknown." Has a better definition of organic form ever been offered? Frost said it again in 1939 in his prose introduction to *Collected Poems*. Of the course of a true poem, he said that "it has an outcome that though unforeseen was predestined from the first image of the original mood—and indeed from the very mood." The principle of the unforeseen but predestined is the very principle of growth of organic form and in its working exemplifies the classical laws of probability and inevitability.

Frost's classical nature comes out in the boldest contrast when we compare him with one of his romantic contemporaries, that rival for whom he had little esteem, Carl Sandburg. Sandburg declared that the past was a bucket of ashes and sought for "new ways to be new," as Frost named the quest for poetic novelty. He practiced the cult of free verse, inspired by the majestic chanting rhythms of Whitman but producing a banjo version of them, as someone has observed. In time Sandburg became a sentimental humanitarian poet, his credo of "the people, yes" provoking Frost to reply, "The people yes and no."

In contrast, Frost went back for inspiration to the pastoral poetry of Vergil and the satires of Horace. Except for one poem, "The Lovely Shall be Choosers," Frost eschewed free verse—"like playing tennis with the net down," he drily remarked—and practiced in the traditional patterns and forms. His triumph was that in becoming a traditional poet, he escaped being merely conventional and succeeded in being creative. He found, as he put it, "old ways to be new."

How did he achieve newness by working in the old ways? Chiefly, I would say, by experimentation in the "sound of sense." Even as youthful poet, he would have none of the "musicality of literature" theory advanced by Poe and Lanier; and quite early he was drawn to the study of verbal images, the connotation of tones of voice, the sound of sense. What possibilities of the dramatic there were in the sound of sense! This was the thing and not any theory of quantitative verse such as Robert Bridges had expounded to him. "The living part of a poem," he had said in refutation to Bridges, "is the intonation entangled somehow in the syntax, idiom and meaning of a sentence."

Frost used a simple illustration that nonetheless gives the whole meaning of his sound of sense creed. Here is a primer version of sense:

> I see a dog.
> The dog is in the house.
> I will put him out.
> He will come back.

Now let us put this sense into tones of voice:

> There's that dog again.
> Get out of here, you brute!
> Oh, what's the use! He'll come back.

The sounds bring the words to life. Now they are energetic, dramatic, charged with tone—now they can be taken into poetry.

"Sound-posturing," Frost called this principle of composition; "writing with your ear to the voice." To an interviewer he once said: "Take the expression, 'oh.' American poets use it in practically one tone, that of grandeur: 'Oh Soul!' 'Oh Hills!'—'Oh Anything!' That's the way they go. But think of what 'oh' is really capable: the 'oh' of scorn, the 'oh' of amusement, the 'oh' of surprise, the 'oh' of doubt—and there are many more. But these are disdained by the academic poets."

For a motto, Frost took for himself "common in experience—uncommon in writing." This, too, was a classical approach to material. Not the wild or extravagant or eccentric or peculiar or extreme areas of experience—but the central, common, broad areas were to be his material; "uncommonness" was to come from experimentation in the writing of the sound of sense.

By adhering to the traditional forms of poetry and by use of material common in experience, Frost maintained a common ground with the reader, and in this, too, his poetry has a classical air. He had no truck with self-expression but held to the great norm of communication, the ancient relationship of poet and hearer whereby there was a sharing of poetic experience. "Only just as much as we can communicate is literature," he said at the New School for Social Research.

In applying his principle of growth in the development of organic form Frost observed the humanistic law of probability. Around him the romanticists were indulging in the cult of self-expression. With the encouragement of such critics as J. E. Spingarn, the romanticists of the second and third decades of our century were cultivating spontaneity and originality and genius. They made a cult of wonderful possibilities and propagated a doctrine of personal expansiveness. This was alien to Frost's conservative temperament. He was drawn to the probable story and away from the improbable-though-possible story. In *North of Boston* and his other books of the 1914–1930 period, he was the poet of the common in man and nature, not the exploiter of the unique and wonderful. In these books he was an observer of another law of humanistic art—the much misunderstood and misrepresented law of decorum or measure or proportion. His feeling for decorous proportion was yet another classical trait.

The range of Frost's poetry is humanistic. He has written only one poem that could be called naturalistic in the literary sense. That is the terrible "Out, Out—" about the severance of a boy's hand by a buzz saw. At the other extreme from naturalism is the religious poem "The Trial by Existence," which appeared in *A Boy's Will*, the only poem by Frost that I would call religious. The point I want to make is that all the space between the raw naturalism of "Out, Out—" and the religious insight of "Trial by Existence" has been occupied by Frost, and this space may properly be called the humanistic range.

Frost was like an intelligent Greek, the New Humanists said, because he was of a positive and critical turn of mind. He came by this turn of mind from the New England culture he had inherited. Born in Mark Twain's America—in San Francisco in 1874—Frost had been brought east in 1885 to be educated in Emerson's New England. Frost's ancestors had come to New England more

than two centuries earlier. His formative life-experiences took place in a sim-
plified world, the world of the New England farmer from about 1885 to about
1915; and it was in this rural culture that he evolved his classical outlook.

Lawrance Thompson, Frost's authorized biographer, has said that Frost
"knows from long experience that strong men and women will work out a life
that is good in that stubborn contest with rocky soil and short summers. . . . As
a New Hampshire farmer himself in the early years, Frost lived with neighbors
of all classes, many of them his superiors in their ability to make a simple but
sufficient living out of a little. He has never forgotten his respect and admiration for the courage and self-dependence he saw about him during those years.
The rigorous trial by existence in rural communities requires ability and cun-
ning if life is to go on. . . . And Frost has given expression in his poems to that
inner strength and satisfaction which comes from living close to the soil."

"Me for the hills where I don't have to choose," Frost said in 1923, when
invited to face the complex and tormenting questions of modern urban civilization.

When I first visited Frost at Amherst in 1927, I found him, to my surprise,
quite opposed to the educational policy of Alexander Meiklejohn, who had been
president of Amherst College from 1912 to 1924. This was surprising for two
reasons. First, I knew that it had been Meiklejohn who had ruled in 1917 that
Frost's lack of any academic degree didn't matter and had appointed him an *ad
interim* full professor of English. Secondly, I knew that Frost had himself been
a teacher of marked originality, and I thought that a Meiklejohn-run college
would be a congenial environment for him. But I learned that Frost had complained of "Meiklejaundice" during the three years (1917–1920) he had served
under the experimental educator and had repeatedly wanted to resign. Finally
he had gone off to the University of Michigan but had returned to Amherst on
Meiklejohn's departure. "Meiklejaundice," I gathered, was romanticism in
higher education.

Meiklejohn had been gone four years when I spent my first weekend with
Frost, but it was repetitiously evident that his theory and practice still stuck in
the poet's craw, for he talked against them persistently and took a lively, hopeful interest in the presidential succession at Amherst (George Daniel Olds was
resigning and Arthur Stanley Pease was in the offing). Frost conceded that the
English-born Meiklejohn, who had been a professor of philosophy at Brown,

was brilliant; but he doubted him as thinker and as administrator. Meiklejohn had put his liberal-radical views on education into two books: *The Liberal College* (1920) and *Freedom and the College* (1923). But Frost preferred the educational philosophy of Olds and Pease and sided with the faculty conservatives in their resistance to Meiklejohn.

Frost took pains to see that I met two of his friends on the Amherst faculty. Handsome English professor George F. Whicher came to tea; and at the faculty club I had a long talk with Professor G. R. Elliott, who was then writing *The Cycle of Modern Poetry* and sought advice about a publisher. Elliott revealed to me a strong religious interest and was later to declare that Irving Babbitt, "a rigorous moral humanist of New England, had indirectly done much for the best interests of religion."

Ezra Pound was even more of a topic than Meiklejohn in my first long session with Frost. I thought that Frost was prompted to reminisce about Pound because I had discussed Pound the night before in a lecture to Amherst students, but I soon found that Frost wanted his biographer to know that he felt deep gratitude to our expatriate poet. I could see that he was ambivalent toward Pound, but I noted few signs of hostility whereas he frankly confessed to the state of being fascinated by the young master.

The critics' recognition of Frost and the public's recognition of him in buying his books were in step with each other in the 1920s. I looked into the matter of Frost's sales when I began writing the biography, and I found his sales position in 1927 most promising. At that date his most popular book was *North of Boston*, which had risen above twenty thousand copies. Next was *New Hampshire*, which had had five printings since its appearance in 1923. *Mountain Interval* had also required five printings. The encouraging thing was that all of Frost's titles were in steadily increasing demand; and *Selected Poems*, which appeared in 1923, had reached its fourth printing by 1927. These figures seem small when placed beside the totals achieved by Frost's books in the early 1960s, but they were impressive in the 1920s and were undisputable evidence of Frost's well-established popularity.

Recognition of Frost by the bestowal of honors was also begun in the Twenties. The chief of these was the Pulitzer Prize for Poetry awarded him in 1924 for *New Hampshire*, published the previous year. In 1930, as the decade ended in the onset of a vast economic engulfment, a *Collected Poems* was published to signalize the solid reputation of the poet.

I very quickly became acquainted with the angry side of Robert Frost, which at first astonished me. The new literary generation of the Twenties was friendly toward him, but he had no feeling of solidarity with them. He had been one of the advisory editors of *Seven Arts*; he had been touted by Amy Lowell as a figure of the new poetry; Waldo Frank had seen him as a precursor of "Our America." But Frost was hostile, as he showed in the satire of "New Hampshire," to the liberal drift of the new generation. One of the journalistic buglers of the liberal writers who were coming to dominate the literary scene was Burton Rascoe, who ran in the New York *Herald Tribune* a diary of his comings and goings in literary society. He had misreported remarks of Frost about Eliot and Joyce at a private gathering, and Frost resented being interviewed without his knowledge. My surprise was great when Frost showed his resentment and told me that he had thought of going to New York to use his fists on the brash journalist.

It was quite noticeable that Frost had no praise for living poets. He never mentioned Edwin Arlington Robinson in all the talks I had with him between 1926 and 1934. He did say that Wallace Stevens, who had been in his class at Harvard but unknown to him at the time, made a formal garden in the wilderness of life; and he once expressed a liking for Thomas Hornsby Ferril. He was impatient with Louis Untermeyer's marital changes and reversals but said never a word about his verse or criticism. That is all I can remember of his references to contemporary poets.

Nor did Frost express any esteem for the new prose writers of the Twenties. He derided the novels of Sinclair Lewis—"Sinkler" or "Sink" Lewis, he called him. But he liked detective and mystery fiction, and was the first to tell me about the Philo Vance stories of S. S. Van Dine (Willard Huntington Wright).

He was good-natured in recalling a meeting he had with H. L. Mencken. Apparently each had liked the other's conversation. An early lyric of Frost's had concluded:

> They would not find me changed from him they knew—
> Only more sure of all I thought was true.

"Mencken and I agreed," Frost said, "about the virtue of not changing our minds. Mencken said that he had changed his mind only once. As a reporter he got sick of witnessing executions and finally decided that capital punishment was a bad thing. But after a while he decided that he had been right in approving of capital punishment and wrong to change his mind on this matter. Capital punishment was a good thing after all. I told him I had never changed my mind on any important thing."

Frost's jealousy of living poets was understandable, though unexpected by his friends who early came to regard him as a poet without rivals. We must remember that from 1892 to 1912—twenty years—Frost had been denied publication so many times while poets he knew to be his inferiors were being published so often that he contracted a deep-seated jealousy. It required decades of reassurance of his acceptance for jealousy to run its course. All these— the resentment of criticism, the anger at the new literary liberalism, the jealousy of his contemporaries—were premonitory symptoms of the massively angry Frost who would emerge fully in the 1930s and threaten to become a reactionary poet, though he never went the full distance to reaction.

Had any poet in America achieved by 1930 a more secure position than Frost's? He was fifty-six years old and had published five volumes of poems garnered from thirty-five years of mature devotion to his craft. He had extended his range from the early lyrics of *A Boy's Will* through the dramatic narratives of *North of Boston* to the symbolic and philosophical poems of *West-Running Brook*. He was New England's poet in the great line from Longfellow and Emerson. And no one (except Edmund Wilson) doubted his permanence. Would poems like "The Pasture," "The Death of the Hired Hand," "The Road Not Taken," "Stopping by Woods on a Snowy Evening," and "Acquainted with the Night" ever disappear from the anthologies? Surely Frost could face the new decade of change—and everyone knew times would change in the Thirties—with the utmost feeling of security in his place in literary history.

Yet Frost was entering the black decade of his life. His personal life was to be filled with grief and death. The rural culture of 1885 to 1915, the rich soil from which his poems had drawn their nourishment, was to diminish and grow impoverished before his eyes as he drove his old automobile across the depressed New England states. The great passage of America from a rural to an urban civilization went on inexorably, while Frost protested and satirized the New Deal and industrial-collectivist trends. And leadership in poetry appeared to pass to T. S. Eliot. Frost was embittered and despairing—but he went on writing and creating some of his finest poems. He called his book in 1936 *A Further Range*, and it indubitably was.

251

After the dreadful decade was over, it was clearly acknowledged that Frost had grown from a regional poet to a national poet. The 1940s would be for Frost a decade of recovery. In the 1950s he achieved a status unimaginable by his admirers in the 1920s: he became the national bard.

He could well have stopped growing in the 1920s. Not many writers, especially not many poets, surpass after the age of fifty-six the achievements of their middle life. But Frost did. He extended and deepened his achievement. Nothing we critics wrote of him in the 1920s can be stretched far enough to encompass the national bardic poet who wrote "A Record Stride," "Neither Out Far Nor In Deep," "The Gift Outright," "Choose Something Like a Star," "A Masque of Reason," and "A Masque of Mercy."

Upon the inauguration of President Kennedy in 1961, Frost's word to us was "We're going to go the length and lead from our strength. . . . Sum it all up in saying, an Augustan age of poetry and power, with the emphasis on the power. That belongs to my poetry, and it belongs to politics all the time."

Two years later he was dead, and it was seen that the Augustan program he had proclaimed exceeded his declining powers. *In the Clearing* showed the relaxation of old age, not the power that had belonged to his books of the 1920s and 1930s. For Frost's greatness, the critics looked back to these books; and more than one has stressed their classicism, as John Frederick Nims did in a memorial essay: "I find Frost classical because his view of existence is tragic (more classical, then, than romantic), and because—obviously—his work has certain affinities with Greek and Latin poetry."

CHAPTER 15

Orage in America

He was standing near the curb in front of the Neighborhood Playhouse, that "place of light, of liberty, and of learning" in the little theater movement of the early Twenties. He was talking to my friends Margaret Naumburg and Jean Toomer. I knew instantly that he was A. R. Orage, "advance man" for the demonstration of ancient dances to be given that night at the playhouse. Jean motioned me to approach, and my wife and I were introduced to Orage. We met a tall Englishman with the big frame of a Yorkshire farmer, dark clad but giving an impression of light.

"I felt his alertness and his relaxation," said my wife afterwards. She had been a dancer at the Neighborhood Playhouse, and her impressions of people were often a sizing-up of their physical characteristics. "I felt in Orage," she explained, "something always in motion but not hurried, not tense, not forced—an easy swiftness which could change its course deftly and resume the original direction with perfect sureness. Quick intelligence, quick feeling and understanding, and an extraordinary speed of perception—a sort of lightning functioning."

As for me, I felt that this man's *note* was intelligence, and I have never met a man who struck it with as much clarity. The hazel eyes, alive and challenging, were intelligent. The strong nose was intelligent. The mouth, ready to smile at paradox, was intelligent. There was a slight suggestion of an elephantlike cast to the whole countenance, and the elephant is reputed to be the most intelligent of beasts. Indeed, the whole build of Orage suggested the elephant but a light and swift-moving elephant, not a lumbering one; and as an elephant he was depicted in the "jungle scene" Alexandre de Saltzmann painted on the barn wall at the Château du Prieuré, seat of the Institute for the Harmonious Development of Man. Katharine Mansfield looked at this wall-scene while she rested her ravaged body in the afternoons. Perhaps it crossed her mind when she picked out her literary mentor Orage in the "jungle" that Ganesa, the Indian god of wisdom, he who wrote down the *Mahabharata* from Vyasa's dictation, had the head of an elephant.

Orage was fifty-one on this February night in 1924. He gave no sign of middle age. No hint of grey in the dark hair, and only a slight recession of the hairline near the part on the left. No sign of corpulence, and in this he differed from the big-bellied Ganesa! His body was firm and strong from a year of hard physical work at the Institute, yet easy in its carriage. "You expected a man who looked like that to talk well," wrote Holbrook Jackson of Orage in the years when they were colleagues in the Leeds Art Club; and this was a way of saying that intelligence was the keynote of his appearance.

A few minutes after we met Orage on the sidewalk, we heard him "talk well" from the stage of the Neighborhood Playhouse. He gave a sort of preface to the demonstration of "various movements of the human body taken from the art of the Ancient East—examples of sacred gymnastics, sacred dances and religious ceremonies preserved in certain temples in Turkestan, Tibet, Afghanistan, Kafiristan, Chitral, and other places." He declared that Mr. Gurdjieff, founder of the Institute for the Harmonious Development of Man, was able to prove that in the Orient certain dances have not lost the deep religious and scientific significance they had in the remote past.

At this introductory lecture—the one discussed in Chapter 12 as Hart Crane's collision with a C Influence—Orage spoke of "a new quality of concentration and attention and a new direction of the mind" to be achieved through the exercises. He said:

> Dancing still has quite a different meaning in the East from what we give it in the West. In ancient times the dance was a branch of real art, and served the purposes of higher knowledge and religion. A person who specialized in a subject communicated his knowledge through works of art, particularly dances, as we spread knowledge through books. Among the early Christians dancing in churches was an important part of the ritual. The ancient sacred dance is not only a medium for an aesthetic experience, but a book, as it were, or script, con-

taining a definite piece of knowledge. But it is a book which not everyone who would can read.

How quickly we learned the truth of the last observation. The two sets of "obligatory exercises," the initiation of the priestess, the dervish dances, the pilgrimage movement called "measuring-one's-length," the folk- and work-dances, the enneagram dance—all these and many others had a strange impact that can only be described as awakening. The design and the detail were extraordinarily precise, and one could well believe that they were an exact language to convey knowledge. But one could not read it, only feel it; and the feeling was—tremendous. Here was an experience produced by art that was entirely different from all former art experiences the audience had ever had, as many confessed in the weeks that followed when Gurdjieff held lectures and formed a class in movement at the Rosetta O'Neill Studio on upper Madison Avenue.

2.

If it cannot be said that the visit of Gurdjieff took America by storm, it can be said that it raised a conversational storm in the circles of the intelligentsia. And this storm was no teapot tempest, as events soon showed.

Orage and a second emissary had arrived in New York in December, 1923, and Orage had given a talk at the famous Sunwise Turn Book Shop in January. He related that G. I. Gurdjieff had been a member of a society called Seekers of the Truth which had made several expeditions into Asia in 1895 and afterwards. These expeditions investigated ancient records and sought for hidden knowledge. Gurdjieff had then appeared in Russia in 1913 and had made preparations to found an institute. Revolutionary turmoil, however, frustrated his plans, and Gurdjieff and his pupils had trekked across Asia Minor and Turkey and on to Germany. Finally, Gurdjieff had established the Institute for the Harmonious Development of Man at Fontainebleau-Avon in a chateau that had once been the residence of Madame de Maintenon.* The effect of this information was to heighten the mystery of Gurdjieff.

The newspapers were facetious in their reporting of Gurdjieff's demonstra-

* According to Gurdjieff, he appeared in Russia in 1911 and first set up an institute at Moscow, later at Tiflis, Constantinople, and other places.

tions at Lesley Hall, Neighborhood Playhouse, Carnegie Hall; but the press accounts were offset by a serious article, "The Forest Philosophers," by C. E. Bechhofer Roberts in the *Century*. The Gurdjieff visit, however, was not nearly the sensation in the press that it was in conversation, where it stirred up quite as much rejection as it did curiosity. All that spring and into the summer months the question of Gurdjieff—a new Pythagoras or a charlatan?—was the most controversial topic at intelligentsia gatherings.

The crowds who came to see the Gurdjieff demonstrations and the several score who joined a class in movement that met every night at the Rosetta O'Neill Studio never looked like the people who attend theosophical lectures or turn out to welcome highly touted swamis. Rather they were the people one saw at the first night of an O'Neill play or at the opening night of the Society of Independent Artists or at a League of Composers concert. I do not know any better word to describe them than *intelligentsia*, a word that has lost its vogue but is still serviceable for identifying the public that in 1924 read the *Dial* and the *New Republic* and *Vanity Fair*, listened to Stravinsky and Schoenberg, looked at Picasso and Matisse, discussed psychoanalysis and the progressive education of John Dewey, and inclined toward socialism. Some of us had heard of Orage, and Orage's reputation was undoubtedly a considerable factor in attracting the intelligentsia to the Gurdjieff meetings.

A couple of years earlier, Van Wyck Brooks had written about the London weekly, which Orage had given up when he burned his bridges and entered the Institute for the Harmonious Development of Man. "Mr. Orage's *New Age*," Brooks had said in the *Freeman*, "occupies a place apart in the literary journalism of our time. It has inspired a unique devotion in its readers; it has been written and edited with a devotion that is equally remarkable."

Knopf had published Orage's *Readers and Writers* in 1922, and Brooks's review said:

> In *Readers and Writers*, a selection from his weekly causerie on books and contemporary thought, Mr. Orage has initiated us into some of the secrets of the [*New Age*]. What are his own chief preoccupations? The importance of what he describes as "free intelligence," the importance of individual responsibility, the importance of disinterestedness, of simplicity in style and judgment in criticism, of a pan-human as distinguished from a national ideal, above all the importance of common sense. What are his characteristic attitudes? An intense belief in the future, an eager curiosity, an ample hospitality; and along with all this, a dry wit

and a bracing skepticism. One does not have to seek beyond the pages of this little book in order to understand the exceptional appeal of the *New Age*.

I must not give the impression that Orage played the central role in the tour of the Gurdjieff pupils. The indisputable triumph of the tour was the program of ancient dances and movements. People who had no use for the ideas of Gurdjieff excepted the dances from their censure; the dances, they said, were strange and wonderful. And indeed it was a unique and profound experience that they gave. There had never before been anything like them in America.

Unthinkingly we regard ourselves as heirs of all the ages, but there are breaks and declines and discontinuities in the history of man; and we inherit only fragments of a knowledge forgotten. The ancient dances collected by Gurdjieff bridged the gaps in the long history of the race and affected us across millennia. Here for the first time Americans saw the ancient *objective* art of dancing.

Orage was a sponsor for the ideas of the Gurdjieff system. People who were usually negative toward the occult and the esoteric hesitated to dismiss without inquiry a system of ideas that had an advocate in the skeptical Orage. "There must be something to it," they conceded, "if Orage has given up his review and gone to Fontainebleau." Again it is Van Wyck Brooks who tells us what an influential figure Orage was in the early 1920s.

Mr. Orage is one of those men who are able to play a lone hand without lapsing into eccentricity, or bitterness, or the coterie-spirit. He is absolutely independent and absolutely fearless; he is that most valuable of critics, the man who loves his own generation and chastens it because he loves it. He never permits an idea to pass him unexamined; he is in the habit of testing his own faith, and he challenges the faith of others with an impartial rigour. "Truth bears no man's name" is a proverb he quotes with approval. . . . There is a steely toughness, a hard, clean lucidity about his thought that is obviously the result at once of an unremitting moral effort and of an unflagging delight in the use of the intellect. In consequence of this Mr. Orage has a terrible eye for the otiose, the conventional, the official, the sentimental, the trivial, and the infantile. One is not surprised to find him remarking that he loves best "the men of the eighteenth century."

Indeed there are times when Mr. Orage reminds one of Dr. Jonson. . . . One can see, however, that the passion of his life is conversation and that his criticism springs out of it. . . .

Mr. Orage makes the classical conception of art as attractive as Addison was supposed to have made virtue. . . . Nevertheless, his predominant mood is one of expectation . . . he has given us one of the most stimulating of all books of modern criticism.

3.

Orage stayed in New York to become a fisher of men after Gurdjieff and his followers sailed for Europe early in June. He met a great many people, talked to small groups in several homes, and resumed his journalism, contributing "Unedited Opinions" to the *New Republic* and a remarkable essay on "New Standards in Art and Literature" to the *Atlantic Monthly*. By the fall, on his return to New York from a quick visit to Fontainebleau where Gurdjieff had met a nearly fatal accident, there were perhaps two hundred interested people prepared to join the groups he formed to meet once a week for instruction in the Gurdjieff system.

There were about thirty in the group Elizabeth Delza and I joined. We met in the apartment of Margaret Anderson and Jane Heap at 24 East 11th Street in the ambiance of the *Little Review*. Several of our friends were in this group— and others soon became friends as we were more and more involved in the fascinating expositions of Orage. Sometimes we had visitors. One night found Van Wyck Brooks and Padraic Colum sitting inconspicuously in a corner.

Orage was the best talker I have ever listened to, a man of beautiful lucid speech such as I imagine Plato was in the Garden of Academe.* He opened his series with a brief discourse on reality. Reality comprises both the actual and the potential, he explained. The actual is what in fact exists or takes place. The potential is what might or may exist or take place. Reality is what exists or happens or what may exist or may happen. Psychology today, he proceeded to say, treats of only one part of reality, the actual; it's oblivious to the potential in human nature. Orage's words seemed tipped with light when he declared that the real potential in relation to men is that they may become Men.

---

* As a young man Orage immersed himself in Plato and was the chief speaker at the weekly meetings of "the Plato group" at Leeds. "It was then," says his memoirist, "that he began to attain his greatest eloquence as a speaker, exercising his oratory less upon socialist platforms and more in philosophic exposition."

4.

That fall of 1924 I got the job of managing editor of a popular inspirational magazine that had sprung up in the wake of Coué's visit to America. It was a bread-and-butter job in which I took no pride; and I was surprised when Orage hinted that he would like to write for this publication from whose masthead barked the words—Health! Happiness! Success!—to attract unhealthy, unhappy, unsuccessful readers. But Orage was a fisher of men, and I surmised that he thought that a series on such topics as "How to Learn to Think," "The Control of Temper," and "How Not to Be Bored" would cause men to bite on his ideas, and he could play them into the net of his groups. He quickly wrote fifteen articles and I used all my editorial art to advertise and feature them, but the fish didn't bite. No letters came in, and the only excited readers were members of the Orage groups who bought the magazine at newsstands.

The articles were too good for the ineffectual, spiritless people my magazine catered to. They were the best pieces on self-improvement I ever found during my editorial life in that field; they were better than Arnold Bennett's excellent *How to Live 24 Hours a Day*, because Orage's exercises in self-improvement needed only a creative attitude to become exercises in self-development. The final article, "Life as Gymnastics," supplied the creative attitude and harmonized perfectly with Orage's weekly meetings on the system of G. I. Gurdjieff:

> There can be little doubt that for most of us, in the present epoch, the image of life as a gymnasium is a greatly needed tonic. . . . The classic Greek conception of life was just that; and everybody knows that the gymnasium, with its lectures and discussions as well as physical exercises, was the most popular institution of Pythagorean Greece. What is not so well known is that the gymnasium was for the Greeks a symbol of life itself. Their God ran this planet as a gymnasium for the exercise of men, and all experiences were to be taken as movements, turns, stretches, exercises in wrestling, running, lifting, and so on. Moderns will find what the ancient Greeks found in this image of life—the evocation of a creative emotion.

These luminous articles, buried for many years in the files of an extinct magazine, were resurrected by a London publisher in 1953. An American edition, newly entitled *The Active Mind*, was imported and welcomed by the current students of Gurdjieff in New York.

5.

In two years Orage consolidated those who had stayed the course in his several groups into one large group of seventy-five or a hundred. We met once a week in the barnlike quarters of Muriel Draper at 24 East 40th Street. There was a modest fee of ten dollars a month for the meetings, and sometimes we made individual appointments with Orage for psychological counseling on a social, not professional, basis. Orage continued to form beginners' groups and to feed them after a while into the big group.

That big group always reminded me of the brilliant first-night crowd in the lobby between acts of a Theatre Guild opening—only people weren't standing but sitting on folding chairs in Muriel Draper's big room. A small bedroom filled one corner in the rear of this room, and up front a door opened into a kitchen from which cockroaches would occasionally wander into the audience at great peril to their lives. I have seen the expensively shod foot of a very rich lady descend with deadly aim upon a cruising cockroach, the while her face was fixed attentively on Orage's forceful words on the mechanical behavior of human beings. Muriel Draper who had been a salon mistress in Florence and London was now in straitened circumstances, but her sparkling personality brightened the shabby room in which she held her famous New Year's Eve parties and in which Orage discoursed on the possible attainment of individuality.

Sitting up front were often to be seen Helen Westley, leading actress of the Washington Square Players and member of the board of the Theatre Guild; Edna Kenton, lifelong student of Henry James who even grew to look like James; and Mary Johnston, historical novelist. Near them would be Mabel Dodge Luhan in town from Taos, with husband Toni wrapped in an Indian blanket seated on the floor beside her. Jessie Dwight, a onetime partner of the Sunwise Turn Book Shop, would be there too; she would marry Orage in a couple of years.

The art world was well represented: vigorous red-bearded Boardman Robinson and Sally; Florence Cane, remarkable art teacher of children; Ilonka Karasz, *New Yorker* cover artist, and her sister Mariska Karasz, needlework artist; Aaron Douglas, Harlem artist; print expert Carl Zigrosser; Elizabeth Sage Hare, art patron.

Editors could be spotted around the room: John O'Hara Cosgrave, retired editor of the *Sunday World Magazine* section and leading spirit of the Dutch Treat Club; Jane Heap of the *Little Review*, and the *Little Review* "office boy,"

Caesar Zwaska; T. S. Matthews, a junior editor of the *New Republic*, and his boss Herbert Croly, who usually sat with Mrs. Croly inconspicuously in the back rows. In the far corner the poet R. Ellsworth Larsson, pallid but intense, also made himself inconspicuous until the meeting broke up when he went to hover near his adored hostess. Other poets who came frequently were Melville Cane, Samuel Hoffenstein, and Schuyler Jackson. The actress Rita Romilly seldom missed a meeting, and just as faithful in attendance was Edwin R. Wolfe, an actor who produced Paul Green's *In Abraham's Bosom* in a Greenwich Village theater.

Writers were, of course, attracted by Orage's reputation. A partial list would include the Knopf novelist Isa Glenn; the short-story writer Israel Solon; Jean Toomer; Lawrence S. Morris, writer for the *Freeman* and the *New Republic*. A young engineer, John Riordan, who was preparing a book of short stories subsequently published under the title *On the Make*, came with his wife Mavis McIntosh, a literary agent. Elizabeth Otis, Mavis' partner in the subsequently well-known McIntosh & Otis Agency, was also an Orage pupil. The young English bookseller Stanley Nott, who had founded in New York the Chaucer Head Book Shop, was another devoted pupil.

In the center of the room could usually be found the aristocratic looking publicist Amos Pinchot and the brooding architect Hugh Ferriss. There were scientists too among this esoteric gathering in quest of esoteric knowledge. The best known was Dr. Louis Berman, who was riding the wave of popular interest in endocrinology. And there was C. Daly King, not yet Dr. C. Daly King. On the whole—a worldly group, sophisticated and successful or well started on the climb to success.

Orage—invariably late because lateness sharpened the mood of anticipation—would enter the big room through Muriel's kitchen where he had stopped for a Volstead Act breaker and would sit easefully in a large chair, not the gilt throne Muriel had salvaged from a theatrical warehouse which everyone avoided. He would smoke one cigarette after another, though not compulsively. (He had experimentally stopped smoking at Fontainebleau until he had reached the point of indifference whether he smoked or not.)

"And what is he telling the good men and ladies," asked Waldo Frank in "Mystery in a Sack Suit," his *New Yorker* profile of Orage, "that they should harken to him—leaders though they are—with humble rapture? He is propounding a simple, matter-of-fact psychologic method. A method too simple, really, to be written down either by him or by me. So what that Method is, you'll have to find out for yourself. What it *does*—or claims to do—is nothing less than the whole and utter overturning of everything you live by."

Frank, it should be said, dropped out after hearing only the first part of a comprehensive method and did not realize that the method was deceptively simple in appearance but strictly scientific in fact. The classic Pythagorean injunction, Know Thyself, could well have been the Orage group motto, for their work was the scientific pursuit of self-knowledge.

Although there was no expressed prohibition, the writers in the groups somehow felt that they were not to write publicly about the Gurdjieff method. Frank perhaps was aware of a discouraging attitude toward writers' propensity to rush into print. One member of the groups did write a short book of exposition of the Gurdjieff ideas as presented by Orage, and with Orage's blessing got it published in 1927. The writer was C. Daly King who adopted the pen name of Robert Courtney; the book was called *Beyond Behaviorism*, and it was published by a small firm I worked for.

King, a disillusioned investigator of psychoanalysis, had been so completely persuaded by Orage's lucid discourse that he had resigned from his junior partnership in a factoring business and entered graduate courses in psychology at Columbia University. He applied himself to Orage's teachings in a professional spirit and qualified in three years to lead a group of his own in a New Jersey suburb. An outstanding student at Columbia, he became a collaborator with his teacher, William Moulton Marston, in writing the important text *Integrative Psychology*, 1931. But before his collaboration with this leading psychologist, King had published a couple of entertaining detective novels in which representatives of various schools of psychology tried to solve crimes by their respective theories.

King's next book, signed with his true name, made no more appreciable impact on American psychology than had *Beyond Behaviorism*, even though the new book appeared in a series sponsored by C. K. Ogden and carried an introduction by William Moulton Marston. Just as King's first book took into account the whole physiological science of man and went beyond it to the primary assumption of all human beings that the world exists and "I" exist, so his second book of exposition of Gurdjieff, *The Psychology of Consciousness*, went beyond integrative psychology by outlining a superior method for changing consciousness from passive to active.

King continued to study with Orage until 1931 when Orage returned to England to found the *New English Weekly.* Later he matriculated as a postgraduate student in psychology at Yale, where he studied neurology under Dr. Harold Saxton Burr.

King's next work was a book privately printed in 1951, entitled *The Oragean Version as Presented by C. Daly King.* The edition was limited to one hundred copies, not for sale, and further publication was expressly forbidden. The reason for this prohibition was King's premise that the Oragean version of the ideas of Gurdjieff was one version of the approach to the hidden learning, which is usually secret and seldom appears on the surface of public history. He noted that the hidden learning had appeared in the East Indian version of the Bhagavad Gita, in the medieval renditions of Orders of Chivalry and the original Rosy Cross, in the earliest Christian and Mohammedan accounts, once in the official religion of ancient Egypt, and perhaps in the initial interpretation of Lamaists in Tibet.

The hidden learning is usually kept secret because when it is indiscriminately disseminated, it is debased and weakened—as had happened with Christianity and Buddhism. One must then ask why Gurdjieff formulated the secret information at his Institute for the Harmonious Development of Man at Tiflis and at Fontainebleau-Avon and in New York without any special safeguards against its disclosure. Because, Orage had hinted, at certain times of desperate crisis the hidden learning is revealed.

The tradition that there exists an esoteric knowledge or hidden learning excites the gullible, both positively and negatively. Some people immediately believe in the tradition, believe in it uncritically and unscientifically. Others at once disbelieve the assertion of the existence of hidden learning, stigmatizing the tradition as a superstition and denouncing its exponents as charlatans without any investigation. It was the fate of the Oragean version of Gurdjieff's psychological teachings that it attracted some who were positively gullible in their "mystical" beliefs, and at the same time it repelled others who were negatively gullible and wrote nonsense about a teaching of which they had no personal knowledge. Men who would not dream of setting forth their opinion of Freud or Marx without earning their right to state it by actual study of the source never hesitated to dismiss Orage without attending his groups or even reading the books of C. Daly King.

The correct attitude toward Orage's teaching was, of course, the skeptic's, and Orage often enjoined upon his groups one of the inscriptions in the study house at the Institute for the Harmonious Development of Man: "You Cannot Be Too Skeptical." For skepticism is investigation and experimentation without prejudice and without gullibility, positive or negative—admittedly an attitude difficult to attain but one essential to the practice of the Gurdjieff method of nonidentifying self-observation.

Some excuse for the ignorance of later hostile commentators on the Oragean version may be found in the inaccessibility of King's early books. But *The States of Consciousness*, which he published in 1963, is an authoritative work that is readily available. Much of Orage's influence and much of his contribution to American culture took place underground, so to speak; but his exposition of the Gurdjieff propositions had a visible, public, scientific result. That result was the planting in the science of psychology as formulated in the United States of a fourth view of the nature of consciousness.

When Orage began his New York lectures, there were three contrasting and long-established views as to the nature of consciousness itself. In the first view (the psychological or subjectivist), consciousness is the primary reality and the nervous system is secondary. This is, of course, the view of psychoanalysis. In the second view (the physiological or objectivist), neural phenomena are the primary factors, and consciousness is a result of the operations of the nervous system. The behaviorist is completely physiological and even denies consciousness. The third view is called parallelism and holds that neurological phenomena are accompanied by conscious phenomena or vice versa, but parallelists are unable to state what the connection between neurological and conscious phenomena may be, and actually beg the question.

To these long-established views, Orage added a new, a fourth view, on which his follower King has written:

> The term, consciousness, refers always and legitimately only to the relationship between the subjective entity, or experiencer, and those end-products of the neural functioning of his body which furnish the experiencer with what in fact he experiences. . . . Most of us are unaccustomed to thinking in terms of field theory and we are unaware that three forces, not merely two, are present in all phenomenal occurrence. When experience occurs, there is certainly 1) an experiencer and there is 2) something that furnishes his experience to him. That

something is precisely the operations of his nervous systems. But there is also a third factor involved: it is 3) the relationship existing between the experiencer and the neural raw material from which his experiences result. And this relationship determines the extent and the type of consciousness operative in the given instance.

Thus the Orage-Gurdjieff view brings about a reconciliation of the subjectivist and objectivist views. It points out that the first is correct in reference to one factor of the whole human integer (the subjective entity, the experiencer), and the second is correct in reference to another factor (the objective organism). But what relates the experience to the end-products of neural functioning is an additional field factor whose function is reconciling. This field factor cannot be described in terms of the items whose mutual relationship it establishes, for it is the *state of consciousness* that establishes the particular relationship between subjective entity and objective organism, and the state of consciousness defines the specific condition resulting, *e.g.*, sleep, waking, self and cosmic consciousness.

6.

In the summer of 1927 I visited the Château du Prieuré at Fontainebleau-Avon for four weeks. Part of me did not want to go. I was enjoying living in New York and didn't want to change my ways. But part of me wanted to wake up, wanted to become a new man. This part prevailed and one sunny afternoon Elizabeth Delza and I were ringing the bell beside the wrought iron gate of the Château du Prieuré. Our ring was answered by two spry boys, Tom and Fritz Peters, nephews of Margaret Anderson who had been made wards of Jane Heap. (Decades later Fritz Peters was to write *Boyhood with Gurdjieff* and other books.) We passed into a courtyard enclosed by pink stone walls. There was a big circular fountain with water splashing from upper to lower basin, and beyond was the beautifully proportioned chateau, dormer windows gazing from a gray slate mansard.

The Institute for the Harmonious Development of Man had been given up in 1924 after Gurdjieff's nearly fatal accident, but Americans could still spend summers at the Prieuré, provided they understood that Gurdjieff had abandoned the Institute phase and was not teaching. He was now writing a three-volume book, a priority undertaking that superseded the intensive personal teaching of the Institute phase.

We were shown to our simple room on the third floor of the wing—good quarters comparable to the "Monks' Corridor" on the third floor of the main building but not as elegant as "the Ritz" on the second floor. I never visited in "the Ritz" but heard about its canopied beds, old mirrors, and painted walls—reminders of the elegance of the age of Louis XIV. Gurdjieff was not around when I came out on the terrace and looked at the formal garden and pool that extended to the kitchen garden and woods that filled the rest of the thirteen-acre estate. When I saw Waldo Frank and Jean Toomer coming toward the château, I joined them.

Waldo, who called himself a mystical naturalist, had won by 1927 a considerable reputation in Europe as a representative of the new American literature. He was accustomed to being received abroad by such writers in France as André Gide and Jules Romains and in Spain as Ortega y Gasset and Unamuno. Although Frank had attended some Orage groups in America, he seemed taken aback when Gurdjieff failed to receive him with a host's interest in American literature and with respect for his own "prophetic" vision. I think he may have envisioned a conversation over glasses of sherry on high philosophy, not knowing that Gurdjieff scorned the talk of intellectuals as "titillation."

Waldo had been walking about the grounds for several hours. He was tired and had begun to suspect he had fallen into the wrong hands for an introduction to Gurdjieff. Toomer had rescued him from the Russians who were showing him the estate. Soon after I joined them we sighted Gurdjieff, a man of only medium height but broad and muscular, his shaven dome eye-catching, coming down the walk with a Russian journalist whose name sounded like Karma. Toomer, who had spent previous summers at Fontainebleau, introduced Waldo and me to Gurdjieff, who immediately invited us to the "Russian bath" that night. The invitation was roguish: we were told that we would have to pay for the bath by telling three "anecdotes"—obviously, Rabelaisian anecdotes were meant.

Gurdjieff usually dashed people's preconceptions when they met him, especially if they thought they were about to meet a holy man from the East. They might find the holy man in a low dive of a restaurant as the composer Thomas de Hartmann did, or writing at a table at the Café de la Paix, or as host at a sort of Abbey of Theleme as the Château du Prieuré sometimes seemed.

Gurdjieff at once bewildered Frank by speaking of his chapter on America in the tales of Beelzebub, the book he was currently writing. Moreover, Frank didn't understand Gurdjieff's fractured English. A couple of times I heard him speak perfect English. I believe that it was a deliberate part of his pedagogy to speak broken English. By making himself hard to understand, Gurdjieff obliged his listeners to give full attention. In order to get his meaning, they had to be active instead of passive toward him.

Gurdjieff led us back to the terrace, then clapped his hands; a girl appeared with little cups of coffee. We—Karma, Frank, Toomer and I—sat on the grass around Gurdjieff who reclined on his side. Frank, who had by now heard enough about "anecdotes," remarked: "I have always objected to anecdotes. They break up the flow of a conversation." Incomprehension. Karma said: "I don't understand." Thinking that his words were not understood, Frank repeated them slowly. "I don't understand the attitude," said Karma. Gurdjieff rose, discharged an explosive speech on the worthlessness of mental titillation, and strode off. He's through with us, I thought, but he turned and waved us to follow to the courtyard where stood his hard-used Citroen. We were going to the Café Henri IV.

At the Henri IV Gurdjieff entered completely into the role of writer. Notebooks appeared, he and Karma looked at them (I think Karma was a temporary Russian translator), and Gurdjieff began to write in Armenian. (G. I. Gurdjieff was the son of a bard and carpenter; he grew up in Armenia, which has a notable literary heritage.) On arrival at the café, Gurdjieff had ordered a round of armagnac. When the drinks came, he proposed the toast: "Health—ordinary idiots." We downed our brandy, except for Waldo who sipped his. Somebody told him to down it. While Gurdjieff concentrated on his writing, we sat quietly at a table nearby. Waldo ventured to observe that Gurdjieff acted like a jovial headmaster. After a while another round of armagnac appeared and we drank to the toast: "Health—candidats for idiots"—infants being the "candidats." Waldo now complained softly to Toomer and me. "How long does this keep up? I haven't had any lunch."

I glanced at Gurdjieff, intensely writing or revising, undistracted by café noises, the passing to-and-fro of waiters, the presence of his guests. He was to me the enlarged picture of a Renaissance writer, a man with a huge appetite for experience, a great store of energy, an immense power of concentration, the fabulous all-around man of the Renaissance. Carlyle I remembered had criticized Jesus for incompleteness: "He had no Falstaff in him." But it could not be said of Gurdjieff that he had no Rabelais in him. On the biggest scale he was all that a writer should be: indefatigable, living life to the fullest, inspired with the highest aim in literature—the writing of a modern scripture.

This summer he was a writer and not a teacher. And yet it came to me on the café terrace that, despite his disclaimer, Gurdjieff was teaching all the time, simply by giving dramatic experience to his American followers and curiosity-seekers. Frank, who had approached Gurdjieff with some feeling of self-importance, was being treated as if he were a man of no importance. The reduction was being performed with flourishes of Eastern politeness. What made the experience especially painful for Frank was the presence of two of his own former "disciples." Frank had "discovered" Toomer and introduced his book *Cane*; and I had written a monograph on Frank's early books, which Lewis Mumford had rightly called "a premature study." Toomer and I had both broken away from Frank's leadership and had been learning from the practice of the Gurdjieff method to think of ourselves as nonentities. Whether Frank learned anything about himself from the psychological demonstration Gurdjieff was giving, I don't know. He seemed merely reactive and painfully affronted.

His ordeal was ours, too, for Gurdjieff's demonstrations were directed at the whole cast, not just at the temporary leading unconscious actor. We were glad when Gurdjieff abruptly closed his notebooks and rushed us back to the Prieuré. Here we joined a soup line in a small garden and filed past a huge casserole from which was ladled our evening meal. Gurdjieff, consigning us to the democracy, disappeared.

After supper we went to the study house, a hangar converted into a sort of hall for classes in music and sacred gymnastics. Here the Russian composer Thomas de Hartmann played Gurdjieff's music with remarkable precision and force. De Hartmann had been a composer of some note in St. Petersburg before the war. His fame had begun with a four-act ballet, *The Pink Flower*, performed at the opera in 1907, with Pavlova, Fokine, and Nijinsky in the cast. But from 1917 he had been Gurdjieff's musician.

At various places in the study house there were mottos painted in a peculiar script that I could not read. I was told that the inscription over the entrance read: "Remember that you came here realizing the necessity of struggling only with yourself and thank anyone who helps you to engage in this struggle."

About ten o'clock the men drifted over to the Russian bath house Gurdjieff had constructed (the women had had their bath in the late afternoon). Here I met several Americans I had known: the poets Melville Cane and Schuyler Jackson, the Chicago importer Fred Leighton, the actor Edwin Wolfe, the fledgling writer Bayard Schindel, and other New Yorkers.

The Russian bath one took at the Prieuré differed somewhat from the Turkish bath one had known in New York; it proved to be an altogether novel experience. The men sat on three or four tiers in the steam room and gradually worked up to profuse sweating. There was a rest period in an outer room. Then a return to the top tier of the steam room. We sat on a long bench, as in a dugout, each man holding a leafy branch. At one end of the dugout there was a loud *bong* as a big valve was opened and live steam rushed in. We could see the steam advance until it enveloped us, and then we used our leafy branches to flick the burning drops of water off our bodies. After a few minutes Gurdjieff signaled for the valve to be shut, and we filed into an outer room for final cleansing rites. During the rest period there had been relaxed conversation and joking but so far as I could observe, no telling of "anecdotes" to pay for the bath. "Anecdotes," I later learned, were called for only on certain occasions.

After the Saturday night bath came the midnight feast in the English dining room. A true feast it was, though I cannot remember the exotic dishes that made the meal an epicurean adventure. Gurdjieff sat in the center of a long head table; facing it were about sixty of us drinking toasts to the twenty-one types of idiots, which Gurdjieff proposed at frequent intervals. "Health—ordinary idiots." "Health—candidats for idiots." "Health—squirming idiots." "Health—compassionate idiots." "Health—squared idiots." We got up to nine or ten of these. On no occasion at which I was present did we go higher, but I never saw anyone tipsy. (One learned how to drink at Fontainebleau.) Infrequently a toast was drunk in water: "Health—wise man." The twenty-first toast was to the Unique Idiot—"His Endlessness," Gurdjieff explained.

Now at last, at the feast, Waldo Frank was receiving the special guest treatment which he had expected on his arrival eleven hours before and which he no longer desired after his reduction to nonentity. But Gurdjieff had seated him and his wife at his left and was playing the host. When the sheep's head was served, Gurdjieff told his special guests that in the East the sheep's eyes were considered the tastiest part and he would honor them by offering the eyes. But neither Waldo nor Alma Frank would accept the delicacy.

After coffee we adjourned to the drawing room, and a reader began one of the long chapters in the tales of Beelzebub. This was a switch to intellectual activity after the previous "instinctive-moving center" activity of the bath and the emotional activity of the music in the study house. Gurdjieff sat to one side and watched attentively the behavior of his audience. It was plain that he was writing to produce intended effects upon an intended audience, and he was checking on the production of designed effects. (Gurdjieff remarked that "to write my book for conscious men would be easy but to write it for donkeys— very hard.") Around four o'clock in the morning, after inviting Waldo and Alma to eat crayfish with him in Montmartre next evening, Gurdjieff closed the reading, and we all retired for a few hours of sound and most refreshing sleep.

To conclude this episode of a literary man's visit at the Prieuré: Since Sunday was a day off for us Americans, we arose late and found Gurdjieff had already gone to Paris. Waldo and Alma Frank also left for Paris, unsure about accepting Gurdjieff's invitation. Not until some years later did I learn from Alma that they had gone to the appointed restaurant to see if Gurdjieff were there, but not intending to join him. However, as they peered in from the street, Gurdjieff looked up, and Waldo felt that they had to go inside. At the dinner Gurdjieff apparently pressed hard on the sensitive spots of Frank's psychology until he could bear the pressure no longer. In what was intended to be a Dostoyevskian scene, Frank stood up and denounced Gurdjieff: "I think you are the Devil." He packed his wife and himself out of the restaurant on this note.

In the Gurdjieff view, Waldo Frank was an armchair mystic, the kind of literary mystic who is just another variety of idiot. Such a person has had no direct contact with and no direct instruction from anyone who lives permanently in a higher state of consciousness. The influences playing upon an armchair mystic are exclusively literary; any entrance he may have made into a higher state of consciousness is accidental, perhaps even pathological. He cannot repeat the entrance at will or stay long in a higher state. He is, in short, an ordinary man with the ordinary illusions: he thinks that he is already a conscious being, that he possesses will and can "do," and that he does not need to undergo special training to complete his evolution. His idiocy is squared because he is vain about his purely literary illusion of self-consciousness.

When Gurdjieff returned from Paris on the following day, Elizabeth Delza and I were invited to go on an automobile trip with him—destination unnamed.

We made a caravan of three cars, for this trip we had been warned would be eccentric. Although it had been rumored that we were going to Mont-Saint-Michel, we were anxious lest Gurdjieff should decide to turn another way. There were unscheduled stops during the day, during which Gurdjieff might rest by the roadside and play on his portable harmonium or write a while in his notebook.

Gurdjieff seemed to be telling us to take nothing for granted, as we departed for we knew not where, to stay we knew not how long. He was shaking up our usual expectations, and giving us a lesson in the undependability of life. For himself, he seemed to be working at least an eighteen-hour day. Up long before us, he had put in three or four hours of writing by the time we were taking croissants and coffee. He drove for long hours with no relief. He played his harmonium at intervals. He presided with great gusto at enormous dinners at the inns where we stayed. One of the secrets of his sustained energy seemed to be the distribution of his efforts among the three main functions of man's psychology, *i.e.*, intellectual, emotional, and instinctive activity. "When body work, mind rest," he remarked to me after driving for some hours.

With relief we found ourselves at last traveling over the causeway to the tiny island of Mont-Saint-Michel. There was no spot in all France I was more eager to see than this famous abbey. Gurdjieff's chapter on art was responsible, for he had therein resurrected from total obscurity a certain monk named Ignatius. This Ignatius had grown up on the continent of Europe, migrated to Africa and joined a brotherhood there which afterwards migrated to Europe and came to be called Benedictines. Ignatius, according to Gurdjieff, had been sent by his abbot to Mont-Saint-Michel for the purpose of directing the building of a temple. Although Ignatius was murdered in his sleep, the "temple" was finally built "at the beginning of contemporary European civilization," in Beelzebub's words, and "exists there even up till now and is called, it seems, 'Mont-Saint-Michel.' "*

Gurdjieff, however, was noncommunicative as he led us about the historic abbey. He took us to the lowest level the official guide knew about and insisted that there was still an even lower level, a "foundation"—presumably the one planned by the murdered Ignatius. The guide denied the existence of any lower level. "They do not know," Gurdjieff said to his group.

On the trip there was a remarkable incident. We were speeding along in the

* Richard II, grandfather of William the Conqueror, began the Abbey Church in 1020 and helped Abbot Hildebert to build it. The ground-plan of Ignatius was, of course, earlier.

darkness of ten o'clock on a country road when Gurdjieff muttered, stopped, and turned his car about. We retraced our route for a couple of miles and came upon one car of our caravan in a ditch. There was a palaver with the Russian and English occupants of this car, and then Gurdjieff braced himself in the ditch in front of the stalled vehicle. With his great shoulders and back, he gave a heave, then lifted and shifted the car on the edge of the road. Its passengers climbed in, the motor started, and off we went, both cars, in a hurry to reach the Prieuré before midnight. What a Herculean back, I thought. "Mr. Gurdjieff took one of these heavy trunks on his back and carried it down as though it were nothing," wrote Thomas de Hartmann in *Our Life with Mr. Gurdjieff,* an intimate account of the years he spent with Gurdjieff from 1917 to 1929.

After the Mont-Saint-Michel trip, my life at the Prieuré settled into a kind of routine, though it was too novel for me to feel it as routine. I got up about six-thirty, breakfasted on big slices of toast and a bowl of coffee, and then joined a "road gang" in the forest. Hour after hour I made "little ones out of big ones," breaking limestone into nut-sized pieces. There was a break for lunch around twelve-thirty and then more road work until late afternoon. Supper was around six-thirty, followed by music in the study house and "book readings" in the large drawing room until ten or eleven at night. Cracking stone in the open air was, of course, an invigorating change for a sedentary intellectual. But this was not the point. We were told that we should learn to work like men, not like ordinary laborers mending a road. That is, we were to be self-aware while we cracked stone and self-observant of the phenomena of our physical toil.

Two days each week I was assigned to kitchen duty. On these days, I got up about five, made a fire in the old stove, laid out forty or fifty huge hunks of bread for toasting, lugged in cans of milk, and made coffee. Then the woman cook of the day came and served breakfast to some forty-odd people with hearty appetites. After breakfast there was a considerable chore for a single scullion—washing the dishes. The kitchen was old-fashioned and certainly not labor-saving ("overcoming difficulties" was part of our creed), and it took a long time to prepare lunch under the supervision of the cook. After lunch, another long bout of dishwashing. In mid-afternoon there was a short rest period before the evening meal was prepared and served. The last dish was dried and kitchen swept by ten o'clock—too late to join the book reading.

It was easy to feel self-pity on such a day and to store up resentment at being left out of the more pleasant road work, the gatherings at mealtimes, and the music and book meetings. Yet it was possible to struggle against self-pity and to cease to resent the menial role. One gained an insight into the purpose of the kitchen scullion work imposed on aspirants to knighthood in the medieval orders of chivalry.

Orage arrived at Fontainebleau about the middle of my stay and began work on the English translation of Gurdjieff's books. I do not know whether Orage visited the grave of Katherine Mansfield in the protestant cemetery at Fontainebleau where he had stood on January 12, 1923, when she was buried; but he must have found that memory of her was still warm at the Prieuré four years after her death. Mansfield's attendant was no longer at the Prieuré; and her friend Olgivanna had departed, to marry Frank Lloyd Wright a few years later. But Olga de Hartmann kept Mansfield's memory green for American admirers like me who asked about her life at the Institute.

7.

Orage returned to New York in the fall of 1927 and resumed weekly group meetings. Continuing the oral tradition of occultism, all instruction was direct, as is the practice in esoteric schools. There were no texts—only discourse, question and answer, only orally communicated knowledge. Orage occasionally recommended collateral reading: *Some Sayings of the Buddha* in the F. L. Woodward translation, Alfred North Whitehead's *Science and the Modern World*, and A. S. Eddington's *The Nature of the Physical Universe* were sometimes cited. But even when the pattern changed from discourse on "the method" to the reading of Gurdjieff's book, as it did this fall, the oral character of the teaching was maintained. We did not have individual access to the manuscript. In groups of fifteen or twenty we listened to a reading of forty or fifty pages at a clip. I used to resent the extra difficulties imposed on comprehension by these reading-aloud sessions. But I came to see that there were advantages, too, in this struggle to understand at a faster pace of reading than my slow critical progress over the printed page.

Every week Orage gave us a commentary on the chapter he had recently translated. The general title for this first series was *Beelzebub's Tales to His Grandson* or *An Objectively Impartial Criticism of the Life of Man*. The purpose of this first series was stated by Gurdjieff as follows: "To destroy, mercilessly, without any compromises whatsoever, in the mentation and feelings of the reader, the beliefs and views by centuries rooted in him, about everything existing on the world." The constructive part of Gurdjieff's teaching was to be embodied in the second and third series of his writings. Meanwhile Orage, who had begun as a Nietzschean, commented brilliantly on the tremendous idol-smashing chapters of Gurdjieff's cosmic parable.

Given the composition of the group, the most eagerly awaited commentary was the one Orage gave on Gurdjieff's chapter dismissing modern art. Orage attempted to explain the concept of objective art. "It is the production of an effect or the conveyance of a meaning by deliberately invented, artificial means. . . . Self-expression has nothing to do with art, for there is seldom any self involved worth expressing. The legitimate purpose of genuine art is the illumination of truth through the emotional experience of *the recipient*, not of the artist." Orage made clear how great a human being a true artist must be.

> He must know the human organism so minutely as to be able to guarantee the effects (and that there shall be no other than the intended ones) of the sensory stimuli with which he proposes to confront it and he must know how to arrange those stimuli in a design, both simultaneous and progressively continuing, such as will produce the emotional result he wishes; finally he must know how to *re*-mind his auditor or observer by these means, not of some personal whim or distortion of his own which only some of them may share, but of a missed fact or a forgotten relationship that is universally and humanly true. And for that purpose he must be of such stature as already to have realized this truth for himself. The genuine artist is much greater than the scientist, because it is demanded that he must have been a genuine scientist first. Real and detailed knowledge is only a prerequisite of his profession and part of its technique; he need also be a human being so far developed normally as to have achieved some realization of those traits which it is the function of art to illuminate.

Art was dying in the West, Orage had concluded; only "movements," and not renascent tidal impulses, could be expected as cultures on the same level interacted. Art was dying because artists no longer took for their aim the impossible and the unattainable. Western art, Orage realized, could not be restored by critics and reason, and certainly could not be restored by artists without unattainable aims. It could at best produce only journeyman art and substitute refinement of technique for culture of the spirit.

Orage's conclusion was that "the source [of Western art] can be affected only by a fresh source, not by any of its issues." Invention, for example, had limitations in the already given. Imagism, cubism, vorticism, futurism, expressionism, Joyce-ism, Steinism, constructivism, Dada-ism were not creation, but only fresh combinations of known elements.

We learn from history that what is needed at this critical moment of Western civilization is a reinforced impulse from a *higher* culture. Orage noted that "the Greek stream, at the moment when it was about to die of its own impulse, received by accident a tributary of Egyptian art which raised its source considerably above its original level [Pythagoras persuaded Greece to go to school to Egypt], for the Greeks, in the absence of Egyptian tradition, and even with it, were 'children.' " Later the art of the Middle Ages was "miraculously saved from imminent death by renaissant contact with the classical sources, which themselves had been reinforced from the Egyptian."*

Orage did not consider the Western case hopeless. "There is a remedy and not an impossible one," he declared: "its name is ancient India. . . . Europe today is ancient Greece writ large. . . Ancient India stands in the same relation to us 'children' of Europe as ancient Egypt occupied toward the 'children' of Greece." Not from Indian philosophy nor from Indian antiquarian scholarship would we receive renascent impulses but from something infinitely more living than philosophies—Indian literature. "We have a literature translatable and translated into our own tongue, of such dimensions and qualities that its chief work alone, the *Mahabharata*, towers over all subsequent literature as the Pyramids look over the Memphian sands."

The greatness of the *Mahabharata* had been a recurrent theme in Orage's causeries in the *New Age*. And he made a final eloquent plea** for the discovery by moderns of this "greatest single effort of literary creation of any culture in human history." Unlike such famous essays of the early Twenties as Eliot's "Tradition and the Individual Talent," Orage's "New Standards in Art and Literature" made no visible impression on the leaders of American literary opinion. But for my own essay, "American Literature and the Unattainable,"

* When Orage appeared in New York in 1924, the thought struck me that he was a Pico della Mirandola of the twentieth century.

** This plea has been shortened in the reprinted versions of Orage's "New Standards in Art and Literature."

the final chapter in my 1928 *Destinations*, Orage's essay was received with absolute silence. Although unnoticed in the literary press, the essay did survive underground; and it will undoubtedly come to light as a seminal essay in the ever-deepening crisis of Western civilization.

In "New Standards" Orage had remarked that "artists have a conscience sensitive to the degree to which they are artists; and no amount of skill in craftsmanship, finesse and technique, or the approval these receive, really stills an artistic conscience that has once waked and cried in the night." Orage could have been recalling Katherine Mansfield when he wrote this, for she had told him at Fontainebleau that "presence or absence of purpose distinguishes literature from mere literature, and the elevation of the purpose distinguishes literature within literature. That is merely literature that has no other object than to please. Minor literature has a didactic object. But the greatest literature of all—the literature that scarcely exists—has not merely an aesthetic object, nor merely a didactic object but, in addition, a creative object: that of subjecting its readers to a real and at the same time illuminating experience. Major literature, in short, is an initiation into truth." With this insight, Katherine Mansfield dismissed her highly praised short stories: "There is not one that I dare to show to God."

Under the impact of Institute life, she had come to criticize her former writing. "I've been a camera. But . . . I've been a selective camera, and it has been my attitude that has determined the selection; . . . my slices of life . . . have been partial, misleading, and a little malicious. Further, they have had no other purpose than to record my attitude, which in itself stood in need of change if it was to become active instead of passive. . . . And, like everything unconscious, the result has been evil."

But Institute life—contact with a higher source of culture—was also renascent contact for Katherine Mansfield. Shortly before her death, she told Orage, "I have found my idea. I've got it at last. . . . Katya has felt something that she never felt in her life before, and Katya understands something she never understood before." Her new plan was "to widen first the scope of my camera, and then to employ it for a conscious purpose—that of representing life not merely as it appears to a certain attitude, but as it appears to another and different attitude, a creative attitude."

She explained what she meant by a creative attitude, saying "at present we see life, generally speaking, in only a passive aspect because we bring only a passive attitude to bear upon it. Could we change our attitude, we should not

276

only see life differently, but life itself would come to be different. Life would undergo a change of appearance because we ourselves had undergone a change in attitude. The old details now make another pattern; and this perception of a new pattern is what I call a creative attitude toward life. . . . What I am trying to say is that a new attitude to life on the part of writers would first see life different and then make it different."

"I see the way," Katherine Mansfield declared, "but I still have to go it." A few weeks later this genius of the short story died with none of her new stories on paper.

Another essay in Orage's 1924/25 campaign to awaken the American intelligentsia to a striving for renascent capabilities created a moderate stir in the *New Republic*. "On Religion" was first of all a criticism of modern science, which Orage declared was completely and indifferently ignorant of any means of knowing if an intelligent God exists. Modern science deals only with potentialities actualized, not with reality or potentiality metaphysically,* but only with actuality, that is to say, the physical. Modern science can throw no light on the religion of the past, and it declines to be interested in the question of a technique for religion, thus declaring itself bankrupt of religion forever.

It is essential to note Orage's elementary definition of religion: "certain specific generalizations as to the World and Man . . . that the Universe is an intelligent and therefore intelligible Cosmos; that the obligation and, at the same time, the highest possible aim of Man is to understand and to cooperate with the intelligent laws that govern it; that in order to accomplish this a special way of life or technique is necessary; and that this technique consists primarily in a method of 'divinizing,' that is to say, of raising to a higher conscious level Man's present state of being."

Orage dismissed the assumption of some people that our remote ancestors possessed a lost faculty, the so-called religious sense; but he entertained the conjecture (made reasonable by his Gurdjieffian knowledge) that there had been a lost technique, a lost method known to the Egyptians, the Buddhists, the Pythagoreans, and the Gnostics. He then found a surprising loophole of escape from the science-religion impasse "precisely, in fact, in the latest conquest of the scientific method, the field of Behaviorism."

The behaviorist observed others and could not detect consciousness. But the method of behaviorism could be extended to observation of one's self, and here

* Vide *The Three Conventions* by Denis Saurat.

one would learn about states of consciousness. "Is self-observation," Orage asked, "together with the usual sequel in the scientific method—verification, hypothesis, experiment and demonstration—equally legitimate with the observation of others; and if it is, can we devise a method to ensure its rigorous pursuit?" His answer, of course, was affirmative. "All that would be necessary would be to be doubly on guard against subjectivity and to be all the more rigorously and objectively scientific in sight of the snares of misunderstanding and self-deception." To know ourselves as we actually are, Orage contended, is the first necessary step to religion; "self-consciousness or awareness of our actuality is, in short, an indispensable element in Religion."

On reaching the center of his argument Orage said, "It has been suggested that in the current theories of Behaviorism ancient Religion and modern Science meet. . . . However . . . they only meet, they do not as yet mingle." Nevertheless the methods of the behaviorists could be applied directly to the study of religion. "We can accept their classification of forms of behavior, together, if necessary, with their means of measuring Man. None of their implications, even in the extreme form of organic mechanism, are positively alien to us. If self-observation be the next step in scientific Behaviorism, and it appears logically to be, the second step of Behaviorism may very well prove to be the first step in the technique of Religion."

"On Religion" provoked several religious thinkers to explore new ways and means in the *New Republic* forum, and Herbert Croly, the editor, wrote a series of editorials on the religious technique Orage proposed. In such editorials as "Realistic Liberalism" and "Socratic Liberalism," Croly urged that liberalism transform itself into a discipline of self-liberation. He proposed that liberal curiosity and sentiment should be married to skepticism and a full realization of the inner life. "The only realistic policy for liberals," he argued, "is to start methodically to stretch and intensify their consciousness in the hope that it will become eventually a more adequate instrument for the watching, the understanding, the unfolding, the harmonizing and the deliverance of their personal lives."

In the end no fruition came from these seeds of renascence sown in the *New Republic*. Croly was incapacitated in 1928 and died in 1930. Orage left New York for London in 1931. Deprived of Croly's editorial statesmanship, the *New Republic* became simply a political journal of conventional liberalism, and the giant topic of a renascence was dropped.

"On Love. Freely Adapted from the Tibetan" was published in the *New Re-*

public two years after Orage came to New York, though it had been written during a summer visit to Fontainebleau. Gurdjieff had invited Orage to his room and talked about conscious love, distinguishing it from instinctive and emotional love. The next day Orage showed the British publisher Stanley Nott the draft of an essay. "I talked with Gurdjieff last night for a long time," he said, "and afterwards I went to my room and wrote till four this morning. This is the result." The result is a small classic, the finest essay on *ars amandi* in English literature. "On Love" reads like the notes of an advanced pupil on the sermon of a master. All the flowers of discourse have been dispensed with. The thought is essential; the tone of authority is present.

"On Love" is an essay on chivalric or conscious love. J. Huizinga has observed that in the age of chivalry "love now became the field where all moral and cultural perfection flowered." "The conscious love motive," the essayist says, "in its developed state, is the wish that the object should arrive at its own native perfections, regardless of the consequences to the lover." The technique is the art of delightful surprises. "Constant efforts to anticipate the nascent wishes of the beloved while they are still unconscious are the means to conscious love."

But readers within range of the *New Republic* had ears only for the prophets of instinctive love—Freud and D. H. Lawrence—and were unresponsive to the revealed secret of felicity in love: "Take hold tightly; let go lightly." And so "On Love" did not inspire in America a cult of love and perfection beyond the radius of the Orage groups. In England, however, "On Love" has been often reprinted and has secured permanence in English literature.

8.

There remains to be noted a direct "live" influence on American writers exerted by Orage in the later years of his New York stay. While editor of the *New Age* he had been a remarkable instigator of writing—Pound acknowledged this in dedicating a book of essays to A. R. Orage—and he had been a mentor to his contributors as well. Katherine Mansfield had written him, "You taught me to write, you taught me to think; you showed me what there was to be done and what *not* to do." In New York, starting in 1928 Orage held private classes in professional writing which attracted many serious and talented aspirants to the laurels of literature.

I attended the first series and found in the group the publicist Amos Pinchot who was writing an attack on Walter Lippmann, the poet Melville Cane who was shortly to write several of his finest poems, including the poem on Houdini, and a historian named Wells. Muriel Draper was there, entangled in salon talk but needing to free her style for the printed page—which she did brilliantly in *Music at Midnight* written after Orage's tutelage.

A writer whose promise interested me greatly was T. S. Matthews, a junior editor on the *New Republic*. He reminded me of what I had heard about Arnold Bennett in his learning-to-write phase. Matthews was writing parodies, reviews, paragraphs for the *New Republic* and turning over fiction projects in his mind. *To the Gallows I Must Go* was written in ten days and dedicated to Orage who had advised Matthews to model his novel on the eighteenth-century testament sometimes composed by criminals about to be hanged. "If you wanted to write a narrative," Matthews reports that Orage said to him, "it was absolutely necessary to tell it to yourself over and over, until you were letter-perfect and there were no gaps in it—like a crook committing to memory a watertight cover story."

Another who regarded Orage as *cher maître* was Lawrence S. Morris who contributed literary essays to the *New Republic*. In 1930 he was offered the literary editorship of that paper but had to decline because of eye surgery. Another in the circle was the novelist Isa Glenn who was later to dedicate her best novel, *Transport*, to Orage. And Isa Glenn's son, Bayard Schindel, who was to accomplish a published book about the boyhood of an army general's son. And Paul Ernest Anderson, later a labor union economist. And Alma Wertheim. And others. All in all, perhaps seventy-five writers—no beginners among them—took the "Orage course" between 1928 and 1930.

The "philosophy of composition" taught in this writing course may be found in an essay entitled "On Style," which Orage wrote by way of introduction to a collection of his causeries from the *New Age* published in New York in 1930.* Orage held that "there is scarcely a literary form now existing that was not cultivated and brought to a high degree of perfection before the invention of letters and the printing press." The ancient relationship of speaker and hearer, Orage declared, stands fundamentally unchanged by all the changes due to

---

* Hoping to attach the book to the vogue of popular "art of . . ." books, the publisher titled the collection *The Art of Reading*. I suggested at the time that the book should be titled *Aids to Literary Reflection*, which Orage accepted.

printing. This is proved by this fact: "that writing is everywhere acknowledged to be at its highest and best when it most closely reproduces the living presence of its author—in short, when it speaks." In the ages before the invention of script, the man was the style. But in the age of printing, type has been substituted for voice.

"The transition from speaking to writing, from hearing to reading, demanded more, in short, than simply a script for the words; it demanded the addition to the verbal text of substitutes for all the rest of the living speaker's obvious properties, his gestures, his eyes, his movements, his whole personality. The conveyance, within the verbal framework of literature, of the man himself, apart from and over and above his mere words, is what is truly defined as style. In literature, the style is the man."

It may not be at once apparent that "On Style" is still another essay growing out of Orage's central thought: the stimulation of a possible renascence in our time; but it could fittingly be added to "New Standards in Art and Literature," "Talks with Katherine Mansfield," "On Religion," and "On Love" to make a wonderfully seminal book that might be titled *The Way to Man's Greatness*.

As his parting contribution to American culture, Orage in 1931 instilled a vision of the Leisured Society. He had begun private life as a socialist; then with A. G. Penty he had formulated the national guilds theory (guild socialism) and attracted such stalwart thinkers as Maurice B. Reckitt, S. G. Hobson, and G. D. H. Cole; finally, he had been converted to the New Economics of Major C. H. Douglas. Shortly before the end of his American stay, Orage took the initiative, rented a room at the New York School of the Theatre, and gave a series of four lectures on social credit. About fifty enrolled in the course, which began with an exposition of the nature of real credit and the failure of financial credit. The concluding lecture, which hit the nerve of economic puritanism, was three decades ahead of American thought on work and leisure (Sebastian de Grazia's massive *Of Time, Work and Leisure* appeared in 1962); but it fired several who heard it to a determination to form a study group on the economics of the Leisured Society. My notes from this fourth lecture, in abbreviated fashion, are recorded here:

> Work is not disagreeable in itself but the element of compulsion is. We resent having no choice of occupation. Often the hours of work are too protracted and the work is not remunerative enough.

281

The inducement to work need not be bestial, based on fear or greed. Men can be appealed to on the grounds of pride or shame.

Leisure is in any case one of the by-products of a progressive society. It should not be attached to production, past or future.

Money should have only an instrumental value, not a real value. Financial economics is concerned with the production and distribution of money. Our problem now is not physical scarcity but plenty.

Pride in creation and shame in communal failure should be our inducement, as in the arts and sports.

Let us make the following observations about a sound society.

1. In it industry does not exist to provide employment or "make money" or exert a moral influence.

2. Money exists only for the purpose of facilitating the production and distribution of goods. Money system should be the ticket office of the productive system.

3. The inducement to produce must consist of a constantly rising standard of living. There should be increasing freedom of choice of occupation by the individual. The inducement of leisure—leisure as a right and practical possibility.

The foregoing are the principles of a free commonwealth. What are the means?

1. The community should assume control over the financial system. No nationalization of industry, no nationalization of the banks. Only an official authority is needed, consisting chiefly of statisticians, to govern the volume of money in relation to supply. A deputied agency to do this.

2. Institution of the Just Price. Should look up Catholic economists before 1694 on the Just Price. They had, however, only a moral, not a statistical reason.

3. Introduction of the principle of dividends for all. In real economics true cost is consumption.

Here was the economics for a new age of renascence. Economics based on building up from the individual to the state, not down from the state to a cell of society, as in the totalitarian conceptions. Economics based on the liberty of the individual, regarding both choice of occupation and command over the environment (consumption). Economics for the increasing distribution of leisure, leisure being defined by Orage as the economic condition of *voluntary activity*.

Soon after Orage returned to England, a study group under the leadership of Schuyler Jackson began meeting at Muriel Draper's home, and from this group of enthusiasts came the founders of the New Economics Group of New York in the fall of 1932. This was the beginning of the American social credit movement of the 1930s, traceable to Orage's 1931 lectures on social credit as the Twenties were expiring.

The break between Orage and Gurdjieff that occured in 1931 signified no dissent by Orage from the teaching of Gurdjieff. After the break, Orage, back in London and editor of the *New English Weekly*, remarked to a friend: "I thank God every day of my life that I met Gurdjieff."

Gurdjieff's school was a school of individuation and the time comes when a man must find his own work in life. At that time Gurdjieff produced a strain and a crisis in their relations and cast the man out. So it had happened with Ouspensky; so it happened with Thomas de Hartmann and other advanced pupils. And so it happened with Orage when Gurdjieff destroyed the position of authority that Orage held for seven years in America.

But Orage approved the ending of his period of American leadership. He felt that he had reached, at least for the time being, the end of his tutelage under Gurdjieff. He felt, too, that he had discharged his debt to Gurdjieff and was free to open the final phase of his career. Resuming his journalistic career, he founded a new weekly review of public affairs, literature, and the arts. This last phase was, alas, cut short by Orage's death in 1934.

It was a coincidence that the literary period of the Twenties—which began on False Armistice Day, 1918—ended in a social coma in 1931 when Orage sailed for England for the last time. As he left New York, long bread lines were forming every day at relief centers, and desperate men selling apples lined the streets around transportation terminals. The volume of American industry had fallen disastrously, wages were way down in amount, and unemployment was climbing toward twelve million. In this depressed environment the spirit of the Twenties could not continue. A new period, the Thirties, made itself perceptible to all.

Munson at Woodstock, 1920.

Photograph of Munson by Man Ray, ca. 1920.

Munson in France, 1921.

Painting of Munson by Ernest Fiene, 1925.

Munson in the 1940s.

Sketch of Munson by Reginald
Pollack, 1965.

Photographs of Munson by
Jeanette Fiene.

Photograph of Munson taken shortly before his death in 1969.

Woodstock, 1924

The awakening mood of the Twenties was pervasive by 1924. One sensitive place where this mood of American risorgimento was most fully experienced was Woodstock, in the foothills of the Catskills some ten miles northwest of Kingston, New York. One of two art colonies in the East—the other being Provincetown, Massachusetts—Woodstock responded with optimism to the new in arts and letters, to a revival of the spirit of Walt Whitman.

> Americanos! conquerors! marches humanitarian!
> Foremost! century marches! Liberated! masses!
> For you a programme of chants.

But William Morris, more than Walt Whitman, was the direct inspirer of the art colony at Woodstock. In 1902 came Ralph Whitehead, a disciple of Morris, to the valley. He climbed a mile and a half up the slope leading to Overlook Mountain, a few miles away and 2100 feet high, and founded a small community, which he named Byrdcliffe. Designed to be an experiment in communal living with cooperative workshops in weaving, ceramics, painting, and sculpture, Byrdcliffe was made up of some twenty-five or thirty cottages, studios, and workshops. Two years later a novelist named Hervey White drifted to an area two and a half miles southwest of the village of Woodstock and built a string of cabins and shacks along a country road. White's colony attracted musicians for whom a rustic concert hall was built in 1916. This tract of woods and fields was called The Maverick. The Art Students League of New York set up summer headquarters in the village, and in a hall on the green the Art Association, founded 1919, held exhibitions throughout the summer.

Woodstock had two magazines in the summer of 1924. Frank Schoonmaker, traveler and wine expert, published a local gossipy sheet called *Hue and Cry*; and *1924*, edited by Edwin Seaver, aimed to become one of the "great little magazines" of the American awakening. Seaver's intention was to change the name each successive year, but *1924* died after several issues and never became *1925*.

That summer I stayed at "Ma" Russell's boardinghouse on the corner of where the dirt road to The Maverick turned off the main road to West Hurley. "Ma" Russell's was a nerve center for the village of Woodstock and The Maverick. Here one felt the electrifying impulses of the Twenties as they stimulated the whole community of artists, actors, musicians, and writers. I remember that I abandoned this summer the project I had been nursing of writing a book to be called *Introducing the Twenties*, which had been announced as "in preparation." But the Twenties, I reflected as I sat on "Ma" Russell's lawn, had already been introduced. Excitement was rising and a peak year seemed not far away. (For those who like to indulge an unscholarly taste for exact dates, the peak came on June 13, 1927, when New York welcomed Lindbergh after his flight to Paris.)

Two books published in 1922 had, I felt, formed the Twenties into a definite period. They were *The Waste Land* by T. S. Eliot and *Ulysses* by James Joyce. The first had given an epical metaphor for modern civilization; the second, I thought, had terminated the development of the old novel and presaged a new kind of novel. Whatever one might say about the depressing effects of the pessimism in *The Waste Land* and *Ulysses*, the two works were extraordinarily stimulating to aesthetic endeavor. As Archibald MacLeish observed many years later, "There was something about the Twenties. . . . I refer, of course, to the now evident . . . fact that an age ended with the First World War. . . . *The Waste Land* provided the vocabulary of our understanding; *Ulysses* formed the sense of history in which we lived."

To the theater Eugene O'Neill was bringing new life. My generation saluted *The Emperor Jones* as a minor classic in modern drama, and we ranked *The Hairy Ape* as a powerful fable of alienation. Now in 1924 we were positive that *Desire Under the Elms* was the work of an *arrived* playwright who could be ranked with such foreign playwrights as Hauptmann, Sudermann, Strindberg, and An-dreyev. The American theater, we knew, was at last grown up.

Young America, symbolized by Greenwich Village and Edna St. Vincent Millay, had its festival at The Maverick at the time of the harvest moon. Artists came in costume, illicit kegs of beer were broached, there were games and pic-nics in the afternoon, and in the evening at the outdoor theater there was a program of dances. Here the authentic spirit of Bohemia flared up, that spirit that died in the 1940s and has only been travestied in later decades at North Beach and the Haight-Ashbury.

Edwin Seaver had been impressed by Waldo Frank's "For a Declaration of War" in *Secession*, Number 7. In an early edition of *1924*, Seaver permitted me to describe our youngest generation. "We study esthetics," I wrote, "and we are curious about critical methods. When we talk about art, there is at least some likelihood that an artist will recognize the subject. Our esthetic interest is then our one band of union, and Eliot and Pound are our closest American masters. Doubtless we shall move out from esthetics, but where? Some of us, I expect—and I am thinking particularly of Kenneth Burke—will continue the Transcendental tradition in American letters, will pick up the mantle of Paul Elmer More when his able brain relaxes.* Others, I hope, will set to work at organizing the significant romanticism of our era into a modern classicism, *i. e.*, into a series of new basic assumptions and definitions which will steep mod-ern life in an inclusive vision."

I can account for Seaver's generosity in giving me ample space for expound-ing the direction I felt that our letters should take only by assuming that he was most sympathetic to that direction. In a long essay on "The Esotericism of T. S. Eliot," I described the literary situation of America from a personal point of view.

America has energy and hope. It has weak traditions and a romantic tem-perament. It is becoming conscious of a fundamental difference between it and Europe. In the words of the Cumaean Sibyl, inscribed at the top of *The Waste Land*, Europe "wants only to die." America wants to live.

* Although Burke wrote only once about Paul Elmer More, the dualism of More was a fre-quent topic in his table-talk for a while.

But America has not realized its responsibility in the present crisis. It has not realized that its national destiny is more than a matter of national self-respect. It has not recognized clearly that the leadership of the human spirit has been resigned and that it, if anyone, must assume it. It has the primary qualifications: untapped energetics and spiritual naivete. It has lately acquired self-reliance. It seems not fanciful to predict that it will next acquire a sense of international responsibility.

And then perhaps it will at last be ready to receive Whitman. It will be expectant and humble, waiting for the Word that will release it, for the Word that will spell a new slope of consciousness. Whitman is not the Word, but he formed syllables of it, immense generative syllables. America will wait while these do their deep hidden work, arousing latent power. . . .

Mr. Eliot lacks those deeper dimensions that the new slope will utilize. He is almost purely a sensibility and an intellect: he seems a unified man: at least one gets no sense of a disastrous internecine conflict in him. He loves beauty, he is wounded by ugliness: the age is severe on "beauty-lovers" who cannot go below the surface. It lacerates unmercifully those whose intellects work only at the tips of their senses, who make an ideal of the senses thinking, of sensuous thought. This formula Mr. Eliot believes accounts for much of the excellence of Elizabethan literature.

The formula for literary masterwork in our age will be more complex, more inclusive, much more difficult. . . . It will involve the correlated functions of the whole human consciousness and it will demand the utmost purification of that consciousness. On a tremendous scale our age duplicates some of the features which introduced so much zest into Elizabethan life. Our vital source in antiquity will be, perhaps, the religious and philosophical cultures of the East instead of Graeco-Roman culture. Our New World will be Higher Space, and our explorers, our Columbuses and Magellans, will be such scientists as Einstein and Bohr. Our artists will have a wealth of new materials: our intellectual world expands and fills with possibilities: it is a time for curiosity and daring.

The last paragraph was intended to be an indication of the epical task lying before Hart Crane, who was already outlining the conception of *The Bridge* in 1923 and 1924. The extract should be carefully dated: Woodstock, July, 1924.

On July 9, 1924, Hart Crane wrote me: "I have just re-read your Eliot article in *1924*, and hope I may congratulate you again on some very accurate estimates and constructive motives."

The Armory Show of 1913 was the reveille of the international modern movement in America. From this event there ensued a growing fraternity of artists and writers who joined in an endeavor to awaken in America the modern spirit that was stirring in the West. Never before had such an extensive dialogue been carried on between American writers and the painters, foreign and native, of the modern era. Woodstock in the Twenties was enlivened by the exchanges of writers and artists.

Painters were in the majority at Woodstock, but there was a liberal sprinkling of writers—Will Durant, Richard LeGallienne, Lawrence Langner, Clemence Randolph, Edna St. Vincent Millay, Walter Weyl—who came and went and fraternized with painters. Among the painters were George Bellows, Henry McFee, Andrew Dasburg, Eugene Speicher, Robert Chanler, Ernest Fiene, Alexander Brook, and Peggy Bacon (poet and novelist, too). William Murrell (Fisher), art critic, did much to bring about communication between the two groups, and such writers as the reviewer Harold Ward, the *Secession/Broom* contributor Slater Brown, and the poet Hart Crane were often in the studios of Ernest and Paul Fiene and other Woodstock artists.

It is interesting to remember that there had been in the American past only one instance of a mutually beneficial relationship of poet and artist. That single instance was Walt Whitman in the early 1850s, who fraternized with the group of artists who founded the Brooklyn Art Union. Whitman knew quite well the painters William Sidney Mount and Walter Libby and the sculptor Henry Kirk Brown and his apprentice John Quincy Ward. He heard debate over the aesthetic ideas of Horatio Greenough. Biographer Gay Wilson Allen says of Walt Whitman's newspaper article about the Art Union: "The knowing comments on lighting, coloring, and texture showed how much Walt had profited from his conversations with the artists, possibly with Libby especially, for whom about this time [1851] he sat for his portrait." Allen adds that "one of the painters of this group may have taught Walt the rudiments of crayon sketching, for in a notebook he left some competent portraits and caricatures of himself and others."

For two generations after the Armory Show, the Whitman-Art Union example of cross-fertilization of the writer and the artist was multiplied many times. Numerous writers and numerous painters and sculptors crossed into each other's camps, stimulating each other and extracting mutual benefit from the dialogue.

Hart Crane was conspicuously one of the mixers. He came to Woodstock in the fall of 1923 and stayed for several months with Slater Brown and Edward P. Nagle. Nagle, the stepson of the sculptor Gaston Lachaise, had grown up in Paris and now did a little writing and painting. He had been at Harvard when Dos Passos was there, and Dos Passos remembers that Nagle introduced his friends to the new currents in art and literature.* Crane became a worshipful friend of Gaston and Madame Lachaise; his poem "Interludium," dedicated "To 'La Montagne' by Lachaise," was published in Seaver's Woodstock magazine, *1924.* "La Montagne" was a sculpture of Madame Lachaise recumbent; the concluding stanza of "Interludium" celebrated her.

Crane had, I think, made his drawing of Slater Brown before he joined Brown and Nagle at Woodstock—that drawing which the *Dial* purchased and reproduced, a fine acknowledgment of Crane's artistic gift. Gift it was, for Crane had little tutoring as an artist. On September 23, 1923, he wrote a friend, "I have been making a number of drawings lately. One of Jean Toomer, one of Waldo, and one of an amusing young lady [probably Sue Jenkins]. They are all very interesting, and even Gaston Lachaise, who was in to see me recently, thought that they were worth while." The drawing of Waldo Frank I happily took to use as a frontispiece for the Homage to Waldo Frank number of *S4N* I was assembling that fall. Crane also made a drawing of me which was lost in that illegal warehouse sale I have earlier lamented. Crane had been occasionally drawing and painting for the past two years. "I find it a tremendous stimulation," he wrote me on June 12, 1921, "and you begin to see so many more things than before whenever you look. My drawings are original, at least, and Sommer professes to see much in 'em."

As a number of Crane's letters reveal, William Sommer and Richard Rychtarik and Willi Lescaze were three Cleveland artists from whom Crane learned something about the graphic arts. Sommer in particular. "I have lately

---

* "It was in Nagle's room I saw my first copies of BLAST, with Eliot's early poems. Diaghilev's Ballet and the novelties at the Boston opera and the Armory Show did the rest."

—Dos Passos

run across an artist here," Crane wrote on April 10, 1921, "whose work seems to carry the most astonishing marks of genius that have passed before my eyes in original form, that is,—I mean present-day work. And I am saying much I think when I say that I prefer Sommer's work to most of Brzeska and Boardman Robinson. A man of 55 or so—works in a lithograph factory—spent most of his life until the last seven years in the rut of conventional forms—liberated suddenly by sparks from Gauguin, Van Gogh, Picasso and Wyndham Lewis, etc. I have taken it upon myself to send out some of his work for publication."

Whereupon Crane and I peddled Sommer water colors and drawings to such likely prospects in the art world as we could think of. Sometimes we got encouraging comments, as I did from the De Zayas Gallery (then inactive); but there were very few actual sales. The most reassuring purchase was made by the *Dial*, which reproduced a couple of Sommers.

What his friendship with Sommer meant to Crane in the way of poetic stimulation may be gauged in the poem he dedicated to William Sommer—"Sunday Morning Apples," which is concerned with the interplay of art and nature, and demands uncut reprinting.

> The leaves will fall again sometime and fill
> the fleece of nature with those purposes
> That are your rich and faithful strength of line.
>
> But now there are challenges to spring
> In that ripe nude with head
>
> > reared
>
> Into a realm of swords, her purple shadow
> Bursting on the winter of the world
> From whiteness that cries defiance to the snow.
>
> A boy runs with a dog before the sun, straddling
> Spontaneities that form their independent orbits,
> Their own perennials of light
> In the valley where you live
>
> > (called Brandywine).
>
> I have seen the apples there that toss you secrets,—
> Beloved apples of seasonable madness
> That feed your inquiries with aerial wine.

Put them again beside a pitcher with a knife,
And poise them full and ready for explosion—
The apples, Bill, the apples!

"I never met Hart Crane," said William Carlos Williams in his *Autobiography*, "though I once bought a picture from him by a man named Sohmer [*sic*], whom he was befriending." Williams does not mention that he selected this picture at a private showing of Sommer I held on a bench in Central Park in the fall of 1922. Kenneth Burke arranged the meeting at which I showed Williams perhaps a dozen things by Sommer. Williams looked with a quickly appreciative eye, and several times exclaimed approval. I can only describe his criterion for pictures as excitatory phallicism, for when he saw a Sommer picture he liked especially, he exclaimed: "That gives me an erection"—certainly a powerful metaphor for approval. Finally he bought one for twenty-five dollars; I think he sent the check to Crane in Cleveland, which is why he remembers buying the picture from him.

Williams was not on the Woodstock scene in 1924—but we of the "youngest generation" were very much aware of him. He had contributed to *Secession* and was now contributing to Seaver's *1924*, proclaiming the virtue of the local and the new. Even more than Hart Crane, Williams reflected the influence of modern painting on poetry. In fact, Williams had been undecided about his career when he was at the University of Pennsylvania. His mother had painted a little and he had formed a friendship with the young painter Charles Demuth. Should I become a painter, Williams asked himself, and says that he coldly (can coldness be imagined of the warm enthusiastic Williams?) calculated all the chances of this career. He took long walks with Demuth and then one day decided: "Words it would be and their intervals: Bam! Bam!"

But after this decision, Williams continued to have "fun" painting on Sunday afternoons in the studio of a middleaged commercial artist in Philadelphia, and in the first years of his marriage he did some amateur painting, amusing his wife once by painting on a narrow wooden panel a group of nudes in grotesque positions on the bank of a stream. In his *Autobiography* he dated his education in modern art from his visit to the Armory Show of 1913. Then came his visits to "291" and his interest in the architectural career of his brother. He knew Marsden Hartley well—"a kind of grandpapa to us all"—and went to parties at Walter Conrad Arensberg's studio where he saw the work of Gleizes,

Cézanne, Man Ray, Marcel Duchamp and other avant-gardists. He asked Arensburg what cubism was about, and the poet-collector gave him a justification of the cult of novelty. The only way man differed from other creatures was in his ability to improvise novelty. Anything in paint, Arensberg contended, that is truly new, truly a fresh creation, is good art.

It is remarkably easy to find similarities between the way Williams will write a poem and the way a painter—Edward Hopper, Charles Sheeler, Brueghel the Elder or Jackson Pollock—will paint a scene. Consider Williams' "Pastoral," for instance. Here he is a realist on the back streets of a New Jersey town "admiring the houses of the very poor"—just as pure a realist as Hopper in painting a corner saloon. Here he is direct and simple—like Hopper; and there is angularity in this poem—"roof out of line with sides"—that brings to mind Hopper's remark that "angularity was just natural to me." The question has been asked of Hopper, what is the significance of his banal subjects, his matter-of-factness, his obsession with the ordinary; and this question may well be turned on Williams by the reader of "Pastoral" when Williams declares that he is fortunate if the fences are smeared a bluish green. The art critic replies that Hopper gives "the poetry of the commonplace, of light, of the moment reduced to its lowest common denominator." But isn't that the yield from "Pastoral"—the poetry of the commonplace, the pleasure of the exact transcription of the scene of "the yards cluttered / with old chicken wire, ashes, / furniture gone wrong." The poetry and the art lie in the way Williams and Hopper see their landscapes—not in the subject, but in the vision.

Poetry is in vision. This is the aesthetic truth that Kenneth Burke seized in reading the celebrated "The Red Wheelbarrow," that miraculous 16-word poem of four stanzas of four words each.

> so much depends
>
> upon
>
> a red wheel
>
> barrow
>
> glazed with rain
>
> water
>
> beside the white
>
> chickens

298

Of this poem, Burke said: "The process is simply this: There is the eye, and there is the thing upon which the eye alights,—while the relationship existing between the two is the poem." This is the poetic of Williams, his way of seeing the object, with what directness and simplicity; and suddenly the thought strikes one—"The Red Wheelbarrow" should be hung beside a Sheeler in the gallery of one's mind. The likeness of vision is extraordinary, yet each man is true to his own medium.

Note what Williams had to say about his friend Charles Sheeler. "I think Sheeler is particularly valuable because of the bewildering directness of his vision, without blur, through the fantastic overlay with which our lives so vastly are concerned, 'the real,' as we say, contrasting with the artist's 'fabrication.'" Could Williams not have said exactly the same of his own value? And was not Williams rationalizing his own quest when he said that Sheeler turned from abstraction to particularization because he sought to realize the uniqueness of things as ends in themselves? "No ideas but in things"—the repeated cry of Williams in *Paterson*. I could add the example of Charles Demuth painting a literary picture around the name of Williams and his poem "The Great Figure," but further evidence of the interplay of painting and poetry in the work of Williams and his painter-friends is superfluity of support for Williams' statement in the *Autobiography*: "There had been a break somewhere, we were streaming through, each thinking his own thoughts, driving his own designs toward his self's objectives. Whether the Armory Show in painting did it or whether that also was no more than a facet—the poetic line, the way the image was to lie on the page was our immediate concern."

Looking back on that summer at Woodstock, it seems to me to have been part of an exceptionally pregnant moment in the history of the Twenties. The first moment of the period was one of release from tension, the almost blissful feeling of peace that came with the Armistice (False and True) in November of 1918. Awakening had followed. And by 1924 great designs had been conceived and were being gestated. Some—*The Waste Land* was an early example—had already been delivered. The air was fresh and heady with the spirit of poetic adventure, with the daring of aesthetic experiment.

But we participants in the making of the Twenties—creators and critics and editors, publishers and readers—were we aware of the extraordinary pregnancy of 1924? I think that many of us were; I think that Whitmanian optimism respecting American literature set the tone of the year. We could not have clearly prophesied that the development of the complex, long poem, the "neo-epic," would be the great contribution of the Twenties to poetry, but we did have an inkling that it might be so. For already in 1922 T. S. Eliot had given us *The Waste Land*, and by the end of 1923 twelve cantos of Ezra Pound's "neo-epic" in progress had appeared in print. Hart Crane had made known to a few his great design for *The Bridge* and had even written some lines of it. We did not, however, know that William Carlos Williams was harboring the germ, though not yet the conceived project, of *Paterson*, his "neo-epic" of which he would not be delivered until the Forties.

The situation in poetry was taking form. Williams had called *The Waste Land* a catastrophe for United States poetry, and Crane had rejected the negativism of Eliot's "neo-epic." Nor was either poet accepting leadership from Ezra Pound. Crane wanted to write a "neo-epic" of affirmation, and Williams even then was searching for "an image large enough to embody the whole knowable world about me"—which brought him to the city of Paterson, New Jersey.

It is interesting that Crane and Williams were not allied in their revolt against the Eliot-Pound leadership. Both had been in the Stieglitz circle, but Williams dropped out. Stieglitz, he said, had talked him deaf, dumb, and blind. To Crane, however, Stieglitz was a prophetic figure. Crane and Williams also differed on Whitman as a source. Whitman was an exhausted source, declared Williams; but Crane was to write the Cape Hatteras section of *The Bridge* to honor Whitman. Williams summarily dismissed Whitman as "a romantic in the bad sense." He admitted that Whitman was the peak of his age but, stoutly, he said that Whitman's age had passed "and we have passed beyond it. . . . We have to do better, we have to look, to discover particulars and to refine."

Therefore when Karl Shapiro eulogized Crane, Williams replied firmly: "I can't agree on Hart Crane. He had got to the end of his method, it never was more than an excrescence—no matter what the man himself may have been. . . . He couldn't do it any longer. He was on his way back from Mexico to—work. And couldn't work. He was returning to create and had finished creating."

But had Crane exhausted his method? Certainly not in 1924—and certainly not in 1932 although he had exhausted his broken spirit by then. His method came from Whitman, Stieglitz, Frank, and—Ouspensky. Williams, as we have seen, was through with Whitman and Stieglitz; Waldo Frank and Ouspensky meant very little to him. Williams was indifferent to the mystical nationalism of Whitman, Stieglitz, and Frank. He was a localist who wrote in United States language, and he wasn't mystical at all. Crane, who was not hostile to Williams' localism, was, above all, a mystical nationalist. Crane wanted, above all, to create an American myth, a myth that should be a bridge from the old American consciousness to a new, expanded higher consciousness. Ouspensky, who meant nothing to Williams, inspired—partly at least—Crane's effort to write an epic of an expanded American consciousness.

Such was the pregnancy of the moment I have subjectively named "Woodstock, 1924," the moment that contained the future achievement of Eliot, Pound, Crane, and Williams. It also contained the seed of Ouspensky, which would come to the surface of American life in the fall of 1924 when Orage returned to New York to form study groups in the Ouspensky-Gurdjieff school of psychology. Woodstock had heard of Gurdjieff's descent on New York in the spring of 1924, and all that summer gossip raged at The Maverick about a second coming to America of Gurdjieff's esoteric school. Hart Crane had already collided with the new mission—and recoiled.

The great adventure of the Twenties was fully embarked upon.

Bibliography

Aaron, Daniel. *Writers on the Left.* New York: Harcourt, 1961.

Alfred Stieglitz. Washington, D. C.: National Gallery of Art, 1958.

Allen, Frederick Lewis. *Only Yesterday.* New York: Harper, 1931.

Amory, Cleveland, and Frederic Bradlee, eds. *Vanity Fair: A Cavalcade of the 1920s and the 1930s.* New York: Viking, 1960.

Anderson, Margaret. *My Thirty Years' War.* New York: Covici, Friede, 1930.

————, ed. *The Little Review Anthology.* New York: Hermitage House, 1953.

Angloff, Charles. *H. L. Mencken: A Portrait from Memory.* New York: Thomas Yoseloff, 1956.

Baum, S. V., ed. *E. E. Cummings and the Critics.* East Lansing: Michigan State University Press, 1962.

Beach, Sylvia. *Shakespeare and Company.* New York: Harcourt, 1958.

Beard, Charles A. and Mary R. *The Rise of American Civilization.* New York: Macmillan, 1927.

Bittner, William. *The Novels of Waldo Frank.* Philadelphia: University of Pennsylvania Press, 1958.

Blackmur, R. P. *Form and Value in Modern Poetry.* New York: Doubleday Anchor, 1952.

Boulton, Agnes. *Part of a Long Story.* New York: Doubleday, 1958.

Bourne, Randolph S. *The History of a Literary Radical and Other Papers.* With an Introduction by Van Wyck Brooks. New York: S. A. Russell, 1956.

————. *War and the Intellectuals: Collected Essays, 1915–1919.* New York: Harper Torchbooks, 1964.

————. *Youth and Life.* Boston: Houghton Mifflin, 1913.

Bowen, Croswell. *The Curse of the Misbegotten.* New York: McGraw-Hill, 1959.

Bradbury, John M. *The Fugitives.* Chapel Hill: University of North Carolina Press, 1958.

Brooks, Van Wyck. *Days of the Phoenix.* New York: Dutton, 1957.

————. *Emerson and Others.* New York: Dutton, 1927.

————. *The Life of Emerson.* New York: Dutton, 1932.

————. *The Ordeal of Mark Twain.* New York: Meridian Books, 1955.

————. *The Pilgrimage of Henry James.* New York: Dutton, 1925.

————. *Scenes and Portraits.* New York: Dutton, 1954.

————. *Three Essays on America.* New York: Dutton, 1934.

Brown, Ashley, and Robert S. Haller. *The Achievement of Wallace Stevens.* Philadelphia: Lippincott, 1962.

Brown, Milton W. *The Story of the Armory Show.* New York: New York Graphic Society, 1963.

Burlingame, Roger. *Of Making Many Books.* New York: Scribner, 1946.

Chaplin, Charles. *My Autobiography.* New York: Simon & Schuster, 1964.

———. *My Trip Abroad.* New York: Harper, 1922.

Chaplin, Charles, Jr. *My Father, Charlie Chaplin.* New York: Random House, 1960.

Cowley, Malcolm. *Exile's Return.* New York: Viking, 1951.

Cox, James M., ed. *Robert Frost: A Collection of Critical Essays.* Englewood Cliffs, N. J.: Prentice-Hall, 1962.

Croly, Herbert. *The Promise of American Life.* New York: Macmillian, 1909.

Crunden, Robert M. *The Mind and Art of Albert Jay Nock.* Chicago: Regnery, 1964.

Cummings, E. E. *EIMI.* New York: Grove Press, 1933.

———. *The Enormous Room.* New York: Modern Library, 1922.

———. *Poems, 1923–1954.* New York: Harcourt, 1954.

Davidson, Jo. *Between Sittings.* New York: Dial, 1951.

Davis, Robert Gorham. *John Dos Passos.* Minneapolis: University of Minnesota Pamphlets, 1962.

Dell, Floyd. *Love in Greenwich Village.* Leipzig: Bernhard Fauchnitz, 1926.

Dembo, L. S. *Hart Crane's "Sanskrit Charge."* Ithaca, N.Y.: Cornell University Press, 1960.

DeVoto, Bernard. *Mark Twain's America.* Boston: Houghton Mifflin, 1932.

Dos Passos, John. *The Best Times.* New York: New American Library, 1966.

———. *The Big Money.* Boston: Houghton Mifflin, 1936.

———. *The Forty-Second Parallel.* 1930.

———. *Nineteen Nineteen.* New York: Washington Square Press, 1961. Originally published 1932.

———. *A Pushcart at the Curb.* New York: Doran, 1922.

Dunbar, Olivia Howard. *A House in Chicago.* Chicago: University of Chicago Press, 1947.

Eastman, Max. *Enjoyment of Living.* New York: Harper, 1948.

Elder, Donald. *Ring Lardner.* New York: Doubleday, 1956.

Eliot, T. S. *For Lancelot Andrewes.* New York: Doubleday, Doran, 1929.

———. *The Sacred Wood.* London: Methuen, 1920.

Fadiman, Clifton, ed. *Fifty Years.* New York: Knopf, 1965.

Faulkner, William. *As I Lay Dying.* New York: Jonathan Cape: Harrison Smith, 1930.

———. *Light in August.* New York: Modern Library, 1932.

Fenton, Charles A. *Stephen Vincent Benet.* New Haven, Conn.: Yale University Press, 1958.

Fitzgerald, F. Scott. *This Side of Paradise.* New York: Scribner, 1920.

Foerster, Norman, ed. *Humanism and America.* New York: Farrar & Rinehart, 1930.

Frank, Waldo. *Art and Vieux Columbier.* Paris: Nouvelle Revue Francaise, 1917.

———. *Chalk Face.* New York: Boni & Liveright, 1924.

————. *City Block*. Darien, Conn.: privately published, 1922.

————. *The Dark Mother*. New York: Boni & Liveright, 1920.

————. *Holiday*. New York: Boni & Liveright, 1923.

————. *Our America*. New York, Boni & Liveright, 1919.

————. *Salvos*. New York: Boni & Liveright, 1924.

————. *Time Exposures by Search-Light*. New York: Boni & Liveright, 1926.

————. *The Unwelcome Man*. New York: Boni & Liveright, 1923.

————. *Virgin Spain*. New York: Boni & Liveright, 1926.

————, ed. *The Complete Poems of Hart Crane*. New York: Doubleday, 1958.

Frank, Waldo, Lewis Mumford, Dorothy Norman, Paul Rosenfeld, and Harold Rugg, eds., *America and Alfred Stieglitz: A Collective Portrait*. New York: Doubleday, Doran, 1934.

Freeman, Joseph. *An American Testament*. New York: 1936.

The Freeman Book. New York: Huebsch, 1924.

Frost, Robert. *Complete Poems of Robert Frost*. New York: Holt, 1949.

————. *In the Clearing*. New York: Holt, 1962.

————. *The Letters of Robert Frost to Louis Untermeyer*. New York: Holt, 1963.

Fuller, Edmund, ed. *Journal into the Self: Being the Letters, Papers and Journals of Leo Stein*. New York: Crown, 1950.

Geismar, Maxwell. *The Last of the Provincials*. Boston: Houghton Mifflin, 1947.

————. *Writers in Crisis*. London: Secker and Warburg, 1947.

Gregory, Alyse. *The Day is Gone*. New York: Dutton, 1948.

Gregory, Horace. *Amy Lowell*. New York: Nelson, 1958.

————, ed. *The Portable Sherwood Anderson*. New York: Viking, 1949.

Gregory, Horace, and Marya Zaturenska. *A History of American Poetry, 1900–1940*. New York: Harcourt, 1946.

Gurko, Miriam. *Restless Spirit: The Life of Edna St. Vincent Millay*. New York: Crowell, 1962.

Harcourt, Alfred. *Some Experiences*. Riverside, Conn.: privately printed, 1951.

Hemingway, Ernest. *A Moveable Feast*. New York: Scribner, 1964.

————. *The Sun Also Rises*. New York, Scribner, 1926.

Hoffman, Frederick J. *Gertrude Stein*. Minneapolis: University of Minnesota Press, 1961.

————. *The Twenties*. New York: Viking, 1955.

Hoffman, Frederick J., Charles Allen, and Carolyn F. Ulrich. *The Little Magazine: A History and a Bibliography*. Princeton, N.J.: Princeton University Press, 1946.

Horton, Philip. *Hart Crane: The Life of an American Poet*. New York: Norton, 1937.

Johnson, Alvin. *Pioneer's Progress*. New York: Viking, 1952.

Joost, Nicholas. *Scofield Thayer and the* Dial. Carbondale, Ill.: Southern Illinois University Press, 1964.

Josephson, Matthew. *Life Among the Surrealists*. New York: Holt, 1962.

————. *Zola and His Time*. New York: Book League of America, 1928.

Kemler, Edgar. *The Irreverent Mr. Mencken*. Boston: Little, Brown, 1950.

Knoll, Robert E., ed. *McAlmon and the Lost Generation*. Lincoln: University of Nebraska Press, 1957.

Knox, George. *Critical Moments: Kenneth Burke's Categories and Critiques*. Seattle: University of Washington Press, 1957.

Kramer, Dale. *Ross and the New Yorker*. New York: Doubleday, 1951.

Kreymborg, Alfred. *Troubadour*. New York: Boni & Liveright, 1925.

Kuehl, John, ed. *The Apprentice Fiction of F. Scott Fitzgerald*. New Brunswick, N.J.: Rutgers University Press, 1965.

Langner, Lawrence. *The Magic Curtain*. New York: Dutton, 1951.

Lewis, Sinclair. *Babbitt*. New York: Harcourt, 1922.

————. *Elmer Gantry*. New York: Harcourt, 1927.

————. *Main Street*. New York: Harcourt, 1920.

————. *The Man Who Knew Coolidge*. New York: Harcourt, 1928.

Lippmann, Walter. *Public Opinion*. New York: Macmillan, 1922.

Litz, A. Walton, ed. *Modern American Fiction*. New York: Oxford University Press, 1963.

Loeb, Harold. *The Way It Was*. New York: Criterion Books, 1959.

Lueders, Edward. *Carl Van Vechten and the Twenties*. Albuquerque: University of New Mexico Press, 1955.

Luhan, Mabel Dodge. *Movers and Shakers*. New York: Harcourt, 1936.

Lynd, Robert S., and Helen Merrell. *Middletown*. New York: Harcourt, 1929.

Macdougall, Allan Ross, ed. *Letters of Edna St. Vincent Millay*. New York: 1952.

Mairet, Philip. *A. R. Orage: A Memoir*. New Hyde Park, N.Y.: University Books, 1966.

Manchester, William. *Disturber of the Peace: The Life of H. L. Mencken*. New York: Harper, 1951.

Matthews, T. S. *Name and Address*. New York: Simon & Schuster, 1960.

Mencken, H. L. *The American Language*. 4th edition: New York: Knopf, 1934.

————. *Happy Days: 1880–1892*. New York: Knopf, 1943.

————. *Heathen Days: 1890–1936*. New York: Knopf, 1943.

————. *Newspaper Days: 1899–1906*. New York: Knopf, 1941.

Millay, Edna St. Vincent. *Collected Lyrics*. New York: Harper, 1939.

————. *Collected Sonnets*. New York: Harper, 1941.

————. *Mine the Harvest*. New York: Harper, 1934.

Mizener, Arthur. *The Far Side of Paradise*. Boston: Houghton, Mifflin, 1951.

Moore, Marianne. *Collected Poems*. New York: Macmillan, 1951.

Munson, Gorham. *Destinations: A Canvass of American Literature Since 1900*. New York: J. H. Sears, 1928.

————. *Dilemma of the Liberated*. New York: Coward-McCann, 1930.

————. *Making Poems for America: Robert Frost*. Chicago: Encyclopedia Britannica Press, 1962.

————. *Robert Frost: A Study in Sensibility and Good Sense*. New York: Doran, 1927.

————. *Style and Form in American Prose*. New York, Doubleday, Doran, 1929.

————. *Waldo Frank: A Study*. New York: Boni & Liveright, 1923.

1913 Armory Show 50th Anniversary, 1963. Henry Street Settlement, N.Y.: and Munson-Williams-Proctor Institute. Utica, N. Y., 1963.

Nock, Albert Jay. *Memoirs of a Superfluous Man*. New York: Harper, 1943.

Norman, Charles. *Ezra Pound*. New York: Macmillan, 1960.

————. *The Magic-Maker: E. E. Cummings*. New York: Macmillan, 1958.

Norman, Dorothy. *Alfred Stieglitz: Introduction to an American Seer*. New York: Duell, Sloan, and Pearce, 1960.

Nott, C. S. *Teachings of Gurdjieff*. London: Routledge & Kegan Paul, 1961.

O'Connor, William Van. *Ezra Pound*. Minneapolis: University of Minnesota Press, 1963.

————. *Sense and Sensibility in Modern Poetry*. New York: Barnes & Noble, 1948.

————. *William Faulkner*. Minneapolis: University of Minnesota Press, 1959.

Orage, A. R. *The Active Mind*. New York: Hermitage, 1954.

————. *The Art of Reading*. New York: Farrar & Rinehart, 1930.

————. *Essays and Aphorisms*. London: Janus Press, 1954.

————. *Readers and Writers*. New York: Knopf, 1922.

Ouspensky, P. D. *The Fourth Way*. New York: Knopf, 1957.

————. *In Search of the Miraculous*. New York: Harcourt, 1949.

————. *Tertium Organum*. 3rd American edition, authorized and revised. New York: Knopf, 1955.

Paige, D. D., ed. *The Letters of Ezra Pound, 1907–1941*. New York: Harcourt, 1950.

Parker, Dorothy, ed. *The Portable F. Scott Fitzgerald*. New York: Viking, 1945.

Payne, Robert. *The Great God Pan: A Biography of the Tramp Played by Charles Chaplin*. New York: Hermitage, 1952.

Poore, Charles, ed. *The Hemingway Reader*. New York: Scribners, 1953.

Pound. *Patria Mia*. Chicago: Ralph Fletcher Seymour, 1950.

Pound, Ezra, and Ernest Fenollosa. *The Classic Noh Theatre of Japan*. New York: New Directions, 1959.

Rajan, B., ed. *T. S. Eliot: A Study of His Writings by Several Hands*. New York: Funk & Wagnall's, 1948.

Rascoe, Burton. *We Were Interrupted*. New York: Doubleday, 1947.

Rascoe, Burton, and Groff Conklin, eds. *The* Smart Set *Anthology*. New York: Reynal & Hitchcock, 1934.

Ray, Man. *Self Portrait*. Boston: Little, Brown, 1963.

Rosenfeld, Paul. *Men Seen*. New York: Lincoln Macveagh, Dial Press, 1925.

————. *Port of New York*. New York: Harcourt, 1924.

Sandburg, Carl. *Abraham Lincoln: The Prairie Years and the War Years*. New York: Harcourt, 1926.

Sanderson, Stewart. *Ernest Hemingway*. New York: Grove Press, 1961.

Schorer, Mark. *Sinclair Lewis*. New York: McGraw-Hill, 1961.

Seldes, Gilbert. *The Seven Lively Arts*. New York: Sagamore Press, 1957; originally published, 1924.

————, ed. *The Portable Ring Lardner*. New York: Viking, 1946.

Seligman, Herbert S. *Alfred Stieglitz Talking*. New Haven: Yale University Press, 1966.

Sergeant, Elizabeth Shepley. *Robert Frost: The Trial by Existence.* New York: Holt, 1960.

Shafter, Toby. *Edna St. Vincent Millay: America's Best Loved Poet.* New York: Messner, 1957.

Sheean, Vincent. *The Indigo Bunting: A Memoir of Edna St. Vincent Millay.* New York: Harper, 1951.

Smith, Chard Powers. *Where the Light Fails.* New York: Macmillan, 1965.

Sprigge, Elizabeth. *Gertrude Stein, Her Life and Work.* New York: Harper, 1957.

Stearns, Harold E. *The Street I Know.* New York: Lee Furman, 1935.

Stein, Gertrude. *The Autobiography of Alice B. Toklas.* New York: Random House, 1933.

————. *The Making of Americans.* New York: Something Else Press, 1966; originally published, 1925.

————. *Selected Writings of Gertrude Stein.* Edited by Carl Van Vechten. New York: Modern Library, 1946.

————. *Three Lives.* New York: Modern Library, 1933.

Swanberg, W. A. *Dreiser.* New York: Scribners, 1965.

Thompson, Lawrance. *Fire and Ice: The Art and Thought of Robert Frost.* New York: Holt, 1942.

————, ed. *Selected Letters of Robert Frost.* New York: Holt, 1964.

Turnbull, Andrew. *Scott Fitzgerald.* New York: Scribners, 1962.

Turner, Susan J. *A History of the Freeman.* New York: Columbia University Press, 1963.

Untermeyer, Jean Starr. *Private Collection.* New York: Knopf, 1965.

Untermeyer, Louis. *From Another World.* New York: Harcourt, 1939.

Van Doren, Mark. *The Autobiography of Mark Van Doren.* New York: Harcourt, 1958.

Van Vechten, Carl. *Peter Whiffle: His Life and Works.* New York: Knopf, 1922.

Walter Weyl: An Appreciation. Privately printed, 1922.

Wasserstrom, William. *The Time of the* Dial. Syracuse, N.Y.: Syracuse University Press, 1963.

————, ed. *A* Dial *Miscellany.* Syracuse, N.Y.: Syracuse University Press, 1963.

Weber, Brom. *Hart Crane.* New York: Bodley Press, 1948.

————, ed. *The Letters of Hart Crane.* New York: Hermitage, 1952.

Williams, William Carlos. *Autobiography.*

————. *The Broken Span.* Norfolk, Conn.: New Directions, 1941.

————. *In the American Grain.* New York: New Directions, 1925.

————. *Selected Essays of William Carlos Williams.* New York: Random House, 1954.

Wilson, Edmund. *Axel's Castle.* New York: Scribners, 1931.

————. *Five Plays.* New York: Farrar, Straus, 1954.

————. *I Thought of Daisy.* New York: Farrar, Straus, and Young, 1953.

————. *The New Freedom.* Introduction by William E. Leuchtenburg. Englewood Cliffs, N.J.: Prentice-Hall, 1961.

————. *The Shores of Light.* New York: Farrar-Strauss, 1952.

Winters, Yvor. *The Bare Hills.* Boston: Four Seas, 1927.

————. *In Defense of Reason.* New York: Swallow Press & William Morror, 1947.

Wolfe, Thomas. *You Can't Go Home Again.* New York: Harper, 1940.

Index

James, Henry, 48, 91, 110, 114, 128
James, William, 20, 91
Jazz Age, 131
jh. *See* Heap, Jane
Johns, Orrick, 35, 36
Johnson, Alvin, 88, 91
Johnson, Gerald W., 121
Johnson, Martyn, 101, 102
Jones, Jenkin Lloyd, 95
Jones, Llewellyn, 109
Jones, Robert Edmond, 58, 69, 72, 115
Josephson, Matthew: and *Secession*, 160–168,
    170–71, 173, 177; and Dada, 179–82;
    mentioned, 44, 158, 218
Joyce, James, 102, 110–11, 142, 178, 194,
    291

Kahn, Otto, 213, 220
Karasz, Ilonka, 260
Kaufman, Beatrice, 140
Kelly, Harry, 116
Kemp, Harry, 72, 122
Kennerley, Mitchell, 134, 167
Kent, Rockwell, 117
Kenton, Edna, 58, 72, 210, 260
Kerfoot, J. B., 51
Key, Ellen, 74, 109
Keynes, John Maynard, 89, 126, 146
King, C. Daly, 261–63
Kirchwey, Freda, 91
Kling, Joseph, 75–76, 179, 190
Knopf, Alfred A., 127, 132–37
Knopf, Blanche, 134
Komroff, Manuel, 140, 141
Kreymborg, Alfred, 16, 33–38, 39, 56, 73,
    117, 135, 163, 180
Kreymborg, Dorothy, 36
Kronenberger, Louis, 139
Krutch, Joseph Wood, 76
Kuhn, Walt, 9–10

Lachaise, Gaston, 104, 295
La Follette, Clara, 99
Laforgue, Jules, 194
Langner, Lawrence, 137, 139, 294
Lardner, Ring, 128, 131

Larsson, R. Ellsworth, 261
Laski, Harold J., 22
Lawrence, D. H., 56, 120, 142, 143
Leacock, Stephen, 113
League of American Writers, 30–31
LeBlanc, Georgette, 209
Lee, Algernon, 117
LeGallien, Richard, 294
Leighton, Fred, 269
Lescaze, William, 199, 295
Leslie, Shane, 130
Lewis, R. W. B., 216, 217
Lewis, Sinclair, 74, 126, 145–46, 250
Lewis, Wyndham, 110
Lewissohn, Ludwig, 92, 104
Lichtner, Julius, 164, 170
Lincoln, Abraham, 65
Lindsay, Vachel, 56, 109
Lippmann, Walter, 20, 22, 29, 72, 88, 90,
    101, 115, 124, 145, 280
Littell, Philip, 69, 88, 91
Little Review, 107–13, 165, 190, 192
Liveright, Horace, 63, 73, 137–41
Loeb, Harold: founder, *Broom*, 158–59, 163;
    and Dada, 179–83; mentioned, 171
Lovett, Robert Morss, 21, 101, 157
Lowell, Amy, 35, 36, 56, 60, 69, 159, 167,
    168–69, 243, 250
Loy, Mina, 35
Luhan, Mabel Dodge. *See* Mabel Dodge
Luks, George, 14
Lunn, George R., 90

McAlmon, Robert, 36, 158
McBride, Henry, 16, 210
MacDonald, William, 91
MacDougall, Allen Ross, 158
Macdougall, Duncan, 64
McFee, Henry, 294
Macgowan, Kenneth, 58, 167
McIntosh, Mavis, 261
Mackenzie, Compton, 126
MacLeish, Archibald, 291
MacVeagh, Lincoln, 78
Macy, John, 157
Main Street, 147–48